AFRICAN AMERICANS ON THE WESTERN FRONTIER

The American West

Washington

Oregon

Montana

Idaho

Wyoming

North
Dakota

South
Dakota

Nebraska

Nevada

Utah

Colorado

Kansas

California

Arizona

New
Mexico

Oklahoma

Texas

100th
Meridian

AFRICAN AMERICANS
on the
WESTERN FRONTIER

Edited with an Introduction by
MONROE LEE BILLINGTON
and
ROGER D. HARDAWAY

UNIVERSITY PRESS OF COLORADO

Copyright © 1998 by the University Press of Colorado

Published by the University Press of Colorado
5589 Arapahoe Avenue, Suite 206C
Boulder, Colorado 80303

The University Press of Colorado is a cooperative publishing enterprise supported, in part, by Adams State College, Colorado State University, Fort Lewis College, Mesa State College, Metropolitan State College of Denver, University of Colorado, University of Northern Colorado, University of Southern Colorado, and Western State College of Colorado.

The paper used in this publication meets the minimum requirements of the American National Standard for Information Sciences—Permanence of Paper for Printed Library Materials. ANSI Z39.48-1992

Library of Congress Cataloging-in-Publication Data

African Americans on the western frontier / edited with an
    introduction by Monroe Lee Billington and Roger D. Hardaway.
        p.   cm.
    Includes bibliographical references (p.   ) and index.
    ISBN 0-87081-491-5 (hardcover : alk. paper) — 0-87081-614-4 (pbk. : alk. paper)
    1. Afro-Americans—West (U.S.)—History—19th century. 2. Afro-
Americans—West (U.S.)—History—20th century. 3. Frontier and
pioneer life—West (U.S.) 4. West (U.S.)—Race relations.
    I. Billington, Monroe Lee. II. Hardaway, Roger D.
    E185.925.A58 1998
    978'.00496073—dc21   98-9958
                                                            CIP

This book was designed and typeset in Adobe Garamond by Stephen Adams, Aspen.

09   08   07   06   05   04   03   02   01   10   9   8   7   6   5   4   3   2

CONTENTS

CONTENTS

FIGURES

AFRICAN AMERICANS ON THE WESTERN FRONTIER

INTRODUCTION

Monroe Lee Billington and Roger D. Hardaway

The African American experience in the American West began in 1528 when a Spanish exploring party shipwrecked off the Texas coast in the Gulf of Mexico. Four survivors of that mishap wandered across Texas, the American Southwest, and northern Mexico until they were rescued by Spanish soldiers in 1536. One of this quartet of conquistadors was an African slave named Estevanico. Some historians have speculated that Estevanico, who was from northern Africa, was brown—an Arab—rather than black. Most scholars, however, have concluded that he was the latter, and official Spanish records refer to him as a "negro." The native peoples this slave and his companions met during their eight-year ordeal told them of other tribes to the north and west of Texas that were so wealthy their cities' streets were paved with gold. Intrigued by these stories, Spanish authorities in Mexico City sent Estevanico in 1539 to guide an expedition to find these fabled towns. The cities existed but the gold did not. Moreover, the natives of these settlements killed Estevanico, ending what many historians eventually came to see as a significant journey by this first known African to explore the American West.

During the next four centuries other African Americans visited or lived in what later became the western half of the United States. Some, like Estevanico, were slaves of Spanish officials, explorers, and settlers. One was a member of the Lewis and Clark expedition that went to the Oregon coast in the early nineteenth century. A few were fur trappers and traders. As whites from the United States began gradually settling the western frontier, they, too, brought Americans of African ancestry with them as slaves or servants. These latter travelers performed much of the work necessary for making pioneering expeditions successful; they cooked, herded cattle, nursed children, hunted, built shelters, and performed a host of other required functions. In short,

African Americans were a small but vital part of the frontier experience that historians have often attributed only to European Americans.

Several generations of historians have been drawn to the study of the American West in the one hundred-plus years since Frederick Jackson Turner issued in 1893 the first draft of his now-famous thesis on the significance of the frontier in United States history. Like Turner, however, most of his disciples ignored the African American contribution to the settlement and development of the western frontier. In the late 1950s and succeeding decades, however, a few scholars began researching black cowboys, soldiers, and other African Americans who were a part of the westward movement of the middle and late nineteenth century. During the civil rights movement of the 1960s—when many people in the United States began focusing on the African American contribution to the nation's history—the number of books and articles produced on western black settlers increased dramatically. That trend has continued until the present time.

By the late 1980s the study of minorities in the West—women, Native Americans, Hispanics, and Asians as well as African Americans—had become so prevalent that some scholars began to refer to what they called the "New Western History." While acknowledging (in some cases, grudgingly) that the Turner Thesis had much to commend it, the "new" western historians challenged Turner's conception of the development of the American West as something done primarily by Caucasian men. Obviously, this book—designed to document and validate the African American frontier experience—supports the idea of studying the American West from a multicultural perspective.

The editors' primary purpose in putting this volume together is rather simple. While much has been written in the last few decades about black people in the American West, the scholarship has dribbled forth in bits and pieces. Few attempts—and none totally successful—have been made to tell the complete story of the presence of African Americans on the western frontier. The editors have devised an overall concept of the western black experience, and they have carefully chosen essays that will convey the various aspects of that story to their readers. The editors hope, of course, that this group of articles will present—as fully as a book of essays can—the essential history of African Americans in the West from 1850 until the end of the frontier era.

The editors have another reason, however, for presenting this compilation. Just as western blacks were not included in the Turner Thesis, they have generally been omitted from textbooks used in college courses on the American West. While much scholarship has been produced recently on African American westerners, textbook authors have been slow to include mention of them in their works. Unfortunately, the same has been true of those who have written texts for use in African American history courses—they have not discovered the American West and the contributions black people made to its development. Thus, the editors expect this volume to be a worthy supplemental textbook in college courses on western American history and on the black experience in the United States. They also hope that scholars will use it to develop courses on the specific theme of the black presence on the western frontier. Hopefully, too, the book will be of interest to those readers who are neither university professors nor students but are, rather, members of the general public who find the topic interesting and want to read a book about it.

For purposes of this volume, the editors define the West as including those contiguous states whose areas are totally or in part west of the one hundredth meridian (or line of longitude). This description encompasses those seventeen states that make up the Great Plains, Rocky Mountain, and Pacific Slope regions. Since this is essentially a collection of previously published essays, however, adhering strictly to that definition has not been possible; a few of the articles include discussion of the states that lie between the Mississippi River and those bisected by the one hundredth meridian. The editors see this as no major departure, however, because the focus of each essay is on one or more of the states in or west of the Great Plains.

Likewise, the editors consider the frontier era to extend from 1850 to 1912. The beginning date is important because much of the West was first organized under provisions of the congressional Compromise of 1850. Concurrently, the number of African Americans moving west increased rather dramatically at mid-century. Several went to Utah with the Mormons in the late 1840s and early 1850s just as many others were participating in the California gold rush. And while it is true that several thousand African Americans were—prior to 1850—in two of the states/territories covered by this volume, blacks in Texas and Indian Territory were almost all slaves with no rights and little freedom until after the Civil War. Consequently, their impact on the settlement and development of the western frontier prior to 1850 was minimal; thus, the editors have chosen not to discuss the pre–1850 experiences of African Americans in Texas and what became Oklahoma.

Moreover, although some historians would claim that the frontier "closed" in 1890 because the U.S. census bureau and Frederick Jackson Turner said it did (and others would argue that it has not closed yet), the editors have chosen 1912—the year the last of the western territories attained statehood—as a logical date to conclude that the frontier period had ended. And, as is the case with the physical constraints of the editors' definition of "the West," a few of the articles included in this volume envelop time periods that stray outside the boundaries the editors have adopted. But these instances are few in number and minor in scope, and most of the essays fit comfortably within the 1850–1912 time frame.

The volume begins with an essay by early black historian W. Sherman Savage on the question of slavery and the status of African American pioneers in the new western territories acquired by the United States in the late 1840s. Newell G. Bringhurst then examines the implementation of slavery in the Mormon theocracy of Utah. Once slavery ended, the rights of freedmen were still uncertain; blacks organized and petitioned governmental authorities for equality in the late 1860s as Eugene H. Berwanger shows in his study of African American activism in Colorado during the Reconstruction era.

Freedom did not come easily to African Americans; nearly 200,000 blacks fought to abolish slavery during the Civil War. As a reward for that service and in recognition of the fact that black men made good soldiers, Congress in 1866 began the process that led to approximately 10 percent of the postwar army being comprised of African American soldiers assigned to all-black units of cavalry and infantry. Monroe Lee Billington surveys the history of these "buffalo soldiers" and their service in the American West during the last third of the nineteenth century. Michael J. Clark examines the experiences of one of the units—the Twenty-fourth Infantry—while it was stationed in Utah in the late 1890s, after the Indian wars were over.

Most ex-slaves and other blacks who went west during the frontier era did so to escape racism in the East and for the economic opportunity the region afforded them. The three most important methods of earning a living in the West during the late nineteenth century were to be found on the mining, cattle, and farming frontiers. Robert A. Campbell discusses black coal miners who went to Washington in the 1890s. Kenneth W. Porter—like Savage, a pioneering historian of the western black experience—examines the work of the several thousand African American cowboys who labored on western ranches and on the trails that went north from Texas into the Great Plains and Rocky Mountain regions. Eventually, the open range that made cattle raising so lucrative was—to a great extent—acquired by homesteaders who wanted to farm it and other settlers who earned their living in the towns that developed to provide goods and services to the soldiers, miners, cowboys, farmers, and townspeople. Randall B. Woods looks at the experiences of "exodusters" who went to Kansas after the Reconstruction era to escape the discrimination that prevailed in the former slave states. George O. Carney then surveys the movement that existed in Oklahoma and Indian territories (as well as in other

4

areas) to establish all-black towns where African Americans could live free of Caucasian influence or control.

While most of the scholarship that exists on black westerners—like that in other areas of the nation's history—is about men, a few researchers have sought to explain the role African American women played in settling the frontier. Glenda Riley presents a general overview of the history of black women in the West with an emphasis on the Great Plains region. Anne M. Butler then explores the lives and experiences of the tiny minority of western African American women who served time in frontier prisons.

Once black pioneers—whether male or female—journeyed to the frontier, they sought to create a "sense of community" in their settlements. This was true whether they lived in all-black communities or in segregated neighborhoods of towns with white majorities. William L. Lang looks at the institutions the black residents of Helena, Montana, established in the late frontier era, including a black-owned newspaper. Gayle K. Berardi and Thomas W. Segady expound upon the role of African American newspapers in furthering the "sense of community" concept of black pioneers on the western frontier. The volume concludes with Roger D. Hardaway presenting a bibliographic essay of the black frontier experience.

Some of the essays in this collection stress the ways in which the experiences of whites and blacks on the western frontier differed. Obviously, European Americans did not suffer the inhumanity of slavery; nor did they have to fight to attain the right to vote or secure the other benefits of citizenship. Other articles—especially those concerning segregated black communities and women prisoners—prove that the West was not free of racial prejudice. But the same was true of all other sections of the United States during the time period this book surveys. Moreover, one theme that runs throughout much of the remainder of the volume is that the experiences of most black westerners were essentially the same as those of most whites. Thus, with some exceptions, the western frontier generally afforded African Americans a substantial measure of equality, the freedom to live their lives as they chose, and the opportunity to become economically successful.

One concern that the editors confronted was how to refer to the people they were discussing. In recent years, "African-American" has become the preferred appellation of black leaders and organizations in the United States. Increasingly, the term is being used in scholarly works without the hyphen, and that is the version the editors have chosen to use along with the universally accepted "black." When some of the authors wrote, however, other designations such as "Negro" and "Afro-American" were in general use. The editors have made no attempt to correct these, preferring to leave the articles (in relation to this matter) in the forms in which they first appeared.

All of the essays in this book are reprinted, of course, with permission of the copyright holders. The eleven authors who are still living were all remarkably cooperative in allowing the editors to use their works. In all cases, the editors asked and received permission to correct typographical errors that appeared in the original versions of the essays. The editors also suggested a few stylistic changes, such as substituting "sixty" for "60," in order to bring some consistency to the narrative; again, the authors were exceptionally cooperative in agreeing to these alterations of their articles. The copyright holders of the works of the two deceased authors—Kenneth W. Porter and W. Sherman Savage—took different (but equally legitimate) approaches to the editors' requests for minor stylistic modifications. *Labor History*, which first published Porter's essay on black cowboys, accepted such changes because they did not substantially alter the author's work. Greenwood Press, the owner of the rights to the book from which the Savage piece is extracted, preferred not to allow any changes in the author's narrative except for the inclusion of minor clarifications in brackets to show that those words are the editors'—not Savage's. The editors made no attempt to reconcile the differences in form that the authors employed in drafting the "notes" sections of their works.

Finally, most of the essays in this book are reprinted in toto, but some have been edited—with permission—to shorten them and to remove any parts that the editors deemed irrelevant to the focus of this project. Again, authors and publishers were extremely helpful in allowing the editors to perform their tasks, and this has, hopefully, made the finished product better than it would have been otherwise. The editors would like to thank the interlibrary loan staffs of New Mexico State University and Northwestern Oklahoma State University for their patient help in locating items the editors needed for background information and in compiling their own original essays; Wilma Nossaman, who did almost all of the typing on the several versions of the evolving manuscript; those people who supplied photographs and maps; and the editorial staff of the University Press of Colorado. Without the cooperation of these many and varied people and organizations, this compilation would not have been possible.

SLAVERY IN THE WEST

W. Sherman Savage

[This article originally appeared as chapter 2, "The Slavery Issue," in W. Sherman Savage, *Blacks in the West* (1976), pp. 22–46, *passim*. Retitled, adapted, and reprinted with permission of Greenwood Publishing Group, Inc., Westport, Connecticut.]

Eighteen fifty was a watershed year in American—and especially western American —history. The 1840s had seen the United States acquire Texas, the Oregon Country, and the Mexican Cession. These areas made up over 40 percent of the land in the rapidly expanding nation. In Washington, Congress quickly granted statehood to Texas and created Oregon Territory; the former would have slavery while any states carved out of the latter would be free of the peculiar institution. Then, in 1850 the nation's lawmakers divided, organized, and sought to define the status of slavery in the land acquired as a result of the Mexican War. The Compromise of 1850 allowed California to enter the Union as a free state and created Utah and New Mexico territories (areas that included Nevada, Arizona, about half of Colorado, and a small portion of Wyoming) with slavery existing in them if the people who lived there should so choose.

The Compromise of 1850 was far from a total success. Both Utah and New Mexico experimented with legalized slavery, but the environment and other factors worked against the practice becoming a permanent part of those regions' political, economic, and social systems. Moreover, the status of blacks in the "free" state of California—seemingly settled by congressional action and the California constitution—remained in limbo for several years. Most early slaveholding pioneers who went to the first Pacific Coast state ignored the law and kept their "slaves" in bondage until forced to set them free. In 1856, in a landmark case brought to trial by Bridget "Biddy" Mason (who spent five years as a slave in "free" California), a judge ruled for the first time that slavery could not exist in the Golden State. Other courts decided cases accordingly until slaveholders began to realize that they must either free their slaves in California or dispose of them before migrating there.

California was not, however, the only western state or territory in which whites illegally enslaved African Americans; a few slaves were to be found from time to time in Oregon Territory (which included Washington and much of Idaho, Montana, and Wyoming) and in other free areas. Thus, the story of slavery's existence in the West is not as simple as it might first appear. Moreover, in 1854 Congress passed the Kansas-Nebraska Act, opening up the possibility of slavery existing in all parts of the old Louisiana Purchase (the institution was already sanctioned in Indian Territory, Arkansas, and Louisiana by the Missouri Compromise of 1820). Finally, in 1857 the U.S. Supreme Court, in the so-called Dred Scott Decision (Scott v. Sandford, 19 Howard 393), ruled that slaveholders could take their human chattels into any U.S. territory—congressional action in creating "free" territories violated the constitutional prohibition against taking property without due process. Consequently, 1850— which had produced a supposed resolution of the issue of slavery in the western territories—ushered in a decade of controversy, conflict, and confusion about the status of African Americans in the West.

In this volume's first essay, W. Sherman Savage—truly a pioneering historian of the western black experience—discusses slavery as it existed in the American West with an especial emphasis on the troubled decade of the 1850s. Savage argues— in a voice echoed by most historians who have addressed the subject since he first did so—that western slavery was not as harsh as its southern counterpart. Savage cannot imagine, for example, that the system that allowed Biddy Mason to sue for her freedom and win in a California court could have existed anywhere in the slaveholding South. Nevertheless, being a slave meant having to move where one's master wanted to go, and many of the first African Americans in the West went to the region in bondage.

When men [and women] began to move west, the area was regarded as free territory that would not be disturbed by slavery. Many people felt that slavery could not exist in the West because it would not be profitable. The commodities that had made it profitable in the South—cotton, rice, sugar cane, and tobacco—were not grown in the West. Both Henry Clay and Daniel Webster assured the country that there could be no slavery in the West because of geographical prohibitions. They did this with firm conviction in the debate on the Compromise of 1850, which, when passed, resulted in self-determination within the territory on the slavery issue. Others spoke against slavery in the West on moral grounds. This position was represented by a former citizen of a slave state, writing in the *Californian,* who opposed the introduction of slavery in California and other parts of the West because, to him, slavery anywhere was wrong. He felt that blacks had equal rights to health and happiness and that every individual's duty to society was to be employed in such a way as to support himself.[1]

Many of the governments established in the West had adopted the slavery provision and related ideas of the Ordinance of 1787, which set up a territorial governing system for the Northwest. The provision of that ordinance which dealt with slavery was Article VI. It stated that "there shall be neither slavery nor involuntary servitude in said territory, otherwise than in punishment of crimes whereof the party shall have been duly convicted. Provided always, that any person escaping into same, from whom labor or service is lawfully claimed, such fugitive may be lawfully reclaimed and conveyed to the person claiming his or her labor or service."

Nevertheless, slavery did exist in the West, largely because of slave owners who moved to the frontier and brought their slaves with them. Many of those who migrated west were from the southern states of Virginia, Kentucky, Tennessee, and the Carolinas. In Oregon in 1850, about 30 percent of the population had come from southern states. These persons were determined to perpetuate slavery in this new territory, and they persisted despite all opposition.

The controversy over slavery in the West was therefore an extension of that issue in the East. The North was determined that slavery should not be established in the new states and territories which were formed out of newly acquired land, especially the section north of the original Missouri Compromise Line. The South was equally determined that its slave economy should be established and perpetuated in as many as possible of the states which were formed from this acquired land. The South hoped that a sufficient number of its own citizens would go to these new states to gain control of their governments in order to maintain the South and its point of view.[2]

The matter of slavery in Missouri was settled with the admission of that state into the Union. But Nebraska and Kansas were admitted after the Kansas-Nebraska Bill was passed by Congress. There were two main reasons for this bill: the building of the Pacific Railroad to the West and the extension of slavery. It was an attempt to effect a compromise between the free and the slave interests of the American Union by prohibiting slavery in Nebraska but acknowledging its possibility in Kansas.

According to the census report of 1860, the black population of Nebraska was eighty-two. When the Civil War began, the black population was still less than a hundred, and a large number of these were free blacks. There were, however, a few slaves in Nebraska. From 1854 to 1857, the territory of Nebraska was divided into six districts, and a yearly census was taken to ascertain how many persons lived in each district and in the territory as a whole. The 1854 census showed four slaves in District One and nine in District Two.[3] The report for 1855 showed five slaves in Richardson County in the southern part of the territory near Kansas and Iowa; Atoe County, in the same general area, had six. According to the 1856 report, there were five slaves in Atoe County, two in Richardson County, and four in Omaha County.[4] It is possible that there were other slaves who were not reported. Several instances of blacks at Fort Phil Kearney are known. For example, a black woman was brought to the fort by a Mrs. Carrington, the wife of an army officer stationed there. Supposedly, there was a need for slaves to furnish the domestic service around the post, and the woman served as a maid to Mrs. Carrington.[5] Another black woman was a servant of the wife of a Lieutenant Ward, and Captain Ten Eyck had a black slave who served as his butler.[6]

The incidence of slavery in Kansas was greater than that in Nebraska. The first census, in 1855, revealed 193 slaves, and in 1856 the number increased to 400. They were owned by fifty slaveholders who had moved into the state and had sought to win Kansas for slavery. But there were also many persons in Kansas who opposed slavery. Some were "poor whites" or persons from the Deep South or the Southwest who did not own slaves. Elise Isely said that the Boston and Hutchinson families represented a cross section of those who came from slave states but were opposed to slavery.[7]

The presence of slaveholders and the Kansas-Nebraska Bill notwithstanding, the constitution of Kansas included a section on slavery providing that there should be no slavery or involuntary servitude in the territory except as punishment for those who had been convicted of a criminal offense.[8] The statutes of the territory of Kansas also provided for slaves in bondage. Any person who was held in slavery had the privilege of petitioning the district court judge for leave to sue as a poor person in order to establish his right to freedom. He was required, however, to give the ground upon which he claimed his freedom. The court then would decide if the ground was sufficient.[9] The slave was not to be removed from the territory nor be harshly treated until his case was heard. The drawback of such a law, as far as the slave was concerned, was that it placed the burden of proof on him, in the interest of protecting the slave owner as well.[10] Lacking formal education or outside assistance, he was usually helpless.

Another act of the territorial legislature of Kansas made it plain that no person who was conscientiously opposed to holding a slave or who did not admit the right to hold slaves in the territory could sit as a juror in a trial when any violation of the act dealing with slaves was being tried.[11]

There were some slaves also in Iowa because of its nearness to Missouri. State records document such cases as that of the black who was given to a bride at the time of her marriage to George Wilson of Agency, Iowa. The condition of the gift was that the boy, Henry Triplett, must be taught a trade and be given his freedom at the age of twenty. This was carried out faithfully, and he was apprenticed to a blacksmith named Stephens. Triplett subsequently became a minister in the Methodist church, but he always revered his former master, Wilson.[12] According to information furnished by his son, George Wilson owned another slave, a black woman whom he held on his farm at Agency and at Dubuque at various times. She was unruly and Wilson could do little to control her. In the southern system, her master would have made an attempt to break her spirit. But in Iowa such action would scarcely have been attempted. Wilson decided upon another method; he traded the slave woman for a pair of mules and never bought another slave.[13] In Linn County in 1860 there was a case concerning a woman named Henrietta. Like many other slaves, she had no other name.[14] Henrietta was born in Virginia and was probably sold to her master in Iowa, although there is a possibility that she had been reared in her master's family and brought to Iowa by them.

The territorial laws of Iowa specified that slavery or involuntary servitude should exist only as punishment for convicted criminals. Fugitive slaves were another matter, however. Slaves frequently escaped from Missouri into Iowa, and the citizens of northern Missouri were so much concerned about them that they formed an organization to help the slave owners in that section reclaim their property. In 1860 four slaves belonging to T. W. Dobyns, John Furgenson, and Chester Cotton escaped to Iowa and were traced as far as Henry County where the trail was lost.[15] Although slavery was prohibited by law, then, it did exist, and the problem of escaping slaves was very serious. One writer reported that as many as 10,000 slaves escaped from the South each year. This figure may be high, but it is known that a large number did escape annually right up to the Civil War. Slavery was therefore a prominent issue in Iowa. Henry Clay Dean, speaking of the Democratic party in Iowa, claimed that it had lost two governorships, two United States Senate seats, and both houses of the state legislature for three successive sessions because it had not concerned itself with the black question.[16]

In Wisconsin and Minnesota there was little demand for slavery. In fact, there was strong opposition. Henry Dodge and the Gratiot brothers were among the greatest influences in its abolition in Wisconsin and Minnesota. David Giddings, a relative of the famous Joshua R. Giddings, was another fearless fighter against slavery. When the Wisconsin state constitution was drafted, it gave suffrage to all white men over twenty-one years of age, but Giddings moved that the word "white" be stricken so that all males, without regard to race, should vote. The section on black slavery was submitted separately. Both sections failed at that time, however.[17]

There were those who migrated to Wisconsin and Minnesota from southern Illinois, Missouri, and southern states. In some cases they brought their slaves with them to perform domestic service.[18] One instance involves Major Lawrence Taliaferro, an Indian agent for many years at Fort Snelling. He inherited a number of slaves, whom he took with him to Fort Snelling after his appointment.[19] Among the slaves brought from Virginia was Harriet, who was purchased from Taliaferro by Dr. John Emerson in order that she could become the wife of Dred Scott.[20] Taliaferro leased his slaves to officers at the fort, which accounts for the way he could keep a number of slaves with so little for them to do. Later, the major freed his slaves, who were valued at $30,000.[21]

In Colorado as well, only a few slaves were found. The soil and climate there were not amenable to the kinds of crop which blacks had traditionally worked. Still, some of the first blacks recorded in Colorado, in the census of 1860, were probably slaves. One writer, for example, says that Joel Estes, discoverer of the beautiful park which bears his name, had with him several black slaves.[22]

Likewise, there were few blacks, slave or free, in Utah.... Consequently, the black has exerted little influence in Utah. Some mention might be made of the Mormon church's position with respect to slavery, however. The Mormons had moved from the Midwest, where they had first settled, because they had been badly treated there. They wanted to move out of the United States, but in this they failed because the United States acquired Utah Territory soon after they settled there. The Mormons wanted to go where their religious freedom would not be disturbed, but the freedom that they sought did not always carry with it political freedom or freedom for all blacks. Elder Orson Hyde, writing in the *Frontier Guardian,* felt that he was called upon to define the attitude of the church on slavery, for there were several men who had brought their slaves with them to their new location. Hyde explained that the slave could leave his master if he chose, for there was no law in Utah which authorized slavery, and no law could prevent slaves from leaving. He went on to say that when a slave owner in the South embraced the Mormon faith, the church decreed that it was for the slave to decide whether or not he wished to remain in the master-slave relationship. Nevertheless, the church left the slave a victim of existing laws, for it would not interfere with the law of the land. While regarding the selling of slaves as a sin, the church let moral responsibility for such an act rest with the individual church member. Hyde advised all the Mormon elders in the North and South to avoid controversies over the slavery question, and he told them that they should oppose no institution which the country recognized.[23] By this definition of its attitude on slavery, the Mormon church recognized the right of the slave to self-determination in his claim of freedom.

Richard Burton writes that slavery was legalized in Utah solely for the purpose of allowing the Saints to purchase slave children who might otherwise be abandoned or destroyed by their parents. He felt that some of the slave parents were so devoted to their children that they would destroy them rather than see them in slavery. Despite this, he was sure that there were only a few slaves in the territory. A most important factor, in his opinion, was the weather, which was not favorable to the crops which required slave labor.[24] He thought that another consideration was the cost of keeping slaves when there was nothing for them to do. Certainly, this was a factor in the whole slavery movement and was the reason why slaves were moved from the northern states to the southern states before the Civil War.

There were, however, some slaves in Utah, despite conditions that were not conducive to their presence in the state. A few slaves came to Salt Lake City with a company which set out from Mississippi on January 10, 1847. The pioneers in the company were John Bankhead, William Lay, and William Crosby, each attended by a slave.[25] A list of slaveholders in Utah supplies the names and other information. Daniel Thomas, one of the original pioneers, brought with him his slave servant, Toby. William Matthews brought his servant, known as "Uncle" Phil. William Lay had with him Hank, whose name appears on the plaque of the original settlers. William Crosby owned two slaves, whose names, Oscar and Griff, also appear on the list of pioneers. James Flake also owned two slaves, Martha and Green. Martha was acquired by Herbert Kimball, who took her to California where he remained for a short time before returning to South Carolina. Before his departure, however, he made arrangement for James Flake to take possession of Martha, and she became the wife of Green Flake.[26] Another pioneer slave owner was William Smith, who owned Herman and Lawrence. All of these men, together with their slave servants, were the pioneers who went to Salt Lake City and had much to do with its organization and development.[27]

The record of what these blacks did when they obtained their freedom is not known in much detail. Green Flake moved from Salt Lake City to Union, a small town in Salt Lake County. Later in life he moved back to Salt Lake City and lived there for a time before moving to Idaho Falls where he died on

October 20, 1900.[28] Frank Perkins, the slave of Ruben Perkins, settled in the West with his master. Whether he remained a slave or became a free man in Utah is not revealed in the available records. Ben Perkins, probably a brother of Ruben Perkins, owned a slave named Ben, whom he sold in Utah to a Texan named Sprouse. Sprouse tried to take Ben to the South, but the latter escaped in the mountains near Denver and returned to Utah where he remained a free man the rest of his life.[29]

There were few blacks and correspondingly few slaves in Idaho, Montana, Nevada, North and South Dakota, New Mexico, and Arizona. [Historian Hubert Howe] Bancroft noted that the only slaves in Arizona, for example, were a few domestic servants who were brought there from time to time. A few others who belonged to the fur companies found work in that industry. One case is recorded of a will, filed in 1818, in which provisions were made for a slave woman, XY, to be given her liberty at the death of her master.[30] This region was then a part of New Spain, however, and the woman might have been an Indian.

Oregon was another state where there were not many blacks, yet few other states matched it in the controversy over slavery. The issue was political rather than economic, and it came into full view when the provisional government was established. A section added to the Oregon Organic Act excluded slavery from the territory, but there were those who felt that slavery ought to be extended to include Oregon.[31] One Oregonian, in an open letter published in the *Sacramento Democratic State Journal,* stated that there were many persons in Oregon who favored slavery.[32]

Oregon outgrew its provisional government and, looking toward statehood, operated under committees. In August 1857 a constitutional convention was called for the purpose of drafting a constitution. One of the first questions which faced that body was slavery. On August 18, 1857, Jesse Applegate of Umpqua County said that the members of the convention had been chosen by the people with the expressed or implied understanding that the slavery issue would not be decided by the constitutional convention but by the people themselves. He introduced a resolution to prevent the convention from discussing the subject. That body, he thought, was not capable of handling such a matter, and discussion would only engender bitter feeling among its members. It would destroy harmony, delay the business unnecessarily, and thus prolong its sessions. The second part of his resolution recommended that the committee on rules be instructed to declare out of order all debate on the subject of slavery, either as an abstract proposition or as a mere matter of policy.[33]

The convention made provision for submitting the whole question of slavery to the people; if the measure passed, it was to be added to the constitution. The bill submitted to the voters stated that "persons lawfully held as slaves in any state, territory or district of the United States, under the law thereof, may be brought into the state and such slaves and their descendants may be held as slaves within the state and should not be emancipated without the consent of their owner." If the citizens voted against the measure, Section VI of the Northwest Ordinance, which stipulated that there should be neither slavery nor involuntary servitude in the state other than as a punishment for crime, would be added to the Organic Law.[34] The measure failed, and slavery was excluded from the territory.

Although the action of the convention seemed to exclude all possibility of slavery in Oregon, the same action had been approved earlier by the state legislature when it was organized. Despite this, slavery did exist in Oregon. One case was that of Lou Southworth, who came to Oregon with Benjamin Seals in 1853. Also in 1853, Amanda Wilhite came across the plains from Missouri and remained a slave in Oregon for many years, a gift from her master to his daughter. Amanda had been born in Liberty, Clay County, Missouri. She later became the wife of Benjamin Johnson, a slave who came across the plains at the same time.[35] Yet another instance of slavery in Oregon involved a man named Robin Holmes, whose children were held as slaves. Their owner, Nathaniel Ford, came to Oregon in 1845 and brought with him three slaves, two men and one woman. The woman married one of the men and became the mother of several children whom Ford continued to claim until 1853. Their parents, Robin and Polly Holmes, claimed their freedom, left Ford, and lived at Nesmith's Mill. When Ford denied them their children, Holmes sought a writ of habeas corpus to obtain possession of them.[36] Judge George Williams directed Ford to bring the children into court and to show cause for their detention.[37] The case came to trial in the summer of 1853, and the children were awarded to Holmes on the ground that slaves had been brought into Oregon where slavery could not exist according to the law and practice.[38]

Slaves are known to have been in California as long ago as the Spanish regime, although their presence then was exceptional. A case in point is that of the slave girl owned by the wife of a Spanish citizen named Ontonio Jose de Cot. Other citizens opposed the presence of the slave and insisted that she be removed from the country. Senora de Cot assured them that it was her intention to leave California as early as possible, and in all probability she did.[39] Bancroft speaks of a slave who had been brought into California from Peru in 1828 and who for some reason went back to Peru.[40] It is possible that she and the slave of Senora de Cot were the same person.

Some pioneers wanted to bring slaves into California from the southern states in the hope of producing cotton there. James Gadsden, famous for the purchase which bears his name, is representative of southerners who felt that cotton could be grown profitably in California's warm climate.[41] Such an ambition bore little fruit, however. For the most part, the slaves who were brought into California were body servants and domestic servants.

The gold rush, of course, made California a focus of public interest. Perhaps for this reason, slavery there received a good deal of attention. Before California came into the Union, slavery was a burning issue. The Compromise of 1850 made it a free state, but in 1852 the California State Legislature passed an act which allowed owners who had brought their slaves into the territory before it was admitted into the Union to keep them, provided they did not remain in California.[42] This action did not mean that the state legislature had sanctioned slavery but that California would not free the slaves who had been brought in before 1850. The owners were given a stipulated time by which to remove their slaves from the state. Some owners complied with the new law within the time specified, while others completely disregarded the law, holding their slaves almost until the Civil War.

In many of the California papers, advertisements appeared which offered black slaves for sale. Perhaps this was in order to comply with the law which demanded that owners get rid of their slaves if they wished to remain in California. In 1851, for example, a slaveholder advertised in one of the Sacramento papers that he had for sale a black named Julius Caesar, whom he would sell for $100. He asked the abolitionists or persons who were opposed to slavery to buy him, but whether Caesar was bought or given his freedom outright is not known.[43]

The case of Charley Bates is evidence that the California law did not protect all blacks there. Bates had been the slave of a man from Mississippi who brought several slaves into California with the idea of giving them their freedom in two years. Not trusting their master, all the slaves except Bates ran away. Bates remained the full two years, secured his freedom, and moved to Stockton. One day he was seen by one of his former master's creditors, who filed against him as chattel property and put him up for sale. He was bought by an abolitionist for $750.[44]

The case of Alvin Coffey is another which shows that the law was not always enforced. Coffey was born about 1822 in Saint Louis County, Missouri, and remained there a slave, working for his master until 1849 when his master decided to leave Missouri and join the gold rush. By October 1849 they reached California and settled in a mining camp. Duval, the master, did not like the

Gold miner. Several hundred African Americans labored in the nineteenth-century western gold fields. This miner was photographed in the Auburn Ravine of California in 1852. (Courtesy, California State Library.)

West and decided to return to Missouri. He took all the money which Alvin had been able to accumulate by working on his own after hours and then sold Alvin to a man named Tindle. This whole transaction was begun and completed in the state of California where slavery did not legally exist. Tindle in turn allowed Coffey to purchase his freedom for $1,500. Freed by his own purchase, Coffey devoted himself to business. He established a laundry, and in a few years he accumulated about $10,000. He was so successful in his business that he was able to make a loan of $2,000 to a minister who had lost his crop. Although the loan was never repaid, Coffey was sufficiently established in business to sustain the loss without apparent injury.[45]

There were two cases in San Jose that involved slavery in California. In one, a slaveholder named Ferguson had brought a black slave named Joe from Kentucky in the 1850s. Ferguson realized that there was always the danger that a slaveholder might be taken to court in California, and this he was determined to prevent. He sold Joe to James Reed, for whom Joe worked for several years in San Jose.[46] The other case is of some importance from the point of view of the master as well as the slave, for it shows one man's humane response to the potential evil of the slave system. Judge Kincade came to town from Missouri, bringing with him two slave couples and their children. He soon realized that he did not need laborers in California and decided to sell one of the couples, Abe and Sarah, and their children.[47] The judge made sure, when he sold them, that the family would not be separated, since he shared the belief of those who felt that such separation was the worst feature of the slave system.

By 1859 most slaveholders realized that, if they took their slaves into California, they were in danger of losing them. In that year, for example, Napoleon Byrnes of Missouri sold most of his slaves in his home state before he started for California. He did, however, keep two, whom he brought into California with him. One of them was known as "Uncle" Pete, who earned his livelihood by whitewashing buildings, a craft more in vogue then than now. "Uncle" Pete became a free man, but he seems to have been happy with Brynes and his family. He constantly came back to visit his former master and insisted on waiting on the table on special occasions. He wanted to leave all of his earnings to Brynes, but the latter kindly refused.[48]

Slavery in California was much like slavery in the acknowledged slave-holding states in that it was characterized by both good men and bad. There were benevolent masters who emancipated their slaves for a variety of reasons. One case of this sort occurred in Butte County, where Franklin Stewart freed a slave named Washington who for more than seventeen years had given faithful service in Arkansas and Missouri as well as California. Stewart made it known that he was entitled, by law and equity, to keep this slave and that he was freeing him of his own volition.[49] The transaction of emancipation was recorded in the court of Butte County, May 4, 1852. In the same county, A. G. Simpson freed his slave, Lewis Taylor.[50] Taylor seems to have been one of those slaves who came to California with their masters under an agreement that they would be freed after a specified period of service. The ironic feature of this case was that the master could not write; his slaves signed his name to documents which he authenticated by his mark. In Mariposa County, Thomas Thorn freed his slave, Peter Green, and the emancipation had a monetary condition attached to it. Peter was to pay Thorn $1,000 or serve for a year, beginning April 1, 1853. Which alternative Green selected is not known, but he did remain in the northern section of California and took a leading part in the Methodist church in Stockton.[51]

While slavery in the West was generally accompanied by humane treatment, the records do show some cases of brutality. In one such case in California, a master was observed beating his slave over the head with a stick because the latter had been associating with free blacks. The master was forcibly restrained from continuing his chastisement, but he threatened to take the black back and have him whipped. Friends of freedom instituted habeas corpus proceedings and secured a writ which was served on the master. However, when the case came to trial, the slave was awarded to the master, who took him back to the South.[52] This occurred in 1850, when the fugitive slave question was before the country. That question probably had a bearing on the outcome of the case.

Because slavery in the West was generally prohibited by law, many slaves brought into the region sought their freedom through legal means. It is true that there were slave cases adjudicated in the southern states, but they were not initiated by the slaves themselves, and in any case the word of a slave was not taken against that of a white man. In the West the burden of proof was on the slave owner to show why his slave should not be freed.

The interpretation of the law varied from state to state, and even from case to case, however. In some cases slave owners were able to regain their slaves. When in 1859, for example, a slave named Peter Fisher escaped from Kentucky to Kansas, he was found, arrested, tried under the Fugitive Slave Law, and returned to his owners.[53]

Because of the relatively large number of blacks in California, the slave question came before the courts there more often than in the other states of the West. In its efforts to regulate slavery in the state, the California Legislature passed an act which gave the slave owner who claimed a slave the authority to procure a warrant for the slave's arrest. Any civil officer could be called upon, and he was forced to serve the warrant and make the arrest. If the slave owner could prove in court that the slave belonged to him, he was authorized by law to take the slave, by force if necessary, but he was required to remove the slave from the state.[54] The state constitution declared that neither slavery nor involuntary servitude could exist in the state of California, but the legislature provided for the punishment of those who helped slaves to escape. They were subjected to a fine, imprisonment, or civil damages which could be collected by the owner. This law was rigidly enforced between the years 1852 and 1854. Antislavery Democrats then amended the law, rendering it ineffective after April 15, 1855.[55]

Many persons in California had migrated from southern states where slavery was legal. Some of these southern pioneers were opposed to slavery in this new state because it meant competition for jobs. These same citizens were in favor of slave owners' being able to recapture any slaves escaping into California. This no doubt was partially the reason for the law which prohibited slaves from living in the state, and it was the reason why the legislature was ready to pass an enabling act to the California Fugitive Slave Law.

Several cases of owners who tried to secure their slaves and return them to servitude came before the California courts. One of these was the case of C. S. Perkins of Mississippi. Perkins claimed three slaves, Carter, Robert, and

Sandy, who were seized on January 1, 1852, and taken before Justice of the Peace B. D. Fry. These slaves could be claimed under both the state and the national laws, which provided for the return of slaves who were fugitives from labor. The charge was vigorously denied by the slaves, each of whom claimed that he did not owe labor to anyone. The slaves declared that for several months they had been in the agricultural business for themselves. They sued for a writ of habeas corpus, which was finally brought before the California State Supreme Court on which Chief Justice C. H. Murray and associate justices Alexander Anderson and Solomon Hydenfelt sat. The writ was denied and the slaves were remanded to their master.[56]

One of the important cases of slavery which came before the courts in California was that of Robert Smith. In 1851 Smith started out from Hancock County, Georgia, with the strongest and best of his slaves and settled in Mississippi. He did not remain there long but moved westward, spending some time en route in Illinois and Missouri. Being a Mormon, Smith went on to the Mormon settlement in Salt Lake City. At the outset there were eight slaves, but by 1856 there were fourteen, among them the slave woman Biddy Mason. Smith went in search of gold but later moved to San Bernardino County, California. Because he had kept the slaves in California, contrary to the state constitution, Smith knew that they were legally free. He then decided to move to Texas, and he told the slaves that they would be free there since they were free in California. Biddy Mason was the first of Smith's slaves to doubt his many promises of freedom. When Robert Owen, one of the early black pioneers in Los Angeles, visited the slaves in Santa Monica Canyon, Biddy Mason made known to him her master's intentions, whereupon Owen had the slaves arrested and put in the county jail.[57] They were brought into court on a writ of habeas corpus, and the court decided that all of them over twenty-one years of age should have their freedom, while those under twenty-one should be placed under the jurisdiction of the court. "When the constitution was framed," the judge said, "those who had slaves were given a reasonable time to get them out of the state. The older slaves could not be held because the time for such holding had passed, and those who were born in California had never been slaves since they were born in a free state."

To summarize the issue of slavery in the West: while for the most part slavery was legally proscribed in the West, there were slaves there. Consequently, many of the problems which faced slaves in other states manifested themselves in the West as well. Slaves were brought to the West and sometimes were kept in defiance of the law. Some slaves who fled to the West in the hope of becoming free were tracked down, arrested, and taken back to slave states.

Biddy Mason. Born a slave, Mason successfully sued for her freedom in a California court in 1857. Later, she worked as a midwife and became one of the first African American landowners in Los Angeles. (Courtesy, University of California at Los Angeles.)

And yet there was a fundamental difference. The South, in reducing the slave to the status of a possession, a thing, deprived him of his human voice. In the West the black man could express himself in court and expect to be heard. Indeed, the burden lay not so much with the black man to justify his freedom but with the slave owner to justify slavery. As a result, a number of black people did pass from slavery to freedom, engaged in a variety of activities, and so took their place among all the people who settled the West.

Notes

1. *San Francisco Californian,* March 15, 1858.
2. Seymour Dunbar, *A History of Travel in America* (Indianapolis, 1915), p. 1226.
3. *Territorial Papers of Nebraska,* vol. 1, 1854–1857.
4. *Census Returns,* 1856.
5. Grace Raymond Hebard and E. A. Brininstool, *Bozeman Trail,* vol. 2, p. 90.
6. Ibid., vol. 1, p. 294.
7. Elise Isely, *Sunbonnet Days* (Caldwell, Id., 1935), p.81.
8. Constitution of Kansas, Bill of Rights, Section VI.
9. *Statutes of the Territory of Kansas* (1855), p. 381. This law became effective September 15, 1855.
10. Ibid., p. 171.
11. *Lawrence Daily Journal-World,* March 13, 1933, General W. H. Teors.
12. George Wilson, Jr., "George Wilson: First Territorial Adjutant of the Militia of Iowa," *Annals of Iowa,* 3rd series, 4 (January 1901), p. 571.
13. Ibid., p. 572.
14. Linn County, Iowa, U.S. Census Office, 8th Census, 1860 (Government Printing Office: Washington, D.C., 1864).
15. *History of Marion County, Missouri,* p. 218.
16. Louis Pelzer, "The History of Political Parties in Iowa from 1857 to 1860," *Iowa Journal of History and Politics* 7 (April 1909), p. 194.
17. Louise P. Kellogg, "The Story of Wisconsin, 1634–1848," *Wisconsin Magazine of History* 3 (1919–20), p. 230.
18. John N. Davidson, "Negro Slavery in Wisconsin," *Wisconsin State Historical Society Proceedings,* Fortieth Annual Meeting (December 8, 1892), p. 82.
19. James H. Baker, "Address at Fort Snelling in the Celebration of the Centennial Anniversary of the Treaty of Pike with the Sioux," *Minnesota Historical Society Collections* 12 (1905–08), p. 297.
20. John D. Lawson, ed., *American State Trials* (1914; rpt., Wilmington, Del., 1971), vol. 13, p. 220.
21. "Auto-Biography of Maj. Lawrence Taliaferro, Written in 1864," *Minnesota Historical Society Collections* 6 (1894), p. 235.
22. James Harvey, "The Negro in Colorado" (M.A. Thesis, University of Denver, 1941). This same evidence is given by Mrs. Ira Williams, granddaughter of Joel Estes.
23. "Slavery among the Saints," *Millenial Star* 13 (February 15, 1851), p. 63 (quoting remarks of Elder Orson Hyde in *Frontier Guardian*).
24. Richard F. Burton, *The City of the Saints and Across the Rocky Mountains to California* (New York, 1861), p. 297.
25. John Brown, "Pioneer Journeys: From Nauvoo, Illinois, to Pueblo, Colorado, in 1846, and over the Plains in 1847," arranged by John Zimmerman Brown, *Improvement Era* 13 (July 1910), p. 810.
26. Jack Beller, "Negro Slaves in Utah," *Utah Historical Quarterly* 2 (October 1929), p. 124. This accounts for her being listed as the slave of James Flake.
27. John Brown, *Autobiography of a Pioneer* (Salt Lake City, 1941).
28. Beller, "Negro Slaves in Utah," p. 125.
29. Ibid., p. 124.
30. Louis H. Warner, "Wills and Hijuelas," *New Mexico Historical Review* 7 (January 1932), p. 84.
31. William P. Lords, *Oregon Laws,* vol. 1, p. 83.
32. *Sacramento Democratic State Journal,* September 15, 1857.
33. *Journal of Constitutional Convention,* quoted in *The Oregon Constitution and Proceedings and Debates of the Constitutional Convention of 1857,* ed. by Charles H. Carey (Salem: State Printing Department, 1926), p. 79.

34. Charles H. Carey, ed., *The Oregon Constitution and Proceedings and Debates of the Constitutional Convention of 1857,* pp. 30–34.
35. Fred Lockley, "Facts Pertaining to Ex-Slaves in Oregon, and Documentary Record of the Case of Robin Holmes vs. Nathaniel Ford," *Oregon Historical Society Quarterly* 23 (June 1922), p. 112.
36. T. W. Davenport, "Slavery Question in Oregon," *Oregon Historical Society Quarterly* 8 (September 1908), p. 196.
37. Lockley, "Facts Pertaining to Ex-Slaves in Oregon," p. 112.
38. Davenport, "Slavery Question in Oregon," p. 196.
39. Theodore H. Hittell, *History of California* (San Francisco, 1897), vol. 2, p. 115.
40. Bancroft, *History of California* (San Francisco, 1884), vol. 2, p. 293.
41. M. Eva Thacker, "California's Dixie Land," *California History Nuggets* 5 (March 1938), p. 174.
42. *Laws of State of California, Acts of Legislature, 1853* (San Francisco: Franklin Printing House).
43. R. M. Baker, *Representative and Leading Men of the Pacific* (San Francisco, 1870), p. 304.
44. George H. Tinkham, *History of Stockton from its Organization up to the Present Time, Including a Sketch of San Joaquin County* (San Francisco, 1880), p. 132. This incident (involving Charley Bates) occurred soon after California came into the Union.
45. Delilah L. Beasley, *Negro Trail Blazers of California* (Los Angeles, 1919), p. 70.
46. "When San Jose Was Young," a series of articles prepared for the *San Jose News,* January 5, 1917–April 22, 1918.
47. Ibid.
48. Mary T. Carleton, comp., "The Byrnes of Berkeley: From Letters of Mary Tanner Byrne and Other Sources," *California Historical Society Quarterly* 17 (March 1938), p. 44.
49. D. L. Beasley and M. N. Work, comps., "California Freedom Papers," *Journal of Negro History* 3 (January 1918), p. 47.
50. Frank Gilbert, "History of California from 1513 to 1850," vol. 1 of F. Gilbert and Harry L. Wells, *History of Butte County, California* (San Francisco, 1882), p. 199.
51. Owen C. Coy, "Evidences of Slavery in California," *Grizzly Bear* 19 (October 1916), pp. 1–2.
52. *San Francisco Daily Alta Californian,* February 16, 1850.
53. Thomas A. McNeal, *When Kansas Was Young* (New York, 1934), p. 8.
54. Tinkham, *History of Stockton,* p. 135.
55. Ibid.
56. Ibid.
57. *Los Angeles Times,* February 12, 1909.

THE MORMONS AND SLAVERY— A CLOSER LOOK

Newell G. Bringhurst

[This article originally appeared in the *Pacific Historical Review*, Vol. 50 (1981), pp. 329–338. Copyright by the Pacific Coast Branch, American Historical Association. Reprinted with permission.]

Utah Territory was an anomaly among western American regions. Whereas most European Americans who went west in the 1840s and succeeding decades were drawn by the area's economic opportunities (mining, cattle raising, farming, etc.), those who went to Utah wanted a remote place where they could exercise religious freedom. The territorial government that Congress created in Utah in 1850 was headed for a number of years by Brigham Young who had led several thousand members of the Church of Jesus Christ of Latter-day Saints to the Great Salt Lake valley in the late 1840s. The Mormons settled the desert valley, established their culture and customs there, and ruled it once the U.S. government granted it territorial status. Utah was, in short, a Mormon theocracy.

Mormon attitudes toward African Americans have been controversial ever since Joseph Smith began the Latter-day Saint religion in 1830. Many black Americans have consistently condemned the Mormons as racists while the church's white leaders have just as steadfastly defended the religion's antiblack practices as being grounded in biblical doctrine. From Smith's home base in New York, the Mormons moved first to Ohio and continued their westward trek to Missouri. But when a church newspaper editorialized in favor of converting free blacks to Mormonism, many slaveholding Missourians, believing this would cause an influx of African Americans to the state, reacted negatively. This concern caused Smith to issue some proslavery statements in an apparent effort to mollify the Saints' non-Mormon neighbors. Still harassed, however, the church's members moved east into the free state of Illinois. When Smith decided to create a third party and run for president in 1844, he surprised many observers by reversing the church's Missouri policy and advocating the abolition of slavery.

Regardless of Smith's—and the Mormons'—changing views on slavery, little doubt exists that the Saints, like most European Americans of that era, believed that blacks were inferior to whites. Smith and a few other prominent Mormons, while denouncing slavery, kept African American "servants" in their homes. When Young led a contingent of church members to Utah in the years following Smith's murder in June 1844, several Mormons took their servants with them. Soon they were joined by a few southern converts who brought more slaves to Utah.

Young's support of slavery in Utah led to the legalization of the peculiar institution in his theocracy for a decade—from 1852 to 1862. The Mormon brand of slavery, however, paled in its harshness when compared to southern bondage. The law required slaveholding Saints to grant their slaves (whom the Mormons still persisted in calling "servants") some basic rights. But, as Newell G. Bringhurst argues in the following essay, the fact that the Latter-day Saints treated their slaves with some significant concessions to their status as humans did not mean that white Mormons believed in the equality of their African American fellow churchmen. The Utah legislature passed several segregation laws, and the church's hierarchy refused to allow black men to become "priests" (a lay status afforded to most white men automatically) or to participate in other denominational rites. Mormon leaders may have exhibited some ambivalence about slavery, but they were united in their belief that they were socially superior to African Americans.

The year 1852 was one of decision for Brigham Young and his Mormon followers. After three years of uncertainty—in the wake of their long, arduous migration to the Great Basin—the Mormons had been granted a territorial government, thanks to the Compromise of 1850. In 1851, Young was appointed Utah's first territorial governor and Mormon residents elected their first territorial legislature. This body, convened initially in late 1851, dealt with a variety of issues, including the legality of slavery in Utah. The Compromise of 1850 allowed the residents of Utah to decide for themselves the status of slavery in the territory.[1] In early 1852, Governor Young asked the legislature to give legal sanction to slavery throughout the territory. Young got what he wanted. On February 4, 1852, Utah became the only territory west of the Missouri River and north of the Missouri Compromise line of 36°30' to legalize slavery.

Several scholars have investigated slavery in Utah. Jack Beller described the presence of slaves among the Great Basin Saints in a pioneering essay in

Amanda and Samuel D. Chambers. Born slaves in Alabama, the Chamberses became devout Mormons and moved to Utah in 1870. (Courtesy, Utah State Historical Society.)

1929.[2] In recent years, Dennis L. Lythgoe and Ronald Coleman have examined the impact of the peculiar institution on Utah's small but visible black population, and Lester E. Bush, Jr., has probed Brigham Young's antiblack prejudices and his refusal to admit blacks to the Mormon priesthood.[3] Little effort has been made, however, to explain why Utah Mormons chose to legalize black slavery in 1852 and perpetuate it until 1862—the year Congress abolished it in Utah and all other federal territories.

At first glance, Mormon support for slavery seems baffling, for most Latter-day Saints had come from nonslaveholding areas of the Northeast and Midwest.[4] Brigham Young himself, as is well known, had been born in Vermont and grew up in a New England and New York environment where strong antislavery sentiments prevailed during the early nineteenth century.[5] Then, too, Mormon willingness to embrace slavery is puzzling in light of the religion's long record of antipathy towards the peculiar institution. This hostility went back to Joseph Smith, the founder of Mormonism, who expressed opposition to slavery in the *Book of Mormon*, published in 1830—the year he organized the Mormon Church. This work, considered by Mormons as holy scripture and on a par with the Bible, condemned all forms of human bondage. Purportedly the history of a pre-Columbian people living in the Western Hemisphere, the *Book of Mormon* approvingly notes God's command that the "Nephites"—a divinely chosen people—shun slavery.[6] Latter-day Saint antipathy toward slavery continued after Smith moved his followers westward from New York to Ohio and Missouri during the 1830s. "It is not right that any man should be in bondage one to another," proclaimed Smith in 1833.[7] Two months later, as the Saints and the Missouri non-Mormons clashed, the Mormon *Evening and Morning Star* questioned the right of several Missourians to hold slaves. In October 1834, W. W. Phelps, editor of the *Star*, boasted that Missouri-based Saints did not have to depend on slave labor, and in that same month two Mormon missionaries, David W. Patten and Warren Parrish, deplored the "power of tyranny that exists in the slave states." As late as 1838 Oliver Cowdery, an important church leader and advisor to Smith, confessed to strong antislavery feelings. "I have been long enough in slaveholding states to know that they never will, neither can they compete with free states in point of policy, enterprise and intelligence." Such views helped promote clashes between the Saints and proslavery Missourians throughout the 1830s.[8]

Mormon opposition to slavery during the 1830s, however, was tempered by the strong desire of Joseph Smith and other Mormon leaders to avoid identification with those abolitionists who advocated the immediate eradication of slavery. These antislavery advocates generated a great deal of hostility—both rhetorical and physical—from northerners as well as southerners, and the Mormons were anxious to avoid being identified with such a group that, like themselves, constituted a despised minority.[9] Abolitionists were particularly active in establishing chapters of the American Anti-Slavery Society and recruiting new members in New England, New York, and Ohio, areas that were also centers of Mormon activity.[10] Cowdery, like Smith, vigorously condemned the "corrupting" and "dangerous" abolitionists who raised the specter of slave rebellion, pauperism, and miscegenation.[11] Mormonism's antiabolitionist position hardened further in 1835 when the church membership approved a resolution that was entered into the *Doctrine and Covenants*, another Mormon scriptural work.

> We believe it just to preach the gospel to the nations of the earth and warn the righteous to save themselves from the corruption of the world; but we do not believe it right to interfere with bondservants, neither preach the gospel to, nor baptize them, contrary to the will and wish of their masters, nor to meddle with or influence them in the least to be dissatisfied with their situations in this life thereby jeopardizing the lives of men. Such interference we believe to be unlawful and dangerous to the peace of every government allowing human beings to be held in servitude.[12]

Such hostility toward abolitionists reflected a Mormon desire to preserve their settlements in the slaveholding state of Missouri—the location of the Mormon "Zion" or central gathering place. It also reflected the attitudes of other northern-based religious denominations and Americans in general during the 1830s.[13] Thus, throughout the 1830s the Mormons looked at slavery in two different ways: they condemned those actively campaigning for immediate abolition, but at the same time they opposed slavery.

Mormon opposition to slavery reached its peak during the early 1840s following expulsion of the Saints from Missouri and the establishment of Nauvoo, Illinois, as their new headquarters. Joseph Smith lashed out against slavery during his campaign for the presidency of the United States on a third party ticket in 1844. In his platform he called for the "break down [of] slavery" and removal of "the shackles from the poor black man." Southern citizens should petition their legislators to abolish slavery through a program of compensated emancipation with the funds coming from the sale of federal public lands. Smith was confident that the "hospitable and noble" southerners would help rid "so *free* a country…of every vestige of slavery."[14] His views were echoed by such important church spokesmen as Sydney Rigdon and Orson Hyde, who wanted to see blacks "liberated from bondage" and slavery done "away with."[15] Mormon newspapers also denounced the "slaveholder who deprives his fellow-beings of liberty," and lamented that slavery's continuing existence made America less than "an asylum for the oppressed."[16]

In light of such opposition to slavery, why did Brigham Young and other Mormon leaders decide in 1852 to legalize slavery in Utah with their "An Act in Relation to Service"? The evidence suggests that the answer is found in developments following the assassination of Smith in 1844 and the removal of the church's headquarters from Illinois to Utah during the late 1840s. In part, this slavery measure was a response to the interests of twelve Mormon slaveholders who brought sixty to seventy slaves into the Great Basin with them when they migrated west.[17] These slaveholders included several who assumed leadership positions in the years following the death of Joseph Smith—Charles C. Rich, a member of the Council of Twelve Apostles; William H. Hooper, a leading merchant who later became Utah's territorial representative in Congress; and Abraham O. Smoot, the first mayor of Salt Lake City.[18] In the words of a contemporary observer, these men constituted a "respectable minority...in favor of slavery."[19] Such prominent individuals notwithstanding, the overwhelming majority of Latter-day Saints eschewed involuntary black servitude throughout the 1850s and early 1860s, and the number of slaves held in Utah actually declined during the 1850s. By 1860 there were only twenty-nine slaves held by twelve owners.[20]

Of greater importance in explaining the Saints' decision to legalize slavery was their desire to win converts among southerners. There were "many Bre^n. [brethren] in the South" with "a great amount" invested "in slaves," Brigham Young noted in January 1852, and they might be persuaded to migrate to the Great Basin if their slave property was protected by law.[21] The 1852 "Act in Relation to Service" was addressed specifically to those "persons coming to this Territory and bringing with them servants justly bound to them."[22]

The Mormons also looked upon southern members of Congress as natural allies when Mormon polygamy came under increased attack in the early 1850s. Prompted by the Mormons' public admission, for the first time in 1852, that they were practicing polygamy and considered it an essential feature of their religion, these attacks coincided with stepped-up northern criticism of slavery following the Mexican War. By the early 1850s, both the Saints and slaveholding southerners looked upon popular sovereignty and states' rights as the best means to protect their respective "peculiar institutions" from outside attack. Jedediah M. Grant, a Mormon apostle and close advisor to Brigham Young, upheld the right of a community to handle its own "Domestic Institutions." The Saints, he explained, stood "with THE SOUTH" as "opponents of centralization."[23] Mormons later reacted enthusiastically to the Kansas-Nebraska Act of 1854, which opened these two regions to the possibility of slave labor—previously barred by the Missouri Compromise of 1820.[24] Some Saints also applauded the Dred Scott decision of 1857, which held that Congress could not prevent southern slaveholders from taking their chattels into any United States territory. Mormons looked upon this decision as establishing a principle favorable to polygamy.

> Congress has no power over the question of Slavery in the Territories and of course none over the question of polygamy. Those [two institutions] can now flourish wherever the people will it in any of the Territories of the United States and Uncle Sam can attend to his own business without troubling himself any further about them.[25]

The *Deseret News*, the church's official newspaper, supported southern attempts to reopen the international slave trade during the late 1850s. The resumption of this trade, noted the *News*, would reduce miscegenation between white slaveholders and their black slaves and also satisfy the increasing demand for slaves in the expanding cotton kingdom. In addition, these incoming African slaves would be given the "benefits" of American civilization.[26]

The bonds of identification between the Utah Mormons and southern slaveholders were far from complete, however. Most Mormon converts during the 1850s continued to come from nonslaveholding regions in the United States and abroad. By contrast, only a tiny percentage of the church's membership was drawn from the South.[27] Mormon missionaries, moreover, faced difficulties in the South because they, like other outsiders in the region, were not trusted and were accused of "running negroes to Salt Lake" and of being "abolitionists." Antagonism between the two groups intensified when Utah refused to follow the South out of the Union in response to Abraham Lincoln's election. Despite Mormon dislike for the Republican Party, which in 1856 characterized slavery and polygamy as the "Twin Relics of Barbarism," Young in 1861 announced that Utah was "firm for the Constitution."[28]

More important in explaining the legalization of Utah slavery than Mormon efforts to curry southern favor or the influence of Utah's tiny slaveholding population was Mormon opposition to the importation of additional slaves into the territory. A careful reading of the 1852 act suggests that, instead of being a device for promoting slavery in the region, it was designed to do just the opposite. The measure consisted primarily of regulations to control the slave owners, not the slaves. Slave owners had to prove that their chattels had come into the territory "of their own free will and choice"; slaves could not be sold or removed from the territory without their consent; and masters had to provide their slaves with "comfortable habitations, clothing, bedding, sufficient food, and recreation." A master was also restricted in the means he chose to "correct and punish his servant" and was admonished to be "guided by prudence and humanity." Moreover, if the slaves were "between the ages of six and twenty years," masters had "to send [them] to school" for "not less than eighteen months." And in contrast to prevailing practices in the slaveholding South, Utah masters could not engage in "sexual intercourse with any of the African race." Violations of this provision carried a fine ranging from $500 to $5,000 and the possibility of imprisonment for three to five years. Offending masters could also be compelled to "forfeit all claims to said servant or servants."[29] Enforcing these regulations were the powerful Utah territorial probate courts, which—contrary to what their title implied—had judicial authority over various civil and criminal violations, not just those involving property.[30]

The 1852 law and the manner of its enforcement could not help but have a dampening effect on slaveholding in Utah. Brigham Young seemed to suggest as much in a message to the Utah legislature in late 1852 when he noted that this statute and other antiblack measures "had nearly freed the territory of the colored population," and by implication had discouraged slaveholding in general. Earlier in the year he had told the same legislature that his own feelings were "that no property can or should be recognized as existing in slaves."[31] He reaffirmed this conviction often in later years, telling a follower in 1855 that "slavery [should not be] entailed upon our young, vigorous, and thriving Territory." A year later he announced to Thomas L. Kane, a non-Mormon friend of his, that "neither our climate, soil, production, nor minds of the people are congenial to African Slavery." Still later, he told the famous newspaper editor Horace Greeley that the Saints have no "very decided propensity in favor of slavery" because it "would prove useless and unprofitable."[32]

Young seems to have reflected accurately the views of other Saints. When a measure to legalize slavery was introduced in the Utah constitutional convention of 1856 it was dropped because only a "few delegates" favored it. Apostle John Taylor, who traveled east in the same year to promote Mormon statehood, assured northerners that "Utah shall not be admitted as a slave state." In the early 1860s, Utah territorial delegates William H. Hooper and John M. Bernhisel also predicted that Utah would enter the Union as a free state.[33]

Though the 1852 law was not designed to promote slavery, it was the product of Mormon racism. Young and most Mormons looked upon blacks as inherently inferior and therefore fit subjects for involuntary servitude. Like other nineteenth-century biblical literalists, Mormons traced the inferiority of black people to their alleged descent from Ham and Canaan, a lineage that destined them "to occupy the position of 'servant of servants.'"[34] In the Great Basin, noted W. W. Phelps, a former Mormon newspaper editor and prominent church spokesman, "the Jehovah Smitten Canaanite [could] bow in humble submission to his superiors."[35] Brigham Young made a similar observation in justifying the act of 1852. "The seed of Canaan," he proclaimed, "will inevitably carry the curse which was placed upon them until the same authority, which placed it there, shall see proper to have it removed." Young found additional support for black servitude in an alleged relationship among blacks, Cain, and the Devil.[36]

Young looked upon Utah's institution of servile bondage as similar to black indentured servitude as practiced in Illinois, Mormonism's former gathering place.[37] He pictured the few Mormon slaveholders as benevolent "masters" over "servants," and he urged them to use their black servants "with all the heart and feelings, as they would use their own children…and treat them as Kindly, and with the same humane feeling necessary to be shown to morall [sic] beings of the human species."[38] The 1852 statute reflected this mood of "benevolent servitude" by its use throughout of the term "servant" rather than "slave."[39]

The 1852 act represented the culmination of a trend that had begun in Nauvoo where Mormon leaders placed restrictions on the political and civil rights of blacks. The Nauvoo city charter permitted only "free white males" to vote, hold municipal office, or belong to the militia, the famed Nauvoo Legion. Marriage between whites and blacks was prohibited, and Joseph Smith himself, as mayor of Nauvoo, once enforced this measure by fining two black men for attempting "to marry white women."[40] Nauvoo blacks were also subjected to extralegal abuse. In 1844 a Nauvoo black named Chism was whipped as a result of charges that he had stolen some goods.[41] Mormon discrimination against blacks intensified in the wake of Joseph Smith's assassination and the migration west. During the late 1840s blacks were formally denied entry to the priesthood. While the precise date when this occurred is difficult to determine, there is evidence that it was established policy by the spring of 1847 when the Saints were encamped in their temporary frontier settlement of Winter Quarters (in present-day Nebraska). Apostle Parley P. Pratt justified denying the priesthood to blacks on the basis of their alleged descent from Ham, which left them "cursed as regards [to] the Priesthood."[42]

The antiblack attitudes of Mormons were not publicized to any significant extent until early 1852 when Brigham Young asked for legislation to legalize black slavery in Utah. Since blacks could not "bear any…priesthood," he stated, they could not "bear rule in any place until the curse is removed from them."[43] The enslavement of Utah blacks made it easier for Mormon territorial officials to discriminate against blacks in other ways—for example, through the enactment of laws prohibiting all Utah blacks (both slave and free) from voting, holding public office, and belonging to the territorial militia.[44] Municipal officials throughout Utah took their cue from the territorial legislature and prohibited blacks from voting and holding public office in later Great Basin settlements. The Mormons also wrote antiblack proscriptions into the constitutions for their proposed state of Deseret in 1856, 1860, and 1862.[45]

The willingness of the Utah Mormons to legalize slavery dramatizes a basic transformation within Mormonism, a religion that originally emphasized equality before God of all mankind, regardless of race. This transformation became increasingly evident during the thirty-five years after 1830, when the *Book of Mormon* had proclaimed that the Lord "denieth none that come unto him, black and white, bond and free, male and female; and he remembereth the heathen; and all are alike unto God, both Jew and Gentile."[46] During the first decade of Mormonism's existence, when church activity was focused in Ohio and Missouri, the Saints placed special emphasis on this message. Even during the early years in Nauvoo, they continued to accept all men, regardless of race, in full fellowship, and they ordained at least two blacks to the priesthood.[47] However, during their sojourn in Nauvoo, church leaders also began to discriminate against blacks in both the secular and ecclesiastical realms. Just as the Nauvoo-based Saints prohibited blacks from voting, holding public office, belonging to the Nauvoo Legion, and intermarrying with whites, they also began to deny them religious equality.[48] Church officials found religious justification for denying the priesthood to blacks and confining their missionary activities almost exclusively to people of white, northern European ethnic stock.[49] This discrimination found its ultimate expression in 1852 in the legalization of slavery in Utah.

Mormon tolerance for slavery in the Great Basin was primarily the by-product of increased Mormon racism and did not represent a Latter-day Saint commitment to slavery as a socioeconomic institution. Thus, the Utah Mormons found it easy to adopt the apparently paradoxical position of upholding slavery as a legal institution while at the same time proclaiming their desire to see Utah admitted to the Union as a free state. The Mormons maintained this position until Congress abolished slavery in Utah and all other federal territories in 1862.

Notes

1. For a discussion of the Compromise of 1850 as it affected the Mormons, see J. Keith Melville, *Conflict and Compromise* (Provo, Utah, 1974).

2. Jack Beller, "Negro Slaves in Utah," *Utah Historical Quarterly,* II (1929), 122–126.

3. Dennis L. Lythgoe, "Negro Slavery in Utah," *Utah Historical Quarterly,* XXXIX (1971), 40–54; Lythgoe, "Negro Slavery and Mormon Doctrine," *Western Humanities Review,* XXI (1967), 327–338; Ronald G. Coleman, "Blacks in Utah History: An Unknown Legacy," in Helen Z. Papanikolas, ed., *The Peoples of Utah* (Salt Lake City, 1976), 115–140; Coleman, "Utah's Black Pioneers: 1847–1869," *OMOJA: A Scholarly Journal of Black Studies,* II (Summer 1978), 95–110; Lester E. Bush, Jr., "Mormonism's Negro Doctrine: An Historical Overview," *Dialogue: A Journal of Mormon Thought,* VIII (Spring, 1973), 22–31. Also, see James B. Christensen, "Negro Slavery in Utah," *Phylon,* XIII, (1957), 298–305; Jan B. Shipps, "Second-class Saints," *Colorado Quarterly,* XI (1962), 183–190; Kate B. Carter, *The Negro Pioneer* (Salt Lake City, 1965); and Fawn M. Brodie, "Can We Manipulate the Past?", *First Annual American West Lecture, University of Utah* (Salt Lake City, Oct. 3, 1970).

4. See especially S. George Ellsworth, "A History of Mormon Missions in the United States and Canada, 1830–60" (Ph.D. dissertation, University of California, Berkeley, 1951); Laurence M. Yorgason, "Preview of a Study of the Social and Geographic Origins of Early Mormon Converts, 1830–1845," *Brigham Young University Studies,* X (1970), 279–282; Yorgason, "Some Demographic Aspects of One Hundred Early Mormon Converts, 1830–1837" (M.A. thesis, Brigham Young University, 1974).

5. Whitney R. Cross, *The Burned-Over District* (Ithaca, N.Y., 1950), 217–226, 264, 274–284; S. Dilworth Young, *Here Is Brigham* (Salt Lake City, 1964), 14–37.

6. *Book of Mormon,* Alma 27:9; see also Mosiah 2:13 and Alma 44:2.

7. While this statement was made within the context of a discussion of the rights and privileges guaranteed under the Constitution, there are suggestions that Smith was primarily concerned with economic rather than human bondage. See *Doctrine and Covenants,* 104:16–18, 83–84. In another revelation six months earlier, Smith affirmed that the U.S. Constitution upheld the "principle of freedom" for "all mankind." *Doctrine and Covenants,* 98:5.

8. *Evening and Morning Star* (Kirtland, Ohio), Feb. 1834; *Latter Day Saints Messenger and Advocate* (Kirtland, Ohio), Nov. 1834; Oliver Cowdery to Warren A. and Lynn Cowdery, June 2, 1838, as reprinted in Stanley R. Gunn, *Oliver Cowdery: Second Elder and Scribe* (Salt Lake City, 1962), 182–183; Warren A. Jennings, "Factors in the Destruction of the Mormon Press in Missouri, 1883," *Utah Historical Quarterly,* XXXV (1967), 56–76.

9. *Latter Day Saints Messenger and Advocate,* Nov. 1835.

10. Leonard L. Richards, *"Gentlemen of Property and Standing": Anti-Abolition Mobs in Jacksonian America* (New York, 1970), *passim.*

11. *Latter Day Saints Messenger and Advocate,* April and May 1836.

12. *Doctrine and Covenants,* 134:12. It was originally published in the *Latter Day Saints Messenger and Advocate,* Aug. 1835.

13. Donald G. Mathews, *Slavery and Methodism* (Princeton, N.J., 1965), 142; Mary Burnham Putnam, *The Baptists and Slavery, 1840–1845* (Ann Arbor, 1913), 11; C. Bruce Staiger, "Abolitionism and the Presbyterian Schism of 1837–39," *Mississippi Valley Historical Review,* XXXVI (1950), 395–401; Madeline Hook Rice, *American Catholic Opinion in the Slavery Controversy* (New York, 1944); Richards, *Gentlemen of Property and Standing, passim.*

14. Joseph Smith, Jr., *Views on the Government and Policies of the United States* (Nauvoo, 1844), 3.

15. Nauvoo *Times and Seasons,* Feb. 1, 1844; New York *The Prophet,* June 29, 1844.

16. *Nauvoo Neighbor,* Sept. 10, 1845; *Latter Day Saints Millennial Star* (Liverpool, England), Sept. 1843.

17. This estimate is based on figures compiled from several sources, particularly Beller, "Negro Slaves in Utah," 122–126; and Kate B. Carter, *The Negro Pioneer, passim.*

18. *Ibid.*

19. Quoted in Frederic A. Culmer, "'General' John Wilson, Signer of the Deseret Petition," *California Historical Society Quarterly,* XXVI (1947), 330.

20. As indicated by a two-page compilation of Utah's black population in 1860 that was prepared by George Olin Zabriskie on the basis of data taken from the federal census of 1860. Copy in the library of the Utah State Historical Society, Salt Lake City. That these census figures are not complete is indicated by Charles W. Nibley *Reminiscences* (Salt Lake City, 1934), 35–36, which notes two black slaves held by John Bankhead of Logan and not included in the 1860 census.

21. "Speach [*sic*] by Gov. Young in Counsel on a Capital Bill relating to the Affrican [*sic*] Slavery," Jan. 23, 1852, Brigham Young Papers, Latter-day Saint Church Archives, Salt Lake City.

22. "An Act in Relation to Service," in *Acts, Resolutions, and Memorials of the Legislative Assembly of the Territory of Utah* (Salt Lake City, 1855), 160–162.

23. Jedediah M. Grant, *Three Letters to the New York Herald* (N.p.,n.d.), letter dated May 1, 1852.

24. Salt Lake City *Deseret News,* April 13, 1854; see also *New York Daily News,* April 26, 1855, as reprinted in New York *The Mormon,* May 5, 1855; John Taylor to Brigham Young, Sept. 16, 1855, John Taylor Papers, L.D.S. Church Archives; and *Latter-day Saints Millennial Star,* Feb. 24, 1855.

25. *Deseret News,* May 20, 1857; see also *Deseret News,* Oct. 7, 1857; *Latter-day Saints Millennial Star,* June 27, 1857; San Francisco *Western Standard,* April 17, 1857.

26. *Deseret News,* April 13, June 1, July 13, 1859.

27. Lamar C. Berrett, "History of the Southern States Mission, 1831–1861" (M.S. thesis, Brigham Young University, 1960), 274–275; Ellsworth, "A History of Mormon Missions in the United States and Canada," 303–306, 335–336.

28. *St. Louis Luminary,* Sept. 29, 1855; *Deseret News,* Aug. 26, 1857; *Latter-day Saints Millennial Star,* Nov. 1, 1856; Gaylon L. Caldwell, "'Utah Has Not Seceded': A Footnote to Local History," *Utah Historical Quarterly,* XXVI (1958), 172–175.

29. "An Act in Relation to Service," 160–162.

30. James B. Allen, "The Unusual Jurisdiction of County Probate Courts in the Territory of Utah," *Utah Historical Quarterly,* XXXVI (1968), 133–142.

31. Brigham Young, "Message to the Joint Session of Legislature," Dec. 13, 1852, Brigham Young Papers (also reprinted in the *Deseret News,* Dec. 24, 1852); Young, "Speech to the Joint Session of the Legislative Assembly, January 5, 1852," in *Journals of the Legislative Assembly of the Territory of Utah* (Salt Lake City, 1852), 108–110, reprinted in *Deseret News,* Jan. 10, 1852.

32. Young to John Taylor, Sept. 8, 1855, Brigham Young Papers; Young to Thomas Kane, April 14, 1856, *ibid.*; Horace Greeley, *An Overland Journey* (New York, 1860), 180.

33. New York *The Mormon,* June 14, 1856; John Taylor to Brigham Young, Jan. 18, 1856, John Taylor Papers, L.D.S. Church Archives; William H. Hooper to Young, Dec. 4, 1861, *ibid.*; John M. Bernhisel to Young, Feb. 19, 1863, *ibid.*

34. Brigham Young, "Speech to the Joint Session of the Legislative Assembly, January 5, 1852." For the popularity of this belief among nineteenth-century Americans, see especially George M. Fredrickson, *The Black Image in the White Mind* (New York, 1971); H. Shelton Smith, *In His Image But...: Racism in Southern Religion, 1780–1910* (Durham, 1972). See also Naomi Felicia Woodbury, "A Legacy of Intolerance: Nineteenth Century Propaganda and the Mormon Church Today" (M.A. thesis, University of California, Los Angeles, 1966).

35. *Deseret News,* July 26, 1851.

36. Brigham Young, "Speech to the Joint Session of the Legislative Assembly, January 5, 1852"; Wilford Woodruff, "Journal," Jan. 16, 1852, Woodruff Papers.

37. A number of provisions in the 1852 statute are remarkably similar to legislation adopted by Illinois in 1819 regulating indentured servants in that state. See Paul M. Angle, "The Illinois Black Laws," *Chicago History,* VIII (1967), 66–67.

38. "Speach [*sic*], by Gov. Young in Joint Session of the Legislature…Giving His Views on Slavery," Feb. 5, 1852, Young Papers, L.D.S. Church Archives.

39. Significantly, when the first draft of this measure was presented as "a Bill relating to Affrican [*sic*] slavery," Brigham Young remarked: "The Caption of this Bill I don't like, I have therefore taken the liberty to alter it. I have said 'an act in relation to manual service' instead of Affrican [*sic*] Slavery." See "Speach [*sic*] by Gov. Young in Counsel on a Capital Bill relating to the Affrican [*sic*] Slavery," Jan. 23, 1852, *ibid.*

40. Joseph Smith, Jr., *History of the Church* (2nd ed., Salt Lake City, 1978), IV, 239–244; VI, 210.

41. Church spokesmen, however, discounted Mormon involvement in the beating. "Journal History," March 30, April 1, 1844, L.D.S. Church Archives; *Nauvoo Neighbor,* May 22, 1844.

42. Church Minutes, April 15, 1847, LDS Church Archives.

43. "Speach [*sic*] by Gov. Young in Counsel on a Bill relating to the Affrican [*sic*] Slavery," Jan. 23, 1852.

44. "An Act to Establish a Territorial Government for Utah," sec. 5, chaps. 35 & 47, in *Acts, Resolutions, and Memorials of the Legislative Assembly of the Territory of Utah* (Salt Lake City, 1855).

45. For the various antiblack statutes enacted on both the territorial and local levels during the early 1850s, see *Acts, Resolutions, and Memorials of the Legislative Assembly of the Territory of Utah, passim.* Copies of the constitutions for the state of Deseret appeared in various Mormon and non-Mormon publications throughout the 1850s and 1860s.

46. *Book of Mormon,* 2 Nephi 26:33; see also 2 Nephi 9:5–22, 25:16, 26:13, 26:25; Alma 1:30, 29:2, 5:49, 17:8, 23:4–18; Helaman 5:18–19, 5:48–52; 3 Nephi 2:12–16.

47. Newell G. Bringhurst, "Elijah Abel and the Changing Status of Blacks within Mormonism," *Dialogue: A Journal of Mormon Thought,* XII (Summer 1979), 22–36.

48. "Minutes of a Conference of the Church of Jesus Christ of Latter-day Saints Held in Cincinnati, June 25, 1843," LDS Church Archives.

49. Mormon scripture was later used to justify this ban. See, for example, *Pearl of Great Price,* Abraham, 1:21–27.

RECONSTRUCTION ON THE FRONTIER: THE EQUAL RIGHTS STRUGGLE IN COLORADO, 1865–1867

Eugene H. Berwanger

[This article originally appeared in the *Pacific Historical Review*, Vol. 44 (1975), pp. 313–329. Copyright by the Pacific Coast Branch, American Historical Association. Reprinted with permission.]

Once the Thirteenth Amendment abolished slavery in 1865, blacks began to push for the same rights that whites enjoyed. But just what freedom meant to African Americans remained in a state of legal flux during the late 1860s. Not until the adoption of the Fourteenth Amendment in 1868 did the Constitution define "citizen" to include black Americans. Nevertheless, the Radical Republicans who controlled Congress after the Civil War made sure that southern blacks were not only free but also were given some measure of equality. The Freedmen's Bureau established schools and provided some of the basic necessities of life on an emergency basis. Federal troops protected ex-slaves from angry white mobs. Registrars and polls watchers ensured that adult black men were allowed to vote and hold office. But Radical Reconstruction was aimed at the South, not the West. So in western areas, African Americans began on their own to organize and petition the U.S. government for equal rights.

Perhaps the most organized African American community in the West during the Reconstruction era was that in Denver. There, a coterie of black men began demanding rights, petitioning the government for the right to vote and for black children to have a government-provided education equal to that afforded white youth. Several black men in Denver comprised an economic and social elite in the

African American community. They were men of some means—businessmen who had almost daily contact with the town's white leaders. It seemed only logical and just to them that they should have the same rights as other free men in the United States.

The leader of the Denver black community—at least on the issue of legal rights—was William Jefferson Hardin, a barber with a large white clientele. An outstanding orator, Hardin served for several years as the unofficial spokesman of Denver blacks. Others, however, also aided the cause of black equality. These men included Henry O. Wagoner and Edward Sanderlin—also barbers—and Barney Ford, a hotelier and restauranteur. Once these men were granted suffrage in 1868, they became important to white Republicans who courted black votes.

But in the first few years after the Civil War, as Eugene H. Berwanger explains in the following essay, Denver's African Americans faced opposition from most whites in the city who, like their counterparts in the rest of the U.S., were not sure what the abolition of slavery meant for black Americans. With little support from Denver whites, Hardin and his allies petitioned the Radical Republican Congress for the right to vote. Congress responded with a law in early 1867 that extended the franchise to adult black men in all of the western territories. Efforts by Denver blacks to secure integrated education for their children were not as successful, however, because they had to deal with local—not national—white leaders. Still, with the right to vote came power and influence for Denver's black community. Consequently, many white Republican officials who had been opposed to blacks having the vote—or even the right to an education—in the 1860s actively sought their electoral support during succeeding decades.

The Civil War did little to alter the pattern of discrimination suffered by blacks in Colorado Territory. As the war came to a close, however, and as the territory anticipated statehood, black settlers began to balk at restrictions on their citizenship.[1] Refusing to be satisfied with the termination of slavery in the South, they waged a vigorous campaign from 1865 to 1867 to obtain the right to vote and to educate their children in public schools. Though neglected by historians, their quest for equality in Colorado is significant, for it constituted one of the few successful civil rights efforts at the state or territorial level in the nineteenth century, and it had important repercussions for manhood suffrage in other territories.[2]

Blacks first began to press for equal suffrage in 1864 when the territorial legislature attached a restrictive amendment to Colorado's voting law. Although election statutes enacted in 1861 had extended the ballot to all "male persons" who were twenty-one years of age and older, the amendment of March 1864 declared that these "male persons" did not include Negroes: blacks and mulattos were expressly denied the right to vote. Local blacks angrily claimed that the amendment deprived them of a privilege they had enjoyed until its passage. White leaders denied the charge. When former territorial governor John Evans in 1866 explained the legislature's action to Congress, he merely observed that black men had not voted before 1864 and, therefore, the amendment had made no practical difference.[3]

Intent on overturning the new discriminatory law, blacks in July 1864 sent a small delegation to the state constitutional convention where they lobbied unsuccessfully for equal suffrage. Because the constitution produced at this convention was rejected at the polls,[4] a second constitutional convention met in 1865. This time the convention submitted the suffrage question, along with the constitution, to a public vote.[5] On September 5, 1865, enfranchised Coloradans approved the constitution by 155 votes but rejected equal suffrage by a vote of 4,192 to 476. The strongest opposition to enfranchising blacks came from the southern part of the territory where many Mexican Americans had settled. The largest number of pro-Negro votes were cast in the heavily Anglo populated regions around Denver and Central City, areas where most blacks also lived.[6]

Colorado Negroes refused to accept the decision.[7] Under the leadership of a group of black barbers in Denver, including Edward Sanderlin (or Sanderline), Henry O. Wagoner, and William J. Hardin, they urged Congress to oppose Colorado's statehood until equal suffrage had been guaranteed to all.[8] Especially outspoken was William Jefferson Hardin, who was to remain the leading civil rights figure in Colorado into the 1870s. Upon his arrival in the Denver area in 1863, Hardin had first gained renown as a lecturer on the accomplishments of Toussaint L'Ouverture in Haiti.[9] Then, following the rejection of Negro suffrage in the public referendum of 1865, he turned his energies to the campaign for black rights in Colorado Territory. He challenged James M. Cavanaugh and John M. Chivington, candidates for Congress, to public debate on equal suffrage; so effective was his plea that Cavanaugh reversed himself and endorsed Negro suffrage.[10] As Hardin's reputation as a black civil rights spokesman grew, he became an enigma to white contemporaries in the territory: Why, they asked, did Hardin, an octoroon, so vigorously pursue the cause of black freedom when he might have easily passed for being a Frenchman or an Italian?[11]

Hardin's efforts went well beyond speechmaking. In a national appeal he wrote and telegraphed prominent easterners, asking them to denounce publicly the lack of equal suffrage in Colorado and to use their influence against the

William Jefferson Hardin. The leading African American civil rights activist in Colorado in the 1860s, Hardin moved to Cheyenne, Wyoming, in 1873 and served in the Wyoming territorial legislature from 1879 to 1884. (Courtesy, Wyoming Division of Cultural Resources.)

territory's admission as a state as long as the suffrage restriction remained in effect. Response to Hardin's call varied. Horace Greeley, editor of the *New York Tribune*, spurned him, insisting that black suffrage, while desirable, should never be a condition for granting statehood.[12] Senator Charles Sumner reacted more favorably and, consistent with his avowed ideals, objected to Colorado's constitution because of its voting restriction.[13] Predictably, criticism in Colorado to Hardin's letters and telegrams was sharp and immediate. The black leader had publicly to clarify his position for local, prostatehood politicians. He was not opposed to statehood, he explained; he sought only "equal rights to all men, then [Colorado's] brightness would [outshine] all the rest [of the states]."[14]

Hardin also sought clarification of the laws under which Negroes could preempt and homestead public land. Blacks had been denied access to public land during the ante-bellum period, and Hardin urged George M. Chilcott, Colorado's delegate to Congress, to inquire into the postwar policy. When Chilcott explained that the federal government had reversed its earlier policy, Hardin encouraged Negroes in Colorado to establish their claims.[15]

The impact that Colorado black leaders had on the federal level was limited by their lack of prominence and their lack of personal acquaintance with national politicians. Locally they could do much more, and here blacks were able to enlist the aid of Alexander Cummings, territorial governor. On December 11, 1865, Hardin, Henry Wagoner, and J. G. Smith asked Cummings to forward to Congress a petition containing the names of 137 blacks who were angered by the voting restriction. To deny equal suffrage, they asserted, was to disregard "the bloody lessons of the last four years."[16] Because the governor opposed Colorado's admission and thought the denial of Negro suffrage would forestall it, he forwarded their appeal to Secretary of State William Seward for transmission to Congress.[17]

The petition sought to prevent statehood by arguing that the number of voters who approved the 1865 constitution was too small to indicate overwhelming sentiment for statehood. More importantly, insisted the petitioners, the state constitution ignored the recent rebellion by making color, not patriotism, the test for the right of suffrage. All restrictions against blacks should be removed, contended the signatories, and Congress should not admit Colorado into the Union "until the word *white* be erased from her State Constitution.... We ask for nothing but even handed justice," they concluded, "and we feel assured you will not turn a deaf ear to our humble and earnest appeal...."[18]

During the next month, January 1866, Hardin, Wagoner, and three other blacks went to the governor with a second petition that dealt not only with disfranchisement, but also with the exclusion of black children from Colorado's public schools. They asked for the abrogation of these restrictions. Cummings forwarded the petition to the legislature along with a personal appeal for equal suffrage and public education for black youth. United in their opposition, the legislators ignored both the petition and the governor's recommendation.[19]

Governor Cummings's role in the quest for Negro suffrage was openly criticized by Frank Hall, territorial secretary, and William Newton Byers, editor of the *Rocky Mountain News*. They believed that the governor was not really sympathetic with blacks and was merely using them in an attempt to defeat Colorado's bid for statehood.[20] Byers characterized the governor's support of civil rights legislation as a "foolishly demented" act. "The governor...," he wrote, "appeals to the negroes for aid...not that he cares a particle for them or their rights. The negroes, stupidly, have fallen into another trap set to win their influence against the State's admission."[21]

While Cummings's main objection to statehood centered on Colorado's financial instability, it is true that he used the exclusion of Negroes from the polls to strengthen his antistatehood argument. Still, this does not mean that he had no personal sympathy for racial justice. Cummings's activities during his brief tenure in office, 1865–1867, indicate an honest compassion for blacks. In his 1865 Thanksgiving Day proclamation, Cummings asked for "equal and exact justice to all men."[22] When he forwarded the blacks' petition of January 1866 to the legislature, he candidly addressed himself to the denial of suffrage: "It seems incredible that such a measure [the 1864 amendment to the 1861 voting qualifications law] could have been adopted at such a time.... It is a fact worthy of notice that this was the only case in the whole nation where public sentiment retrograded during our fearful struggle." Supporting, in the same message, Negro demands to send their children to public schools, he declared lack of education to be one of the "features of the accursed spirit of slavery, from whose thralldom the nation has just emerged.... Justice to the living, and gratitude to those who died that the Nation might live, forbid that the state of things against which these petitioners protest, should longer prevail."[23]

Cummings revealed fair-minded concern once again in January 1867 when he vetoed a bill excluding Negroes and mulattos from juries. In defending his action, he characterized the legislature's measure as a "surprising" attempt to thwart the national will. The lawmakers, nevertheless, passed the bill over the governor's veto.[24] Typically, editor Byers was critical of Cummings's stand: the governor's "henchmen in the legislature," said Byers, had introduced the bill, knowing it would pass, in order to strengthen the governor's stand against statehood.[25]

The *News* was just as sharp in its denunciation of Negro demands. Admitting the injustice of taxing blacks for the support of schools from which their children were excluded, Byers suggested separate facilities. He defended his proposal by writing, "Much as we may be in favor of granting to the negro his rights, we do not propose to eat, drink or sleep with one, and neither do we believe it right that our children should receive their education in negro classes."[26]

Byers's major criticism came in response to the blacks' antistatehood petition before Congress. Along with John Evans and Jerome Chaffee, U.S. senators-elect, and George Chilcott, delegate-elect to Congress, the *News* labeled as fraudulent many of the signatures on the document. In its view, Colorado's black population was too small to produce the 137 names on the petition. Byers, moreover, characterized the petition as part of the antistatehood movement being led by Democrats. Negroes, he claimed, could be easily persuaded to sign petitions merely to have their names presented before Congress. Reiterating, as he often did, past Republican beneficences toward blacks, Byers warned them that cooperation with Democrats could damage their rapport with Republicans: "One cannot fail in depising the ungrateful viper who would sting the breast of him that warmed it into being."[27]

The *News,* however, reserved its most vituperative criticism for Hardin. Byers denounced him as "the man who…no doubt is indebted largely to his seven-eighth [sic] Saxon origin, for his superior intellect, and we have never seen anything 'nigger' about him, save in this instance, where his vanity has betrayed him into an act of treachery that the future will make him sorely repent."[28] Hardin's civil rights activities, wrote Byers, were undertaken merely to get "his name in the papers." Byers saw further opportunity to ridicule the black leader as the Denver municipal election approached in 1866. In jest, he suggested that Hardin be nominated for mayor and he printed political advertisements announcing Hardin's candidacy.[29]

Even as late as 1868, Hardin was still the focus of editorial criticism. The Democratic *Gazette* reported that a black accused of murder in Central City had been shot while trying to escape into the mountains. Hardin would do well to keep away from Central City, warned the *Gazette,* because authorities there "have a very summary way of disposing of obnoxious darkies…, and even his elegant form might go uppum stumpum, if he was to shoot his mouth off in the style he usually does in Denver, on the 4th of July."[30]

Hardin was subject to more insidious forms of harassment as well. On July 4, 1866, when a black Denver resident was shot, apparently without provocation, Hardin was convinced that he was the intended victim.[31] Several months later, a number of white women in the city received obscene letters that invited them to write to Hardin. Fortunately, he was able to disclaim any involvement, but not before one of the young ladies had entered his barbershop armed with a revolver. The *News,* on this one occasion at least, chose to defend his moral integrity and describe the attack on his character as disgraceful.[32]

Although the *News* was generally critical of Hardin, the *Denver Daily,* a Radical Republican newspaper established in 1867, came out in full support of the black leader and his aims. The editor lauded Hardin's ability as a public speaker and praised as irrefutable his arguments for equal rights. Reporting on a public meeting of blacks in 1867, the editor wrote, "We thanked God with these colored people, for what they have realized, and promised ourselves to pursue our pleading for them, as we have done in the past, till, as a race, they get what God gave them in creation.... God speed the right."[33]

Despite such reactions in Colorado to civil rights activities, the blacks' petition requesting denial of statehood failed to impress a majority of Congress. Over Radical Republican opposition to the restricted suffrage provision in the Colorado constitution, Congress voted in April 1866 to admit the territory.[34] Statehood was not to be realized with congressional endorsement alone, however; Andrew Johnson vetoed the bill, arguing that the territory had too small a population to be a state. Since this contention had earlier found support among many senators, it came as no surprise when the upper house failed to override the President's veto.[35]

Though Johnson's veto message ignored the civil rights arguments in the blacks' petition, the petition nonetheless had important consequences. Its exposure of the denial of black suffrage in Colorado Territory came at a time when equality at the polls was arousing much interest in Congress. Discussion among lawmakers over the admission of the territory from January to May 1866 offered Radical Republicans the opportunity to keep raising the issue of restricted voting in the territories.[36] Finally, under their leadership and after months of legislative maneuvering, Congress in January 1867 forbade restricted suffrage because of color in all United States territories.

The timing of and debate over the territorial suffrage act indicates the influence of the Colorado situation on the measure. On May 15, 1866, Andrew Johnson vetoed Colorado's admission into the Union, a move that left the area a territory and, under the 1864 legislative restriction, limited voting to whites only. On the same day, James Ashley of Ohio introduced in the House of Representatives a bill regulating territorial government. Of its nine provisions, five required territorial legislatures to pass laws severely restricting the activities of corporations within their boundaries, two concerned salaries of federal appointees in the territories, one denied territorial governments the power to grant divorce, and the last gave all citizens (except Indians) the right to vote. Ashley characterized his bill as being primarily an attempt to prevent special interest groups from securing unlimited favors in the newly settled regions. He did not refute two criticisms: one, that several of the provisions were illogical inasmuch as territorial legislatures could not be compelled to pass laws limiting their own powers; and, two, that the first eight provisions were a mere veil to force Negro suffrage upon the territories. The measure passed the House by a vote of 97 to 43, with 51 members not voting. The Senate failed to take action due to Delaware Senator Willard Saulsbury's filibustering and the closing of the session.[37]

Early in the next session, following an extensive discussion of the franchise restriction when Colorado's admission was again being considered, Senator Benjamin Wade reintroduced the territorial bill. He declared that the bill did indeed relate to the suffrage question in Colorado, and he amended it to strike out all provisions except that on suffrage. Though 21 senators abstained, the measure easily passed the upper house on January 10, 1867, by a vote of 24 to 7.[38] Rushed to the lower house on the same day, the amended bill was approved within two hours. It became law without the President's signature on January 31, 1867.[39] Thus did blacks in Colorado ultimately gain the right to vote through national legislation when whites in the territory were still unwilling to grant it.

White Coloradans, despite earlier and strong objections to the enfranchisement of blacks, quietly accepted Negro suffrage when it came in 1867. Although rumor of mob action to discourage Negroes from voting in the municipal elections of that year circulated in Denver and Central City, no violence took place.[40] How may Colorado's calm acquiescence be explained? Republican editorial columns reveal two possible explanations: journalists and politicians alike were quick to perceive the advantage of gaining the new black votes for one party or the other, and settlers in the territory were beginning to accept the fact that congressional authority took precedence when it came into conflict with territorial legislation and opinion.

D. C. Collier, editor of the *Daily Miner's Register* in Central City, claimed that Democrats in Colorado had submitted to equal suffrage in order to entice the black vote. He was, in effect, reflecting the editorial strategy of Republican newspapers.[41] Both the *Register* and the *Rocky Mountain News*, during the two months preceding the municipal elections, exhorted blacks to recall demonstrated Republican sympathy when casting their votes. Hinting that the Negro vote had strategic significance, Byers told blacks that suffrage offered them the chance to counter "the ignorant foreign vote" usually cast for Democratic candidates.[42] Equally anxious to curry favor with black voters, Collier came out in support of the territorial suffrage law and praised Negroes as "informed citizens." Though he believed that most southern ex-slaves were too unenlightened to vote, he contended that, "in Colorado, negro suffrage is intelligent suffrage…. We have the law, and we believe it to be one which does justice to a large class of our fellow citizens…. We believe the negro in this Territory fully capable of exercising the elective franchise. We rejoice that their manhood has been recognized and ensured by the great Union party of the nation." Collier's strong determination to capture the black vote for Republicanism caused his partisanship to become clearly evident: "In voting, they will vote for justice and good order, for a Union on the basis of freedom…. We are sure they know which party always stood up for their manhood, and which party has rescued them from slavery and oppression which the Democracy shout to perpetuate."[43]

The final collapse of overt opposition to Negro suffrage came as Coloradans realized Congress's determination to ensure equality at the polls. Republican editors during 1866 had regularly extolled the idea of popular sovereignty and had expressed disdain for any federal measure that would stipulate unrestricted suffrage in the territories.[44] They contended that Congress should legislate Negro suffrage for the loyal states before forcing it upon them.[45] Yet as the territorial bill reached its final stages of debate and as its passage became a certainty, they yielded to the inevitable. A most striking example of the change in attitude appeared in the *Rocky Mountain News:* "That Congress has full right and power to legislate for the Territories was argued and conclusively settled, affirmatively,…and no sane man who reads the Congressional reports, can doubt for a moment that Ashley's bill creating impartial suffrage will pass and become law in the present session. There is not the slightest doubt as to this fact, for Congress is determined to push this question to the wall, and forever nail it there…."[46] The *Daily Miner's Register,* reflecting a similar view, announced simply that the new suffrage act was law and must be obeyed. "Let those who are opposed to the measure," declared editor Collier, "remember that they can gain nothing by opposition but will act far more wisely to accept the position and not combat the inevitable."[47] Bitterly disappointed with the turn of events, George West, a leading Democratic journalist, nonetheless agreed with Republican editors: "We never can believe that any thing of the sort [Negro suffrage] can take place here at present—but if our Congress does so enact we will bow our head to the laws and obey…."[48] The *News* made perhaps the most concise appraisal of Colorado's mood on

Negro suffrage. Most would find suffrage distasteful, Byers consoled his readers, "yet it was coming to that and the issue may as well be accepted first as last."[49]

Black Coloradans reacted quickly and favorably to the territorial suffrage act. At a public gathering on February 21, 1867, they heard Hardin speak on "Equal suffrage and the duty of the colored voters in Colorado." He emphasized the obligation of blacks to vote Republican. Democrats, said Hardin, had impeded the progress of Negroes and were "hereditary enemies" of black people.[50] In order that an intelligent vote of whatever persuasion might be encouraged, black leaders in Denver arranged for Lewis H. Douglass, son of Frederick Douglass, to teach evening classes on government and politics.[51] Lewis and Frederick, Jr., arriving in Denver in 1867 to seek work as typographers, had become involved in the struggle for equality within the territory. During their short stay in Colorado, until 1868, their presence added prestige to the movement.[52]

Black Coloradans cast their ballots for the first time in April 1867. Following the election they held a public meeting and passed a series of resolutions praising white citizens for quietly accepting Negro suffrage.[53] On two occasions, once by telegram and once by petition, Negro leaders informed Congress that since equal suffrage had gained acceptance among all Coloradans, they no longer opposed Colorado's admission as a state.[54]

Confident in their newly achieved right to vote, black leaders soon took up anew the education issue. There was evidence of personal discord, however, among Denver's black leadership, which for a time prevented a united effort. After a fistfight broke out on August 1, 1867, among Denver Negroes who were celebrating the anniversary of emancipation in the West Indies, a verbal dispute ensued between Hardin and Frederick Douglass, Jr. Hardin foresaw reverberations from the fight within the white community. "Utterly depraved and degraded," it would appear as a "disgraceful nigger frolic" to whites. Black citizens, he warned, faced possible ostracism, "not on account of their color, but on account of their disgusting behavior." Douglass quickly rose to defend Denver's blacks, describing Hardin's remarks as "impolitic and damaging." The debate might well have continued had not Denver editors declined to publish further correspondence on the subject.[55] Only on the school issue were Negro leaders once more to unite in protest.

The main complaint of Negroes regarding education was that they paid taxes to support public schools from which their children were excluded. Appeals to local and territorial officials in 1865 and 1866 had produced no results. Under Lewis Douglass's leadership in June 1867, blacks again expressed dissatisfaction about the lack of educational facilities for their youth. Colorado

Republicans had better provide schooling for black children, declared Douglass, or face the loss of Negro support in Denver.[56] Although Douglass himself did not state clearly whether he sought segregated facilities or full integration, Hardin and Sanderlin went before the Denver Board of Trustees for Schools and demanded integrated education. Integration was unacceptable to the board; the offer of separate facilities, conceded by school authorities, was just as unacceptable to the two Negro leaders.

In an attempt to force the integration issue at the opening of the fall school session, 1867, black parents in east Denver sent their children to the local public school. D. B. Hatch, principal and teacher who subsequently resigned over the matter, called for the expulsion of the Negro children. Initially unresponsive to Hatch's protest, the board of trustees finally compromised with black leaders: all children could remain in one building, but with whites restricted to one floor, blacks to another.[57] The accord was short-lived; by 1868 Negro school children were being shunted among various rented facilities, and in 1869 they were consigned to the African Baptist Church. Finally, in 1873, Denver schools were integrated despite opposition from the white community.[58]

As early as 1867 black dissent in Colorado Territory had achieved suffrage and school facilities for Negro youth. With these primary aims realized, the force of the protest declined. "Equality before the law" had been the solitary goal of Colorado blacks, said Hardin, and he optimistically believed that it had been achieved with the territorial suffrage act.[59] Black leaders in the Rocky Mountain region do not appear to have been interested in economic reform. While some eastern liberals, white as well as black, were suggesting land redistribution in the South in order to ease the burden of poverty among ex-slaves,[60] Denver's Negro leaders expressed no desire for similar reform in Colorado. Perhaps they were simply preoccupied with suffrage; perhaps, like many of their contemporaries, they believed that erasing racial distinction from the laws was the first step to full equality. In any case, their individual financial status may offer perspective regarding their lack of concern about economic injustices. While the average per capita wealth for Denver's black population in 1870 is listed at $90, census figures at the same time credit Henry Wagoner with personal assets of $6,300; Edward Sanderlin, $2,500; William Green, $1,700; and Hardin, $1,500. Clearly, despite possible census inaccuracies, theirs was an advantaged position.[61]

Any remaining thrust of the black protest diminished as its leadership became interested in politics or moved out of the territory altogether. The Douglass sons, unable to find local employment as printers, returned to Washington, D.C., and devoted their efforts to the *New National Era*, a fledgling black newspaper.[62] Hardin's zeal as reformer lessened as his political ambitions grew. He remained spokesman for Denver blacks, but delivered addresses mainly at Republican territorial conventions, where he praised the party and urged Negro support.[63] Rewarded with a minor position at the Denver mint in 1873, he was dismissed for "incompetence" after a bigamy charge was leveled against him.[64] Frustrated by his failure to advance in politics and plagued by marital problems, he moved to Cheyenne in 1873 and served in the Wyoming territorial legislature in 1879 and 1882.[65]

The struggle for equal rights in Colorado is peripheral to the central theme of Reconstruction history, yet it is integral to the whole of that history. It stimulated congressional enactment of equal suffrage for blacks in all territories three years before the ratification of the Fifteenth Amendment. It suggests that black Americans in the West, not just in the East or the South, were affected by the reform rhetoric of the period. It reveals, in addition, the change in white thinking toward Negro suffrage in one small section of the country. Admittedly, white Coloradans acceded to equal suffrage out of a sense of inevitability, but having accepted the change they never retracted it. The editor of the *Central [City] Herald* may well have been speaking for many white Coloradans in late 1868 when he wrote: "So far as we are concerned, negro suffrage is dead and buried, and while we could never be induced to vote for it, we have nothing further to say against it."[66] Black Coloradans overlooked this grudging compliance and chose instead to express open optimism about the nation and their future in it. As Hardin observed in 1870, "This glorious republic is the blood-bought heritage of all. There is not one law for the white man, one for the red man and another for the black; but equal laws for all men."[67]

Notes

1. Restrictions in Colorado Territory paralleled those in the northern states. Specifically, laws prohibited blacks from serving on juries, giving testimony against a white person, marrying white persons, and voting. *Provisional Laws and Joint Resolutions of the General Assembly of Jefferson Territory* (Omaha, 1860), part II, chap. XX, sec. 212, chap. XXVI, sec. 378; part III, chap. XII, sec. 5. See also Harmon Mothershead, "Negro Rights in Colorado Territory," *Colorado Magazine*, XL (1963), 212–223, for a general discussion.

2. None of the standard works on Colorado, such as Frank Hall, *History of the State of Colorado* (4 vols., Chicago, 1889), or LeRoy Hafen, *Colorado and Its People* (2 vols., New York, 1948), explore the significance of the Negro protest movement. Of all the major studies on Reconstruction, only W.E.B. DuBois, *Black Reconstruction in America, 1860–1880* (New York, 1935), 233, and Rembert W. Patrick, *The Reconstruction of the Nation* (New York, 1967), 135, give passing mention to the territorial suffrage act. The most extensive comment on the measure is found in a footnote in William Gillette, *The Right to Vote: Politics and the Passage of the Fifteenth Amendment* (Baltimore, 1969), 30.

   For the impact of Reconstruction on Negro thinking about equal rights, see Peter Kolchin, *First Freedoms: The Responses of Alabama's Blacks to Emancipation and*

Reconstruction (Westport, Conn., 1972), and Roberta Sue Alexander, "North Carolina Freedmen's Conventions of 1865 and 1866: Increasing Radicalism" (Paper delivered before the Association for the Study of Afro-American Life and History Convention in New York, 1973). In the West itself, only a civil rights protest in California rivaled that of Colorado in importance; even so the endeavor was less successful. California Negroes spoke out against their inability to offer testimony in courts and the lack of educational facilities. Following a decade of protest, the California legislature in 1863 repealed the law that had forbidden blacks from testifying against whites. However, in *Ward v. Flood* (1874), the California Supreme Court rejected an appeal to integrate the state public school system. Richard Bardolph, *The Civil Rights Record: Black Americans and the Law, 1849–1970* (New York, 1970), 91; Ralph J. Roske, *Everyman's Eden: A History of California* (New York, 1968), 277–278; Robert Cruden, *The Negro in Reconstruction* (Englewood Cliffs, N.J., 1969), 69.

3. *General Laws of the First Session of the Colorado Territorial Legislature, 1861* (Denver, 1861), 72–73; *General Laws of the Third Session…, 1864* (Denver, 1864), 79–80; Denver *Daily Rocky Mountain News,* Feb. 8, 1866; Mothershead, "Negro Rights," 218–219.

4. The suffrage issue played no part in the rejection of the 1864 state constitution. Most Coloradans, fearing that the expenses of statehood would be too great a financial burden, preferred territorial status. Mexican Americans in the southern counties resented their separation from New Mexico Territory and incorporation into Colorado Territory in 1861, and they opposed any move making this disconnection permanent. See Howard Roberts Lamar, *The Far Southwest, 1846–1912: A Territorial History* (New York, 1966), 205–225, for a detailed explanation of the complexities of the statehood movements of 1864 and 1865.

5. During the 1840s public referenda had been adopted in the Old Northwest and became common throughout the North and West on questions dealing with Negro rights. Eugene H. Berwanger, *The Frontier Against Slavery: Western Anti-Negro Prejudice and the Slavery Extension Controversy* (Urbana, 1967), 45–46, 93, 111; Gillette, *The Right to Vote,* 25–30.

6. *Cong. Globe,* 39 Cong., 1 sess. (1866), 1351; *Daily Rocky Mountain News,* Sept. 19, 1865.

7. Some observations regarding Colorado's Negro population during the 1860s are appropriate at this point. At the beginning of the decade the territory contained 46 blacks, 23 of them living in Denver. U.S. Bureau of the Census, *1860 Census, Population* (Washington, D.C., 1864), 546–548. The summary of a territorial census taken in 1865 includes no information about the black population; in fact, it merely gives the number of people in each county. Because numbers of inhabitants were an important factor in the argument between prostatehood and antistatehood forces, the raw data may have been destroyed by the disputants. In any case, the work sheets seem to have been lost. Dolores C. Renze, state archivist of Colorado, to the author, March 26, 1971. In a memorial to Congress in 1866, John Evans and Jerome B. Chaffee, U.S. senators-elect from Colorado, and George Chilcott, representative-elect, insisted that there were not more than 150 Negroes in the territory. *Cong. Globe,* 39 Cong., 1 sess. (1866), 1327. This figure seems small but not wholly inaccurate inasmuch as 137 black males signed a petition to Congress in 1865. The 1870 census indicates 456 Negroes in the territory, 230 living in Denver. The majority of Colorado blacks enumerated in 1870 had immigrated from Missouri, Kentucky, and Virginia. U.S. Bureau of the Census, *1870 Census, Population* (Washington, D.C., 1872), 95–96, 328–342. After examining the handwritten work sheets, I have concluded that 394 blacks is a more accurate figure for the 1870 Negro population. Census takers signified the race of every individual by the letters W (white), B (black), and M (mulatto), but in many instances where M appears, it is evident from the name and birthplace that these individuals were Mexican, not mulatto. "Population Schedules of the Ninth Census of the United States: Colorado," National Archives (Ms, microfilm, Fort Lewis College Library, Durango, Colorado).

8. For information on the professions of the black leaders, see J. E. Wharton, *History of the City of Denver from Its Earliest Settlement to the Present Time* (Denver, 1866), 106–124; The *Rocky Mountain Directory and Colorado Gazetteer for 1871* (Denver, 1871), 274, 291, 297, *passim*.

9. *Daily Rocky Mountain News,* Nov. 4, 1865; Black Hawk *Daily Mining Journal,* Nov. 15, 16, 18, and 20, 1864.

10. *Daily Rocky Mountain News,* Nov. 4 and 8, 1865. At the conclusion of the debate, the mostly white audience voted to reject Negro suffrage, although it agreed that Hardin had proved his own right to the ballot.

11. *Ibid.,* Jan. 15, 1866; *Daily Mining Journal,* Nov. 18, 1864; *Cheyenne* (Wyoming) *Daily Sun,* Nov. 9, 1879. The *Cheyenne Daily Sun* published a lengthy political biography of Hardin following his election to the Wyoming legislature in 1879.

12. Hardin to Greeley, Dec. 15, 1865, and Greeley's reply in *New York Tribune,* Jan. 15, 1866.

13. Hardin to Sumner, Jan. 15, 1866, in *Cong. Globe,* 39 Cong., 1 sess. (1866), 2138. Hardin's name is misspelled "Harding" in the *Globe.* Sumner consistently voted against statehood for Colorado during the first session of the 39th Congress, even though some senators supported admission in order to secure additional votes in the quarrel with President Andrew Johnson over Reconstruction. Sumner's opposition continued until the passage of the Edmunds Amendment, which stipulated equal suffrage as a condition for statehood. *Ibid.,* 1329–1331, 1352, 1365; 39 Cong., 2 sess. (1867), 360–364.

14. *Daily Rocky Mountain News,* Feb. 8, 1866.

15. *Ibid.,* Feb. 9, 1866.

16. Wagoner, Smith, and Hardin to Cummings, Dec. 11, 1865, in U.S. Dept. of State, *State Department Territorial Papers: Colorado Series,* Vol. I (Microfilm, Colorado State University Library, Fort Collins), hereafter cited as *Colorado Territorial Papers.*

17. Cummings to William H. Seward, Dec. 23, 1865, in *Colorado Territorial Papers,* Vol. I.

18. "Petition of Colored Citizens to Congress," undated, in *Colorado Territorial Papers,* Vol. I. The territorial papers contain both printed and manuscript copies. They differ only in minor changes in capitalization and in the spelling of four signatures.

19. Territory of Colorado, *House Journal, Fifth Session* (Black Hawk, Colo., 1866), 82–84; "Petition of Colored Citizens" (Hardin, Wagoner, Albert Arbor, A. C. Clark, and W. E. Randolph) to Cummings, Jan. 20, 1866; Cummings to Seward, Jan. 29, 1866; special message of Cummings to the Colorado legislature on Negro suffrage, all in *Colorado Territorial Papers,* Vol. I. The governor forwarded copies of the petition and his message to Seward.

20. Hall, *History of Colorado,* I, 375; *Daily Rocky Mountain News,* Feb. 8, 1866.

21. *Daily Rocky Mountain News,* Jan. 24, 1866. The *News* also roundly rebuked Allen A. Bradford, delegate to Congress, for presenting to the House from "W.J. Hardin and one hundred other niggers" a petition demanding that the word "white" be stricken from the state constitution. Bradford and Cummings were the only whites who were sufficiently involved on behalf of the blacks to receive criticism from the press. *Ibid.,* Feb. 23, 1866.

22. Cummings to Seward, Dec. 11, 1865, in *Colorado Territorial Papers,* Vol. I.

23. Territory of Colorado, *House Journal, Fifth Session,* 82–84; special message on Negro suffrage, in *Colorado Territorial Papers,* Vol. I.

24. Territory of Colorado, *House Journal, Sixth Session* (Central City, Colo., 1867), 144–145; *General Laws of the Sixth Session of the Colorado Territorial Legislature* (Central City, Colo., 1867), 69.

25. *Daily Rocky Mountain News,* Feb. 9 and March 5, 1867.

26. *Ibid.,* Jan. 24, 1866.

27. *Ibid.,* Jan. 15, 1866.

28. *Ibid.*

29. *Ibid.,* Jan. 30 and March 15, 1866.

30. *Daily Denver Gazette,* Feb. 21, 1868.

31. *Cheyenne Daily Sun,* Nov. 9, 1879.

32. *Daily Rocky Mountain News,* Sept. 6, 1866.

33. *Denver Daily,* Dec. 22, 1867.

34. *Cong. Globe,* 39 Cong., 2 sess. (1866), 2135–2136, 2138, 2180.

35. "Message of President Regarding the Admission of Colorado," *Sen. Ex. Doc. 45,* 39 Cong., 1 sess. (1866), ser. set no. 1238; *Daily Rocky Mountain News,* June 26, 1866.

36. *Cong. Globe,* 39 Cong., 1 sess. (1866), 210, 2134, 1327–2180, *passim.*

37. *Ibid.,* 2148, 2210, 2600–2603, 3476, 3525–3529.

38. *Ibid.,* 39 Cong., 2 sess. (1867), 364–365, 382.

39. *Ibid.,* 398–399, 890; Central City *Daily Miner's Register,* Jan. 16, 1867. The denial of equal suffrage in the Nebraska state constitution may have stimulated votes for this territorial suffrage act, but it had played no role in initiating the measure. Nebraskans approved their constitution on June 2, 1866, and it was presented to Congress on July 23. Ashley's bill had been introduced two months earlier, following prolonged debate on the suffrage restriction in Colorado. *Cong. Globe,* 39 Cong., 1 sess. (1866), 4044; *Nebraska City News,* June 30, 1866.

40. *Daily Rocky Mountain News,* April 1 and 3, 1867.

41. Republican editors were uncertain whether Negro suffrage was indeed national Republican policy. See the *Daily Miner's Register,* Jan. 7 and Nov. 19, 1868; *Daily Rocky Mountain News,* June 16 and Nov. 12, 1868.

42. *Daily Rocky Mountain News,* Jan. 3, 6, and 12, 1867.

43. *Daily Miner's Register,* Jan. 16, March 20 and 28, 1867, July 1, 1868. Some may express surprise at the continued editorial appeals, since the territory contained no more than 150 eligible black voters, and only 120 of them cast ballots in the 1867 municipal election in Denver. (*Daily Rocky Mountain News,* April 1 and 3, 1867). Despite the small numbers, however, the Republicans stood to benefit. For example, the black vote in Denver's Arapahoe County determined a Republican victory in the 1868 congressional race. Allen Bradford secured a mere seventeen vote margin over his Democratic opponent, David Belden. Walter L. Shelly, "The Colorado Republican Party: The Formative Years" (M.A. thesis, University of Colorado, Boulder, 1963), 67–71.

44. Although during the 1850s "popular sovereignty" meant the right of individual territories to decide whether they should be free or slave, it gradually came to mean noninterference generally in territorial affairs by the government in Washington. See Robert W. Johannsen, *Frontier Politics on the Eve of the Civil War* (Seattle, 1955), 131–142, for a detailed explanation.

45. *Daily Rocky Mountain News,* Jan. 23 and 27, 1866; *Daily Miner's Register,* Jan. 27, 1866; *Daily Mining Journal,* Jan. 30, Feb. 8 and May 24, 1866.

46. *Daily Rocky Mountain News,* Jan. 6, 1867.

47. *Daily Miner's Register,* March 24, 1867.

48. Golden *Colorado Transcript,* Jan. 16, 1867. During the campaign of 1868, the Democratic *Central [City] Herald* criticized the territorial suffrage act as an example of federal interference. The *Register* curtly replied that, while Congress had previously endorsed popular sovereignty, it was well within its right to impose restrictions on territories. *Daily Miner's Register,* July 1, 1868.

49. *Daily Rocky Mountain News,* Jan. 3, 1867.

50. *Ibid.,* Feb. 16 and 22, 1867.

51. *Ibid.,* Jan. 16, 1867.

52. Philip Foner, *The Life and Writings of Frederick Douglass* (4 vols., New York, 1955), IV, 218–219; *New York Times,* Aug. 8, 1869.

53. *Daily Rocky Mountain News,* April 3, 1867.

54. Hardin and Lewis Douglass to Sumner and Ashley, Jan. 11, 1867, in *ibid.,* Feb. 7, 1867; *Cong. Globe,* 40 Cong., 1 sess. (1868), 950; Denver *Daily Colorado Tribune,* Feb. 18, 1868.

55. *Daily Rocky Mountain News,* Aug. 2 and 6, 1867; *Daily Colorado Tribune,* Aug. 8, 1867.

56. *Daily Rocky Mountain News,* June 6, 1867.

57. *Ibid.,* Oct. 3 and 15, 1867; *Daily Colorado Tribune,* Oct. 3 and 4, 1867. Democratic newspapers ignored the integration struggle; Republican editors made only slight comment. The *News* approved Hatch's resignation, claiming that his anti-Negro bias made him unacceptable as teacher of any children. The *Tribune,* in determining that blacks in Denver were currently contributing $211,000 in property taxes, chided whites for opposing integration while permitting their children to be educated with Negro money.

58. *Manual of the Public School in East Denver, 1873,* in *Ninth Annual Report of the Board of Education, District 1, Arapahoe County, Colorado* (Denver, 1883), 17; Jerome C. Smiley, *History of Denver* (Denver, 1901; reprinted, 1971), 739–740. With Denver's development into a large urban center in the twentieth century, segregated schools again became an issue.

59. *Daily Rocky Mountain News,* May 3, 1870.

60. See Cruden, *Negro in Reconstruction,* 37; Kenneth Stampp, *The Era of Reconstruction, 1865–1867* (New York, 1965), 126–127.

61. "Population Schedules of the Ninth Census: Colorado" (Ms.). Other sources suggest substantially greater assets. In 1865 Hardin estimated Sanderlin's personal wealth to be $30,000 to $40,000. Hardin to Greeley, in the *New York Tribune,* Jan. 15, 1866. Sanderlin himself in later life admitted that he had built a $30,000 gift from his white father into a considerable fortune. *Denver Republican,* March 17, 1890.

62. Arna Bontemps, *Free at Last: The Life of Frederick Douglass* (New York, 1971), 273; *New York Times,* Aug. 8, 1869.

63. Elmer Ellis, *Henry Moore Teller, Defender of the West* (Caldwell, Idaho, 1941), 88.

64. *Daily Rocky Mountain News,* July 23, 1873; *Daily Denver Tribune,* July 23, 1873.

65. *Cheyenne Daily Sun,* Nov. 9, 1879; *Wyoming Historical Blue Book: A Legal and Political History of Wyoming, 1868–1943* (Denver, 1946), 298–299, 305.

66. *Central Herald,* n.d., in *Daily Rocky Mountain News,* Nov. 16, 1868.

67. *Ibid.,* May 3, 1870.

BUFFALO SOLDIERS IN THE AMERICAN WEST, 1865–1900

Monroe Lee Billington

[This is an original article written specifically for inclusion in this volume.]

Nearly 200,000 African Americans were in the military services of the United States during the Civil War. At the beginning of the conflict, the U.S. army resisted the idea of using black soldiers based upon unfounded fears that they would not follow orders and would run away when fighting started. Once the military establishment began utilizing black troops, however, it discovered that they did indeed make good soldiers. Consequently, as part of the postwar move to give freedmen equal rights, Congress in 1866 created the nation's first all-black infantry and cavalry regiments. The law establishing these black units indicated, however, that even the Radical Republicans in Congress harbored prejudicial attitudes towards African Americans. The blacks regiments were not only segregated, but also were commanded by white officers. Moreover, blacks were not allowed into service branches other than the infantry and cavalry.

The two cavalry regiments comprised approximately 20 percent of the army's postwar horsemen; the two (originally four) infantry regiments made up about 5 percent of the military's foot soldiers. All told, the army's troop strength averaged twenty-seven thousand at any one time in the last thirty-five years of the nineteenth century, and about 10 percent of those soldiers were black. Additionally, with the exception of federal troops sent to the South during Reconstruction and a few stationed in eastern posts, most of the army's forces—including almost all of its African American soldiers—were stationed in the frontier West.

Western soldiers fought Indians to make the West safe for occupancy by settlers from the United States. They guarded wagon trains, stagecoaches, and railroads taking Americans to the frontier. They aided local law enforcement efforts to round up cattle rustlers and other outlaws. In addition, they built roads, strung telegraph wire, and performed other perfunctory duties that aided the movement of the nation westward to fulfill its so-called manifest destiny not only to own but also to control and settle the western territories.

Perhaps the most important function of the army in the late nineteenth century—at least in the eyes of most Americans—was fighting the resisting Indians who had lived in the West for centuries. African Americans not only fought in these Indian wars, they distinguished themselves by having low desertion rates, winning Medals of Honor, and generally performing their assigned duties in exemplary fashion. Moreover, they contributed to the local white communities that began forming on the frontier by spending their money in these towns, entertaining townsfolk by forming bands and baseball teams, and by continually patrolling the vast frontier expanses looking for outlaws and Indians.

In the following article, Monroe Lee Billington surveys the activities of the black troops (denominated "buffalo soldiers" by their Indian adversaries) during the late nineteenth century. He shows that while white westerners did not always appreciate the work the African American troopers performed, they were invariably willing to benefit from the presence of black soldiers on the frontier. And he demonstrates that by fighting, scouting, keeping the peace, playing games and music, spending money, and engaging in a variety of other activities, the buffalo soldiers contributed significantly to the growth and development of the American West.

Before the outbreak of the American Civil War, many of the eighteen thousand enlisted men in the U.S. army—which included no African Americans—had been scattered throughout the trans-Mississippi West, protecting travelers and settlers from Indians who resented and resisted these migrants moving into their homelands and hunting grounds. When the war began in 1861, army officials recalled the vast majority of these soldiers to the East. Because of the lower military profile, western Indians stepped up their attacks on white intruders. The Sioux outbreak in Dakota Territory in 1862 was the most famous of these, but other Indians, including the Apaches and the Comanches in the Southwest, also fought those who intended to take their lands. Such action on the part of the Indians convinced the nation's political and military leaders that if the West was to be made safe for European and American settlers, a great segment of the army had to be relocated there upon the conclusion of the war.

In view of the Indian threat and because thousands of Civil War soldiers' enlistments had not ended when hostilities ceased, the army sent a large number of these men to the western frontier. Consequently, some of the nearly 200,000 black Civil War soldiers—who had comprised about 10 percent of the Union's wartime forces—were assigned to posts on the frontier in 1865 and 1866.[1] For example, the Fifty-seventh Infantry and the One Hundred Twenty-fifth Infantry had been organized in the last year of the Civil War. From August to November 1866 the army stationed six companies of the Fifty-seventh at New Mexico's forts Union and Bascom. Within a month after these soldiers left New Mexico, the entire regiment was disbanded. From August 1866 until October 1867 eight companies of the One Hundred Twenty-fifth were stationed at seven New Mexico forts. Most of them then transferred to Fort Riley, Kansas, for discharge from military service. In December 1867 this regiment, too, was disbanded.[2] The fate of the Fifty-seventh and the One Hundred Twenty-fifth infantries paralleled other Civil War regiments sent to the frontier, their men being mustered out and their units disbanded by 1868.

While African Americans had been permitted to serve in the military during the Civil War, as well as all previous American wars, they had never before been allowed to serve during peacetime. Because black troops performed numerous heroic acts during the Civil War, black leaders and their white supporters advocated that blacks be permitted to enlist in the postwar army. The Army Reorganization Act of 1866 provided for two of ten cavalry regiments (the Ninth and Tenth) and four of forty-five infantry regiments (the Thirty-eighth, Thirty-ninth, Fortieth, and Forty-first) to be for black enlisted men. White commissioned officers and black noncommissioned officers led these regiments. When the army disbanded the remaining Civil War units, many war veterans along with new recruits took advantage of the new law and joined the postwar army. The Army Reorganization Act of 1869 provided for the retention of the Ninth and Tenth cavalry regiments, but it combined the four black infantry regiments into two—the Twenty-fourth and Twenty-fifth.[3]

Between the Civil War and the Spanish-American War, approximately 141,000 enlisted men served in the U.S. army. Included in these numbers were fourteen thousand black men, about 10 percent of the total. On average, at any one time 2,700 black men were under arms.[4] During this so-called era of the Indian wars, most American soldiers, including almost all those of African descent, were stationed in the area stretching from the one hundredth meridian to the Pacific Coast and from Canada to Mexico. The majority of their posts were in the Great Plains and Rocky Mountain states.

The black troopers came to be called "buffalo soldiers." How and why this name was applied is in doubt. Some writers have suggested that the Indians first used it because of the similarity of the hair and the color of the American plains animal and the African Americans. Others have said the men got the name because in wintertime they wrapped themselves in buffalo robes. Still others have suggested that from a distance a black cavalryman and the horse he rode blended together to look like a single animal, a bison. Finally, it has been theorized that the Indians originated the term because of their respect for the buffalo and the black men, both being worthy opponents in a fight. In any case, the soldiers accepted the name as complimentary, and the Tenth Cavalry even incorporated a likeness of the wild animal on its regimental crest. Although the Indians probably first gave the name to members of the cavalry, it came to be applied to infantrymen, too.

Between 1866 and 1869, all four of the army's black infantry regiments served at various posts on the frontier. When those units were reorganized as two, they also were assigned to the West. In 1870 the Twenty-fourth and Twenty-fifth regiments began their tours of duty at nearly a dozen forts in Texas, remaining there for a decade.[5] When the Twenty-fourth moved out of Texas in 1880, it transferred to forts Reno, Sill, Supply, and Elliott in Indian Territory. In 1888 that assignment was followed by a move to the area under the jurisdiction of the army's Department of Arizona at forts Apache, Grant, Thomas, and Bayard—the latter being in New Mexico.[6] The men of the Twenty-fourth remained in Arizona and New Mexico until 1896. At that time, the army transferred them to Fort Douglas in Utah where they remained until 1899. The Twenty-fifth's moves paralleled the Twenty-fourth's. In 1880 the Twenty-fifth moved from Texas to Dakota Territory. Eight years later, it moved to Montana Territory's forts Missoula, Shaw, and Custer. The main body of the regiment remained in Montana until the early 1890s.[7] In 1898–1899 some of the men of the Twenty-fifth found themselves in Arizona and New Mexico.[8] Clearly, black infantrymen in the postwar army were stationed at a large number of military forts scattered throughout the American West.

If the primary responsibility of the cavalrymen was to subdue the Indians, the major task of the infantrymen was to maintain and guard military forts. Thus, infantrymen served as support groups to cavalrymen, and almost every frontier post usually had at least one company of each, working in tandem. While cavalrymen expended most of their efforts fighting Indians, infantrymen devoted their attention to necessary but mundane day-to-day activities in and around their often isolated and lonely posts. Garrison duty was unglamorous and harsh, but it was vital for success. Black infantrymen spent countless hours performing skilled and unskilled tasks. They built military roads and installed and maintained telegraph lines. They erected new buildings and repaired old ones; served as carpenters, plasterers, painters, and bricklayers; and dug water wells and cellars for storing pickled meats, molasses, and vegetables. They quarried and hauled stone for fencing post gardens and cemeteries.[9] The need for wood for fuel was a matter demanding attention at frontier forts, and these men searched for, chopped, and gathered their posts' wood supplies.[10]

On numerous occasions, black infantrymen served in quartermaster departments, working as teamsters, blacksmiths' helpers, and corral builders. From time to time, they served as clerks in subsistence departments and as bakers, cooks, stewards, and clerks in post hospitals. The considerable expense of obtaining fresh vegetables from distant sources led the army to authorize commanders at western posts to purchase seed potatoes, garden seeds, and agricultural implements so that troopers could plant and cultivate their own vegetables. Throughout the West, post and company gardens supplied much fresh produce for both blacks and whites, providing a valuable component of the officers' and enlisted men's diets.[11] These and countless other activities of black infantrymen helped accomplish the army's mission.

Even though cavalrymen were by definition associated with activities related to horses, in places and at times when cavalrymen were absent or otherwise unavailable, mounted infantrymen acted as horse soldiers. When Indians tried to capture posts' horses, black infantrymen were called upon to protect the vital herds and then to mount army mules and chase the Indians away. When Indians stole animals from private citizens, these infantrymen tried to retrieve them.[12] They protected miners, ranchers, farmers, and travelers; escorted army paymasters and protected lines of supply; and guarded water wells and springs.[13]

When occasion warranted, post commanders sent mounted infantrymen to seek out and subdue Indians by capturing or killing them. In addition to activities of short duration—such as when troopers chased away Indians from posts or settlements—numerous scouting expeditions were planned in advance and lasted from a few days to several weeks. Often black participation in these excursions was substantial.[14]

When black infantrymen were in New Mexico in the late 1860s, they participated not only in numerous small-scale and several major scouts but also in at least one grand expedition. The latter began in the spring of 1869, organized and led by a captain in the Thirty-eighth Infantry. Launched from Fort Selden in southern New Mexico and comprised of nearly two hundred black enlisted men and five white cavalrymen, this large command explored a vast region of southwestern New Mexico, including the San Andres, Sacramento, and Guadalupe mountains and the essentially barren desert between them. Traveling a circuitous route through mountain passes and across virtually waterless country, the expedition developed a detailed map of a region perhaps not before seen by white or black men. They learned that the desolate region was home to only a few Indians who constituted no serious threat to others. In an expedition that lasted sixty-three days, the main body of this command traveled 1,241 miles, an average of more than nineteen miles a day.[15] This and other expeditions and scouts were testimonies to the black infantrymen's contributions to military objectives in the West.

While black infantrymen served more or less all over the American West, the Ninth and Tenth cavalrymen were concentrated in the states of Kansas and Texas and the territories of Oklahoma, Arizona, and New Mexico. Fewer numbers served in the states and territories of Nebraska, the Dakotas, Colorado, Wyoming, and Utah. They performed three decades of continuous service on the Great Plains and in the Rocky Mountain West, especially the Southwest.

Shortly after the formation of the Ninth Cavalry, the entire regiment, under its commander, Col. Edward Hatch, marched to southwest Texas, to face the daunting task of standing guard over thousands of square miles of raw frontier. They worked to make life and property secure on one of the most turbulent and strife-ridden frontiers in the history of the American westward movement. Operating from the Guadalupe Mountains to the Rio Grande, the men of the Ninth relentlessly pursued their objectives, including freeing the Pecos River country of troublesome Indians. Riding their mounts over thousands of dusty miles in blistering heat, they had cleared southwest Texas of resisting Indians by 1875.[16]

In the meantime, the Tenth Cavalry was organized and commanded by Col. Benjamin Grierson. Its early headquarters were in Kansas, but some of its companies were stationed across the border in Oklahoma. Later, other companies were moved to the Red River valley of Texas and Oklahoma, where they rode hundreds of miles pursuing Cheyennes, Comanches, and Kiowas who had left their reservations to commit depredations. The Red River War was over by early 1875, when the main body of the Cheyennes surrendered. Black soldiers were an important factor in bringing that confrontation to an end.[17] After the Red River War, the army relocated the companies of the Tenth to west Texas. For several years, these cavalrymen worked in a harsh environment as they cleared the Staked Plains of Mescalero Apaches.[18] Bravery and hardship went hand in hand.

The various Apache tribes constituted a major barrier to the settlement of New Mexico and Arizona territories. Anticipating a serious Indian outbreak, the army moved the entire Ninth Cavalry from southwest Texas to New Mexico in 1876.[19] The Ninth's major adversary was Chief Victorio, a Warm Springs Apache who resisted the government's efforts to move his people to a

Tenth Cavalrymen. African Americans constituted about 20 percent of the army's cavalry forces during the late nineteenth century. These members of the Tenth Cavalry were photographed while on escort duty in Montana in 1894. (Courtesy, Montana Historical Society. Photo by A. B. Coe.)

reservation in Arizona. Black cavalrymen chased him and his warriors across New Mexico Territory for six years. Victorio's band was considerably smaller than the number of soldiers available to control it, but its hit-and-run tactics served it well. Furthermore, the Indians' knowledge of the countryside and its environment, and their flights to safety beyond the United States-Mexico border, placed the cavalrymen and their leaders at a disadvantage.[20]

Eventually, however, the army prevailed as the Ninth, with support from the Tenth in west Texas, applied constant pressure. After the soldiers halted several of their chases of Victorio's band at the international boundary, Colonel Hatch finally ordered them into Mexico. These American troopers helped a Mexican force corner the heretofore elusive chief. In 1880 Mexican soldiers found and attacked Victorio's warriors, killing their leader. Although Mexican soldiers had ended Victorio's life, the men of the Ninth Cavalry had played an important role in the chief's demise.[21]

But the death of Victorio did not completely halt Indian resistance in New Mexico. Some of the chief's followers remained in the territory, requiring the army's attention. Throughout most of 1881 the army and the Warm Springs

Apaches sparred with each other, the latter being led by a Victorio supporter named Nana. Much deadly fighting ensued. To combat Nana's band, Colonel Hatch assumed personal command of his forces on one occasion and placed every available fighting man in the field. Although Ninth cavalrymen never won a decisive battle against Nana and his warriors, they gradually pushed the band farther south until its leader and members fled into permanent hiding in the mountains of northern Mexico.[22]

For many years, the Colorado Utes were not in the direct line of American westward advance, but the discovery of precious metal near Pike's Peak in 1859 stimulated a great influx of outsiders onto their lands. Ute resistance was inevitable. For nearly two decades, Utes harassed or killed settlers, burned cabins, and stole stock. In the late 1870s the army moved detachments of the Ninth from New Mexico to southern Colorado where black soldiers fought furious battles with the Indians. As a result, the Utes were forced to reside on reservations.[23]

After the west Texas frontier was pacified, the army transferred the Tenth Cavalry to Arizona in 1885 to oppose the bands of Chiricahua Apache leaders such as Mangus and Geronimo. Years of prior military campaigning in Arizona had driven a majority of these Apaches onto reservations, but many so-called renegades remained at large. As men of the Tenth hunted these Indians, fights occurred at desert watering holes as well as in the Chiricahua Mountains of southeastern Arizona. White units also were involved in these activities. Soon thereafter, black soldiers played a major role in the defeat of Mangus, the remaining rebellious Apache leader of a remnant of Indians who had formerly followed Geronimo.[24]

A final Indian-army confrontation occurred in December 1890. The Battle of Wounded Knee, a gruesome engagement in South Dakota between white cavalrymen and Sioux, resulted in the deaths of at least 150 Indian men, women, and children. The fact that more than twenty soldiers also died did not impress the remaining Sioux. When they began to express their anger at the battle's slaughter, the army sent men of the Ninth from Nebraska to control a potentially dangerous situation. Within two weeks, these men moved more than four thousand Indians to South Dakota's Pine Ridge Reservation. With this final action, the era of the Indian wars was over.[25]

Because of feats of heroism, eighteen black enlisted men, four of whom served as "Seminole-Negro" Indian scouts, received Medals of Honor (often, but incorrectly, referred to as congressional Medals of Honor).[26] When Congress awarded the medals it was not only directly recognizing the valor of these specific men but also indirectly applauding the efforts of all African American soldiers.

The medal winners—and their comrades in arms—deserved the accolades they received in view of the grueling ordeals they had experienced.

After the pacification of the Indians, the government instituted major changes in the military presence in the West. Nearly a hundred forts were no longer needed, and by the end of the century all but about a dozen of them had been abandoned. Related to these actions was the fact that as railroads were extended into the West, the army could, if necessary, move men and animals over long distances easily. A few large forts could do what dozens of smaller posts had done previously. The army did not, however, reduce the number of men under arms, and the forts that remained were heavily garrisoned, with several hundred men being located at some of them at any given moment. Forts Duchesne in Utah and Bayard in New Mexico were prime examples of the concentration of African American troops in the final decade of the nineteenth century.

While minor Indian resistance had to be dealt with in the 1890s, the men of the army's western garrisons in that decade usually had little to do. The army kept them busy with practice marches and maneuvers, exercises in the field, camps of instruction, and target practice and competitions.[27] One time-consuming job for some of the men was closing down the forts designated to be abandoned.[28] The army's educational program, established shortly after the Civil War, was considerably enlarged in the nineties, and many black soldiers spent hours participating in it.[29]

Leisure activities also helped pass the time. Many men benefited from libraries and reading rooms established at almost every post or garrison. Amusement halls with stages for theatrical performances, lectures, and lyceums were at most forts. These buildings also were used for dancing, parties, and social gatherings of all sorts. Moreover, many post exchanges had recreation rooms with billiard tables for the enlisted men to use.[30]

One important leisure-time activity was baseball. Soldiers in the postwar West had taken up the popular sport early on, finding time to play the game during the years that troops were called upon to suppress Indians. Companies often had their own teams, some of which were composed of both officers and enlisted men. When conditions and time permitted, the teams competed with others whose members were stationed at the same post. Sometimes all-post groups played other forts' teams or those made up of civilians from nearby communities. Black teams played white ones, while some squads were composed of members of both races. In the humdrum days of the 1890s, soldiers found ways to fill the available time with what would soon become a national pastime.[31]

A few years after the end of the Indian wars, the army moved large numbers of white and African American soldiers from the West to Cuba to fight in the Spanish-American War. Most of the blacks who remained in the West during the 1898 conflict soon thereafter were sent—along with many veterans of the Cuban hostilities—to the Philippine Islands to pacify the inhabitants of the nation's most recently acquired territory.[32] By 1900 all but a handful of black soldiers had been removed from the American West.

Even though the primary job of the United States army after the Civil War was to protect people and property from Indians, it also performed other functions. Its additional activities during that era justified it being considered a national police force.[33] Both African American and Caucasian soldiers in the American West assisted local authorities and federal marshals with their jobs. They escorted civilians, stagecoaches, and freighters; guarded railroad construction workers and mail carriers; and chased robbers, horse thieves, and cattle rustlers. Members of both the Ninth and Tenth cavalries watched over government survey crews along the international boundary between the United States and Mexico. Also, in a period when Mexico's government was unstable, detachments of black soldiers patrolled the Rio Grande valley to keep turmoil from spreading into the United States. When members of losing or outgunned political and military factions sought refuge north of the border, black soldiers escorted them back to their own country.[34]

After disposing of Victorio and Nana in New Mexico, the army assigned the Ninth the job of preventing "boomers" from illegally moving from Kansas to Oklahoma. In the mid-1880s, over two thousand boomers filtered in from various points along the border, requiring the constant attention of six companies of black cavalrymen. The soldiers conducted countless patrols to intercept these determined immigrants, many of whom were belligerent and ready to fight. Explosive situations sometimes led to conflict and bloodshed. After the government arrested the boomers' leaders—making it clear that it would not tolerate their illegal activities—Kansans stopped their attempts to "invade" the "Promised Land," and black soldiers drove out the majority of those already in Oklahoma.[35]

The government also used the army to help control labor violence. When laborers working for giant industrial corporations organized unions to advance their interests, strike duty became one of the army's peacetime functions. The military often intervened in contests of wills between organized workers and powerful corporation owners. In over fifty instances from the late 1870s until the end of the century, soldiers acted sometimes as peacekeepers but most often as strikebreakers. When thousands of laborers struck against several railroads in

1894, creating a presumed national emergency, the government ordered commanders of six of the nation's eight military departments to act. Immediately, the army made available sixteen thousand soldiers to protect railroad property and to break strikes. By 1900 duty related to railroad strikes had involved almost two-thirds of the men in the army.[36]

From early July through the middle of September 1894, soldiers from the military departments in the West were in the field supporting federal marshals in opening rail traffic, defending property, and restoring order. When railroad workers in southern Colorado protested deteriorating economic conditions, owners called upon the army for help. Five companies of the Twenty-fourth Infantry—over two hundred men—traveled by rail from southeastern Arizona and southwestern New Mexico to Trinidad, Colorado.[37] This military presence immediately became a visible symbol of the power of the national government.

The situation in southern Colorado was volatile; the strikers were in bad humor. They had burned railroad bridges, applied soap to rails, put sand in brake boxes, and assaulted railroad employees. But these activities ceased once the soldiers arrived. The strikers were hesitant to damage railroad property directly under military guard. Thus, after two months, the soldiers left Colorado and returned to their posts in Arizona and New Mexico. The mayor, chief of police, and other officials and prominent citizens of Trinidad commented upon the exceptional and highly commendable conduct of the black enlisted men during their stay in Colorado.[38]

Another civil disturbance in which the army was involved was New Mexico's Lincoln County War, one of the most famous events in the history of the American West.[39] In the 1870s Lincoln County constituted the southeastern quadrant of New Mexico Territory, an area larger than the state of Kentucky. In the mid-1870s landowners and local businessmen who operated a mercantile business throughout the county obtained lucrative contracts with the government to supply large amounts of beef and flour to Mescalero Apaches and to provide beef, grains, and vegetables to Fort Stanton, situated some nine miles northwest of the town of Lincoln.

Problems arose for these men and their profitable enterprises when a former Texas rancher and a wealthy young Englishman joined forces to compete with the entrenched group. The competition and conflict between these two economic and political factions resulted in intrigue, corruption, violence, and murder. The events overwhelmed territorial politics, brought down a governor, caused the U.S. departments of the Interior and Justice to send in a special investigator, and involved the president of the United States and New Mexico's most famous outlaw, Billy the Kid.

When both sides hired several dozen professional gunmen to protect their interests, Lincoln County was in a state of anarchy. Under these conditions, the county sheriff called upon the military for assistance. Col. Nathan Dudley, the commander at Fort Stanton, accepted the invitation to intervene—contrary to direct orders from his superiors to refrain from doing so. With a force of thirty black cavalrymen and white infantrymen, Dudley rode into the town of Lincoln. The commander had declared his neutrality in the dispute, but in fact he favored the faction of which the sheriff was a member. Although the combatants burned some houses and killed a few people after the soldiers arrived, the situation was soon contained and the troops with their gatling gun, brass howitzer, and two thousand rounds of ammunition had helped bring the conflict to an end.

For years historians have sorted contradictory information and attempted to make valid interpretations of the turbulent events in Lincoln County. Whatever else they have decided, they correctly have concluded that Colonel Dudley directly affected the outcome. He could not have done this without the support of his soldiers; therefore, enlisted men of the Ninth Cavalry were important contributors to the final outcome of the Lincoln County War.[40]

Following the Civil War, the American people regularly praised the veterans of that great conflict. They held celebrations and awarded numerous accolades and honors to those citizens who had served as temporary soldiers. For these men, the U.S. government was generous with monuments, commemorations, and pensions. All of this, however, was in stark contrast to the treatment afforded the professional soldiers who served the country in the postwar period. After 1866 a pervasive anti-military ethos enveloped men who served in the army. Although they served during the period of the Indian wars, the government considered them peacetime soldiers, and they did not command the respect directed toward the thousands of citizen-soldiers who had fought in the Civil War. Another strike against them was that this postwar army was composed primarily of lower-class urban workers, European immigrants, and African Americans—people for whom other Americans often expressed contempt.

Except for soldiers who comprised an army of occupation in the recently defeated southern states during the Reconstruction era and for a few artillerymen who served in forts along the Atlantic and Gulf coasts after 1877, most men in the post-Civil War army served on the frontier protecting Americans from attacks by the original occupants of that land. Farmers, ranchers, miners, migrants, and railroad construction workers often called upon the military establishment, assuming without question that help would be forthcoming.

Under these circumstances, one might assume that all westerners were appreciative of the soldiers' efforts. Such was not the case. Members of the nonmilitary population, in fact, often criticized the soldiers for not taking action or for not acting quickly enough. And when soldiers were unsuccessful in a specific mission, the wrath of an unappreciative population often poured out. To be sure, some frontiersmen praised the soldiers, but for each person who could say that the army protected him, another—and perhaps more—was critical.

Among the services the multipurpose army provided after the Civil War was its economic contribution to western development.[41] It strengthened local economies when it purchased in great quantities meat, vegetables, lumber, fuel, forage, and other supplies. Although soldiers' paychecks were individually small, when a hundred or more men were at a post, their collective income added significantly to the local economy. But even those westerners who made money because of the presence of troopers did not necessarily respect them. Beef contractors, producers of agricultural products, horse and mule dealers, freighters, saloon keepers, and others were glad the army was in the West, but they did not necessarily like its enlisted men and they did not hesitate to prey upon them.[42]

The civilian population's prejudice toward peacetime soldiers increased when those soldiers were African Americans. Prejudiced whites often harassed black soldiers. Disputes in bars, brothels, and gambling houses invariably took on racial overtones if black troopers were involved.[43] Moreover, white civilians who murdered black soldiers were seldom punished for such crimes. By contrast, black soldiers suspected of violating the law often became the targets of unrestrained abuse at the hands of white citizens and local authorities.

When Civil War-era politicians debated whether African Americans were to be a part of the peacetime army, military officers generally spoke against it, even though black men had distinguished themselves during the war. When the decision was made to allow African Americans in the postwar army, military leaders were quick to support segregated regiments. Establishing separate units for blacks, preventing blacks from serving in other branches of the army besides the infantry and the cavalry, and—in the beginning—paying black troops less money than whites were obvious signs of prejudice.[44]

In terms of structure, the postwar black regiments were exactly the same as those for whites, except that they were assigned chaplains with specific instructions to educate the black troops. Educated northern black soldiers did not need rudimentary schooling, but illiterate former southern slaves could profit from it. A more enlightened group of enlisted men meant a better army, and the educational program proved to be quite successful.[45]

Officially, the same rules and regulations governed the entire army; therefore, duties and routine experiences of African Americans were similar to those of white soldiers. Because the army was small and faced a demanding mission on the frontier, white leaders—like it or not—depended on black soldiers to carry their share of field and garrison duties. Shortages of manpower prevented prejudice from remanding blacks to noncombatant status.

Although African Americans constituted about 10 percent of the enlisted men in the army between 1865 and 1900, black enlisted men comprised only 4 percent of those who won the coveted Medal of Honor during that same period. The lower percentage was more likely a function of white prejudice in awarding the medals than a measure of black bravery. Some officers of black regiments complained that prejudice among high-ranking military and political leaders was responsible for this discrepancy in recognition.

Officers of black units often protested that supplies, equipment, and animals sent to their men were inferior. The military records reveal numerous specific instances of discrimination in regard to which units received the best animals and supplies.[46] But when the army converted to the improved Springfield rifle in the 1870s, black units got their issues at approximately the same time as white units received theirs. In other instances, army authorities gave both races the privilege of testing new weapons and equipment. Here, apparently, was an area where the army did not practice discrimination.[47]

Clearly the army was discriminatory in regard to the presence and promotion of black commissioned officers. Although the rules were not prohibitive, not a single African American enlisted man rose from the ranks to a commission between 1866 and 1898. During that time, only twenty-two black youths received appointment to the U.S. Military Academy. Of the twelve who passed the West Point entrance examination, only three—Henry O. Flipper, John H. Alexander, and Charles Young—were able to overcome four years of social ostracism, discrimination, and many other tribulations to graduate from the academy.[48] Of the dozens of men to whom the army accorded commissions to serve as chaplains, only five were African Americans.[49] Sheer numerical facts present a self-evident case for discrimination against blacks in the army's officer corps.

Even though the army insisted that its official policies were non-discriminatory, it could not guarantee its soldiers equality or social acceptance. Most white Americans—both military and civilian—believed blacks were inferior to whites, and official policy could not change those beliefs. Many high-ranking army officers freely expressed their reservations about blacks serving in

Charles Young. One of three African American graduates of the U.S. Military Academy in the late nineteenth century, Young served in the American West as an officer of the Tenth Cavalry. (Courtesy, Nebraska State Historical Society.)

the military; some of them, in fact, supported political efforts to eliminate African Americans from the army.[50]

Officers often acted upon their prejudices. Some preferred to resign from the army rather than accept appointment to a black regiment. Others, such as Eugene A. Carr and Frederick Benteen, remained in the military service but slowed their promotions when they turned down opportunities to command black units.[51] George A. Custer, who refused a lieutenant colonelcy with the Ninth Cavalry but wangled the same rank in the Seventh, is the best known of those officers whose racial prejudice directly affected their careers. No doubt Custer's military career and niche in history would have been far different had he fought the Apaches and helped kill Victorio rather than fighting Sitting Bull and the Sioux who killed him at the Battle of the Little Big Horn.

Many officers commanding African Americans allowed their prejudices to show. The records are filled with black soldiers' charges that officers directed abusive language toward them, often employing racial epithets.[52] The charges were frequent enough to indicate that many of the blacks' complaints were probably justified. Far too many officers knowingly or unknowingly created conditions encouraging racism in an era when prejudice was pervasive. Racism was often just beneath, if not actually above, the surface of both the civilian and military societies.

Although prejudice permeated the prevailing climate and some officers publicly expressed their contempt for black soldiers, others came to respect and even praise them. Both Edward Hatch and Benjamin Grierson, longtime commanders of the Ninth and Tenth cavalries, expressed their appreciation numerous times. Zenas R. Bliss, leader of the Twenty-fourth Infantry, showed genuine concern when his enlisted men were treated unfairly. When George Lippitt Andrews of the Twenty-fifth Infantry suspected another officer of racial prejudice, he reported him to the assistant adjutant general of the Department of Dakota and asked that he be reprimanded.[53] John J. Pershing willingly commanded black troops and defended his men against unjustified criticism. His nickname "Black Jack" devolved from his identification with black troops.[54] The military records are filled with statements of praise from numerous other white officers who worked closely with African Americans. "Reliable," "trustworthy," "faithful," "courageous," and "devoted to duty" were terms and phrases that officers attached to specific black troopers.

These officers admired the black soldiers as fighting men. An officer of a white cavalry regiment at a post that had black infantry companies wrote: "It does not take very long for one to change entirely his ideas in respect to these [black] troops. They make excellent soldiers."[55] After a tough engagement with Indians in Colorado, a white captain awarded black troopers what he considered the highest possible accolade when he called them "the whitest men" he had ever seen.[56] Colonel Bliss pointed out that during the Indian wars, African Americans had served gallantly, and he believed that they ranked among the best soldiers on the frontier.[57] When Gen. John Pope wrote that a group of black troopers had done "everything that men could do," he unknowingly made a statement that could have been used as the collective epitaph of the black soldiers who served during the Indian wars.[58] An objective assessment of the record is that African Americans as a group were, by any standard, competent—even exceptional—fighting men.

In conclusion, despite hardships and racial prejudice, the black soldiers who served in the American West after the Civil War made important contributions. First, they helped subdue resisting Indians. Second, they intervened in numerous and various civil disturbances. Third, they provided a positive impact upon the economy of the West. Finally, they participated in a temporary military society that interacted with a white civilian population, resulting in a cultural exchange between the two races. In short, the buffalo soldiers aided in bringing a new civilization to the American frontier.

Notes

1. Frederick H. Dyer, *A Compendium of the War of the Rebellion* (New York, 1959), vol. 3, 1718–1740; Dudley Taylor Cornish, *The Sable Arm: Negro Troops in the Union Army, 1861–1865* (New York, 1966), 126–131, 232–235, 254–255, 288; *The Army Lineage Book, Volume II: Infantry* (Washington, D.C., 1953), 22.
2. Dyer, *Compendium of the War*, vol. 3, 1718–1740. See also S. C. Agnew, *Garrisons of the Regular U.S. Army: New Mexico, 1846–1899* (Santa Fe, 1971), 123–125.
3. Robert M. Utley, *Frontier Regulars: The United States Army and the Indian, 1866–1891* (New York, 1973), 11–12, 15; Mary Lee Stubbs and Stanley Russell Connor, *Armor-Cavalry, Part I: Regular Army and Army Reserve* (Washington, D.C., 1969), 19–20; *Army Lineage Book, Volume II: Infantry*, 25–26.
4. Russell F. Weigley, *History of the United States Army* (New York, 1967), 567.
5. Arlen L. Fowler, *The Black Infantry in the West, 1869–1891* (Westport, Conn., 1971), 18.
6. *Ibid.*, 74, 80–81.
7. *Ibid.*, 50, 60.
8. S. C. Agnew, *Garrisons of the Regular U.S. Army: Arizona, 1851–1899* (Arlington, Va., 1974), 115–117, 119; Agnew, *Garrisons of the Army: New Mexico*, 64–65, 104–105.
9. Monroe Lee Billington, *New Mexico's Buffalo Soldiers, 1866–1900* (Niwot, Colo., 1991), 26, 29.
10. Darlis A. Miller, *Soldiers and Settlers: Military Supply in the Southwest, 1861–1885* (Albuquerque, 1989), 122.
11. Billington, *New Mexico's Buffalo Soldiers*, 29–30, 31, 32.
12. James Monroe Foster, Jr., "History of Fort Bascom, New Mexico, 1863–1870" (M.A. thesis, Eastern New Mexico University, 1955), 55–56.
13. James Monroe Foster, Jr., "Fort Bascom, New Mexico," *New Mexico Historical Review*, 35 (1960), 48–49; Fowler, *Black Infantry in the West*, 27–28, 52.
14. *Ibid.*, 23–24.
15. Billington, *New Mexico's Buffalo Soldiers*, 19–22.
16. William H. Leckie, *The Buffalo Soldiers: A Narrative of the Negro Cavalry in the West* (Norman, Okla., 1967), 7–12, 17–18, 81–112.
17. *Ibid.*, 7–8, 12–17, 113–140.
18. *Ibid.*, 141–171.
19. Utley, *Frontier Regulars*, 357; Leckie, *Buffalo Soldiers*, 174–175.

20. Billington, *New Mexico's Buffalo Soldiers*, 47–59, 87–93; John P. Clum, "The Apaches," *New Mexico Historical Review*, 4 (1929), 107–127; *Annual Report of the Commissioner of Indian Affairs to the Secretary of the Interior for the Year 1877* (Washington, D.C., 1877), 34–35; *Annual Report of the Secretary of War, 1880* (Washington, 1881), vol. 1, 86, 88.

21. Billington, *New Mexico's Buffalo Soldiers*, 93–97; *Annual Report of the Secretary of War, 1880*, vol. 1, 109; vol. 2, 94–95.

22. Billington, *New Mexico's Buffalo Soldiers*, 103–108; *Annual Report of the Secretary of War, 1881* (Washington, D.C., 1881), vol. 1, 118, 126, 127. Although devoting little attention to black troopers, these general studies of major Indian groups with which those soldiers had to deal are worthy of note: Dan L. Thrapp, *The Conquest of Apacheria* (Norman, Okla., 1967) and *Victorio and the Membres Apaches* (Norman, Okla., 1974); Donald E. Worcester, *The Apaches: Eagles of the Southwest* (Norman, Okla., 1979); and C. L. Sonnichsen, *The Mescalero Apaches*, 2nd ed. (Norman, Okla., 1972).

23. Leckie, *Buffalo Soldiers*, 205–209.

24. *Ibid.*, 239–245.

25. *Ibid.*, 255–258.

26. Preston E. Amos, *Above and Beyond in the West: Black Medal of Honor Winners, 1870–1890* (Washington, D.C., 1974), 1–38. See also W[alter] F. Beyer and O[scar] F. Keydel, *Deeds of Valor: How America's Heroes Won the Medal of Honor* (Detroit, 1900–1901), 2 vols.

27. Billington, *New Mexico's Buffalo Soldiers*, 153–155; Fowler, *Black Infantry in the West*, 65–66; Ronald G. Coleman, "The Buffalo Soldiers: Guardians of the Uintah Frontier, 1866–1901," *Utah Historical Quarterly*, 47 (1979), 422.

28. Billington, *New Mexico's Buffalo Soldiers*, 150–152. For a detailed account of the closing of a small fort, see Monroe Billington, "Black Soldiers at Fort Selden, New Mexico, 1866–1891," *New Mexico Historical Review*, 62 (1987), 65–80.

29. Fowler, *Black Infantry in the West*, 92–108; Billington, *New Mexico's Buffalo Soldiers*, 159–163.

30. *Ibid.*, 156, 157.

31. Don Rickey, Jr., *Forty Miles a Day on Beans and Hay: The Enlisted Soldier Fighting the Indian Wars* (Norman, Okla., 1963), 187.

32. Billington, *New Mexico's Buffalo Soldiers*, 179.

33. Michael L. Tate, "The Multi-Purpose Army on the Frontier: A Call for Further Research," in Ronald Lora (ed.), *The American West* (Toledo, Ohio, 1980), 171–208; Barton C. Hacker, "The United States Army as a National Police Force: The Federal Policing of Labor Disputes, 1877–1898," *Military Affairs*, 33 (1969), 259. See also Samuel P. Huntington, *The Soldier and the State: The Theory and Politics of Civil-Military Relations* (New York, 1957); and Robert W. Coakley, *The Role of Federal Military Forces in Domestic Disorders, 1789–1878* (Washington, D.C., 1988).

34. Billington, *New Mexico's Buffalo Soldiers*, 141–142.

35. Leckie, *Buffalo Soldiers*, 245–251.

36. Jerry M. Cooper, *The Army and Civil Disorder: Federal Military Intervention in Labor Disputes, 1877–1900* (Westport, Conn., 1980), 115.

37. Billington, *New Mexico's Buffalo Soldiers*, 143.

38. *Ibid..*, 144–145.

39. Facts and interpretations of the Lincoln County War are still in dispute. The following books will inform their readers, even though they are not always in agreement: Maurice G. Fulton, *History of the Lincoln County War*, edited by Robert N. Mullin (Tucson, 1968); William A. Keleher, *Violence in Lincoln County, 1869–1881: A New Mexico Item* (Albuquerque, 1957); Frederick W. Nolan, *The Life & Death of John Henry Tunstall* (Albuquerque, 1965); and John P. Wilson, *Merchants, Guns, and Money: The Story of Lincoln County and Its Wars* (Santa Fe, 1987).

40. For more information on the role of African American soldiers in bringing the Lincoln County War to an end, see Billington, *New Mexico's Buffalo Soldiers,* 79–86; Robert M. Utley, *Four Fighters of Lincoln County* (Albuquerque, 1986), 45–46; and Dee Dwight Greenly, "The Military Career of Nathan Augustus Monroe Dudley, 1843–1889" (M.A. thesis, New Mexico State University, 1986), 87–88.

41. Tate, "Multi-Purpose Army," 198–199; Miller, *Soldiers and Settlers,* 37ff.

42. Thomas D. Phillips, "The Black Regulars," in Allan G. Bogue, Thomas D. Phillips, and James E. Wright (eds.), *The West of the American People* (Itasca, Ill., 1970), 140.

43. Billington, *New Mexico's Buffalo Soldiers,* 66–67; *Cimarron News and Press,* quoted in *Mesilla News,* April 8, 1876; *Las Vegas Gazette,* Oct. 7, 1876; Norman Cleaveland and George Fitzpatrick, *The Morleys—Young Upstarts on the Southwest Frontier* (Albuquerque, 1971), 121; Chris Emmett, *Fort Union and the Winning of the Southwest* (Norman, Okla., 1965), 372; and Frank N. Schubert, "Black Soldiers on the White Frontier: Some Factors Influencing Race Relations," *Phylon,* 32 (1971), 412.

44. Jack D. Foner, *Blacks and the Military in American History: A New Perspective* (New York, 1974), 61–62; Fowler, *Black Infantry in the West,* 121–126.

45. Billington, *New Mexico's Buffalo Soldiers,* 187–188; Bruce White, "ABC's for the American Enlisted Man: The Army Post School System, 1866–1898," *History of Education Quarterly,* 8 (1968), 479–496.

46. For examples, see Billington, *New Mexico's Buffalo Soldiers,* 188–189. But careful researchers have found much evidence that white troops also experienced shortages of supplies and received inferior animals.

47. Thomas D. Phillips, "The Negro Regulars: Negro Soldiers in the United States Army, 1866–1890," unpublished manuscript cited in Marvin Fletcher, *The Black Soldier and Officer In the United States Army, 1891–1917* (Columbia, Mo., 1974), 23.

48. Foner, *Blacks and the Military,* 64. For information on West Point's first black graduate, see Theodore D. Harris (ed.), *Negro Frontiersman: The Western Memoirs of Henry O. Flipper* (El Paso, Tex., 1963), and Theodore D. Harris, "Henry Ossian Flipper: The First Negro Graduate of West Point" (Ph.D. diss., University of Minnesota, 1971). Other black West Point cadets and graduates have received little scholarly attention, except for Flipper's contemporary, Johnson C. Whittaker, whose story of racial tribulations at the army's premier military academy is recounted in John Marszalek, *Court-Martial: A Black Man in America* (New York, 1972).

49. For brief accounts of these African American chaplains, see Earl F. Stover, *Up From Handymen: The United States Army Chaplaincy, 1865–1920* (Washington, D.C., 1977), 88–92.

50. Edward M. Coffman, *The Old Army: A Portrait of the American Army in Peacetime, 1784–1898* (New York, 1986), 365–366; Fowler, *Black Infantry in the West,* 129–130.

51. Coffman, *Old Army,* 366.

52. For an extreme example of a white officer's prejudice and its tragic consequences, see Billington, *New Mexico's Buffalo Soldiers,* 192–199.

53. Fowler, *Black Infantry in the West,* 129.

54. For a sketchy account of Pershing's command of African American troops in Montana in 1896, see Donald Smythe, "John J. Pershing at Fort Assiniboine," *Montana: The Magazine of Western History,* 18, no. 1 (1968), 19–23.

55. Quoted in Coffman, *Old Army,* 368–369.

56. Quoted in *ibid.,* 369.

57. *Ibid..,* 332.

58. Quoted in *ibid.,* 371.

IMPROBABLE AMBASSADORS: BLACK SOLDIERS AT FORT DOUGLAS, UTAH, 1896–1899

Michael J. Clark

[This article originally appeared as "Improbable Ambassadors: Black Soldiers at Fort Douglas, 1896–99" in the *Utah Historical Quarterly*, Vol. 46 (1978), pp. 282–301. Retitled, adapted, and reprinted with permission.]

Historians have written much about the buffalo soldiers who helped make the American West safe for white settlers in the late nineteenth century. The cavalrymen have received the majority of scholarly attention because they did more Indian fighting than the infantry did; their experiences, therefore, seem more exciting to most students of the frontier. Some historians, however, have sought to insure that the infantrymen receive the recognition they deserve. They have pointed out that the infantry fought Indians, too. But perhaps more important—as Monroe Lee Billington showed in the previous essay—was the infantry's more mundane work building roads, guarding stagecoaches, and repairing military buildings.

In the following article, Michael J. Clark looks at the experiences of the Twenty-fourth Infantry during a four-year period in the late 1890s. The essay is unique not only because it is about the infantry rather than the cavalry but also for at least two other reasons. First, the Twenty-fourth, between 1896 and 1899—except for a brief stint in Cuba during the Spanish-American War in 1898—was stationed at a fort adjacent to Salt Lake City, Utah; all of the black regiments at all other times in the late nineteenth century were at isolated posts far from highly populated urban areas. Second, the article focuses on the Twenty-fourth at a time when the Indian wars were over. Thus, this essay differs significantly from most of those that have been written about the buffalo soldiers in the American West.

Clark offers some interesting insights into the relationships that existed between the black troopers and the white westerners they were assigned to protect. In the beginning, Salt Lake's leaders resisted having several hundred black soldiers stationed so near their city. They especially feared that some of the soldiers would attack the community's white women. Various of the state's officials sought unsuccessfully to prevent the unit's transfer to Utah. Consequently, when the troops arrived, the soldiers and their commanders did all they possibly could to prevent unpleasant racial confrontations and to impress favorably the capital city's nervous white citizens.

These efforts succeeded, causing the attitudes of the city's residents to change after several months' contact with the buffalo soldiers. Thousands of Salt Lake's white citizens showed up to give the men of the Twenty-fourth Infantry a rousing send-off when they left for Cuba in April 1898, and another large crowd welcomed them back to the city several months later. The interactions between the black soldiers and the white Utahans proved that members of the two races could peacefully coexist and that they could benefit from each other's presence when given the rare opportunity to do so as they were on the western frontier in Utah in the last half decade of the nineteenth century.

Although the record is clear, few people know that on the east bench, overlooking Salt Lake City and touching the boundaries of the University of Utah, more than six hundred Black people—soldiers of the United States Twenty-fourth Infantry, wives, children, and others—lived, worked, and attended school for almost four years in one of the most attractive locations in the western United States. Twenty-one graves in the little Fort Douglas cemetery, with weatherworn markers that become less legible each year, serve as quiet reminders that Black people exceeded the geographical boundaries historians have generally assigned them. Two additional graves mark the resting place of Black cavalrymen from the famous Ninth Cavalry stationed at Fort Duchesne, Utah, prior to the turn of the century and at Fort Douglas following the departure of the Twenty-fourth Infantry.

Although Black United States Army regiments were stationed throughout the West during the late nineteenth century, knowledge that they were a regular and integral part of the army is not widespread.[1] After 1866, members of the Twenty-fourth Infantry, Twenty-fifth Infantry, Ninth Cavalry, and Tenth Cavalry served as far north as Vancouver, British Columbia; as far west as the Presidio in San Francisco; and as far south as Mexico. Black men in uniform, as well as their wives and children, were prominent at Fort Bayard,

New Mexico; Fort Grant, Arizona; Fort Douglas, Utah; Fort Duchesne, Utah; Fort Logan, Colorado; Fort Missoula, Montana; Fort Davis, Texas; and numerous other posts throughout the West and served in some cases to augment comparatively small Black civilian populations.

The relative dearth of published material on the army's Black rank-and-file and the considerable difficulties involved in uncovering information may partially account for the limited attention given Black enlisted men. Additionally, officers and cavalry units have been considered more attractive by writers and historians. This does not mean that Black units and their men have gone entirely unobserved. Their critics appear to have been more vocal, if not more numerous, than their eulogizers. As late as 1900, Black soldiers continued to be characterized as "illiterate," "lazy," "a drinker," "a gambler," "set apart by nature," "a natural horseman," and inconsequential in the development of the West.[2] Subsequent discussions by historians have challenged these characterizations, but the definitive study is yet to be made.

In attempting to delineate in more detail the presence of the Twenty-fourth Infantry in Utah, the author's examination of local newspapers and army records for that period raised several questions that warranted further investigation: Why was the Twenty-fourth stationed in Utah? What impact did the unit have upon Salt Lake City? What was it like to be a Black soldier during this period? Where did the men come from? How did the presence of Black soldiers affect the development of Salt Lake City's Black community and its historical presence in Utah? Were there any long-term effects of the regiment's presence in Utah?

During early September 1896 word circulated between military posts that the adjutant general was considering a plan to relocate several regiments. Although details of the proposed reassignment of troops were not fully known, there were those soldiers who wished for new duty assignments and those who were anxious to remain where they were. Some civilian populations refused to cheer the pending change. In Salt Lake City, for example, the Sixteenth Infantry, a white unit, grudgingly prepared to leave Fort Douglas for Boise Barracks and Fort Sherman in Idaho and Fort Spokane, Washington. According to a local newspaper report, the unit's football and baseball teams were greatly disappointed because they had hoped to win championships in Utah.[3] In addition, younger soldiers were probably concerned with leaving girl friends, and older soldiers faced the prospect of moving families and household effects. A group of Salt Lake City residents, after attending a dance at Fort Douglas, "went home happy and expressed sorrow at its being the last dance they would attend at the post for several years."[4]

The Fifteenth Infantry, as luck would have it, was transferred from Illinois to forts in the Southwest that had been garrisoned by the Twenty-fourth Infantry. These New Mexico and Arizona posts had reputations for being "hellholes," and members of the Fifteenth Infantry were probably convinced that they were being punished for some wrongdoing. On the other hand, it appears likely that most members of the Twenty-fourth Infantry were happy with the regiment scramble and felt that, after thirty years, the unit was finally getting in Fort Douglas the kind of duty station it deserved. At that point, all four of the army's so-called Black units—each unit had white officers—were stationed in the West.[5]

The arrival of the Twenty-fourth Infantry in Salt Lake City more than doubled Utah's Black population. The Ninth Cavalry, stationed at Fort Duchesne in Uintah County, had 584 Black soldiers, and the Twenty-fourth's strength was rather constant at 512. One may speculate that Utah's total Black population, civilian and military, exceeded eighteen hundred in the fall of 1896 and reached twenty-three hundred in 1898 after the Twenty-fourth returned from the Spanish-American War.

Both rumor and fact preceded the arrival of the Twenty-fourth Infantry in Salt Lake City, and some citizens expressed concern, or at least interest, at news appearing in the *Salt Lake Tribune* and *Salt Lake Herald* reporting the War Department's decision to station the Twenty-fourth at Fort Douglas.[6] On September 20, 1896, almost one month before the advance companies of the Twenty-fourth arrived in Salt Lake City, the *Tribune*, in an editorial entitled "An Unfortunate Change," voiced attitudes that Black soldiers would ultimately have to confront during their tour of duty in Utah. The editorial reflected upon the close ties that had existed between the city and members of the Sixteenth Infantry and implied that such relationships would not be possible with members of the Twenty-fourth. It also pointed out that the residential portion of the city lay between the central city and Fort Douglas. As a result, "colored" soldiers would have to travel on streetcars to and from the post, and this would bring them in direct contact with whites and especially with white women. The editorial argued that there were differences between Black and white soldiers when they were drunk. A Black soldier "will be sure to want to assert himself" when on a car with white ladies. It would be best, the editorial concluded, to lay the facts before the secretary of war and

> he might still be induced to make the change and send the colored men to some other station where they would be just as comfortable, where they would not be a source of apprehension and discomfort to the people of a large city like this.[7]

Following the editorial lead, Sen. Frank J. Cannon met with Secretary of War Daniel S. Lamont and asked that some regiment other than the Twenty-fourth be sent to Fort Douglas. According to the *Deseret News*, at least a part of Senator Cannon's appeal to the secretary had to do with the undesirability of locating "a colored regiment" in the immediate neighborhood of the University of Utah. However, the secretary, although sympathetic to Cannon's appeal, "found it impossible to change the order."[8] The *Salt Lake Herald* must have reflected what was on the minds of a good many citizens when it reported: "Some people say that there is a good deal of politics mixed up in the move of the Twenty-fourth Infantry to Fort Douglas."[9] Julius F. Taylor, a Black and editor of the *Broad Ax,* noted that Secretary of War Lamont was a Democrat and for that reason would not withdraw the order to transfer the Twenty-fourth.[10] Taylor's speculation is not persuasive, and it appears that politics played no significant part in the secretary of war's decision.

In addition to criticizing Senator Cannon for his part in trying to prevent the Twenty-fourth from being stationed at Fort Douglas, Taylor was critical of the *Salt Lake Tribune* for being the only newspaper in Salt Lake City to raise "any sort of objection to the location of the Twenty-fourth." Taylor also charged the *Tribune* with being "the accepted organ of the Republican party."[11] By way of contrast, the *Salt Lake Herald* editorialized on October 10, 1896, "Glory and Honor to the Sixteenth Infantry! Welcome to the Twenty-fourth Infantry." The *Herald's* welcome indicated that there was no unified view regarding the Black soldiers. Some opposed their coming, others did not. Depending on the source, the issue was considered racial, political (owing, possibly, to the recently fought battles over statehood and the practice of polygamy), or a matter of reward for meritorious service.

William G. Muller, a white officer of the Twenty-fourth, in his unpublished history of the regiment, considered the *Salt Lake Tribune's* editorial the most prominent occurrence connected with the unit's tour of duty in Utah. Although he could not recall the dates the regiment was stationed at Fort Douglas, he did recollect that feelings against the "negro soldiers" were "bitter" and prejudiced. Later, he observed, when the regiment returned to Salt Lake City from Cuba, "it had the hearts of the people."[12] Muller also remarked that a year after the Twenty-fourth's arrival the *Tribune* printed what amounted to an apology to the unit.

Morale may have been an important factor in the relocation of the Twenty-fourth Infantry. During the thirty years the regiment was stationed in the southwestern territories, various requests had been made for transfer to more desirable duty stations. In January 1895 the requests became more specific, asking for a "station near a large city." George W. Murray, apparently a civilian supporter of the Twenty-fourth, in a memorandum to the secretary of war, offered several key points for consideration: 1) the difference in treatment between Black and white units; 2) "every unit in the infantry regiment in the Army has had or now have [*sic*], a station near a large city except the Twenty-fourth"; and 3) "depression and demoralization results [*sic*] from service too long in the wilderness."[13] Murray's memorandum was received in the adjutant general's office on February 7, 1895, and was submitted to Lt. Gen. J. M. Schofield in command of the army. He suggested that "this regiment be given a northern station if it is found practicable to do so."[14]

No immediate action followed Murray's recommendation to Secretary of War Lamont, but on January 22, 1896, Col. J. Ford Kent, commanding officer of the Twenty-fourth, added to what must have been an increasing number of requests to have the Twenty-fourth moved to a northern station. Writing from the regiment's headquarters at Fort Bayard, New Mexico, Colonel Kent requested a "good station" and announced that "a natural feeling prevails that it is on account of their color that the regiment is debarred from the better locations."[15] Kent sought support for his request by noting that General Schofield, by then "the late Commanding General," had supported his request. Schofield had given a favorable endorsement for relocation on February 15, 1895, and had inspected Kent's post in May. Kent, in his letter to the adjutant general, noted that Schofield informed him in May that "it had been decided, in the event of a possibility in changes in station, that the 24th Infantry should be sent to Fort Douglas...."[16] Several months passed before the final decision was made.

In September 1896 the *Salt Lake Herald* reported: "Colored Men Will Come."[17] The response was primarily one of surprise, for the change had not been expected until spring. The city was alive with discussion of the pending arrival of the "Colored Gentlemen" from Forts Bayard and Huachuca.[18] The uncharitable editorial that had appeared in the *Salt Lake Tribune* on September 20 was followed on September 23, 1896, by an article entitled "Capt. Hoffman's View" which reflected favorably upon the Twenty-fourth Infantry. Capt. William Hoffman, apparently a resident of Salt Lake City, said he was acquainted with the regiment and that its members were "well-behaved." "The men will keep to their own race," he said, and "we generally will know only the officers and their families." After his own regiment, the Eleventh, Hoffman volunteered, the "Twenty-fourth is my very first choice...." Hoffman did not discuss how he became acquainted with the merits of the Twenty-fourth, but his views may have moderated the more impetuous citizens' concerns over the prospect of having uniformed Black soldiers walking the streets of Salt Lake City.

Captain Hoffman concluded "that there is no chance whatever that the War Department order will be changed." If Hoffman's belief in the army's intractability and Senator Cannon's "Vain Attempt to Have Them Sent Elsewhere"[19] did not convince the people of Salt Lake City that the arrival of the Black soldiers was imminent, the debarkation at the train station "of about 100 colored women and a number of dark sports who follow the regiment from post to post" must have.[20] Fifty enlisted men were married and brought their families with them.[21] It is difficult to estimate how many children and other civilians arrived in connection with the unit. Most families lived on or near the post.

According to newspaper reports, the new residents of Fort Douglas were pleased with their assignment and "gratified at having been transferred from Texas to the promised land."[22] Members of the unit apparently wanted the people of Salt Lake City to have a good impression of them, for as one member of the regiment stated: "I do not say this from conceit, but you will find our regiment better behaved and disciplined than most of the white soldiers. It is not an easy matter to get 600 men together without there are one or two unruly fellows among them."[23]

Some questioned whether the newly arrived Black chaplain connected with the unit, Allen Allensworth, should be considered an officer. In some accounts he was considered the exception to the all-white officer ranks. Others regarded him much like a civilian. Born a slave in Louisville, Kentucky, Allensworth was appointed to the position of army chaplain by President Grover Cleveland. The fact that Allensworth was picked by a Democratic president endeared him to Julius Taylor, editor of the *Broad Ax,* and gave Allensworth the distinction of being the only Black army chaplain at that time.[24] Allensworth was married and had two daughters, Eva and Nellia.

The arrival of the Twenty-fourth was not without its impact upon the city's Black community. When the soldiers arrived on the Union Pacific, it was reported that "almost every colored resident in the city" met them at the station.[25] There would be greater contact between the fort and the Black citizens of the city in the months to come.

Concern over how the newly arrived soldiers would make use of the diversions the city had to offer was probably great. The city boasted a number of establishments that might appear attractive to the soldier looking for some way to pass the time. One, located "on the east side of Commercial Street, near Second South," was called the "policy shop" and allegedly offered gambling, food, and liquor. There, according to a newspaper account, "Merchants, street-loungers, youth, prostitutes and even men in the employ of the city contribute their mite in the hope of fabulous winnings."[26] Yet the strictness of military

Allen Allensworth. A Baptist minister, Allensworth served as a chaplain of the Twenty-fourth Infantry for twenty years. He retired in 1906 as a lieutenant colonel, the highest rank attained by a black officer up to that time. (Courtesy, Spirit Productions.)

discipline and the earnestness of white officers and top sergeants in enforcing it limited the pursuit of pleasure somewhat. According to the *Broad Ax:*

> Rev. Allensworth desires to inform the good people of our beautiful city that he would be more pleased if all the saloons, gambling houses and immoral houses would absolutely refuse to entertain the negro soldiers, for he believes that there are a thousand white men who are willing to go to hell with the black man, but there are a very few who care to go to heaven with him. He hopes that the police will arrest every brazen faced woman, be she black or white, who attempts to travel on the street cars to and from the fort.[27]

Despite Allensworth's appeal, Black soldiers did make use of the city for saintly as well as more mundane purposes.

Military routine at Fort Douglas offered little excitement for the enlisted members of the Twenty-fourth Infantry. While in the Southwest, the regiment's duties had included "expeditions against the Indians...guarding strategic points, building roads, hunting horse thieves, and doing anything else which called for hard work and no fame."[28] By contrast, the Utah experience included practice marches, attendance at the post school, exercises in the gym during periods of cold weather, work at improving the post's water system, maintenance of the post garden, janitorial work, clerk duties, work in the post exchange, drills, commissary work, maintenance of post stables, and black-smithing. From time to time, an enlisted man might have an opportunity for detached service or recruiting and travel, for example, to Fort Logan, Colorado, or to one of the eastern cities.

For all of its regularity, however, enlisted men appeared to prefer military over civilian life and there was a high percentage of reenlistments. The average number of enlisted men in the regiment between February 1, 1897, and April 1, 1898, was 513. During that time, the average number of probable vacancies was approximately twelve per month. In many cases, however, the vacancies failed to materialize as individuals changed their plans and remained in the service or accepted discharge and reenlisted within a short period of time. The post band was apparently considered excellent duty. For the same period, the average number of probable vacancies in the band amounted to slightly more than one-half vacancy per month.[29] One controversy that may have affected vacancies during the months of November and December came in reaction to the treatment received by an enlisted man, Private Barnes, from Captain Augur. Augur had struck Barnes because he "was not doing his job." Apparently, Barnes had witnesses and was prepared to press his case against Augur. In a letter to the commanding officer of Company D, Twenty-fourth Infantry, the

Mansfield Robinson. A soldier in the Twenty-fourth Infantry, Robinson was one of several thousand African Americans who served in the U.S. army's western outposts during the late nineteenth century. (Courtesy, Edward M. Coffman.)

company adjutant declared that Colonel Kent had investigated the occurrence and observed that "Augur was sorry." The adjutant stated that "Kent seems to be supporting his officer."[30] Barnes's fellow enlisted men displayed their displeasure by indicating they would not, in some cases, reenlist.

Private Barnes's willingness to bring charges against a white officer provides a rare glimpse at the activities and encounters that produced courts-martial and other disciplinary measures. The attractiveness of disciplinary problems as news items makes it possible to get a closer look at the atmosphere that existed at the post as well as to determine, to some extent, what the soldiers did on their frequent visits to the city. However, disciplinary measures were fewer before the unit's departure for the Spanish-American War in Cuba than after the men returned.

In addition to his military routine at Fort Douglas, the Black soldier was involved in various societies and clubs, athletics, and other activities. A number of enlisted men belonged to "Noah's Ark Lodge, G.U.O. of O.F. [Grand United Order of Odd Fellows], which is the lodge of the Twenty-fourth Infantry." Lt. Peter McCann, who before January 1899 was a first sergeant in the Tenth Cavalry, helped set up the lodge when he served with the Twenty-fourth while it was stationed in New Mexico.[31] In addition to Noah's Ark Lodge, some soldiers belonged to the Society of Prognosticators, organized while the regiment was stationed at Fort Bayard, New Mexico.[32] Like many of the soldiers' societies, the Society of Prognosticators "operated under rules known only to the organization...."[33] A less secret society composed of enlisted men was the Christian Endeavor Society. This group met once a week and invited guests to speak on a variety of topics. On one occasion, Miss Nellia Allensworth, daughter of the post chaplain, spoke on "Confidence."[34] Mr. Wake of Salt Lake City, on another occasion, chose as his topic "Our Missionary Work."[35] The society regularly invited members of the Allensworth family and Sgt. James M. Dickerson to speak. The Frederick Douglass Memorial Literary Society was also active on the post. It sponsored instrumental solos, lectures, and debates on such topics as: "Resolved, that there is no future for the negro in the United States" (the debate was decided in the affirmative).[36] This society also supported an amateur dramatic club.[37] Enlisted men also joined the Love and Hope Lodge No. 3858 which had ninety-five members. Affiliated with the "Grand United Order of Odd Fellows, a Colored order," the lodge was founded at Fort Huachuca, Arizona, near the Mexican border. In Salt Lake City the soldiers founded "city lodges of the order" and on occasion participated in events with civilians. W. W. Taylor, editor of the *Plain Dealer,* and Horace Voss were members of city lodges.[38]

The Williams and Prince Minstrel Company was organized by the men at Fort Douglas and provided entertainment at the post as well as in the city.[39] Dancing was another favorite activity. Enlisted men gave "hops" and invited Black civilians; a dancing school was conducted by Corporal and Mrs. Batie;[40] and the New Year's holiday in January 1898 provided an occasion for the enlisted men to hold a masquerade ball at the post.[41] Post social life demonstrates the extent to which Black civilians and soldiers mingled and the lengths to which the Black soldier went to improve the quality of his life and that of his fellow soldiers. There was enough activity on the part of enlisted men that the *Salt Lake Herald* could report, "enlisted men want their own social hall for entertainment and dances and to hold meetings of their secret clubs."[42]

Athletics were also important to the men. Sports fans from the city followed the Fort Douglas baseball team, the Colored Monarchs, which competed against the Ninth Cavalry's team from Fort Duchesne and civilian teams from Salt Lake City. The team's popularity led the Salt Lake City Street Car Company to donate on one occasion ten dollars "to the post baseball fund." Individual players had their followers in the city, but sometimes, as in the case of James Flowers, "a good athlete and baseball player lacked the necessary qualifications of a soldier." Baseball "cranks" were disappointed when Flowers was dishonorably discharged from the service.[43]

The reputation of the Twenty-fourth Infantry's band—heralded by some as the best in the army—reached Salt Lake City before the regiment. The band was as well received as the athletic teams. The *Salt Lake Herald* reported that members of the band "seem to feel they are a part of this city and it is their duty to do all they can to make matters pleasing."[44] At least one officer at the post was less pleased than were Salt Lake City citizens about the use of the band. "I am aware," one first lieutenant lamented in a letter that found its way to the adjutant general's office, "that a regimental band has other purposes for its existence than the furnishing of music for a post dance once a week." He obviously wanted the band to play exclusively at the post to prevent "unpleasant mixing of blacks and whites," apparently at establishments in the city.[45]

Senior officers at the post were decidedly interested in maintaining a good image and went to great lengths to see that requests from the city were accommodated. As a result, the band played for civic occasions when its presence was requested. In addition, individual bandsmen performed community services. Band member Walter E. Loving, for example, orchestrated music for a group called the High School Minstrels, and the music was played at the New Grand Theatre. Apparently a gifted musician, Loving gave free vocal lessons and directed concerts.[46]

A year after the Twenty-fourth Infantry arrived in Utah, the *Salt Lake Tribune* printed an editorial that represented a change in its view regarding the Black soldiers. When the regiment's transfer had been announced, the *Tribune* recalled, the newspaper had complained that

> Fort Douglas lies above and beyond the most pronounced residence portion of the city and that soldiers would ride on cars, drunk as well as sober, and that an intoxicated colored soldier is more offensive than an intoxicated white soldier.

Admitting that this judgment had proved false, the editorial continued that the soldiers had been well behaved, had "less rowdy characteristics" than any white regiment, and were less addicted to drinking.[47] The editorial represented an achievement for the Twenty-fourth. Relations had been good between the post and the community and, officially, at least, everyone appeared satisfied.

Almost nineteen months after the regiment's arrival in Utah the routine of post life at Fort Douglas was interrupted by speculation that should it become necessary to send troops to Cuba, the four "colored" regiments would be the first to depart for the war zone. "It is acknowledged," reported the *Denver News,* "by men of experience in southern climates that white men from the cool regions of the northern states would fare badly in the treacherous climate of Cuba." The Colorado paper's prophecy that Black units would be "given ample opportunity to win glory," was accurate.[48] One month later "both officers and men seemed to be rubbing up a trifle on Spanish for they accosted one another with 'buenos noches, compadre' and 'adios' was the parting salutation."[49] As enlisted men and officers prepared to depart and some wives and children prepared to visit relatives in the East, events at the post were reported with regularity and fanfare.

The announcement of the Twenty-fourth's orders to prepare to depart for Cuba had its impact upon some Salt Lake City citizens:

> Local dealers generally are deploring the issue which makes it necessary for the companies to leave Fort Douglas as by them is distributed each month in this city about $8000.... There is a class that is perfectly willing to see them go, but the merchant is not numbered among them.

On a less mercenary note, patriotic civilians wanted to know exactly when the Twenty-fourth would leave, for "Everybody wants to see Uncle Sam's men when they start to battle for the honor of their country...."[50]

Interest in the movement of the troops was intense throughout the city. It was reported that they would leave on April 19, at 7:30 P.M., but their departure was put off for a day. The delay disappointed thousands of citizens who had prepared to see the regiment off. The Twenty-fourth did leave on April 20, however, and the newspapers estimated that "15,000 to 20,000 people were on and about the depot grounds."[51] Included in that throng were wives, children, and girl friends who "sat for hours under the trees with their soldier lords and sires."[52]

As reported in the *Salt Lake Tribune* the following day, "the element of color seemed entirely eliminated."[53] An editorial in the *Deseret Evening News* spoke of the "mighty coincidence" of Blacks freeing Cubans through war, as Blacks were freed themselves, that "will mark another epoch in the tremendous evolution of human society."[54] Ladies, reported the *Salt Lake Tribune,* who did not like to ride on streetcars with Black soldiers were, on the preceding day, shaking the hands of these same soldiers. William Gibson of Vernal, who was at the depot, recalled that he had seen Patrick E. Connor march through the city in 1862. Having seen both marches, he said he was "satisfied."[55]

Members of the Twenty-fourth Infantry distinguished themselves in Cuba. That campaign does not fall within the scope of this study, but it may be important to note that the work done with yellow fever patients had lasting effects. "Out of the 456 men who marched to Siboney, only 24 escaped sickness...and of this number, only 198 were able to march out." As a result, within "the most famous regiment of african [*sic*] blood since Hannibal slaughtered 70,000 Romans," thirty-six suffered death and many more men were to carry lifelong disabilities resulting from yellow fever.[56]

On September 2, 1898, the Twenty-fourth returned to Fort Douglas amid cheers of their countrymen, and by December the war was officially over. The strength of the command was increased to 958 men, the warm welcome receded, and the routine of the post was quickly resumed. There were differences, however. Approximately half of the enlisted men at the fort were new to Salt Lake City; because of the acceleration in recruitment for the war effort, the average age for soldiers at the fort was probably lower than it had been; and reenlistments, transfers, and discharges increased. In general, the soldiers seemed to exhibit a slightly different attitude, a restlessness.

When the Twenty-fourth arrived at Fort Douglas in 1896, members of the unit seemed well satisfied with the change in station. Subsequent reports indicated that a general feeling of well-being continued. However, just prior to the unit's departure for Cuba the *Broad Ax* reported:

> Within the past ten days we have conversed with a number of the Twenty-fourth regiment and they all expressed a great desire to get away from Salt Lake

City and to be located at some other point where it would be more congenial for them and their families.

The report is not surprising. It was as difficult for Black people to live in Utah as it was in most other states at the turn of the century. If Taylor was accurate in reflecting the general attitude of Black soldiers toward Salt Lake City, his report offers considerable contrast between what appeared to be the feeling at the time of the regiment's departure for Cuba and the confessed feelings of a "number of the Twenty-fourth regiment."[57]

The record is not clear. As mentioned earlier, the officers of the Twenty-fourth, as well as enlisted men, were sensitive about the Utah assignment and sought to make sure that there were few negative incidents involving Black soldiers. Prior to the unit's departure from the Southwest, Colonel Kent had made it clear that measures would be taken to prevent confrontations between enlisted men and Caucasian residents of Salt Lake City. Soldiers were only to visit the city in full uniform, curfews would be enforced, soldiers would not be able to work in the city, and they were to defer to whites as a matter of policy. The regiment's record, prior to its departure for Cuba, indicates that measures devised for maximum discipline were effective when coupled with the apparent desire on the part of enlisted men to make a good showing.

Experience in a national war and volunteer work in yellow fever camps in Cuba, however, was bound to have some impact on the soldiers. They had risked their lives and some of their fellows had died. It is conjecturable that the returning soldiers felt less reticent and more like they had earned a better place in society. Two enlisted men, Beverly Perea[58] and a Sergeant Williams, had been made commissioned officers only to be reduced to ranks again. Additionally, the unit faced the prospect of being sent to the Philippines. These factors appeared to affect the enlisted men. One thing is certain: disciplinary problems increased.

Not long after the regiment's arrival in Utah, on November 17, 1896, H. B. Ballantyne and W. P. Gunn had had the dubious distinction of being the first members of the Twenty-fourth to appear in the Salt Lake City police court. Both were fined for drunkenness, and Gunn received an additional fine for "packing a machete in such a manner as to lay himself liable to carrying a concealed weapon."[59]

Few soldiers followed the path of Ballantyne and Gunn until after the regiment's return from Cuba when a dozen enlisted men were cited for a variety of infractions in the first few months of 1899. These offenses and the punishments included: offensive and indecent language to a noncommissioned officer (fine and fifteen days), scandalous conduct in the presence of ladies (two months at hard labor), assault upon another soldier (fine and twenty days), fraudulent enlistment (dishonorable discharge), theft and desertion (one year at Fort Leavenworth prison). From the examples cited one can see that scandalous conduct in the presence of ladies—which probably meant the use of distasteful language on a streetcar—was a relatively serious offense, more so than assault upon another soldier. Community relations were obviously considered important, and infractions involving civilians, especially women, were handled firmly.[60]

That soldiers would engage in various types of misconduct does not seem unusual, but racial stereotypes tended to prevail in newspaper reports of such incidents. For example:

> George Warren, a colored soldier, and Robert Brooks, a colored porter, stole a suit of clothes from another colored man and were captured by Sergt. Burbidge. During the trial yesterday the judge was compelled to listen to a ten minutes' display of oratory on the part of Warren, whose subject was: 'Craps, and how they should be played to be successful.' Warren was sentenced to thirty days, while Brooks who pawned the clothes, was given fifty days. "Golly, thirty days to say nuffin 'bout what I'll get when I reaches de fote," said Warren as he ambled away.[61]

Even as military and civilian officials were dealing with the little flurry of disciplinary problems among the enlisted men in early 1899, rumors were circulating that the Twenty-fourth would be transferred soon. The rumors proved true, and the men soon took up new assignments in San Francisco, Alaska, Montana, Washington, and Vancouver, British Columbia. Two detachments of twenty-five men each were sent to Sequoia and Yosemite parks in California "for the benefit of the health of the colored men, many of whom are nearly broken down from the effects of Cuban fever."[62] And in July 1899 four companies of the Twenty-fourth arrived in the Philippines for a three-year tour of duty.

The Twenty-fourth Infantry, departing on two occasions from Utah, first for the Spanish-America War and second for the campaign in the Philippine Islands, may be the most prominent United States Army regiment to serve from the state. The unit has not, however, been regarded as a regiment having close ties with the state. Personal relationships that may have been established during the regiment's stay at Fort Douglas have been obscured by time, and the Twenty-fourth Infantry, the "Buffalo Soldiers," remain indistinct in local memory. The fanfare of the unit's arrival in Salt Lake City, its participation in jubilee celebrations and other state occasions, the baseball games, concerts, and other human dramas struggle to become part of the state's history. Perhaps this is as it should be. Few of the soldiers made Utah their home, and not many of their descendants live in the Beehive State today.

Nevertheless, members of the Twenty-fourth, perhaps over fifteen hundred different individuals, were significant additions to the Salt Lake City population in both an economic and a social sense. The economic impact of the regiment upon the surrounding community was, of course, a duplication of the contact of prior and subsequent military units. Socially, however, the local community, for the first time in history, experienced the influx of a relatively large and cohesive military group that greatly augmented the already existing Black community. Although the Twenty-fourth Infantry had not been located near a large city for a thirty-year period and Salt Lake City had never had a large Black population, the two sides managed. Generally speaking, suspicion and uncertainty gave way to confidence and resolution, stereotypes to a tenuous familiarity; and with the advent of war, the two worlds met in the camp of self-interest. Black soldiers, members of the Ninth Cavalry and Twenty-fourth Infantry and later, the Twenty-fifth Infantry, became improbable ambassadors. More than two thousand different soldiers carried a like number of versions about their stay in the "Great Basin Kingdom" to the far corners of the United States.

Notes

1. Oswald Garrison Villard, "The Negro in the Regular Army," *Atlantic Monthly* 91 (1903): 724. Villard observed that "It was not until the battle of Santiago…that the bulk of the American people realized that the standing army comprised regiments composed wholly of black men. Up to that time only one company of colored soldiers had served at a post east of the Mississippi."
2. Ibid. The notable success of Black jockeys in the Kentucky Derby between 1875 and 1902 may have contributed to one stereotype. See, for example, Middleton Harris, *The Black Book* (New York: Random House, 1974), p. 151. Earlier there was discussion in the U.S. Senate regarding the ability of Blacks as horsemen. During a debate Sen. Henry Wilson of Massachusetts observed that Blacks "are the best riders in America connected with our army. We have some colored regiments west of the Mississippi that were raised in Kentucky, who understand the management of horses as well as any man in this country, admirable riders." U.S. Congress, Senate, "Military Establishment," *Congressional Globe,* 39th Cong., 1st sess., March 14, 1866, p. 1385.
3. *Salt Lake Tribune,* September 27, 1896.
4. *Salt Lake Tribune,* October 4, 1896.
5. U.S. Congress, House, *Annual Report of the Secretary of War,* 54th Cong., 1st sess., 1895, p. 84. The Ninth Cavalry and Twenty-fourth Infantry were stationed in Utah, the Tenth Cavalry and Twenty-fifth Infantry in North Dakota and Montana.

6. *Salt Lake Tribune,* September 19, 1896: "The order from Washington first reached Fort Douglas in the press dispatches and caused considerable surprise, not to say consternation. There had been considerable gossip in army circles during the summer, foreshadowing a change, but it had about died down, and the close of the summer season led the people at the post to suppose that no change would be made until spring." See also *Salt Lake Herald,* September 19, 1896.

7. *Salt Lake Tribune,* September 20, 1896.

8. *Deseret Evening News,* October 8, 1896.

9. *Salt Lake Herald,* September 21, 1896.

10. *Broad Ax,* October 30, 1897. In 1896 there were two newspapers run by Blacks, the *Broad Ax* and the *Plain Dealer.* Taylor apparently backed the Democratic party while the *Plain Dealer* backed the Republican party. Taylor seemed to think that Lamont supported Blacks and would not change the transfer order. Taylor's position appears unusual as the Republican party, "the party of Lincoln," was overwhelmingly supported by Black voters until the New Deal.

11. *Broad Ax,* October 31, 1896. It is difficult to ascertain whether Taylor constructed or accepted a local view regarding the Republican party or by coincidence viewed both the *Tribune* and the Republicans critically. The issue may warrant greater investigation if Taylor's view of the Republican party was widely shared by Blacks in the West.

12. William G. Muller, "The Twenty-fourth Infantry Past and Present," 1923, p. 12.

13. Murray to Daniel S. Lamont, January 31, 1895, Records of the Office of the Adjutant General, General Correspondence, 1890–1917, AGO 1500, RG 94, National Archives, Washington, D.C.

14. Schofield to Murray, February 15, 1895, ibid.

15. Kent to adjutant general, January 22, 1896, ibid.

16. Ibid.

17. *Salt Lake Herald,* September 19, 1896.

18. *Salt Lake Herald,* September 20, 1896.

19. *Deseret News,* October 8, 1896.

20. *Salt Lake Tribune,* October 11, 1896.

21. *Broad Ax,* September 24, 1896.

22. *Salt Lake Herald,* October 16, 1896.

23. *Salt Lake Tribune,* October 16, 1896.

24. *Broad Ax,* October 24, 1896.

25. *Salt Lake Tribune,* October 23, 1896.

26. *Salt Lake Tribune,* March 28, 1896.

27. *Broad Ax,* October 24, 1896.

28. John M. Carroll, ed., *The Black Military Experience in the West* (New York: Liveright Publishing Corp., 1971), p. 92.

29. Adjutant, Twenty-fourth Infantry, to commanding officer, Company D, Twenty-fourth Infantry, October 23, 1897, Letters Sent, Adjutant General's Office, 1897–1906, RG 94.

30. Ibid.

31. *Salt Lake Tribune,* January 20, 1899.

32. *Salt Lake Tribune,* January 11, 1899.

33. Ibid.

34. *Salt Lake Tribune,* February 6, 1898.

35. *Salt Lake Tribune,* February 20, 1898.

36. *Salt Lake Tribune,* January 11, 1899.

37. *Salt Lake Tribune,* February 6, 1898.

38. *Salt Lake Tribune,* May 3, 1897.

39. *Salt Lake Tribune,* February 3, 1899.

40. *Salt Lake Tribune,* April 2, 1899.
41. *Salt Lake Herald,* January 4, 1898.
42. *Salt Lake Herald,* January 31, 1897.
43. *Salt Lake Tribune,* May 20, 1897, March 5, 1899; *Salt Lake Herald,* June 7, 1897.
44. *Salt Lake Herald,* June 1, 1897.
45. Company B, Twenty-fourth Infantry, to adjutant general, November 28, 1896, Letters Sent, Company B, Twenty-fourth Infantry, September 6, 1895, to May 19, 1899, RG 94.
46. *Salt Lake Tribune,* January 23, February 6, 1898.
47. *Salt Lake Tribune,* October 24, 1897.
48. *Denver News* as compiled in "Journal History of the Church," March 15, 1898, Archives Division, Historical Department, Church of Jesus Christ of Latter-day Saints, Salt Lake City. A year and two months later, on May 18, 1899, the *Salt Lake Tribune* reported: "The removal of the companies of the Twenty-fourth to Alaska but goes to illustrate the uncertain side of a soldier's life. Just a little more than a year ago, the government concluded to send the men to Cuba, for the reason that black men can stand the hot weather better. Now they are sent to the other extreme and the reason is given that they can withstand cold weather with much less discomfort than white men."
49. *Salt Lake Tribune,* April 16, 1898.
50. *Salt Lake Tribune,* April 18, 1898.
51. *Deseret Evening News,* April 20, 1898.
52. *Salt Lake Tribune,* April 20, 1898.
53. *Salt Lake Tribune,* April 21, 1898.
54. *Deseret Evening News,* April 21, 1898.
55. *Salt Lake Tribune,* April 21, 1898.
56. T. G. Steward, *The Colored Regulars in the United States Army* (New York: Arno Press and the New York Times, 1969), pp. 224–25, 235; A. Prentiss, ed., *The History of the Utah Volunteers in the Spanish-American War and in the Philippine Islands...* (Salt Lake City, 1900), p. 125.
57. *Broad Ax,* April 23, 1898.
58. Beverly Perea to adjutant general, March 9, 1908, Records of the Office of the Adjutant General, General Correspondence, 1890–1911, AGO 127989, RG 94.
59. *Salt Lake Herald,* November 17, 1896.
60. See, for example, the *Salt Lake Tribune,* January 8, February 6, 14, 28, March 14, April 9, 1899.
61. *Salt Lake Tribune,* January 24, 1899.
62. *Salt Lake Tribune,* May 1, 1899.

BLACKS AND THE COAL MINES OF WESTERN WASHINGTON, 1888–1896

Robert A. Campbell

[This article originally appeared in the *Pacific Northwest Quarterly*, Vol. 73 (1982), pp. 146–155. Reprinted with permission.]

Throughout history, one of the most important factors in the movement of people from one geographic area to another has been the perceived belief that the new location offered better economic opportunity than that left behind. For years, the American West seemed to offer little economic incentive to people from the United States. Prior to the late 1840s only a few Americans ventured west of the one hundredth meridian. Fur trappers and traders went to the northern Plains, the Rocky Mountains, and the Pacific Slope during the first few decades of the nineteenth century. A few people went to California and Oregon to farm. Some merchants sent goods west along the Santa Fe Trail and by water to the Pacific coastline to make money from the inhabitants of land owned first by Spain and then by Mexico.

    In the late 1840s, however, several events led additional Americans westward. The United States settled the Oregon dispute with Great Britain and created an official territorial government for Americans in the Pacific Northwest. Mormons went to Utah to build their Zion outside the jurisdiction of the U.S. and to farm the desert areas of the Great Basin. Finally, and perhaps most importantly, after the Mexican War gave the United States ownership in 1848 of a vast tract of land in what is today the American Southwest, Americans in northern California discovered gold. This sparked a "gold rush" that carried thousands of Americans to the west coast by 1850.

The mining frontier that thus began in California spread eastward to Nevada, Colorado, Arizona, New Mexico, Montana, Idaho, Wyoming, and even South Dakota. And as miners and those who made their living providing goods and services to them fanned out across the American West, blacks were part of the process. Prior to 1865 some went as slaves of white masters while others were escapees from bondage. Later, free blacks joined the mining frontier just as they did the cattle and farming frontiers—for the economic opportunity it offered in the form of gold, silver, copper, and other precious metals.

As railroads traversed the West during the late nineteenth century, a new underground mineral became important—coal. Railroad companies often created coal companies as subsidiary enterprises to cut the cost of fueling their trains. And western capitalists, like those in the East, sought to conserve money as much as they could. This included fighting labor unions and paying miners the lowest possible wages. Railroad companies often hired Chinese coal miners, as the Union Pacific did in Wyoming, because they would work for less than would white miners. African Americans, however, were often barred from the coal mines—because of racial prejudice. But railroads and coal companies welcomed black miners when whites went on strike. Faced with either giving in to the strikers or attempting to break the strikes by bringing in outside laborers, western coal mine owners often turned to black miners to do the dangerous and low-paying work of strikebreaking.

In the following essay, Robert A. Campbell illustrates how wealthy white mine owners employed imported (and underpaid) blacks to counter a white miners' labor union in Washington in the 1880s and the 1890s. He notes that while some African Americans rebelled at the idea of being used to defeat a labor union's bargaining power, others went along with their exploitation willingly because they desperately needed the work.

Newcastle is a semirural suburb of Seattle, and some of its abandoned coal mines today serve as a "solid waste disposal site." All that remains of Franklin, thirty miles southeast of Seattle, are scattered pieces of rusted mining equipment. Yet in the late nineteenth century, Newcastle and Franklin were not only active coal mining towns, but also the locations of violent conflict between Washington coal operators and the reform-labor organization the Knights of Labor. This strike was made more bitter by the employment of black mine workers, a common practice in the mining industry and one that contributed significantly to the defeat of the Knights in western Washington.[1]

Coal miner. Many African Americans worked in western coal mines in the late nineteenth century. (Courtesy, National Mining Association.)

The intense conflict between the coal operators and the mine workers had its roots in a series of related issues. Mining itself was dirty, dangerous work in which men risked their lives daily in murky darkness sometimes a thousand feet below the earth's surface. Poor ventilation, explosive gas, floods, and cave-ins were all part of the job, but such conditions did not unite company and workers in common cause, particularly since the workers often believed that the company sacrificed their safety for reduced costs.[2]

Another disadvantage for mine workers was the tremendous power the operators had over them. Most Washington mining communities were company towns. As an individual, a worker was completely dominated by the overwhelming presence of the company. After his ten-hour shift in the pits, a man went home to his company house or the company boardinghouse, ate food from the company store, and later drank in the company saloon where he complained to his fellow workers about high prices, rapidly accumulating debts, and the "truck system" (wages paid in store credit rather than cash). If he worked for the Oregon Improvement Company (OIC)—the leading independent operator and owner of the mines at Newcastle and Franklin—and wanted to go to Seattle, he traveled on the company railroad, the Columbia & Puget Sound.[3]

In Washington the nature of the mining industry itself also contributed to poor relations between workers and operators. Although coal played an important role in Washington's economic development in the 1880s, mining remained a high-risk and often unprofitable business. Mining the isolated, complex beds was unusually expensive, and domestic and foreign competition for the market in San Francisco was stiff. Compared with nearby Vancouver Island coal and with British and Australian coal, the Washington product was mediocre. High risks and potentially low profits made costs a keen concern of the operators. The one cost over which they had direct control was labor, and they were not willing to share that control with workers. Unions were to be resisted because they increased costs with demands for higher wages and improved working conditions, and because they interfered with a company's right to conduct its business as it saw fit.[4]

Discontentment over their living and working conditions made mine workers receptive to the idea of organizing. When Knights of Labor organizers appeared at Newcastle in 1881, they had little trouble establishing a local assembly (or lodge as it was often called in Washington). By 1885 the Knights were active at Franklin, and by 1888, largely at the initiative of the local workers, the Knights were represented in virtually all the major mining towns in western Washington.[5]

Not surprisingly, the Knights were anathema to the operators. The concerns of Knights of Labor lodges went beyond narrow economics and reflected the broad needs of their communities. At Newcastle and Franklin the organization was the only countervailing force to the dominating OIC. In regard to work, the Knights wanted more than higher wages: they demanded some say in the hiring and firing of employees, distribution of work assignments, and mine safety. Outside the pits they wanted some control over company housing and the operation of the company store. At Newcastle they even demanded that the saloon be converted to a reading room, presumably to be stocked with Knights literature. To the OIC all of these demands were a clear infringement on its right to conduct its affairs without interference from employees.[6]

Seeking to unite all workers, the Knights espoused heterogeneous political and social reform. But in Washington the initial success of the organization was a result of its leadership in the violent anti-Chinese movement that swept across the economically depressed Pacific Northwest in late 1885 and early 1886. Though the importation of Chinese labor was prohibited by the Chinese Restriction Act of 1882, John L. Howard, OIC general manager in San Francisco, considered the smuggling of Chinese from British Columbia a "laudable business." The OIC could hire Chinese for half the wages it paid white workers. Most coal operators employed cheap Chinese labor, and in response the white mine workers became the "shock troops" of the anti-Chinese movement in Washington. In 1885 they appeared to win a major victory. With strikes, very effective boycotts, physical attacks on the Chinese, and widespread public support, mine workers forced the operators to fire their Chinese employees.[7]

The mine workers' victory, however, was a hollow one since it depended upon fostering divisions between different groups of workers. The whites regarded the Chinese with fear and hatred: fear for their own economic security, and hatred of the Chinese as people and as willing tools of the operators. No attempt was made to understand what the whites and Chinese had in common as workers. Moreover, after the expulsion of the Chinese, the OIC and other operators adamantly resisted any further demands of the Knights. Having reluctantly fired the Chinese employees at Franklin and Newcastle, Howard informed the head office in New York that the OIC would not submit again to "the dictation of a lot of demagogues and scum"—his vivid description of the Knights.[8]

The Knights and the OIC remained antagonists. The company said it would offer decent conditions and a fair day's pay for a fair day's work. The employee, as an individual, could accept or reject the offer, nothing more. No combination or union could speak for the workers because the company recognized such groups only as beneficial societies that entertained their members and paid for their funeral expenses. To force the Knights into line the OIC used spies, lockouts, wage cuts, blacklists, and armed guards: it even covertly supported a competing union. To the OIC's direct action the Knights responded with strikes, boycotts, demands for recognition, and occasionally violence. In 1886 and again in 1888–1889, work at the OIC mines was disrupted for months because of disputes between the company and the Knights.[9]

Labor relations in Washington's coal industry changed significantly in 1888. In August the Northern Pacific Coal Company, a subsidiary of the Northern Pacific Railroad, imported over four hundred blacks from the Midwest to break a strike in its mines at Roslyn, sixty miles east of Seattle. With cheap black labor the company broke the strike—and the local assembly of the Knights. The company retained its black employees, and union labor remained a moot issue at Roslyn until the turn of the century.[10]

In September 1888, in response to the events at Roslyn, John Howard advised the OIC office in New York to consider the employment of blacks:

It would take such a new element as negroes, with whom the whites would not assimilate, to prevent any further combinations. The experience of the mine owners on this Coast with regard to imported white labor is that it is simply a temporary relief, and that as soon as the new element has become inoculated with the ideas of the old, (and it does not take very long to do that in this country), history repeats itself with the mine owner.[11]

After the bitter strike of 1889 the OIC officers began to debate seriously the possible use of blacks in the mines. But they could not agree on when to bring in the blacks, nor could they decide if the company should do the hiring or use the services of a labor contractor.[12]

Uncertainty prevailed at Franklin and Newcastle until November 1890 when the OIC, saddled with $240,000 in suits and attachments, went into receivership. With the reorganization of the company in 1891, the local officers were determined to solve their labor problems once and for all. Charles J. Smith, general manager in Seattle, urged the new OIC executives in New York to install non-white labor in the mines. Widespread popular opinion prohibited the use of Chinese, so Smith recommended that the OIC bring in Negroes from the Midwest and South. With black workers the mines would be operated more economically: blacks would accept lower wages than their white counterparts, and, Smith argued, racial animosity would keep the workers divided and eliminate the effectiveness of efforts to organize labor.[13]

By the spring of 1891 the OIC executives were still withholding their approval of using blacks in the mines. Noting the reluctance in New York, T. B. Corey, OIC superintendent of mines in Seattle, implemented another plan. He attempted to force the Newcastle miners (Franklin was closed for repairs) to sign an "Ironclad Contract" that reduced wages and set tough production quotas. Further, the contract forbade a miner to stop work, join in any "strike" or combination for the purpose of obtaining or causing the company to pay their miners an advance of wages, or pay beyond what is specified in this contract, nor will he in any way aid, abet, or countenance any "strike," combination or scheme for any purpose whatever.... And if the said second party shall violate any of the provisions of this contract in this regard at any time, he shall thereby forfeit all claims for coal previously mined and not paid for.[14]

On March 30, 1891, the Newcastle miners unanimously rejected the contract. The state executive board of the Knights in Seattle claimed the contract would result in the "virtual surrendering by the employees of their individuality to the company," and would create "a system of bondage equal [to] if not worse than chattel slavery." The OIC withdrew the contract, and Corey appeared to have resigned. Actually, he had not. With the rejection of the contract by the Newcastle miners, OIC officers in New York finally gave their approval to use blacks in the mines, and Corey was sent to Iowa, Illinois, Indiana, and Missouri to recruit black workers. In Saint Louis he distributed a handbill that read: "Wanted for the New Coal Mines in the New State of Washington!...500 colored coal miners and laborers for inside and outside work.... Good wages will be paid above men. Steady work for three years. No strike or trouble of any kind. The finest country on earth."[15]

Corey had no difficulty hiring the needed workers, and on May 13, 1891, over five hundred blacks, including fifty women and children, left Saint Paul, Minnesota, bound for Franklin. The front page of the Seattle *Post-Intelligencer* carried a large headline on Sunday, May 17—"THE BLACK TRAIN"—and bold type reading, "Oregon Improvement Company Colonizing Its Mining Camps With Non-Union Labor." Very early that morning the blacks arrived at Franklin under the protection of guards—damned "Pinkertons" by the white strikers—from Portland's Thiel Detective Agency, which had been helpful to the OIC in previous disputes. Anticipating trouble, the guards immediately strung a barbed wire fence around the mine buildings and living quarters. Franklin's main street became a "deadline," and no unauthorized whites were permitted within the fenced compound. The school playground, a common meeting area, was also fenced off, and one hundred white and fifty black guards enforced the peace. The next day the Franklin mines opened with all black workers, though eventually the OIC intended to have a mixed labor force at both Newcastle and Franklin. Technically, the blacks were not strikebreakers because the OIC had discharged practically all of its Franklin employees six months earlier when it closed the mine for repairs. But such distinctions meant little to the white mine workers.[16]

The response of white workers to the blacks was varied. A group of people "representing all classes of labor" met at Wilkeson in Pierce County and resolved: "That we will no longer submit to the introduction of the negro race amongst us, and that we cannot and will not recognize the negro as worthy of association with us; neither will we submit to association with them in any manner whatsoever." The mine workers at Newcastle took more direct action: they went on strike. Almost immediately, sympathy strikes were called at Black Diamond and Cedar Mountain. For other reasons Gilman (now Issaquah) was already on strike, which left Franklin as the only operating mine in King County. News of the county-wide strike pleased C. J. Smith, who was "working a combination with the mine owners so that none of the miners will be taken back again except on contract, and when such contracts are made all the disturbing and agitating elements will be eliminated from all the mines."[17]

Suddenly, the stakes of the conflict had been raised dramatically. Other operators had joined with the OIC, and the mine workers were gathering support for a direct confrontation. Each side had reached the limit of its understanding and tolerance, and each was determined to settle matters. Caught somewhere between were the blacks at Franklin.

In Seattle the executive board of the Knights quickly realized the seriousness of the situation. To withstand the pressure of the operators, the mine workers needed wide-ranging labor support. Hence, on May 18—the day after the blacks arrived—the Knights arranged a meeting with the Western Central Labor Union (WCLU), a council that had originally united trade unions and Knights assemblies. The political, militant Knights had dominated the WCLU in its early period, but only that winter they had been expelled over a jurisdictional dispute by the increasingly powerful but more conservative trade unions.[18]

Considering the competition between them, the two labor groups displayed remarkable cooperation. They established a joint strike committee, the purpose of which was to raise relief money for the strikers and to speak with the blacks to "see if they could not be induced to return whence they came." No one suggested that the blacks be asked to join with the white mine workers. Although at this point the mine workers' anger was directed primarily at the OIC, the most the whites were willing to offer the blacks was the opportunity to leave unharassed as soon as possible. Organized labor formally asked C. J. Smith for permission to speak with the black workers, but he refused the request. The Franklin deadline was meant to keep the blacks in as well as the whites out.[19]

In order to bolster morale and dramatize their cause, the Knights and the WCLU organized a huge fund-raising picnic and demonstration at Franklin on May 24, one week after the arrival of the blacks. Over nine hundred people attended, including representatives from all the surrounding mining camps. An outdoor band entertained, and local labor leaders gave rousing speeches, most of which were directed at the black workers who watched the festivities on the other side of the deadline. The speakers urged the blacks to leave and cease defending corporate tyranny. Two Seattle Knights, neither of whom was a mine worker, even offered to help organize the blacks. Their sentiments, however, were not expressed in the resolution passed at the end of the day: "We the miners and mine laborers of King and Pierce counties in the state of Washington,...do protest against the inhuman action of the Oregon Improvement Company in importing cheap colored labor to take the place of honest white labor." Hostility to the blacks had been temporarily repressed while the strikers concentrated on their employers, but the hostility was not far below the surface.[20]

The striking mine workers saw the black "strikebreakers" as naive corporate pawns collected from the slums of America. But they also assumed that once the blacks learned how mining labor relations were conducted, they would realize how they were being used by the company and leave. These were mistaken assumptions.[21]

Who were these black workers? Contrary to white belief, most were not urban slum dwellers ignorant of mining labor disputes. Granted, about one hundred were from Saint Louis, and these men were probably unfamiliar with the mining industry. Yet another one hundred came from Braidwood, Illinois, where T. B. Corey had broken a strike in 1877 with the use of black labor. Corey claimed that many of the blacks from Braidwood were "my old men." At least another one hundred blacks were experienced mine workers from Moberly, Missouri. The rest came from small towns in the South and Midwest. One of "Corey's men" from Braidwood stated that of the five hundred blacks who came to Franklin, at least three hundred were experienced mine workers.[22]

For the most part then, the blacks at Franklin were familiar with the actions of white operators and workers. Many of the blacks knew each other and had worked together before. They had their leaders, their aid societies, and a collective experience. Some of the blacks even brought their wives and children; they intended to be at Franklin for some time, perhaps permanently. In short, the blacks knew why they were there, and they planned to stay.[23]

It is true that Corey lied to the blacks when he told them there was no trouble at the mines. But by June 1 only about seventy-five of the blacks had broken their contracts with the OIC and decided to leave. A number of those who departed felt cheated, having believed that no labor disputes existed at Franklin. Many who left simply did not want to be involved in any trouble; one anonymous miner said, "I don't know much about who is right. Perhaps they are both right, but they've all got guns and a dead nigger gets awfully cold."[24]

Once the blacks were at Franklin it was not easy for them to leave. Most were quite poor, and they were in debt to the OIC for their train fare west. Moreover, the OIC guards watched the blacks carefully to prevent escape. It appears, however, that most who did leave were those who had no previous mining experience. The experienced black mine workers knew why they were there, and the vast majority of them chose to remain.[25]

Why were the blacks willing to remain at Franklin? Part of the reason was economic self-interest. They were trying to earn a living, support their families, and live a respectable life in a society that did its best to perpetuate their former status as slaves. Their opportunities were limited, and they had to take advantage of those that were available. Charles H. Johnson, a vocal black miner, clearly understood his lot when he wrote the editor of the *Post-Intelligencer,* "We are aware that prejudice is against us here; but where can we go? It is against us everywhere.... Let them call us scabs if they want to. We have concluded that half a loaf is better than none."[26]

The black mine workers also received encouragement from the leaders of Seattle's tiny black community. With the blessing of the OIC, the Reverend Hesekiah C. Rice established the Committee of Colored Citizens to aid the blacks at Franklin. Rice appealed to racial pride to inspire the black workers:

> The only way we [blacks] can get employment as workingmen in the North is to go in a great crowd to a place and take possession of it as we have done here. But we don't want to drive the white men out [of] here. We are willing to work side by side with them, but we claim our rights as American citizens to go where we please and work at any trade we please.[27]

The Reverend L. S. Blakeney made an even more pointed appeal:

> The Oregon Improvement Company is your friend[;] stay with them and they will stay with you. You all understood that you were to pay back the money advanced as fare, and as honorable men I counsel you to remain and work out the debt.... Let one colored man do an unworthy action and his whole race is blamed for it.[28]

Loading coal. An African American miner performs one of the tasks required to extract coal from western mines of the late nineteenth century. (Courtesy, National Mining Association.)

The conservative black ministers proved to be quite influential. On May 24, while the band entertained the whites at their picnic, the black workers held a meeting. After listening first to the whites and then to Rice and his fellow committee members, they agreed that

> we came here to stay, and will use all lawful means to accomplish said end. In coming to Franklin we have exercised the right of every American citizen.... [We] expect to enjoy all the rights and immunities guaranteed to all true patriotic American citizens, and as such we deem it our right and privilege to remain not only in Franklin but in any other locality within the jurisdiction of the United States.[29]

The black workers at Franklin were not ignorant tools of the OIC. For reasons of economic self-interest and racial pride they chose to remain and ally themselves with the OIC against the white strikers. They were not so different from black mine workers in other areas of the country. Richard L. Davis, a black Virginian who mined coal in Ohio and in later years served on the

United Mine Workers board, aptly described the awkward position in which blacks found themselves:

> Now, if there is anything that I do despise it is a blackleg [strikebreaker], but in places in this country that they will not allow the negro to work simply because of his black skin, then I say boldly that he is not a blackleg in taking your places. He is only doing his plain duty in taking chances with the world. We ask no one to give us anything. All we want is the chance to work and we assure you we want just as much wages as the whites.[30]

In terms of worker solidarity one might question the wisdom of such beliefs, but the key point about the blacks at Franklin is that they made rational decisions within the framework of limited options that were available to them.[31]

In the end, labor solidarity had little meaning for the whites either. The demonstration of May 24 was the peak of resistance to the OIC. The negative response of the black workers was both a practical and a psychological setback for the white strikers. Racial animosity skyrocketed, and labor groups began to quarrel among themselves. The Knights and the WCLU renewed their squabbles over jurisdiction. The WCLU told the Knights that it would coordinate all strike action or withdraw its support. It wanted all workers, except those at Franklin and Newcastle, to return to work because they had no justifiable dispute with their employers; it believed that public support could be gained from the workers' show of good faith toward their employers. The Knights balked at this idea, arguing that all mine workers had to stand together against the operators and against the blacks. In order to make their intentions clear, a group of mine workers met at Cedar Mountain on June 13 and declared "that we, the miners and mine laborers of King county, hereby agree to let the coal companies of the county to have their choice of either employing all white miners or all colored men, and we will not return to work unless all white miners are employed."[32]

The next day a reporter found Corey writing "Approved. T. B. Corey, superintendent of mines, Oregon Improvement Company" on the union notices ordering all strikers away from the mines. Asked why he was in such a puckish mood, Corey replied that labor was playing into the operators' hands. The demand by the strikers for all black or all white miners "made the issue one of race between the white and colored miners, and not one of wages or conditions of work between the coal companies and their employes." Corey's analysis was correct. The mine workers vented their hostility on the blacks, and their attacks on the company became less strident. The coal operators were left in the enviable position of watching various groups of workers—black mine workers, white mine workers, trade unionists—quarreling among themselves. Worker resistance to the operators had quickly fragmented.[33]

Toward the end of June the strikers started to drift back to the mines. On June 28 the OIC began transferring black workers from Franklin to Newcastle, which resulted in violence. A small scuffle at Franklin between black miners and striking whites flared into a shoot-out in which over one thousand rounds were exchanged. When the smoke cleared, two people were dead and four seriously injured. Governor Elisha Ferry acceded to the deputy sheriff's call for the National Guard; for nearly a month the militia enforced a tense peace at the mining camps, while more and more strikers gave up and either returned to work or left the state.[34]

Though the mines remained quiet, there was no cooperation between blacks and whites. On Independence Day a member of a "committee of citizens" in support of labor said of the blacks: "You take 500, or 600 niggers, put firearms in their hands and they will not only menace the peace, but [also] the purity of the mothers and daughters." The *Post-Intelligencer* soberly reported that "race animosity has reached such a point that the negroes regard any white man as an enemy until they know him, and negroes traveling on the road who have nothing to do with the quarrel have had to prove their identity to escape abuse." Despite such hostility, C. J. Smith announced the end of the strike in late July. In all the mining towns the returning strikers were forced to sign Ironclad Contracts, which reduced wages and forbade them to strike or join any combination.[35]

Resistance to the operators dragged on through 1891. On September 5 the mine workers met at Cedar Mountain and voted to stay out. Though still quarreling with the Knights, the WCLU helped to organize a boycott of "scab" coal, continued to raise money for the strikers, and even sent a representative to the Tacoma Trades Council to explain the situation and ask for assistance. But by November it was obvious that the mines were operating very smoothly without the strikers, and the boycott was a failure. The operators had indeed won.[36]

Though the Knights in eastern Washington remained very active in reform politics until 1900, the mining assemblies in western Washington were fatally wounded in the strike of 1891, and they succumbed in the panic of 1893. In that year many former Knights joined the new Western Federation of Miners (WFM) in Montana. As individuals, the refugee Knights were welcome at the organizational meeting of the WFM, but the last struggling assemblies were not invited to attend because they had agreed to wage scales that were too low. In 1894 labor strife again rocked the Pacific Northwest, but the coal mines, except for a very brief strike at Roslyn, remained quiet. The OIC, in fact all the operators, continued to reap the benefits of the previous victory, and C. J. Smith proudly exclaimed, "our force is the only bulwark against a general Miners['] strike in Washington." Not until 1901 did another coal mining union appear in Washington.[37]

Under the auspices of the OIC, Washington coal operators managed to suppress union activity for a decade, but the OIC itself enjoyed such benefits for only a few years. On October 4, 1895, the company went into receivership for the second and final time. Smith, who was appointed receiver, tried without success to save the company. The OIC was not able to reorganize, and it ceased to exist when it was purchased by the Pacific Coast Company in 1896.[38]

The demise of the OIC and the collapse of the Knights of Labor in western Washington had little direct significance outside the state; even within Washington the economic concerns of most people were tied to the lumber industry, not coal mining. But the defeat of the Knights had important implications, for it was symptomatic of serious problems within organized labor.

In the national mining industry using blacks as low-paid regular employees and as strikebreakers was a tradition among operators. Completion of the transcontinental railroads and development of a truly national transportation system after the Civil War aided employers in restructuring their local work force with "aliens" to make it more efficient or docile. In the early 1870s imported black workers broke strikes in Illinois, Indiana, and Ohio. In late 1874 Ohio coal operators brought several hundred blacks from the South when a strike was called by the Hocking Valley Miners' National Association (MNA). Under the protection of armed guards the blacks broke the strike in a few weeks, and the MNA, one of the earliest "national" mining unions, collapsed.[39]

As race relations deteriorated in the latter part of the century, employers often hired blacks and mixed them with different ethnic groups to fragment the labor force. During the 1880s and 1890s this was a common practice in Pennsylvania, where thousands of East Europeans worked under contract in the mines. Successful mixing of blacks, Hungarians, Italians, and white Americans kept the workers divided and quarreling among themselves. Racial and ethnic animosity superseded any notions of class consciousness.[40]

Few blacks lived in the American West prior to 1900. In Washington at the turn of the century, for example, they constituted less than 1 percent of the population. Yet their presence, even the possibility of their presence, elicited much hostility from white residents. Despised as a race, blacks were feared because they raised the threats of economic competition and miscegenation. Consequently, in the developing labor movement after the Civil War, there was little interracial cooperation. Even the Knights, who embraced the ideal of organizing all workers, made little attempt to organize the few blacks in the West because white workers refused to have anything to do with them. Prejudice overwhelmed any notions of labor solidarity.[41]

In the OIC mines the Knights of Labor played into the hands of the employers. Although they spoke of the common bonds that united all workers, Knights too often practiced the virulent racism so common in the United States. Using a mixed labor force, the OIC was able to fragment the workers and thwart organized labor. One could argue that the Knights were shortsighted, but they merely reflected the dominant values of their culture. More important, they were not debating race relations; they were defending their jobs and homes in a highly irregular industry. To them the blacks were not fellow workers but tools of corporations bent on lowering wages and eliminating unions. Ironically, the presence of the blacks did briefly unify the white workers, but the foundation of that unity—racial animosity—helped bring about their defeat.

Notes

1. I thank Norbert MacDonald and Marvin Lazerson, both of the University of British Columbia, for much useful criticism of previous drafts of this essay.
2. From 1886 Washington's coal mines were annually examined by government inspectors, but "the majority of inspectors seemed more interested in 'boosting' Washington industry than improving the safety and health conditions of the mines"; see Mark J. Stern, "To Bring Forth the Hidden Wealth: The Knights of Labor in the Coalfields of King County, Washington, 1885–1891," B.A. thesis (Reed College, 1973), 17. Mine safety was one of the key issues in a long, bitter strike at the Oregon Improvement Company (OIC) mines in 1886; ibid., 43–45.
3. On the polarizing effects of the company town, see Robert A. Campbell, "An Added Objection: The Use of Blacks in the Coal Mines of Washington, 1880–1896," M.A. thesis (University of British Columbia, 1978), 29–33; Stern, 19–20. Established by Henry Villard in 1880, the OIC had only moderate success during its sixteen-year existence. It owned the mines at Newcastle and Franklin, four small railroads, and a steamship company, and had general offices in New York, Seattle, and San Francisco; see Campbell, 7–10.
4. For a complete analysis of the coal mining economy in Washington, see Campbell, 1–11. See also C. William Thorndale, "Washington's Green River Coal Company [Country]: 1880–1930," M.A. thesis (University of Washington, 1965), 28, 49, 55; Frederick E. Melder, "A Study of the Washington Coal Industry with Special Reference to the Industrial Relations Problem," M.A. thesis (University of Washington, 1931), 25–29; A. Norbert MacDonald, "Seattle's Economic Development, 1880–1910," Ph.D. dissertation (University of Washington, 1959), 15–18, 187; Seattle *Post-Intelligencer*, April 19, 1884, Jan. 1, 1885 (hereafter cited as *P-I* with appropriate date); Thomas Greeve to John Waterbury, report, March 9, 1896, pp. 29–39, Box 53a, Oregon Improvement Company (OIC) Records, University of Washington Libraries, Seattle. Also see John L. Howard to Elijah Smith, Sept. 25, 1885, April 1, 16, 1886, Boxes 56 and 57, OIC Records.
5. Thorndale, 48–49; Melder, 53–57. The best general works on the Knights are Norman J. Ware, *The Labor Movement in the United States, 1860–1895* (New York, 1929); Gerald N. Grob, *Workers and Utopia: A Study of Ideological Conflict in the American Labor Movement,*

1865–1900 (Evanston, Ill., 1961); T. V. Powderly, *Thirty Years of Labor, 1859 to 1889* (1889; reprinted, New York, 1967).

6. Stern, 20–21, 43–54.
7. The diverse reform interests of the Knights ranged from poverty relief and prohibition to socialism and the People's party; see Carlos A. Schwantes, *Radical Heritage: Labor, Socialism, and Reform in Washington and British Columbia, 1885–1917* (Seattle, 1979), 34–35, 42–47, 52–56, and Schwantes, "Leftward Tilt on the Pacific Slope: Indigenous Unionism and the Struggle Against AFL Hegemony in the State of Washington." *Pacific Northwest Quarterly*, Vol. 70 (1979), 25–26. Two good accounts of the Chinese in the West are Robert E. Wynne, "Reaction to the Chinese in the Pacific Northwest and British Columbia, 1850 to 1910," Ph.D. dissertation (University of Washington, 1964), and Alexander Saxton, *The Indispensable Enemy: Labor and the Anti-Chinese Movement in California* (Berkeley, 1971). See also Jules A. Karlin, "The Anti-Chinese Outbreaks in Seattle, 1885–1886," *Pacific Northwest Quarterly*, Vol. 39 (1948), 103–30; Karlin, "The Anti-Chinese Outbreak in Tacoma, 1885," *Pacific Historical Review*, Vol. 23 (1954), 271–83; Schwantes, "Race and Radicalism: The Legacy of the Knights of Labor in the Pacific Northwest" (MS); Howard to E. Smith, July 20 [26?] (quotation), 24, 1884, Box 54, OIC Records; Wynne, 242, 274–75.
8. *P-I*, Sept. 30, 1885; Howard to E. Smith, Sept. 25, 1885 (quotation), Box 56, OIC Records.
9. *P-I*, Sept. 30, 1885. In the fall of 1888 the Knights faced competition from the Miners and Mine Laborers Protective Union. The OIC attempted to keep the two unions quarreling by employing Miners Union men any time the Knights were on strike. The Miners Union never had much support, and it disappeared by 1890. See Thorndale, 48–58; Campbell 48–49; Alan A. Hynding, "The Coal Miners of Washington Territory: Labor Troubles in 1888–89," *Arizona and the West*, Vol. 12 (1970), 221–36; Stern, 55–64, 69–74.
10. For the trouble at Roslyn, see Hynding, the Seattle newspapers, and the annual report of Territorial Governor Eugene Semple, in 50th Cong. 2d Sess., 1888. House Executive Document 1, pt. 5, pp. 913–17 (Serial 2638).
11. Howard to E. Smith, Sept. 14, 1888, Box 59, OIC Records.
12. C.J. Smith to E. Smith, Sept. 27, 1890, Box 48, and Oct. 17, 23, 30, 1890, and to W.H. Starbuck, Feb. 23, March 3 (telegram), 1891, Box 49; and Howard to E. Smith, Oct. 9, 1890, Box 63—all in OIC Records.
13. Joseph Simon to E. Smith, Nov. 27, 1890, and C.J. Smith to Starbuck, Jan. 16, 28, Feb. 4, 23, 1891, Box 49; also C.J. Smith to Starbuck, May 7, 27, 1891, Box 50, OIC Records.
14. *P-I*, May 18, 1891.
15. *Ibid.*, April 2 (quotation), May 18, 1891: Seattle *Press-Times*, May 19, 1891 (handbill).
16. *P-I*, May 17, 18, 20, 1891; *Press-Times*, May 18, 1891; C.J. Smith to Starbuck, May 27, 1891, Box 50, OIC Records.
17. *Press-Times*, May 23, 1891 (Wilkeson response); C.J. Smith to Starbuck, May 27, 1891 (quotation).
18. The Seattle fire of 1889 brought prosperity to organized labor, especially in the building trades. As business unionism became more popular, the influence of the Knights waned. See Schwantes, "Leftward Tilt," 26; Melvin G. De Shazo, "Radical Tendencies in the Seattle Labor Movement as Reflected in the Proceedings of Its Central Body," M.A. thesis (University of Washington, 1925), 2–6. The weekly minutes of the WCLU are a valuable source, though the earliest ones available date from August 1891, well past the climax of the coal mining dispute. See Minutes of the Western Central Labor Union, Box 18, Central Labor Council—King County Records, University of Washington Libraries (hereafter WCLU Minutes).
19. *Press-Times*, May 19, 1891 (quotation); *P-I*, May 19, 20, 22, 1891.
20. *Press-Times*, May 25, 1891; *P-I*, May 25, 1891 (quotation).
21. Stern, 84–85.

22. *Ibid.*, 77, 84–85; *Press-Times,* May 19, 1891 (quotation). T.B. Corey was a former superintendent for the Chicago, Wilmington & Vermillion Coal Company of Braidwood, Illinois, where in 1877 blacks had been used as strikebreakers.

23. Stern, 86. There were 150 married blacks who did not bring out their families; Stern, "Black Strikebreakers in the Coal Fields: King County, Washington—1891," *Journal of Ethnic Studies,* Vol. 5 (Fall 1977), 62.

24. *P-I,* May 19 (quotation), June 1, 1891.

25. Stern, "Black Strikebreakers," 65.

26. *P-I,* July 5, 1891.

27. *Ibid.*, May 19, 1891.

28. Stern, "To Bring Forth the Wealth," 95; *Press-Times,* May 21, 1891 (quotation).

29. *Press-Times,* May 25, 1891.

30. Herbert G. Gutman, "The Negro and the United Mine Workers of America," in *The Negro and the American Labor Movement,* ed. Julius Jacobson (Garden City, N.Y., 1968), 78.

31. Stern, "Black Strikebreakers," 68–69.

32. *P-I,* May 28, June 14 (quotation), 1891.

33. *Ibid.*, June 15, 1891.

34. *P-I,* June 29, 30, July 3, 4, 7, 23, 1891; C.J. Smith to Starbuck, July 4, 30, 1891, Box 50, OIC Records. Smith was overly optimistic about his new work force. On July 13 about thirty blacks at Newcastle went on strike to protest the replacement of black mine workers with returning whites. The OIC gave in and rehired the dismissed blacks; see clipping, OIC Scrapbook, p. 183, Box 69, OIC Records. On the role of the National Guard in the mining disputes, see Patrick H. McLatchy, "The Development of the National Guard of Washington as an Instrument of Social Control, 1854–1916," Ph.D. dissertation (University of Washington, 1973), 237–60.

35. C.J. Smith to Starbuck, July 30, Aug. 3, 1891, Box 50, OIC Records; *P-I,* July 4, 1891 (quotations). The mine workers' defeat contributed to the rise of populism; see Thomas W. Riddle, "The Old Radicalism in America: John R. Rogers and the Populist Movement in Washington, 1891–1900," Ph.D. dissertation (Washington State University, 1976), 121–27.

36. WCLU Minutes, Sept. 9, Oct. 14, Nov. 4, 1891. See also Tacoma Trades Council Minutes, May 21, June 25, Aug. 27, 1891, Central Labor Council—Pierce County Records, University of Washington Libraries.

37. Schwantes, *Radical Heritage,* 34, 52–54, 119–22; C.J. Smith to C.B. Tedcastle, May 9, 1894 (quotation), and to Starbuck, July 2, 7, 1894 (telegrams), Box 52, OIC Records; Richard E. Lingenfelter, *The Hardrock Miners: A History of the Mining Labor Movement in the American West, 1863–1893* (Berkeley, 1974), 220. The United Mine Workers established a local in Washington in 1901, and the Western Federation of Miners established a local in 1903; see Melder, 63, 66–68; Thorndale, 108.

38. Artemas Holmes to E. Smith, Oct. 7, 1895, and Corey to E. Smith, July 13, 1896, Boxes 53 and 53a, OIC Records. Somewhat desperate as the OIC failed, C.J. Smith, who had worked so hard to have blacks employed in the company mines, blamed "Corey and the colored men" for the OIC's troubles, and to the horrified amazement of the other OIC officers, he began to fire blacks in 1896. See Frank Kelley to B.F. [sic] Corey and H.W. McNeill to E. Smith, both Aug. 17, 1896, Box 53a, OIC Records.

39. Herbert G. Gutman, "Reconstruction in Ohio: Negroes in the Hocking Valley Coal Mines in 1873 and 1874," *Labor History,* Vol. 3 (1962), 243–64; Gutman, "The Negro and the United Mine Workers," 51–52, 64–65, 96–100; Ware, 210–11.

40. Darold Barnum, *The Negro in the Bituminous Coal Mining Industry,* The Racial Policies of American Industry, Report 14 (Philadelphia, 1970), 19–20; Sterling Spero and Abram Harris, *The Black Worker* (New York, 1931), 209–13. Essential for an understanding of the origins of American racism are: Winthrop Jordan, *White over Black: American Attitudes*

toward the Negro, 1550–1812 (Chapel Hill, 1968); Edmund Morgan, *American Slavery, American Freedom: The Ordeal of Colonial Virginia* (New York, 1975); George M. Fredrickson, *The Black Image in the White Mind: The Debate on Afro-American Character and Destiny, 1817–1914* (New York, 1971).

41. *Thirteenth Census of the United States, Taken in the Year 1910,* Vol. III, *Population* (Washington, D.C., 1913), 996; Fredrickson, 130–90. And see the following articles in *Labor History:* Kenneth Kann, "The Knights of Labor and the Southern Black Worker," Vol. 18 (1977), 49–70; Melton A. McLaurin, "The Racial Policies of the Knights of Labor and the Organization of Southern Black Workers," Vol. 17 (1976), 568–85; William W. Rogers, "Negro Knights of Labor in Arkansas: A Case Study of the 'Miscellaneous' Strike," Vol. 10 (1969), 498–505. For a general study, see Quintard Taylor, Jr., "A History of Blacks in the Pacific Northwest, 1788–1970," Ph.D. dissertation (University of Minnesota, 1977).

BLACK COWBOYS IN THE
AMERICAN WEST, 1866–1900

Kenneth W. Porter

[This article originally appeared as "Negro Labor in the Western Cattle Industry, 1866–1900" in *Labor History*, Vol. 10 (1969), pp. 346–374. Retitled, adapted, and reprinted with permission.]

One of the most important economic activities that brought African Americans to the late nineteenth-century West was the cattle industry. During the Civil War, many domestic cattle simply wandered off from Texas farms whose owners were away fighting the war. These cattle joined the wild herds of "longhorns" that had roamed for years throughout northern Mexico and southern Texas. After the war, enterprising capitalists began rounding up these stray cattle, establishing ranches, improving the herds by selective breeding, and selling the surplus animals they produced. These ranch owners hired thousands of men to work with their cattle—on the ranches, out on the open range, and on the trails taking cattle they wished to sell to market.

Cattle buyers included the U.S. government which bought beef to feed soldiers stationed at frontier posts and Indians confined to western reservations. The majority of western beef, however, was sold in the East where the population was increasing dramatically due, in part, to millions of immigrants coming to the United States to work in the factories proliferating because of the industrial revolution. Drovers had to move cattle from Texas north to the cow towns (or railheads) that were being established along the railroads that tied the West to the eastern part of the country.

In the process of helping the cattle industry grow into a multimillion dollar business from the mid-1860s to the mid-1880s, the cowboy became—to many Americans—a symbol of life in the West. The so-called "myth of the cowboy" romanticized the low-paying, hard-working, lonely existence of cattle herders by emphasizing the freedom that they supposedly experienced out in the West's wide-open spaces. Cowboys became the heroic lead characters in hundreds of dime novels and stories in mass-market magazines. The cowboy myth continued into the twentieth century and, in fact, grew larger as Hollywood producers turned out hundreds of movies and television programs with "western" themes. The greatest discrepancy between the cowboy myth and reality, however, was that many of the real cowboys were black while few of those in books and films were. Several historians have speculated about why the mythmakers omitted black cowboys from the fictionalized version of the West. For one thing, most Americans (and, consequently, most book readers and film viewers) were white, and authors and movie producers wanted to cater to their audiences. For another, most white Americans would presumably have balked at the idea of African Americans being portrayed in a positive, even heroic, light.

Kenneth Wiggins Porter was one of the pioneering historians who sought to dispel the myth that almost all cowboys were white. In the following essay, he discusses the jobs of cowboys in general and those of black cowboys in particular. He estimates that of the thirty-five thousand or so cowboys employed in the western cattle industry of the late nineteenth century about 25 percent—eight thousand to nine thousand—were black. Other historians believe that the number of black cowboys was closer to five thousand; regardless of who is more accurate, however, the fact is that thousands of African Americans were cowboys. One reason for this great number of black employees in the cattle industry was that Texas, where the business began before spreading north into the Great Plains and the Rocky Mountains, was a slave state and, thus, had a large black population during the time that many Americans regarded much of the West as the cattle kingdom.

The range-cattle industry, in its various aspects, and in its importance to the United States and particularly to the Great Plains for the post–Civil War generation, has been the subject of numerous studies. This industry was rendered possible by such factors as vast expanses of grazing land, projected railroad lines across the Missouri and onto the Great Plains, the rise of heavy industry and the consequent demand for beef of less-than-high quality by the meat-hungry industrial population. But like the steel, mining, packing, and other industries, it also needed a labor force—workers with special abilities and qualities—for although the cowhand or cowboy possibly was no more than a "hired man on horseback,"[1] he was a hired man with skills in riding, roping, and branding that could not be easily acquired. Most of his working hours were spent in such routine tasks as riding the range and turning back drifting steers; rounding up, branding, and castrating calves; selecting beeves for the market; and, even on the "long drive," jogging along and daily "eating dirt" on the flanks or in the rear of a few thousand "cow critters." But he also needed the inborn courage and quick thinking to use these skills effectively while confronting an enraged bull, swimming a milling herd across a flooded river, or trying to turn a stampede of fear-crazed steers.

But the general public, under the influence of decades of "western" movies and, more recently, television shows, has come to regard the cowboy's workaday activities as altogether secondary to fighting off hostile Indians, pursuing rustlers and holding "necktie parties" for them, saving the rancher's daughter from Mexican raiders, and engaging in quick-draw gunfights in dusty streets. From similar sources this same public has also learned that cowboys, with the exception of an occasional low-browed villain or exotic and comic-accented *vaquero*, were all of the purest and noblest Anglo-Saxon type, as in Owen Wister's *The Virginian*.

In reality, as George W. Saunders of the Texas Trail Drivers Association has authoritatively estimated, of the fully thirty-five thousand men who went up the trail from Texas with herds during the heroic age of the cattle industry, 1866–1895, "about one-third were Negroes and Mexicans."[2] This estimate is closely confirmed by extant lists of trail-herd outfits that identify their members racially. These lists also demonstrate that Negroes out-numbered Mexicans by more than two to one—slightly more than 63 percent whites, 25 percent Negroes, and slightly under 12 percent Mexicans.

The racial breakdown of individual outfits, of course, varied widely. Some were nearly all of one race, such as the 1874 outfit that was all-Negro, except for a white boss, or the 1872 outfit that consisted of a white trail-boss, eight Mexicans, and a Negro; but more typical were the two 1877 outfits composed, respectively, of seven whites and two Negro cowboys, and a Negro cook; and seven whites, two Negroes, and a Mexican hostler. Many outfits had no Mexicans at all, but it was an exceptional outfit that did not have at least one Negro and enough outfits were nearly all-Negro, or a third or more Negro, to bring the number up to the estimated 25 percent of the total.[3] A trail-herd outfit of about a dozen men would on the average consist of seven or eight whites, including the trail boss, three Negroes—one of whom was probably the cook, while another might be the horse wrangler, and the third would simply be a trail hand—and one or two Mexicans; if a Negro was not the wrangler, then a Mexican often was. Needless to say, this is not the typical trail outfit of popular literature and drama.

The racial make-up of ranch outfits, with their seasonal and day-by-day fluctuations, was not so well recorded as that of the trail-herd outfits, but available information indicates that ranch hands, in Texas at least, were white, Negro, and Mexican in proportions varying according to locality and to ranchowner tastes; probably the overall proportions differed little from those of trail outfits. A ranch in the Indian Territory during the late 1890s, for example, was staffed by eight cowhands, two of whom were Negroes.[4] Negro cowhands were particularly numerous on the Texas Gulf Coast, in the coastal brush east of the Nueces [River] and at the mouth of the Brazos [River] and south of Houston, and parts of the Indian Territory; in some sections they were in the majority, and some ranches worked Negroes almost exclusively.[5]

Negro trail drivers swarmed west and north with herds from the Texas "hive" and, though most returned, a few remained as ranch hands as far north as Wyoming, the Dakotas, and even Canada and as far west as New Mexico, Arizona, and even California and Oregon.[6] Negroes occupied all the positions among cattle-industry employees, from the usually lowly wrangler through ordinary hand to top hand and lofty cook. But they were almost never, except in the highly infrequent case of an all-Negro outfit, to be found as ranch or trail boss.

Negroes and also Mexicans were frequently wranglers, or *remuderos*[7]—in charge of the saddle horses not immediately in use—usually regarded as the lowliest job in the cattle industry, except for the boy who sometimes served as wrangler's assistant.[8] There were exceptions, however, including some Negro wranglers who became "second in authority to the foreman" in a few camps.[9] Such wranglers were "horse men" in the highest sense: capable of detecting and treating illness and injury, selecting the proper horse for each job, and taking the ginger out of unruly animals. Among these wranglers-extraordinary were Nigger Jim Kelly, the horsebreaker, horsetrainer, handyman, and gunman of the notorious Print Olive; and the famous John Chisum's "Nigger Frank," "who spent a lifetime wrangling Long I horses" and whom a white cattleman declared "the best line rider and horsewrangler I ever saw."[10]

The majority of Negroes on the ranch or "long drive" were neither wranglers nor yet authoritative cooks (of whom more later). They were top hands or ordinary hands who, on the long drive, rode the point, the swing, the flank, or the drag, according to their experience and ability. The point—the position of honor—was at the front of the herd where the steers were strongest, most restless, and most likely to try to break away. There the most experienced top hands rode. Farther back, the cattle were somewhat less troublesome, while in the rear, where the tired beasts were comparatively easy to manage, could be found the fledgling cowboys of the drag, "eating the dust" of the entire herd. Negroes rode in all these positions.[11]

These Negro cowboys, whether on ranch or trail, were generally regarded as good workers who got along well with others and who took pride in their work. A white Texan, a former cowboy and rancher, went so far as to write that "there was no better cowman on earth than the Negro."[12] Old, experienced Negro cowhands frequently served as unofficial, one-man apprentice systems to white greenhorns. This was particularly true, of course, when the fledgling was the employer's son or relative. Will Rogers, for example, got his first lessons in riding and roping from a Cherokee Negro employee of his father.[13] Almost any young would-be cowboy who showed the proper spirit, however, might have the good fortune to be "adopted" and "showed the ropes" by one of these black veterans, who would sometimes take on the inexperienced boy as partner when white cowboys were unwilling to do so.[14]

Although every top hand had to be a skillful rider and roper, some were so outstanding as to be considered "bronco busters" and/or ropers *par excellence* rather than as merely uncommonly able cowboys. A white ex-cowpuncher-writer states that Negroes were hired largely for their ability to cope with bad horses that the white cowhands did not want to tackle. "The Negro cow hands of the middle 1880s...were usually called on to do the hardest work around an outfit.... This most often took the form of 'topping' or taking the first pitch out of the rough horses of the outfit.... It was not unusual for one young Negro to 'top' a half dozen hard-pitching horses before breakfast."[15]

The list of Negro bronc riders—the comparatively few whose names have survived—is still a long one. A few of the better known, partly because they attracted the attention of published writers, were the following: Isam, Isom, or Isham Dart of Brown's Hole, "where Colorado, Wyoming, and Utah cornered," who, although now remembered principally as a reputed rustler, was also "numbered among the top bronc stompers of the Old West";[16] Nigger Jim Kelly, whom old-time cowboys considered the peer of any rider they had seen in the United States, Canada, or the Argentine;[17] a mulatto named Williams in the Badlands of South Dakota, who was a horse-trainer rather than a horsebreaker and whose methods won the admiration of Theodore Roosevelt;[18] and Jim Perry, the famous XIT cook, who was even better known as "one of the best riders and ropers ever to hit the West."[19]

Other Negro cowhands were particularly renowned as ropers, such as Ab Blocker's Frank, who was, according to a white cowboy, "the best hand with a rope I ever saw," and whose roping skill once saved his employer from an angry steer;[20] Ike Word, according to Charles Siringo, "the best roper" at a roundup

Isom Dart. A cowboy and occasionally a rustler of cattle and horses, Dart (originally "Ned Huddleston") plied his trades in Utah, Colorado, and Wyoming. He died in 1900 when shot from ambush by famed gunslinger Tom Horn. (Courtesy, Denver Public Library, Western History Department.)

near Beeville, Texas;[21] Jim Simpson, "about the best roper" on his part of the Wyoming range;[22] and, more recently, the Negro rancher Jess Pickett who, according to a white neighbor, was "the world's best roper."[23]

Naturally enough, many of the famous Negro riders, such as Isom Dart and Jim Perry, were almost or quite as renowned as ropers. One of the most spectacular at both riding and roping was "Nigger Add," "one of the best hands on the Pecos," who would as a matter of course "top off" several bad horses of a morning. Walking into a corral full of tough broncs, he would seize any one he chose by the ear and nose, lead him out of the bunch, and then show him who was boss. As a roper he was even more sensational, and had the unusual technique of roping on foot, a practice that would have killed an ordinary man. He would tie a rope around his hips, work up to a horse in the corral or in the open pasture, rope him around the neck as he dashed by at full speed, and then, by sheer strength and skill, flatten the horse out on the ground where a lesser man would have been dragged to death.[24] Indeed, the prowess of such Negro riders, horsebreakers, and horse-trainers was so outstanding as to contribute to the commonly held belief of the time that there was some natural affinity between Negroes and horses.[25]

Riding, roping, and branding were not the only skills required of a top cowhand. Singing to the cattle, particularly on night herd but sometimes during the day's march, was not only a practical necessity for calming the animals and reducing the danger of a stampede, it also had recreational and esthetic values for the drivers. Negro trail hands were conspicuous in this practice, although Negro chuckwagon cooks were the most noted cow-country musicians, singers, and composers. "Nigger" Jim Kelly, the Olives' versatile horsebreaker and gunman, is also credited with composing a humorous song, "Willie the Cook," which he sang to accordion accompaniment furnished by a white trail hand. "Teddy Blue," a white cowhand whose autobiography is a cow-country classic, tells movingly of his first memory of the "Ogallaly song," which had a verse for every river on the trail, beginning with the Nueces and ending in 1881, when he first heard it, with the Ogallala.[26]

High in the hierarchy of cow-country employees was the ranch or trail cook,[27] who ranked next to the foreman or trail boss and, in camp, ruled supreme over an area of sixty feet around the chuckwagon. In addition to culinary skill—including the ability to prepare a meal in a blizzard, cloudburst, or high wind—the cook also had to be an expert muleskinner or bullwhacker, capable of driving two or three yoke of oxen or a four-mule team attached to the chuckwagon over the most difficult terrain, including flooded rivers. He could do more than anyone else to make life pleasant and many a cowboy selected an outfit because of the reputation of its cook. In compensation for duties that few men could satisfactorily perform, the cook normally was paid from $5 per month more than the ordinary cowhand up to even twice as much.

The cowboy cook was also commonly credited with other qualities less essential and certainly less endearing than the ability to cook and drive the chuckwagon. He was frequently something of a despot; bad-tempered, hard-featured, and unlovely. But numerous accounts of Negro cow-country cooks suggest that the traditional "hard character" pattern fitted them much less than it did whites. The cow-country cook of the Texas and Texas-influenced range, if not typically a Negro, was at least very frequently one.[28]

The cook was frequently in sole charge not merely of the kitchen but of the ranch house itself, and on the long drive was of course frequently left alone to protect the chuckwagon and its contents in any emergency, whether crossing a river or encountering Indians. A Negro cook distinguished himself in an episode of 1877 in which the other members of his outfit played no very heroic roles. Four white men and three Negroes were working cattle in Coleman County, Texas, when Indians suddenly swooped down upon them. All took refuge in a cave except "old Negro Andy, the cook," who stayed by the wagon, fought off the Indians, and saved the supplies.[29]

The Negro cook often possessed other skills beyond the culinary. So many Negro cooks, in fact, were noted riders and ropers that something of a pattern emerges. The wild-game cook extraordinary, Black Sam, was such a good rider that "frequently one of the boys would get him to 'top' a bad horse." Jim Perry of the XIT was not only the best cook that ever lived, according to a white hand, but he was also the best rider as well. Jim Simpson, roundup cook and fiddler, who had come up from Texas in the 1880s with a herd of longhorns, was at one time also "about the best roper" in that part of the Wyoming range.[30]

All cowboys, we have noted, were expected to be able to "sing" in order to soothe the restless cattle. Just as they were expert riders and ropers, Negro cooks were frequently singers, musicians, and even composers. Although hard-worked, they were about the only men in an outfit with the opportunity to carry and play a musical instrument. "The Zebra Dun," a song about a supposed greenhorn who surprised everyone by riding an outlaw horse, is said to have been composed by Jake, who worked for a Pecos River ranch.[31] One chuckwagon cook who supplemented his menu with deer and turkey that he shot himself, also sang and played the guitar.[32] Another, Old Bat, the Slaughter cook, played both the fiddle and the fife. Jim Perry, the XIT cook, was not only the best cook, the best rider, and the best Negro in the world, but also the best fiddler. Jim Simpson, Negro cook and roper of the Wyoming range, was also the regular fiddler for the Saturday night dances.[33]

Negro cooks, in addition to riding and roping, singing and playing, sometimes possessed skills so various as to be unclassifiable. One of the most versatile of Negro cooks was John Battavia Hinnaut ("Old Bat"), probably the most useful man on the Slaughter spread. Although primarily and officially a roundup cook, he was a first-class ranch-hand, a musician, an expert teamster and coachman, an Indian fighter, a mighty hunter, and also served as the boss's valet, practical nurse, and bodyguard.[34]

That the Negro cow-country cook frequently possessed unusual abilities was due in part to limitations imposed because of racial discrimination. He was much more likely than the average white man to have been brought up about the kitchen and stables of a plantation or ranch and there, at an early age, to have become acquainted with cooking and horses. He was less likely to regard kitchen chores as somehow beneath him. The unusually able and ambitious white cowboy could look forward to possible promotion to foreman or trail boss; the Negro of equal ability knew he had little chance of attaining such a position. To become a ranch or roundup cook was about as much as could be expected. Age, inexperience, or physical handicap might preclude a white man from any ranch job outside of the kitchen; but for the superior Negro cowboy to preside over a chuckwagon or ranch kitchen meant an increase in pay and prestige.

The Negro cowhand, however able, could, as we have seen, rarely rise to a position higher than chuckwagon or ranch-house cook. The principal obstacle to his becoming a ranch foreman or trail boss was a general belief that a Negro simply did not possess the qualities necessary for such a position. But even if a ranch owner or group of cattlemen were confident that a Negro had the necessary intelligence, initiative, and general capacity, there was always the practical consideration that such a man, even if in charge of an all-Negro outfit, would on occasion have to deal with white foremen and trail bosses who might refuse to recognize his authority, and that expensive trouble might ensue. A Negro, however great his ability, thus had difficulty in attaining greater authority than could be exercised over a chuckwagon or kitchen. The phenomenal success of Ora Haley, who for three decades was the dominant figure in the range-cattle business of northwestern Colorado, is said to have been partly due to his Negro top hand Thornton Biggs, who although he "taught a whole generation of future range managers, wagon bosses, and all-around cowpunchers the finer points of the range-cattle business," himself "never became a range manager or even a foreman." The fairer-minded recognized the handicaps under which their Negro cowhands labored. Jim Perry, redoubtable cook, rider, and fiddler of the XIT ranch, once wryly remarked: "If it weren't for my damned old black face I'd have been boss of one of these divisions long ago."[35] "And no doubt he would have," a white employee commented.

And yet a very few Negroes of exceptional ability, and sometimes under unusual circumstances, did make the grade. There was the master west Texas rider and roper, "Nigger Add" or "Old Add," who, by 1889 if not earlier, was the LFD's range boss, working "South Texas colored hands almost entirely." One of his qualifications was that he was a "dictionary of earmarks and brands" but probably more important was his universal popularity among cattlemen from Toyah, Texas, to Las Vegas, New Mexico.[36] Nigger Add's outfit consisted "almost entirely" of Negroes—and one wonders who the exceptions were. Probably they were Mexicans.

Some especially able and trustworthy cow-country Negroes fulfilled roles for which there was no equivalent among white cowhands; as confidential assistants, factotums and, when it was necessary to transport large sums of money, bodyguards, and "bankers." Colonel Charles Goodnight wrote of Bose Ikard, his right-hand man: "I have trusted him farther than any living man. He was my detective, banker, and everything else." Bose would sometimes have on his person proceeds from his employer's cattle sales amounting to as much as $20,000, since it was reasoned that a thief would be unlikely to search a Negro's belongings.[37]

John Slaughter's "Old Bat" played a similar role. Officially a roundup cook, he could also do almost any ranch work, but his major importance was as general factotum in anything connected with Slaughter's personal needs— valet, practical nurse, and, above all, bodyguard. When Slaughter was on a cattle-buying trip, Bat always went along to guard the approximately $10,000 in gold that Slaughter usually carried in his money belt, watching while his employer slept.[38] Print Olive's handyman and bodyguard was Nigger Jim Kelly—wrangler, horsebreaker, gunman—who in the fall of 1869 accompanied his boss back from Fort Kearney, Nebraska, their saddlebags stuffed with currency and gold, and who in 1872, with a quick well-aimed bullet, saved Print's life after he had been shot three times and was about to be killed.[39]

For a generation and more, cow-country Negroes distinguished themselves as riders and ropers, cooks and bodyguards, as well as in the more common and still highly necessary positions of wranglers, ordinary cowboys, and top hands. What compensation, financial and psychological, did they receive for their services? And how did their wages, working, and living conditions, and opportunities for advancement and a "good life," compare with those of white hands of corresponding abilities and of Negroes outside the cattle country?

Nat Love. One of several thousand African American cowboys on the western frontier in the late nineteenth century, the flamboyant Love published his autobiography in 1907. In his later years, he worked as a Pullman porter and a bank security guard. (Courtesy, Nebraska State Historical Society.)

In view of the racial situation that then prevailed throughout the United States, particularly in the South and the West, it can be assumed that Negro cowmen encountered discrimination and segregation. The question therefore is not: Did discrimination and segregation exist? But rather: What was their extent and character? And how uniform were they? For although racism was general, it did vary from region to region, from state to state, and even from community to community. It also varied from period to period, probably increasing rather than diminishing during the years in question. Racial discrimination in the cattle country falls into several categories: wages and working conditions on the job; personal and social relations on the ranch or on cattle trails; and in town or at the end of the cattle trail.

Discrimination was probably least evident on the job. As to wages, cow-punching was, of course, by no means a highly paid occupation, regardless of race. Wages of various categories of cowhands varied widely not only from year to year and from region to region, but even within the same year and region and sometimes within the same outfit as well. Wages were generally low, but increased somewhat from the 1860s into the 1890s and were higher on the northern Range than in Texas and Kansas. An ordinary hand in the South received from a minimum $15 per month immediately after the Civil War, to $20-$30 through the late 1860s, 1870s, and into the 1880s, to as much as $45 in the 1890s. An experienced top hand would receive $5 or $10 per month more than a less experienced man, and trail hands were paid somewhat more than ordinary ranch hands. Especially experienced trail hands, below the rank of trail boss, occasionally drew double wages of as much as $60 or even $75; but a "green" boy would receive half-wages of $10-$15. The wages of trail bosses and foremen normally ranged during this period from $100 to $150. Cooks' salaries, as we have seen, might be as little as that of a top hand or as much as double an ordinary cowhand's, but customarily were $5 or $10 more than those of the best-paid cowhand in the outfit. In the North, cowhands usually got about $10 a month more than those in the South. In all cases compensation included food and, in the case of ranch hands, sleeping accommodations, such as they were.[40]

Strange though it may seem, there is no clear-cut evidence that Negro cowhands were generally or seriously discriminated against in the matter of wages, though this was obviously so with Mexicans, who sometimes received one-half to one-third that of white cowboys earning $20–25.[41] "Teddy Blue," to be sure, says of the Olive outfit, for which he worked in 1879, that they hated Mexicans and "niggers" but "hired them because they worked cheaper than white men." He gives no details, however, and the notoriously violent Olives may have been no more typical in their wage policy than in their conduct generally. On the other hand, one trail boss stated: "I have worked white Americans, Mexicans, and Negroes and they all got just the same salary."[42] Wages were so much under the control of the individual employer that no doubt Negroes were sometimes discriminated against; but such discrimination seems not to have been characteristic and, when it occurred, was never nearly as serious as that to which Mexicans were subjected.

Negroes were not discriminated against in the work permitted them—below the rank of foreman and trial boss. An experienced Negro would not be told to help the wrangler or to "eat dust" on the drag while a white greenhorn rode at point. The Negro, to be sure, was occasionally given unpleasant chores, but due to individual unfairness rather than to accepted custom. They might be given jobs that no one else would do—such as killing the calves dropped during the night on a cattle drive.[43] They were sometimes tricked or bullied into doing more than their share of work.[44] But there is no evidence that Negroes were normally expected to do double night-herding duty or guard the cattle while the whites went on a spree—merely that some cowboys were cheats or bullies who were ready to take advantage of Negroes or, for that matter, of inexperienced white cowhands.

Discrimination and segregation off the job, whether on the ranch or the cattle trail, would have been difficult. The sleeping arrangements were usually such as to defy any idea of racial segregation. Ranchowner, trail boss, Negro and white cowhands—particularly in bad weather—frequently not only slept in the same shack or tent but also shared the same blankets.[45]

A good deal of hazing and practical joking is inevitable in a community made up largely of rough and uneducated men. Negro hands, particularly those who were young, inexperienced, or timid, probably were subjected to more than their share of such horseplay. But no one in the cattle country—Negro or white, tenderfoot or old timer—was entirely immune to such treatment.[46] In the case of rough treatment that went beyond hazing and became grossly insulting or physically injurious, the Negro cowhand—nearly always a minority member of an outfit composed principally of whites—was in a difficult position. He was almost never a gunslinger. If he were, and if he succeeded in shooting a white opponent in a quarrel, it might have had very serious consequences for him. Negro cowhands rarely used, or attempted to use, a gun in a quarrel within their own outfit. One exception occurred in 1872, when Jim Kelly got the drop on a white cowboy with whom he had had words; but the boss, Print Olive, finally intervened on behalf of the threatened man.[47] Kelly, however, was not only a gunman; he was Print Olive's gunman as well, so nothing happened to him.

The Negro cowboy engaged in the same amusement as the white—on a basis ranging from apparently complete integration to rigid separation. The extent of this segregation depended upon how well the parties knew one another and, more importantly, upon whether or not the whites included women. To understand the character and degree of this segregation, and the way in which it was regarded by both whites and blacks, one must remember that the white men and women of the cow country were largely southerners, or westerners with a southern exposure, while the Negroes, if not former slaves, were usually the children of ex-slaves. Both whites and Negroes were thus acquainted, by personal experience or recent tradition, with racial *discrimination* far more severe than anything practiced in the post-bellum cow country, even though racial *segregation* under slavery was less rigid than it became during the late nineteenth century.

When ranch work was slack, particularly in the winter, the hands sometimes held a dance, either a "bunkhouse 'shindig'" in which the participants were all males or a "regular dance" with girls from neighboring ranches or from town if one was close enough. On these occasions the Negro hands had the opportunity to shine, as musicians or dancers or both. Although serving as musicians at either type of dance, they were more conspicuous as dancers in the womanless bunkhouse affairs. Indeed, they might not appear on the dance floor with white women, though, singly or in groups, they might present dancing exhibitions as part of the entertainment.[48]

Segregation in a cattle town, where the Negro cowhand was more of a stranger and white women were present, was much more clear-cut than on the familiar ranch. But even here the restrictions were not always as rigid as one might perhaps expect. On the town's streets and among members of the same outfit, segregation might be non-existent. A French baron, returning in 1883 from a visit to the Black Hills, was astonished to see a group of cowboys throwing the lasso and wrestling in front of the door to the hotel bar, with a Negro participating "on a footing of perfect equality." Consequently, he naively assumed that race prejudice had disappeared,[49] but had the cowboys *entered* the bar this illusion would probably have vanished, even though the region was the northern Range, not Gulf Coast Texas.

Even in Texas, however, segregation in the saloons was apparently informal. Whites, it seems, were served at one end of the bar, Negroes at the other. But should a white man and a Negro choose to drink and converse together in the "neutral zone" between the two sections probably no objection would be raised. If the Negro, however, moved from the saloon to a restaurant, he would encounter a completely segregated situation, partly because of the symbolic value attached to sitting down and eating together—as opposed to standing up at the same bar[50]—but principally because women might be guests in the dining room or cafe. In a town without a colored restaurant, the Negro might have food handed to him at the back door of a cafe—perhaps he might even be permitted to eat in the kitchen—but more probably would, like many white cowboys, prefer to purchase groceries and eat sitting on a hitching rail.[51] Negroes, of course, were not lodged in "white" hotels—unless they were in attendance with prominent white cattlemen—but cowboys, black and white, usually felt that they had better use for their money than to spend it on hotel rooms. They preferred to spread their "hot rolls" in a livery stable or some other sheltered spot.[52]

The most rigorously segregated cowtown establishments, at least so far as Negro cowhands were concerned, were brothels staffed with white prostitutes. However, the larger cowtowns at least, such as Dodge City, were also equipped with *bagnios* occupied by "soiled doves of color," while smaller communities usually had a few "public women" of color who operated independently. The rule that Negroes must not patronize white prostitutes did not of course bar relations between white cowhands and colored women.[53] The cowtown gambling-house, on the other hand, was apparently entirely unsegregated. A gambler who intended to separate a Negro trail hand from his wages through the more than expert use of cards and dice could hardly do so without sitting down with him at the same card or crap table.[54] The Negro cowhand was accustomed to a degree of segregation and apparently did not resent it—at least not to the extent of risking his life in defiance of the practice. Clashes between Negro cowhands and whites were exceedingly rare.

Without the services of the eight or nine thousand Negroes—a quarter of the total number of trail drivers—who during the generation after the Civil War helped to move herds up the cattle trails to shipping points, Indian reservations, and fattening grounds and who, between drives, worked on the ranches of Texas and the Indian Territory, the cattle industry would have been seriously handicapped. For apart from their considerable numbers, many of them were especially well-qualified top hands, riders, ropers, and cooks. Of the comparatively few Negroes on the northern Range, a good many were also men of conspicuous abilities who notably contributed to the industry in that region. These cowhands, in their turn, benefited from their participation in the industry, even if not to the extent that they deserved. That a degree of discrimination and segregation existed in the cattle country should not obscure the fact that, during the halcyon days of the cattle range, Negroes there frequently enjoyed greater opportunities for a dignified life than anywhere else in the United States. They worked, ate, slept, played, and on occasion fought, side-by-side with their white comrades, and their ability and courage won respect, even admiration. They were often paid the same wages as white cowboys and, in the case of certain horsebreakers, ropers, and cooks, occupied positions of considerable prestige. In a region and period characterized by violence, their lives were probably safer than they would have been in the southern cotton regions where between 1,500 and 1,600 Negroes were lynched in the two decades after 1882.[55] The skilled and handy Negro probably had a more enjoyable, if a rougher, existence as a cowhand than he would have had as a sharecropper or laborer. Bose Ikard, for example, had a rich, full, and dignified life on the west Texas frontier—as trail driver, as Indian fighter, and as Colonel Goodnight's right-hand man—more so undoubtedly than he could ever have known on a plantation in his native Mississippi.

Negro cowhands, to be sure, were not treated as "equals," except in the rude quasi-equality of the round-up, roping-pen, stampede, and river-crossing—where they were sometimes tacitly recognized even as superiors—but where else in post-Civil War America, at a time of the Negro's nadir, did so many adult Negroes and whites attain even this degree of fraternity? The cow country was no utopia for Negroes, but it did demonstrate that under some circumstances and for at least brief periods whites and blacks in significant numbers could live and work together on more nearly equal terms than had been possible in the United States for two hundred years or would be possible again for nearly another century.

Notes

1. May Davison Rhodes, *The Hired Man on Horseback: A Biography of Eugene Manlove Rhodes* (Boston, 1938), ix–xiii.
2. John Marvin Hunter, editor, *The Trail Drivers of Texas* (Nashville, 1925), 453.
3. *Ibid.,* 987, 255, 717, 157, 505, 472, 817, 138–139, 805, 718–719; R. J. (Bob) Lauderdale and John M. Doak, *Life on the Range and on the Trail,* Lela Neal Pirtle, editor (San Antonio, 1936), 169.
4. John Hendrix, *If I Can Do It Horseback* (Austin, 1963), 205.
5. John M. Hendrix, "Tribute Paid to Negro Cowmen," *The Cattleman,* XXII (Feb., 1936), 24. See also J. Frank Dobie to KWP, Jan. 30, 1953; J. Frank Dobie, *The Longhorns* (Boston, 1941), 309.
6. William A. Keleher, *The Fabulous Frontier: Twelve New Mexico Items* (Albuquerque, 1962), 162–163, 245, 271; Theodore Roosevelt, *Ranch Life and the Hunting Trail* (N.Y., 1920; 1st ed., 1888), 10–11. See also Floyd C. Bard as told to Agnes Wright Spring, in *Horse Wrangler: Sixty Years in the Saddle in Wyoming and Montana* (Norman, 1960), 12–13; Sir Cecil E. Denny, *The Law Marches West* (Toronto, 1939), 187.
7. J. Frank Dobie, *A Vaquero of the Brush Country* (Dallas, 1929), 12–13; Lauderdale and Doak, *op. cit.,* 11; Hunter, *op. cit.,* 679, 204.
8. Douglas Branch, *The Cowboy and His Interpreters* (N.Y., 1926), 42–43; Ross Santee, *Men and Horses* (N.Y., 1926); Agnes Morley Cleaveland, *No Life for a Lady* (Boston, 1941), 111;

William T. Hornaday, "The Cowboys of the Northwest," *Cosmopolitan*, II (Dec., 1886), 226; Edward Everett Dale, *Cow Country* (Norman, 1942), 46–47.

9. Branch, *op. cit.*, 42–43. "For my money he [the wrangler] was one of the most capable fellows around an outfit." Hendrix, *If I Can Do It Horseback*, 185–186.

10. Harry E. Chrisman, *The Ladder of Rivers: The Story of I.P. (Print) Olive* (Denver, 1962), 34–35, 77, 102, 147, 217, 378; Dane Coolidge, *Fighting Men of the West* (Bantam Books, 1952; 1st ed., 1932), 14, 32, 41; Frank Collinson, *Life in the Saddle*, Mary Whatley Clarke, editor (Norman, 1963), 145.

11. Charles A. Siringo, *Riata and Spurs: The Story of a Lifetime Spent in the Saddle as Cowboy and Ranger* (Boston, 1931; 1st ed., 1927), 27.

12. Ramon F. Adams to KWP, Feb. 6, 1953; Roosevelt, *op. cit.*, 10–11; Ellsworth Collings, "The Hook Nine Ranch in the Indian Territory," *Chronicles of Oklahoma*, XXXIII (Winter, 1955–56), 462; Angie Debo, editor, *The Cowman's Southwest, being the Reminiscences of Oliver Nelson, Freighter, Camp Cook, Frontiersman, in Kansas, Indian Territory, Texas, and Oklahoma, 1876–1893* (Glendale, 1963), 98–99, 107–108; Hendrix, *If I Can Do It Horseback*, 161, 205.

13. Homer Croy, *Our Will Rogers* (N.Y. and Boston, 1953), 19–20, 250, 334; Donald Day, *Will Rogers: A Biography* (N.Y., 1962), 11–16; Chrisman, 77; John Rolfe Burroughs, *Where the West Stayed Young: The Remarkable History of Brown's Park…* (N.Y., 1962), 109.

14. Collinson, *op. cit.*, 25–26; James Emmit McCauley, *A Stove-up Cowboy's Story*, with an introduction by John A. Lomax (Dallas, 1956; 1st ed., 1943), 12.

15. Hendrix, "Negro Cowmen," 24.

16. Burroughs, *op. cit.*, 192–195; Coolidge, *op. cit.*, 79; Dean Krakel, *The Saga of Tom Horn: The Story of a Cattlemen's War* (Laramie, 1954), 9–12.

17. Chrisman, *op. cit.*, 34–35, 77, 217, 378; Harry E. Chrisman, Denver, to KWP, Oct. 23, 1965.

18. Lincoln A. Lang, *Ranching with Roosevelt* (Philadelphia, 1926), 286.

19. Lewis Nordyke, *Cattle Empire: The Fabulous Story of the 3,000,000 Acre XIT* (N.Y., 1949), 138.

20. Edward Seymour Nichols, *Ed Nichols Rode a Horse*, as told to Ruby Nichols Cutbirth (Dallas, 1943), 8–9.

21. Charles A. Siringo, *A Texas Cowboy* (Signet Books, 1955; 1st ed., 1886), 82–83.

22. Bard, *op. cit.*, 67.

23. Fred Herring, Lometa, Texas, to KWP, July 20, 1965.

24. J. Evetts Haley, *George W. Littlefield, Texan* (Norman, 1943), 181–186.

25. Frederic Remington, "Vagabonding with the Tenth Horse," *The Cosmopolitan*, XXII (Feb., 1897), 352.

26. E. C. Abbott, ("Teddy Blue") and Helena Huntington Smith, *We Pointed Them North: Recollections of a Cowpuncher* (N. Y., 1939), 261–264.

27. The standard work on the cow-country cook is, of course, Ramon F. Adams, *Come an' Get It: The Story of the Old Cowboy Cook* (Norman, 1952). Almost every general work on the cowboy or the cattle country, and many reminiscences and special studies, also contain useful information.

28. Rufus Rockwell Wilson, *Out of the West* (N.Y., 1933), 377; Emerson Hough, *The Story of the Cowboy*, (N. Y., 1934; 1st ed., 1897), 138–139; J. Frank Dobie, *Cow People* (Boston, 1964), 132; Hunter, *op. cit.*, 485, 43, 307, 535, 295–303, 416–417, 981, 688, 231, 606–607, 81, 679.

29. J.S. Hart, "Jesse Hart, Callahan County Pioneer," *Frontier Times* (Jan., 1953), 86.

30. Dobie, *Vaquero*, 137–139; Cordia Sloan Duke and Joe B. Frantz, *6,000 Miles of Fence: Life on the XIT Ranch of Texas* (Austin, 1961), 172n., 84; Bard, *op. cit.*, 67.

31. John A. and Alan Lomax, *Cowboy Songs* (N.Y., 1938), 78–81, xvii–xix.

32. Max Krueger, *Pioneer Life in Texas* (San Antonio, 1930), 58–71.

33. Allen A. Erwin, *The Southwest of John H. Slaughter* (Glendale, 1965), 147–149, 159; Dobie and Frantz, *op. cit.*, between 102 and 103; Bard, *op. cit.*, 102; Dobie, *Vaquero*, 137–139.

34. Colonel Jack Potter, *Cattle Trails of the Old West* (Clayton, N.M., 1939), 79–80; Erwin, *op. cit.*, 102, 147, 150, 159, 307–308, 317, 323.

35. Burroughs, *op. cit.*, 71; Duke and Frantz, *op. cit.*, 171–172.

36. N. Howard (Jack) Thorp, *Songs of the Cowboys* (Boston, 1921), 166–168; Thorp, "Banjo in the Cow Camps," *Atlantic*, CLXVI (Aug., 1940), 195–196; Thorp, *Pardner of the Wind* (Caldwell, Ida., 1945), 22, 285.

37. J. Evetts Haley, *Charles Goodnight: Cowman & Plainsman* (Boston and N.Y., 1936), 166–167, 207, 215, 242–243; *The West Texas Historical Association Year Book* (Oct., 1942), 127.

38. Erwin, *op. cit.*, 102, 147–150, 159, 307–308, 317, 323.

39. Chrisman, *op. cit.*, 93, 124, 321, 358–359, 401.

40. All the general works on the cattle industry and most of the personal reminiscences give more or less attention to wages. Perhaps most generally useful is Louis Pelzer, *The Cattleman's Frontier…1850–1890*, (Glendale, 1936), 166, 246.

41. James W. Freeman, editor, *Poetry and Prose of the Live Stock Industry* (Denver and Kansas City, 1905), I, 559; James Henry Cook, *Fifty Years on the Old Frontier as Cowboy, Hunter, Guide, Scout, and Ranchman* (New Haven, 1925; 1st ed., 1923), 8–9.

42. Abbott and Smith, *op. cit.*, 39; Lauderdale and Doak, *op. cit.*, 183–185.

43. Haley, *Goodnight*, 136.

44. Dobie, *Vaquero*, 97, 34–36, 46–47,; James C. Shaw, *North from Texas: Incidents in the Early Life of a Range Cowman in Texas, Dakota, and Wyoming, 1852–1882*, Herbert O. Brayer, editor (Evanston, 1952) 34–36, 46–47.

45. Siringo, *Riata and Spurs*, 27; Haley, *Littlefield*, 55, 90, 93, 100–101, 114, 134; J. Evetts Haley, *Jeff Milton: A Good Man with a Gun* (Norman, 1948), 19.

46. Debo, *op. cit.*, 108; Dobie, *Longhorns*, 107–108; Hunter, *op. cit.*, 205; Ray M. Beauchamp, "The Town That Died Laughing," *Frontier Times* (Summer, 1960), 30–31, 50–52; Clifford P. Westermeier, editor, *Trailing the Cowboy: His Life and Lore as Told by Frontier Journalists* (Caldwell, Ida., 1955), 202–203.

47. Chrisman, *op. cit.*, 104, 201; Harry E. Chrisman, Denver, to KWP, Oct. 23, 1965.

48. Duke and Frantz, *op. cit.*, 102–103, 189–190; Ross Santee, *Lost Pony Tracks* (Bantam Books, 1956; 1st ed., 1953), 158–159.

49. Edmond Mandat-Gracey, *Cow-Boys and Colonels: Narrative of a Journey across the Prairie and over the Black Hills of Dakota*, translated by William Conn (Philadelphia and N.Y., 1963), 325–326.

50. Harry Golden, *Only in America* (Permabooks, 1959; 1st ed., 1958), 105–107, presenting his "Vertical Negro Plan" for abolishing segregation, advances the theory that no southerner objected to mingling with Negroes so long as neither party sat down!

51. See Rhodes, *op. cit.*, 86–88, for the attempt of a Negro to eat in a white restaurant in a New Mexico cowtown.

52. George Bolds, *Across the Cimarron: The Adventures of "Cimarron" George Bolds, Last of the Frontiermen*, as he related his life story to James D. Horan (N.Y. 1956), 48–49; John L. McCarty, *Maverick Town: The Story of Old Tascosa* (Norman, 1946), 149.

53. Nyle E. Miller and Joseph W. Snell, *Why the West Was Wild* (Topeka, 1963), 614–615, 127, 453; Burroughs, *op. cit.*, 71; William R. Cox, *Luke Short and His Era* (Garden City, N. Y., 1961), 54–55; Westermeier, *Trailing the Cowboy*, 209, 213; Walker D. Wyman and Bruce Sibert, *Nothing But Prairie and Sky: Life on the Dakota Range in the Early Days* (Norman, 1954), 142–143.

54. Lauderdale and Doak, *op. cit.*, 161; Haley, *Jeff Milton*, 95; Rhodes, *op. cit.*, 86–88; W. M. Hutchinson, editor, *A Bar Cross Man: The Life & Personal Writings of Eugene Manlove Rhodes* (Norman, 1956), 3–5.

55. Walter White, *Rope & Faggot: A Biography of Judge Lynch* (N.Y., 1929), *passim*; Jessie Parkhurst Guzman, editor, *Negro Year Book, 1941–1946* (Tuskegee, Ala., 1947), 306–307.

INTEGRATION, EXCLUSION, OR SEGREGATION? THE "COLOR LINE" IN KANSAS, 1878–1900

Randall B. Woods

[This article originally appeared in the *Western Historical Quarterly*, Vol. 14 (1983), pp. 181–198. Copyright by the Western History Association. Reprinted with permission.]

The passage of the Kansas-Nebraska Act in 1854 turned Kansas into a battleground between proslavery and antislavery advocates. A few southerners moved to the new territory with their slaves, but Congress—with some southern members having resigned—made Kansas a free state in 1861. Then, after congressional Republicans abandoned southern blacks and agreed to end the Reconstruction experiment in 1877, thousands of ex-slaves left the South. The vast majority of these migrants headed to the North, but several thousand went west. These "exodusters" saw Kansas as the promised land. It was where John Brown had become a hero to the abolition movement by killing white southerners in the late 1850s. And for those African Americans moving from Mississippi, Louisiana, and other southern states, Kansas was the nearest western territory that had not been a part of the old slavery empire.

Many exodusters were disillusioned with Kansas. Some went back to the South, others joined fellow ex-slaves in the North, and still others pushed on west to eastern Colorado and other frontier territories and states. But many stayed in Kansas where they filed homestead claims and began farming; some even banded together and founded all-black agricultural colonies like Dunlap and Nicodemus. Other exodusters opted for an urban existence and created African American communities in larger established towns such as Topeka and Kansas City. But whether they lived

The Shores Family. Hundreds of African American families homesteaded in Kansas, Nebraska, and other western states in the late nineteenth century. The Shores family posed for this photo in front of their Custer County, Nebraska, home in 1887. (Courtesy, Nebraska State Historical Society.)

in segregated rural settlements or in black neighborhoods in "white" cities, blacks found themselves members of a Kansas society dominated by the Caucasian race.

In the following article, Randall B. Woods examines the lives of black Kansans from the time of the post-Reconstruction exodus to the end of the nineteenth century. Specifically, he looks at their relationships in dealing with individuals and organized groups within white society. While he finds that racial prejudice existed in late nineteenth-century Kansas, he concludes—as have most historians who have studied western race relations in other frontier regions of that era—that it was not as widespread nor as pervasive as that experienced by African Americans who chose to remain in the Jim Crow South rather than make the trek west. But while this was the case, it was also true that Kansas—and the West in general—was not a utopian promised land for black pioneers. Life in the frontier West was difficult for all of its inhabitants, but it was doubly so for African Americans because they had to bear the burden of prejudice imposed upon them by the majority (white) segment of society.

Black Americans everywhere anticipated that the Civil War would bring in its wake unparalleled opportunities for their race. Had not the slavemasters been driven from the field of battle in ignominious defeat? Afro-Americans of all conditions, classes, and sections looked forward eagerly to the fruits of full citizenship. Rather quickly Negroes realized that the North's commitment to equal rights was transitory and that the South was merely biding time, waiting for the chance to exclude the freedman from participation in the political process and relegate him to a servile status in the region's economic system. By 1876 North and South were ready to make their peace. Northern businessmen, a dominant element in the Republican party, were anxious to finance the industrialization of the South and were more than willing to abandon the Negro in return for that privilege. Believing the campaign for black suffrage and equal rights to be a threat to "orderly economic development" and to the survival of the Republican party in the South, northern business leaders announced that the racial question was now passé and urged the nation to move on to the more pressing problems of industrialization and commerce. Thus, reconciliation and nationalism became the order of the day, but they were accomplished at the expense of the Afro-American.[1] Following the Compromise of 1877, the black man's condition deteriorated not only in Dixie but throughout the country. The Negrophobia that began building with the fall of Radical Reconstruction culminated in the late 1880s and 1890s. Various southern states incorporated disenfranchisement provisions into their constitutions and mandated racial separation on railroads. School segregation and the convict lease system became widespread throughout the South. Lynchings reached an all-time high in 1892. The situation was better for blacks in the North, but even there they increasingly encountered extralegal discrimination and segregation. Their economic situation became ever more precarious as competition from millions of European immigrants forced blacks out of even menial jobs.[2]

But what of blacks living in the American West during the last quarter of the nineteenth century? Was Jim Crow—that is, institutionalized discrimination and segregation—as pervasive for them as for their brethren east of the Mississippi? Or did the frontier environment, with its alleged emphasis on rugged individualism, enterprise, and pragmatism, allow human beings to work out their destinies regardless of race?[3] Insofar as one western state, Kansas, is concerned, the answer lies somewhere in between.

In April 1879 the *New West Monthly* promised blacks intent upon immigrating to the Sunflower State that they could expect to find "a school for every child;—a field to labor;/ respect that sees in every man a neighbor; the richest soil a farmer ever saw/ and equal rights to all before the law."[4] The *New*

West's portrait of Kansas was overdrawn. Black Kansans encountered discrimination in public services and in the administration of justice; segregation in hotels, restaurants, and theaters; and exclusion from white hospitals, churches, and neighborhoods. And yet during the same period there were integrated schools at one level or another in all regions of Kansas; public facilities were open to Negroes on both an integrated and segregated basis; and all the major and minor political parties actively courted the black vote. Except in public schools in the larger cities and in the state militia for a period, legally mandated segregation and exclusion were nonexistent. While Kansans were willing, for the most part, to allow blacks access to facilities and institutions considered essential to the individual's health and safety—on an integrated basis if necessary—they were not willing to condone "social equality," that is, racial mixing in neighborhoods, places of amusement, churches, and fraternal societies. In short, they were committed to what George Fredrickson has called the doctrine of parallel development. According to this white view of racial uplift, blacks would be accorded equal protection under the law and equal opportunity in the marketplace. If the proper genes and moral fiber were present, blacks would progress simultaneously, though separately, with whites.

The black community in Kansas actually began taking shape between 1860 and 1870 when several thousand newly emancipated slaves moved to the state. They were joined by a smaller number of free blacks from the North who perceived Kansas to be a land of political and especially economic opportunity.[5] This influx was a mere prelude, however, to the in-migration of tens of thousands of oppressed blacks from the South that occurred from 1879 to 1881. The Great Exodus, as this extraordinary population movement came to be known, actually began in the late 1870s when at the urging of two ex-slaves— Benjamin "Pap" Singleton of Tennessee and Henry Adams of Georgia— several hundred downtrodden Negroes left the South and established colonies in Kansas. Among the best known were Dunlap Colony, established in 1878 in Morris County in eastern Kansas; Morton City, founded in 1877 in Hodgeman County in the west-central part of the state; and Nicodemus, established in 1877 in Graham County in western Kansas.[6] Then, in early 1879, boatloads of indigent blacks began arriving in St. Louis from Louisiana, Texas, and Mississippi. By the end of February, anywhere from fifty to six hundred were arriving daily. From St. Louis the exodusters moved on via the Missouri River to Wyandotte and the "promised land" beyond. A large number spread out and settled in the larger towns of eastern Kansas—Lawrence, Topeka, Atchison, Kansas City, and Leavenworth—where most found jobs as laborers. In October and November 1879 a group of exodusters, primarily from Texas, settled in Labette County in southeast Kansas, most of them in the towns of Chetopa, Oswego, and Parsons. Intent on becoming independent landowners, a small number of the more ambitious immigrants moved on to Nicodemus or founded new rural colonies in Coffey and Chatauqua counties. The number of blacks who arrived in Kansas during this period is difficult to calculate with any precision. Although some estimates are as large as eighty thousand, most sources state that between forty thousand and sixty thousand made the trek.[7]

The 1870–1882 migration of blacks to Kansas, particularly the much-publicized post–1878 phase of the movement, was the product primarily of the deteriorating racial climate in the South following the collapse of Reconstruction. It was a series of specific events in the late 1870s, however, that crystallized black dissatisfaction and served as a catalyst for the Great Exodus. Among the most important was an 1878 crop failure, which caused widespread suffering and intense economic frustration among black sharecroppers. In addition to the economic factor, blacks in the South, particularly in Louisiana, believed that constitutional proscription was imminent and that they had best leave while they still had the freedom to do so. Still another spur to migration was the pressure exerted by special interests—land companies and railroads, for example—that would profit from rapid population of the West. No less significant was Kansas's historical appeal as the home of John Brown. The state had never permitted slavery and had consistently voted for Lincoln's party. And finally, there was what Nell Painter has dubbed the Kansas Fever idea. According to Painter, southern blacks responded to the racial violence, proscription, and economic exploitation that was their lot in the 1870s by developing and proclaiming the Kansas Fever myth, in which the federal government promised all black people who wanted to go to Kansas free transportation, free land, and free supplies and subsistence for the first year.[8]

By 1882 the Great Exodus was over. Even before its end, however, black and white had set about working out a permanent *modus vivendi*. Black Kansans probably fared better at the hands of whites in politics than in any other field. The word *white* appeared in three places in Kansas's first constitution adopted at Wyandotte in 1859, the first time in a clause barring blacks from voting. Article V extended the franchise to every white male person of twenty-one years and upward.[9] In 1867 Kansans reaffirmed their racism, defeating by nearly a two-to-one vote a constitutional amendment striking the word *white* from the suffrage clause.[10] Indeed, Kansas voters did not actually amend the constitution to provide for adult male suffrage until 1918. Nevertheless, blacks were effectively enfranchised in 1870 when Kansans ratified the Fifteenth Amendment to the United States Constitution.[11] Although there were innumerable attempts by both

Democrats and Republicans to purchase black votes, there was no concentrated effort during the late nineteenth century to disfranchise Negroes. And although they comprised no more than 6 percent of the population, black Kansans cast from 15 to 20 percent of the votes; and during any given year between 1878 and 1900, blacks played no small part in the political history of the state.[12]

The political clout of the black population was enhanced by the fact that it was concentrated in the state's populous, eastern counties. In 1880 one out of every six persons in greater Topeka and one out of every five in Kansas City, Kansas, was a Negro. A decade later almost two-thirds (31,633) of the state's black population lived in ten counties, and a majority (28,170) lived in cities of over 2,500. Kansas Republicans in particular could ill afford to ignore black voters and politicians. By 1880 there were forty-three thousand Negroes in the state, and the vast majority consistently cast their lot with the GOP. The revival of the Democratic party in the mid-1880s and the emergence of the Populists in the early 1890s served to enhance the importance of the black vote in the eyes of the GOP leaders, particularly given the fact that the Democrats and Populists actively competed for the black vote and nominated blacks for city, county, and state office. Negroes took advantage of the situation to secure a disproportionate number of appointive positions and nominations and to compel the GOP to consult blacks in formulating policy.

The constitutional convention that met at Wyandotte not only barred blacks from voting but also excluded them from serving in the state militia.[13] Anticipating that they eventually would be able to compel the legislature to integrate the national guard, blacks during the 1880s proceeded to organize "independent" militia units—the Lawrence Guards and the Garfield Rifles of Leavenworth, for example.[14] And in fact, in 1888, following a concerted campaign of protest and lobbying, they persuaded the legislature to strike the word *white* from the militia clause in the constitution.[15] Nonetheless, black units had to wait until the political turmoil of the 1890s made it possible for them to be officially incorporated into the Kansas National Guard. Governor John W. Leedy, a Populist elected in 1896 on a fusion ticket of Democrats and Populists, was subsequently unable to hold his political coalition together. Alarmed by Republican William McKinley's presidential victory in 1896 and facing reelection in 1898, Leedy actively courted the black vote. As a result, when the Spanish-American war erupted and black Kansans clamored for an all-black volunteer outfit, Leedy accepted a Negro regiment as part of the state's quota and agreed to appoint only Negro officers to command it.[16]

The framers of the 1859 constitution did not exclude Negroes from public schools as they had from the polls and the militia, but they did provide for the establishment of separate systems. In fact, the 1867 session of the state legislature enacted a law stipulating that tax monies collected for school purposes be kept separate and that each race was to benefit from only those facilities and instructors for which it could pay directly.[17] The Kansas legislature ratifying the Fourteenth Amendment in 1868 did not believe the amendment applied to public education and made no attempt to alter the state's legally mandated system of segregation. In 1874, however, Kansas solons passed a civil rights measure making it a crime for the regents or trustees of any state university, college, or other school of public instruction to "make any distinction on account of race, color, or previous condition of servitude."[18] When in 1878 the legislature passed and the people ratified an amendment to the constitution striking the word *white* from the educational clause, it seemed that legalized Jim Crow in Kansas schools was at an end. The very next year, however, Kansas lawmakers once again reversed themselves when a Republican legislature decided that cities of the first class (ten thousand population or more) had the authority to establish separate primary schools for whites and blacks.[19] This was the *de jure* situation as of 1879, but Kansas school districts did not always follow the letter of the law.

Cities of the first class did generally provide separate schools for blacks. In Leavenworth, for example, black children of elementary school age were educated either in the North Leavenworth or South Leavenworth Colored School. The building in the northern part of the city was evidently quite inferior to those structures reserved for whites; one observer described it as a "hut" situated in a "low, dirty-looking hollow close to a stinking old muddy creek, with a railroad running almost directly over the building."[20] In 1865 Topeka city officials rented a small frame building to be used as a primary school; blacks were taught in the attic while whites learned their ABCs in the lower rooms. Although the system had expanded by the 1881–1882 school year to include fourteen elementary schools, segregation still ruled supreme: two of the facilities were all-black and twelve were all-white. Wichita and Lawrence in the 1880s and 1890s and Atchison in the 1890s were the only three Kansas cities of the first class that boasted mixed elementary schools.[21]

Cities of the second class, such as Ft. Scott, were divided into wards. Each ward had its own elementary school, and since blacks were concentrated in one or two areas of the city, de facto segregation was the result.[22] Grade schools in some of the state's smaller towns, such as Hiawatha and Emporia were fully integrated, but faculties in these mixed institutions were usually white.[23] In a few communities the white backlash that followed the exodus of 1879 led to segregation where integration had previously existed. In Olathe, for example, whites and blacks attended the same school in the 1870s, but following an influx into the community of several hundred Negroes from 1879 to 1881, the school board decided it would be better if blacks had their own school with their own teachers.[24] As was the case in cities of the first class, separate facilities in the smaller towns were grossly inferior.[25]

Rural counties were divided into school districts, each having a country schoolhouse with all elementary grades taught in one room. These schools were generally mixed; it must be noted, however, that outside the all-black colonies of Nicodemus and Dunlap, the number of blacks living in outlying areas was relatively small.[26]

High schools in the larger cities and some Kansas colleges were integrated. Indeed, in cities of the first class the black community graduated proportionately only slightly fewer children from high school than did whites.[27] Ironically, it was more difficult for blacks to gain admittance to secondary schools in towns of the second and third class than in those of the first.[28] Wathena admitted colored students to its high school for the first time in 1895, and even then integration was temporary.[29] After a number of white parents strenuously objected, the school board ordered the black scholars expelled. In Jefferson County the superintendent made certain that the high school remained all-white by requiring black applicants to take a special examination.[30] At the college level, Washburn College and the Emporia State Normal School both admitted Negroes, while the state university at Lawrence admitted and graduated blacks on a regular basis.[31] The medical school during this period, however, drew a rigid color line.[32]

There were definite disadvantages to attending a mixed school. One white school teacher in Lawrence discriminated in the manner and degree of punishment he administered; he whipped white transgressors with a switch and blacks with a cowhide.[33] Others made derogatory statements about Negroes in class and graded discriminatorily.[34] A white instructor in the rural school at Gladden near Wathena installed separate water buckets for whites and blacks. When several black students partook of the water for whites, he expelled them. Some black leaders claimed that white instructors in all-black primary schools had been ordered by their school boards to neglect their students, thus retarding their progress and keeping them out of the mixed high schools.[35]

Blacks seeking access to public facilities encountered exclusion, segregation, and integration. Those establishments applying the color line perhaps most frequently were hotels. When the Shawnee County delegation to the Republican congressional convention (called to choose Republican nominees for the forthcoming senate and house races) sought lodging at the Coolidge Hotel in

Topeka, they were turned away because three of their number were colored.[36] That same year no less a figure than ex-state auditor Edward P. McCabe was denied lodgings at the Blossom House Hotel in Kansas City because he was black (although he could have passed for white had he chosen to do so).[37] In 1888 a white innkeeper in Leavenworth turned away the illustrious Frederick Douglass. The Tennessee Jubilee Singers, while touring the state in 1896, were refused accommodations by three different hotels in Wichita.[38] In addition, a majority of Kansas restaurants either excluded or segregated blacks.[39] One of the famous 1883 Civil Rights cases involved a Negro, Bird Gee, who was physically ejected from the City Hotel Restaurant in Hiawatha.[40] Restaurants in Coffeyville, Lawrence, Topeka, and Leavenworth also refused to admit Negroes. Segregation was apparently less frequent in restaurants than exclusion, but there were Jim Crow sections in some establishments. A letter to the editor of the Leavenworth *Advocate* in 1890 from an irate black customer complained of a restaurant "between 4th and 5th streets" that forced Negro patrons to retire to a dark room in the rear of the establishment "with a curtain drawn over him as though he was going to have his picture taken."[41]

And yet segregation and exclusion were by no means universal in hotels and restaurants. Refused accommodations in Leavenworth, Douglass moved on to Topeka, where he was received and feted at one of the largest hotels in the city. Rebuffed by the Coolidge Hotel in Emporia, the Shawnee County Republican delegation was welcomed at the nearby Merchants Hotel. In 1878 the Topeka *Colored Citizen* praised the Taft House Hotel and adjoining restaurant as establishments that "never discriminate as to color."[42] Even in Leavenworth— headquarters of the proslavery element in Kansas prior to the Civil War and a hotbed of Democracy in the late nineteenth century—there were hotels and restaurants open to blacks on an integrated basis.[43]

In transportation, blacks could ride street cars without having to worry about being relegated to a designated section. The first separate coach did not appear on a Kansas railroad until 1892.[44]

Black urban dwellers in Kansas, no less than their brethren in Illinois, Michigan, and New York, had to put up with residential segregation and discrimination in public services. Blacks who came to Kansas in the 1860s and 1870s and purchased homes in Topeka, Wyandotte, Leavenworth, Atchison, Lawrence, or some other eastern town tended to cluster, but they were not excluded from all-white neighborhoods.[45] Apparently, the thousands of blacks who poured into the state during the exodus heightened the white community's desire to see blacks restricted to a certain section of a particular city and led to the creation of what could accurately be called ghettos—"Mississippi Town,"

"Juniper Bottoms," and "Rattlebone Hollow" in Kansas City, and "Redmonds-ville" and "Tennesseetown" in Topeka. It is unclear just what the exact tipping point—that is, the percentage of blacks in each given community necessary to trigger segregation—was for each Kansas town. What is clear is that in each town whose black population totaled 7 percent or more, residential segregation existed.[46] Apparently, in Kansas, just as in other areas, residential segregation was the product primarily of white hostility rather than black clannishness. "To people living outside of Kansas this may seem strange but it is nevertheless true," reported the editor of the *American Citizen* in 1889. "There are houses and lots and additions in and near this city [Topeka] where no negro can rent or buy at any price, let him be ever so talented, cultured or refined, and there are others where if he rents or buys, his life and property are in danger."[47] John R. Davis, a black minister living in Topeka, who was warned via a note on his door to leave the white suburb of Oakland or suffer irreparable damage to his health, complained that many of Topeka's finest white citizens—teachers, lawyers, doctors—moved into the worst white slums rather than live by a Negro. Those whites who dared to stand up for the black man's right to live where he wanted were denounced and ostracized.[48]

Blacks in Leavenworth, Lawrence, Topeka, and Kansas City not only had to live in designated areas, but they had to endure discrimination in public services as well. Streets in Tennesseetown or Mudville were either riddled with potholes or went unpaved completely; sidewalks were often nonexistent; and white fire departments frequently took two to three times as long to answer a call in black sections as they did to respond to an alarm in white areas.[49]

Black Kansans applying for jobs in the public sector, such as firemen, policemen, janitors, and sanitary workers, and those seeking admittance to state institutions encountered some discrimination, but it was the exception rather than the rule. In every Kansas town of the first class and in some of the second, the police force was integrated. The city marshal of Lawrence as of 1880 was a Negro. Some of the urban fire departments were integrated, and Kansas City could boast an all-black fire company. In Topeka alone in 1889 there were thirteen black policemen and nine black firemen.[50] Apparently, all of the state-funded "charitable institutions" of Kansas, such as the State Insane Asylum, School for the Blind, and Asylum for Imbecilic and Idiotic Youth, were open to blacks. These institutions were extremely crowded, however—waiting lists usually contained from fifty to two hundred names—and not only blacks but whites without political influence found it difficult to gain admission.[51] There was some segregation within these institutions, but not on a systematic basis. In 1894 the parents of fourteen-year-old Eva Vance, a student at the blind institute, complained in the *Leavenworth Advocate* that their daughter was forced to sleep in a poorly ventilated room with two other colored inmates. Negro editor B. K. Bruce insisted, however, that this was the first complaint lodged concerning the treatment of Negroes in public institutions in the history of Kansas.[52]

Equality under the law and due process were realities only for black Kansans of property and influence. The poor and undereducated—that is, the vast majority of Negroes in the state—encountered discrimination at virtually every stage of the legal process. Negroes were more likely to be lynched than whites, although the lynching of whites was by no means uncommon in frontier Kansas.[53] In 1879 the residents of Ft. Scott hung and then burned the body of one Bill Howard, an alleged black outlaw.[54] In 1887 Richard Woods, a colored youth accused of assaulting and raping a fifteen-year-old white girl in Leavenworth, was taken from the county jail by a mob of white men who tied him by the neck to the pommel of a saddle and dragged him for more than a mile.[55] Blacks accused of raping white women were lynched near Hiawatha in 1889 and Larned in 1892.[56] And yet lynchings in Kansas were rare in comparison to the southern states, and the number per annum declined steadily from 1870 through 1900.[57] A disproportionate number of inmates at the state prison at Lansing—approximately 25 percent of the prison population throughout the last quarter of the nineteenth century—were black.[58] This imbalance was in part due to the fact that the crime rate among urban-dwelling blacks was higher than that among whites. It must be noted, however, that blacks were more likely than whites to be arrested as suspects, they were more likely to be convicted, and they were almost certain to receive longer sentences.[59] In May 1890, for example, two men—one white and one black—were convicted of the identical crime of selling liquor. The white was pardoned, while the black received both a jail term and a fine. In 1896 the *Leavenworth Herald* insisted that a Negro man had recently been sentenced to twenty-six years in prison for breaking into a white citizen's house and stealing a bottle of wine.[60] Others were incarcerated for taking food; often the value of the stolen item was increased in order that the black offender might be convicted of grand larceny rather than a misdemeanor. Whites accused of crimes against Negroes were less likely to be convicted; and if found guilty, whites were more likely to receive lighter sentences than if the offenses had been committed against whites.[61] There was some discrimination in jury selection, but blacks served on state district court juries throughout the late nineteenth century, even in cases involving two whites. The determining factors in the selection process seem to have been economic and social standing rather than color.[62] Black lawyers were admitted to practice in all areas of the state where there were sizable black communities, and for several years the city attorney of Kansas City was a black man, B. S. Smith.[63]

In social organizations and institutions regarded as nonessential to the individual's health and safety, white Kansans tended to draw the color line rigidly.[64] Virtually all white churches in the state and several YMCA chapters excluded blacks.[65] Theater and opera house owners generally insisted on segregating their audiences except when their facilities were being used for political gatherings.[66] With the exception of the Knights of Labor and one or two other organizations, labor unions in Kansas excluded blacks from membership or compelled them to form separate chapters.[67] Black individuals and organizations were often excluded from public functions and celebrations. In 1890 the Grand Army of the Republic (GAR) prevented a detachment of colored veterans from attending the unveiling of a monument to Ulysses S. Grant in Leavenworth. In 1889 the Topeka colored fire company was turned away from a picnic given in gratitude by a citizen whose house had been saved by local fire fighters.[68]

Although Kansas blacks were generally excluded from white-collar jobs, virtually all types of skilled and unskilled labor were open to them. Railroads hired blacks as porters, construction workers, and brakemen. The meat-packing houses in Topeka and Kansas City were important sources of employment. The Armour facility at one time employed several hundred Negroes.[69] Blacks also found work as hod carriers, carpenters, waiters, and stone masons.[70] The coal mines around Pittsburg, Leavenworth, and Oswego were major employers of Negroes. One Riverside Coal Company mine near Leavenworth was worked by 126 blacks and four whites. The four whites, to be sure, were the check-weighman, engineer, pit boss, and top foreman.[71]

While Negroes suffered from discrimination and sometimes exclusion at the hands of management, the chief hindrance to their efforts to find a secure means of livelihood was the hostility of white labor. In 1880 one C. H. Peck, who was in the process of building a meat-packing house at Atchison, hired a number of laborers at $1.25 per day rather than at the usual $1.50. Among the new employees were three blacks. White workers blamed the Negroes for their cut in wages, an angry mob formed, and the three blacks fled. The enraged workers did not stop there, but proceeded to Seip and Company Brick Yard and compelled more than a dozen black employees to run for their lives. In 1894 in Leavenworth the management of the electric streetcar system promoted James Brown, colored, from shop foreman to motorman. A majority of the white employees voted to strike, but changed their minds when management expressed indifference and publicized the fact that the waiting list for positions within the municipal transit system numbered more than two hundred. Not surprisingly, white working-class hostility produced in Negro leaders a rather deep-seated conservatism. "It is a well-known fact," editor George A. Dudley wrote in the *American Citizen* in 1894, "that the opposition to and oppression of the Negro in this country do not come from the wealthy and intelligent classes but from the laboring and less intelligent masses."[72]

There were no antimiscegenation laws on the books in Kansas. Newspapers around the state contained numerous accounts of mixed marriages, most of which were tolerated. Editorial and private comments indicate that the lack of violent reaction to these cases was due to the fact that whites believed these relationships were aberrations limited to the dregs of society rather than the product of a commitment to racial amalgamation.[73]

The mixed racial situation in late nineteenth-century Kansas—segregated housing, integrated police forces, segregated and integrated schools in the same community, exclusion and segregation in "nonessential" social institutions and public facilities, integrated politics—was a function primarily of white attitudes. True, blacks were hardly passive and in many instances acted collectively to determine their own fate. On a number of occasions armed Negroes intervened to prevent lynchings. Black leaders used their political clout to blunt various racist initiatives by white supremacists and to have the word *white* removed from the state constitution.[74] Yet in a state where the black population amounted to no more than 6 percent at any given time, it is reasonable to assume that the attitudes of the white majority constituted the determining factor in race relations.[75]

There were in Kansas, of course, a group of extreme Negrophobes, ex-Confederates, Irish immigrants, and blue-collar workers who feared job and welfare competition from blacks. To one degree or another, the social status of these individuals as perceived by them depended upon the maintenance of an ironclad caste system.[76] The extreme Negrophobes constituted a minority of the general population, however, and an even smaller minority of those who controlled the economic and political life of the state. Racial prejudice in Kansas peaked during the height of the exodus when whites—fearful that the influx of blacks would bring in its wake job competition, increased taxation, contagious disease, and a crime wave—resurrected a number of ugly stereotypes in their efforts to halt the flood.[77] Once it became clear that the migration was temporary and that Negroes would continue to constitute only a small minority of the population, most whites ceased to feel threatened. A number of factors militated thereafter against the emergence of extreme racism. Among the more important was the state's historical background. There had never been, save perhaps briefly during the 1879–1881 period, any genuine fear of black political and economic domination. Kansas had not experienced the "trauma" of Reconstruction; there was no debt to settle with Negroes, carpetbaggers, and scalawags. For the most part, those whites who controlled Kansas and thus who were in a position to determine racial policies, both *de jure* and de facto, were old Free-Soilers and members of the GAR. Eugene Berwanger points out that most Free-Soilers in Kansas and throughout the West were urban immigrants from the East or non-slaveholding southerners who hated slavery and Negroes equally.[78] This may have been true, but following the Civil War this group was locked into a Republican party that came under repeated and sometimes successful challenge from Democrats and Populists. Prejudiced though they were, many Free-Soilers realized that one way to retain power in Kansas was to make use of the black vote. Once committed to voting rights for blacks, this element found it difficult to oppose the Negro's civil rights in other areas. Joining the old Free-Soilers in supporting civil and political rights for blacks were the Quakers, Presbyterians, and Congregationalists who had moved to Kansas after the war and were imbued with a sense of mission toward the Negro.[79]

Moreover, Kansans in general were self-consciously western, convinced that they had a reputation to maintain for frontier hospitality, openness, and freedom. Kansas should be to the freedman of the South what America was to the European immigrant—a refuge from tyranny and oppression, a land where due process and equality before the law were the inalienable rights of all citizens.[80] In addition, as Kenneth Wiggins Porter has pointed out, the fluidity and individuality of the frontier made it possible for the Negro to be seen, within limits, as a distinct personality rather than a preconceived stereotype.[81] "If a man, white or black, is decent, respectful, and respectable," insisted a prominent white newspaper editor and Union veteran, "he should be treated in a decent and respectful manner."[82] Finally, the extreme prejudice against the Indian that prevailed in Kansas during the last quarter of the century may also have worked to the black man's advantage. At least Negroes were capable of farming and laboring; at least they had sense enough to try and learn the white man's ways and to want to become assimilated.[83]

For most white Kansans, then, a rigid system of Jim Crow was unnecessary. Blacks did not constitute enough of a political or economic threat to warrant total ostracism. Whites were certainly anxious to control the black population, but exclusion or pervasive segregation seemed unsuited to the state's particular history and circumstances. The doctrine of parallel development did. According to this approach to race relations, the Negro was not genetically inferior. He possessed the capacity for intellectual development, moral growth, and material advancement common to all human beings.[84] Whites had an obligation to provide their black brethren with an education and moral guidance, but once these services were rendered, it was the white man's duty to leave the Negro alone to pull himself up by the bootstraps. "The black man has now in his hands in this country all the resources of progress and future power," editorialized the Kansas City *Star*. "If he chooses to remain ignorant, he will be cheated and despoiled…but if he chooses to walk up the ascending way…then he sees into the high atmosphere of freedom and enlightenment."[85] There was a fine line between justice and charity that if crossed would destroy the individual initiative of the Negro and negate any real chance he had for independence and self-reliance. Moreover, Negro advancement did not require assimilation. "Social equality," defined by white Kansans as racial mixing in areas considered nonessential to the individual's health and safety—that is, neighborhoods, places of amusement, churches, and fraternal societies—was irrelevant to attainment of the American Dream. Those who advocated integration in these situations ignored the obvious natural differences between the two races.

The principal of parallel development that underlay race relations, and in fact largely determined racial conditions in late nineteenth-century Kansas, was a compromise between white Kansas's self-image and its sublimated prejudices; in practice, it did much to freeze an unjust status quo. The idea that equal rights led to equal opportunities was based on the assumption that all competitors started at approximately the same place. Whites, who controlled at least 90 percent of the property in Kansas, had not had to deal with slavery, the share-crop/crop-lien system, and pervasive racial prejudice. In brief, the theory and practice of parallel development produced a racial climate in which blacks enjoyed a relatively high degree of physical and psychological freedom, but which was hardly egalitarian.

Notes

1. August Meier, *Negro Thought in America, 1880–1915: Racial Ideologies in the Age of Booker T. Washington* (Ann Arbor, 1963), 22, 26.
2. Ibid., 19.
3. The publication of C. Vann Woodward, *The Strange Career of Jim Crow* (New York, 1955) marked the beginning of a decade of intensive research into post-Civil War race relations. Joel Williamson, Frenise Logan, Roger Fischer, Howard Rabinowitz, and a host of other scholars wrote in-depth studies designed to confirm or deny the hypothesis outlined in Jim Crow, namely that institutionalized discrimination and segregation did not appear in the South until the 1890s and that it was the product primarily of the politics of the 1890s. In addition, during this same period, scholars of the black experience have produced a number of quality monographs dealing with northern race relations prior to World War I. Each has

found essentially the same pattern of exclusion from public and private health facilities; discrimination in hiring; separation in restaurants, hotels, transit systems, and places of amusement; and rigid residential segregation. With the notable exceptions of K. W. Porter's articles on the pre-Civil War frontier, William H. Leckie's study of the black soldier, Philip Durham's work on the Negro cowboy, and Eugene Berwanger's history of western Negrophobia during the slavery extension controversy, little attention has been paid to the American West from students of the black-white dialogue. Joel Williamson, *After Slavery: The Negro in South Carolina during Reconstruction, 1861–1877* (Chapel Hill, 1965); Frenise A. Logan, *The Negro in North Carolina, 1876–1894* (Chapel Hill, 1964); Roger A. Fischer, *The Segregation Struggle in Louisiana, 1862–77* (Urbana, 1974); Howard N. Rabinowitz, "From Exclusion to Segregation: Southern Race Relations, 1865–1890," *Journal of American History,* LXIII (September 1976), 325–50; Leon F. Litwack, *North of Slavery: The Negro in the Free States, 1790–1860* (Chicago, 1961); David M. Katzman, *Before the Ghetto: Black Detroit in the Nineteenth Century* (Urbana, 1973); Allan H. Spear, *Black Chicago: The Making of a Negro Ghetto, 1890–1920* (Chicago, 1967); Kenneth Wiggins Porter, *The Negro on the American Frontier* (New York, 1971); William H. Leckie, *The Buffalo Soldiers: A Narrative of the Negro Cavalry in the West* (Norman, 1967); Philip Durham, "The Negro Cowboy," *American Quarterly,* VII (Fall 1955), 291–302; and Eugene H. Berwanger, *The Frontier against Slavery: Western Anti-Negro Prejudice and the Slavery Extension Controversy* (Urbana, 1967).

4. "Negro Immigration," *New West Monthly,* I (April 1879), 131.

5. Leland Smith, "Early Negroes in Kansas" (master's thesis, Wichita State University, 1932), 27.

6. *Topeka Colored Citizen,* January 11, 1879. See also Robert G. Athearn, *In Search of Canaan: Black Migration to Kansas, 1879–80* (Lawrence, Kansas, 1978), 76.

7. Marie Deacon, "Kansas As the Promised Land: The View of the Black Press, 1890–1900" (master's thesis, University of Arkansas, 1973), 5–6; Roy Garvin, "Benjamin or 'Pap' Singleton and His Followers," *Journal of Negro History,* 33 (January 1948), 14; Robert A. Swann, Jr., "The Ethnic Heritage of Topeka, Kansas: Immigrant Beginnings" (n.p., Institute of Comparative Ethnic Studies, 1974), 65–68, unpublished manuscript, Kansas Historical Society; Lee Ella Blake, "The Great Exodus of 1879 and 1880 to Kansas" (master's thesis, Kansas State University, 1942), 56; and Nell Blythe Waldron, "Colonization in Kansas from 1861–1890" (doctoral dissertation, Northwestern University, 1925). Nell Painter points out that the sustained migration of some 9,500 blacks from Tennessee and Kentucky during the 1870s far exceeded the much-publicized migration of 1879, which netted no more than about four thousand people from Louisiana and Mississippi. Nell Irvin Painter, *Exodusters: Black Migration to Kansas after Reconstruction* (New York, 1977), 146–47.

8. *New Orleans Louisianian,* February 15, 1879; John P. St. John to R. H. Lanier, *Topeka Commonwealth,* June 14, 1879; Billy D. Higgins, "Negro Thought and the Exodus of 1879," *Phylon,* XXXII (Spring 1971), 43–44; H. H. Hill to J. P. St. John, November 28, 1879, and A. Neely to J. P. St. John, September 17, 1879, Letters Received, Negro Exodus, John P. St. John Papers, Kansas Historical Society; Painter, *Exodusters,* 177–78.

9. *History of the State of Kansas* (2 vols., Chicago, 1883) I, 295. Noting that during the 1850s the vast majority of whites living in Kansas were either from Missouri or the Old Northwest, Eugene Berwanger argues that most Free-Soilers living in the Sunflower State were anti-Negro. One of the principal reasons they opposed slavery was general Negrophobia and the belief that a large slave population would ultimately produce a large free black population. Only a small number of former New Englanders within the movement were racial egalitarians. Berwanger, *Frontier against Slavery,* 97–98.

10. Ibid., 214–15.

11. *General Statutes of Kansas (Annotated) 1949* (Topeka, 1950), 61.

12. See William H. Chafe, "The Negro and Populism: A Kansas Case Study," *Journal of Southern History,* XXXIV (August 1968), 406–8, and Willard B. Gatewood, Jr., "Kansas

Negroes and the Spanish-American War," *Kansas Historical Quarterly*, XXXVII (Autumn 1971), 300.

13. *Western Recorder*, May 31, 1883.

14. *Topeka Colored Citizen*, February 8, 1879; *Lawrence Journal*, January 15, 1880; *Leavenworth Advocate*, December 14, 1883.

15. *General Statutes of Kansas (Annotated) 1949*, 64.

16. Gatewood, "Kansas Negroes," 305–6.

17. Memorandum to Paul Wilson, Files *re Brown vs. Topeka Board of Education* (1954), 1–2, Kansas Historical Society.

18. Ibid., 3–4.

19. *Leavenworth Advocate*, May 4, 1889.

20. Ibid., June 29, 1889.

21. *History of Kansas*, I, 545, II, 1226; *Leavenworth Advocate*, April 5, 1890, May 11, 1889; *Parsons Weekly Blade*, October 22, 1892.

22. *History of Kansas*, II, 1073, 1453.

23. *Western Recorder*, August 29, 1884; *Topeka Colored Citizen*, November 8, 1879; *Leavenworth Herald*, September 29, 1884.

24. *Leavenworth Advocate*, May 3, 1890.

25. See *Leavenworth Advocate*, December 21, 1889.

26. *History of Kansas*, II, 1255.

27. *Leavenworth Herald*, June 5, 1897; *Afro-American Advocate*, May 26, 1893; *American Citizen*, June 15, 1888; *Colored Patriot*, May 18, 1882.

28. *Topeka Capital*, May 3, 1895.

29. *Leavenworth Herald*, September 28, 1895.

30. *Topeka Colored Citizen*, October 12, 1898.

31. *Times Observer*, September 26, 1891; *Topeka Colored Citizen*, September 27, 1879; *American Citizen*, February 23, 1888.

32. *Afro-American Advocate*, November 25, 1892.

33. *American Citizen*, March 15, 1889.

34. *Historic Times*, October 24, 1891.

35. *Leavenworth Herald*, February 1, 1896; *American Citizen*, January 25, 1888; *Topeka Colored Citizen*, June 21, 1879.

36. *Topeka Capital*, June 19, 1886.

37. Ibid., November 21, 1886.

38. Ibid., November 20, 1888.

39. *Leavenworth Times* in *Leavenworth Herald*, February 8, 1896.

40. *Hiawatha World*, October 25, 1883.

41. *Leavenworth Advocate*, November 8, 1890. See also *Afro-American Advocate*, May 20, 1892; *Historic Times*, September 26, 1891; *American Citizen*, November 22, 1889; *Kansas State Ledger*, September 30, 1892.

42. *Topeka Colored Citizen*, September 20, 1878.

43. *Leavenworth Herald*, January 12, 1895.

44. *Afro-American Advocate*, August 12, 1892.

45. Smith, "Early Negroes," 27.

46. Nellie McGuinn, *The Story of Kansas City, Kansas* (Kansas City, 1961), 76, and Swann, Jr., "The Ethnic Heritage," 65.

47. *American Citizen*, February 15, 1889.

48. Ibid., February 18, 1889.

49. *Topeka Colored Citizen*, September 20, 1887; *American Citizen*, February 5, 1892.

50. S. S. Petersen to L. U. Humphrey, August 16, 1890, Letters Received, box 5, L. U. Humphrey Papers, Kansas Historical Society; *Leavenworth Herald,* January 12, 1895; *American Citizen,* February 24, 1898.

51. B. D. Eastman to L. U. Humphrey, November 26, 1890, Letters Received, box 2, Humphrey Papers.

52. *Leavenworth Herald,* October 13, 1894.

53. See, for example, *Topeka Colored Citizen,* June 16, 1898.

54. St. John to J. H. Sallee, March 27, 1879, Governor St. John Letters Sent, XIV, St. John Papers.

55. *Topeka Capital,* February 1, 1887.

56. *Atchison Blade,* September 17, 1892; *Topeka Capital,* September 10, 1889.

57. Genevieve Yost, "History of Lynchings in Kansas," *Kansas Historical Quarterly,* II (May 1933), 192.

58. *Topeka Capital,* January 9, 1885; *Leavenworth Times* in *Leavenworth Herald,* January 11, 1896.

59. See, for example, *Herald of Kansas,* March 19, 1880; *Topeka Capital,* January 10, 1885; *Afro-American Citizen,* March 25, 1892; and *Kansas City Gazette,* September 23, 1897.

60. *Leavenworth Herald,* April 4, May 1, 1896.

61. See, for example, *Kansas City Gazette,* January 12, 1899; *Topeka Capital,* November 23, 1890; *Leavenworth Herald,* January 11, 1896; *Kansas City Gazette,* June 2, 1898.

62. *Kansas Herald,* February 6, 1880; *Topeka Capital,* May 4, 1890; *American Citizen,* December 13, 1889.

63. *Kansas City Gazette,* June 21, 1900. See also *Topeka Capital,* January 5, 1888.

64. *Topeka Colored Citizen,* November 4, 1897.

65. *Topeka Capital,* January 3, 1886; *American Citizen,* August 3, 1888.

66. *Topeka Capital,* February 7, 1889.

67. See, for example, *Leavenworth Advocate,* March 21, 1891; *Topeka Capital,* March 1, 1897.

68. *American Citizen,* February 7, 1890.

69. *Ft. Scott Colored Citizen,* June 7, 1878; *Atchison Globe,* July 17, 1882; *Leavenworth Advocate,* August 9, 1890; *American Citizen,* February 21, 1896; *Kansas State Ledger,* May 13, 1896.

70. *Leavenworth Herald,* August 14, 1897; *American Citizen,* August 2, 1889.

71. *Leavenworth Herald,* January 25, 1896.

72. *American Citizen,* July 13, 1894. See also *Topeka Colored Citizen,* April 14, 1898.

73. See *Leavenworth Times,* May 1, 1878; *American Citizen,* January 25, 1895; *Leavenworth Herald,* December 7, 1895; *American Citizen,* June 21, 1895.

74. *Afro-American Citizen,* March 25, 1892; *American Citizen,* June 4, 1897. Berwanger contends that prior to the Civil War the vast majority of people who moved first into the Old Northwest and from there into the Great Plains, California, and the Pacific Northwest were anti-Negro. Antislavery crusades in Ohio, Indiana, and Illinois, emphasizing as many did negative characteristics popularly attributed to blacks, exacerbated racial animosity. Berwanger, *Frontier against Slavery,* 1–2, 18, 24–25, 31, 38–42, 63, 76–77, 97–98.

75. John D. Bright, *Kansas: The First Century, 1854–1954* (New York, 1956), 367.

76. See N. W. Duffield to G. W. Glick, June 18, 1883, Letters Received, box 1, G. W. Glick Papers, Kansas Historical Society; *Kansas Democrat* in *American Citizen,* September 27, 1889; *Atchison Globe,* July 21, 1882; *Leavenworth Advocate,* July 13, 1889.

77. See, for example, A. N. Moyer to St. John, April 17, 1879, and Anonymous to St. John, March 4, 1880, Letters Received, Negro Exodus, St. John Papers; *Topeka Colored Citizen,* March 22, 1879; *Emporia Ledger* in *Herald of Kansas,* April 9, 1880.

78. Berwanger, *Frontier against Slavery,* 1–2, 18, 24–25, 31, 38–42.

79. *Topeka Capital,* March 2, 1890; *Lawrence Journal* in *Topeka Capital,* April 25, 1879; *Kansas City Star* in *Topeka Colored Citizen,* November 4, 1897; *Topeka Capital,* January 6, 1886; M. E. Griffith to St. John, April 20, 1880, Letters Received, Negro Exodus, St. John Papers.

80. Harrison Kelley to John A. Martin, January 24, 1885, Governor Martin Letters Received, box 1, John A. Martin Papers, Kansas Historical Society; *Topeka Capital,* January 10, 1890.

81. Porter, *American Frontier,* 360–424, 470–94.

82. *Topeka Capital,* July 2, 1886.

83. For attitude of white Kansans toward Indians see, for example, *Topeka Capital,* January 7, 1886.

84. *Eureka Republican* in ibid., July 2, 1886. Miscegenation involving men and women of both races occurred in Kansas, but such incidents were rare and were generally frowned upon by both white and black. See *Leavenworth Times,* May 1, 1878; *American Citizen,* January 25, 1895; *Leavenworth Herald,* December 7, 1895; *American Citizen,* June 21, 1895.

85. *Kansas City Star* in *Topeka Colored Citizen,* November 4, 1897.

OKLAHOMA'S ALL-BLACK TOWNS

George O. Carney

[This article originally appeared as "Historic Resources of Oklahoma's All-Black Towns: A Preservation Profile" in the *Chronicles of Oklahoma*, Vol. 69 (1991), pp. 116–133. Copyright by the Oklahoma Historical Society. Retitled, adapted, and reprinted with permission.]

Oklahoma's development was unique among western states. Congress denoted most of its area as part of "Indian Territory" in the early nineteenth century. For several years prior to the Civil War, Indian Territory was home to many black slaves who were brought from the South to the West by members of the so-called Five Civilized Tribes. When slavery ended, most of Indian Territory's black residents chose to remain there. For one thing, the U.S. government promised these freedmen that they would receive land allotments. For another, many Native American slaveholders had treated their slaves more like family members than property; much intermarriage occurred between Indians and blacks in Indian Territory both during and after the slavery era. Thus, of all parts of the U.S., the frontier West seemed to offer to Indian Territory's ex-slaves the best hope for economic and social opportunity.

Beginning in 1889, the U.S. government opened up much of the territory to settlement by non-Indians, carving Oklahoma Territory out of the western half of Indian Territory in 1890. A few thousand blacks joined a greater number of whites in the ensuing land "runs." Many of the newly arrived African Americans agreed with several thousand Indian freedmen (and their descendants) that the best way for blacks to thrive in the "twin territories"—which merged again in 1907 to form the state of Oklahoma—was to pool their land parcels and create all-black towns.

Like similar agricultural colonies in Kansas, Colorado, Texas, California, and New Mexico, Oklahoma's all-black towns were centers of commerce for farming communities. Unlike the colonies in these other western states, however, several of Oklahoma's African American communities survived the economic and social transformations that occurred in the West and elsewhere in the U.S. in the twentieth century. The 1990 census revealed the continued existence of thirteen of these Oklahoma municipalities, almost all of which were founded by African American pioneers in the last decade of the nineteenth century and the first few years of the twentieth.

George O. Carney, a geographer with a doctoral degree in history, began a systematic study of Oklahoma's existing all-black towns in 1983. In the following essay, he surveys the history of the communities, paying particular attention to the way the towns' builders altered the West's landscape. The black settlers erected homes, schools, churches, and government buildings where they lived, learned, worshipped, conducted business, and, in general, established the sense of community that helped them survive and even prosper. Many of the structures that the black pioneers built decades ago remain standing as reminders of the lasting impact African American homesteaders had on the development of the western frontier.

The arrival of Oklahoma's first black residents was a result of the removal of the Five Civilized Tribes from the southeastern United States during the 1830s and 1840s. The Chickasaws, Choctaws, Cherokees, Creeks, and Seminoles, who were all slaveholders, brought their black slaves and a number of "free" blacks over the Trail of Tears to Indian Territory. Following the Civil War and the adoption of the Thirteenth Amendment to the United States Constitution, federal officials met with Indian leaders at Fort Smith, Arkansas, to draw up treaties that provided for the termination of slavery and the adoption of freedmen into the tribes with rights to annuities and lands. A majority of the former slaves eventually received allotments ranging from forty to one hundred acres.[1] By 1870 blacks in Indian Territory numbered more than six thousand.[2]

In March 1889 President Benjamin Harrison by special proclamation opened to settlement a portion of present-day Oklahoma known as the Unassigned Lands. The run that followed in April brought approximately fifty thousand people into the area. Black people joined the rush to stake claims, and according to the 1890 census nearly three thousand blacks resided in Oklahoma Territory and an additional eighteen thousand lived in Indian Territory.[3] Subsequent land openings in the 1890s attracted more black settlers from the surrounding states of Arkansas, Kansas, and Texas. Others journeyed longer distances from the Deep South. At the turn of the century the black population in Oklahoma Territory had increased to almost nineteen thousand and approximately twice that number was located in Indian Territory.[4]

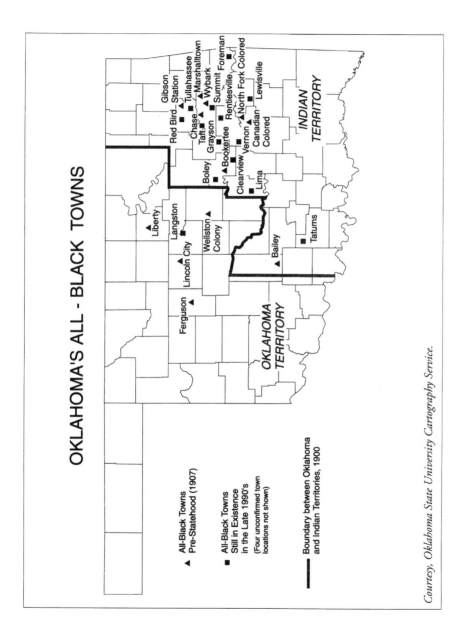

OKLAHOMA'S ALL - BLACK TOWNS

▲ All-Black Towns
Pre-Statehood (1907)

■ All-Black Towns
Still in Existence
in the Late 1990's
(Four unconfirmed town
locations not shown)

—— Boundary between Oklahoma
and Indian Territories, 1900

Courtesy, Oklahoma State University Cartography Service.

Most of the increase in black population resulted from the determined activities of black "boosters," individuals who regarded Oklahoma Territory as a favorable place to settle. Promotional literature described the region as an area where blacks could obtain free land, exercise their rights as citizens, and escape racial discrimination. The most active promoter of Oklahoma Territory was E.P. McCabe who came to the area in 1889 from Kansas where he had been a prominent Republican Party politician and state auditor. He reasoned that if blacks populated Oklahoma in sufficient numbers they could organize an all-black state or at least constitute a political balance of power. He purchased 320 acres of land near Guthrie, attracted settlers to the site, and built the town of Langston (named in honor of John M. Langston, a black Virginia Congress-man).[5] McCabe started the Langston *Herald,* a newspaper he used for promotional and political purposes. He portrayed Oklahoma territory in glowing terms inasmuch as it provided opportunities for blacks to start anew and flee from the suffering of past racial injustices:

> What will you be if you stay in the South? Slaves liable to be killed at any time, and never treated right: but if you come to Oklahoma you have equal chances with the white man, free and independent. Why do southern whites always run down Oklahoma and try to keep the Negroes from coming here? Because they want to keep them there and live off their labor. White people are coming here every day.[6]

McCabe's idea created controversy in the Twin Territories. If Oklahoma became an all-black state, whites and Indians feared that blacks would have political influence over them through positions in state government. Rumors circulated that McCabe's major objective was to become territorial governor, which created additional fears even if Oklahoma did not become an all-black state. Local politicians argued that if McCabe sought the governorship, a violent struggle would ensue. Others predicted his life would be in danger if the president appointed him governor.

In addition, southern white politicians and cotton plantation owners rejected the all-black state plan because it would deplete their cheap labor force. Even though blacks were legally free, they still provided much of the manual labor for southern cotton farms. White southerners tried to discourage black emigration to Oklahoma by promoting the idea that the land was unsuitable for farming.[7]

Several events occurred to resolve these conflicts. Republican Party leaders in Washington, D.C., decided against the appointment of McCabe to the territorial governorship. Instead, he was named deputy auditor of Oklahoma

Territory, a position he held until statehood in 1907. Black migration into the territory slowed for a variety of reasons including the cost and hardships of moving, family ties to home, fear of the unknown, and an unfamiliar agricultural environment. Many of those who did migrate were eventually aided by Oklahoma freedmen who housed and fed the newcomers until they became established.[8] Because of blacks' fear of migration to Oklahoma and white political opposition, McCabe's dream of an all-black state failed. He then turned his attention to the development of all-black towns in the Twin Territories. Mainly through McCabe's promotional efforts, twenty-eight communities and one agricultural colony were founded prior to statehood. Because a majority of blacks lived in Indian Territory, twenty-four of the communities were located there while the remaining four and the lone colony were in Oklahoma Territory. Tullahassee, reported to be the oldest all-black town, was founded in Indian Territory about 1859. Most of them, however, were established between the land run in 1889 and statehood in 1907. Lincoln City was organized in 1889 followed by Langston in 1890—the first two in Oklahoma Territory. Many of the all-black towns in Indian Territory were founded near Muskogee shortly after the turn of the century. These included Taft, Boley, and Vernon.[9]

The all-black towns of Oklahoma were founded for various reasons and were similar in many respects to other western frontier communities. Some blacks wanted to live with people of their own race, which gave them a sense of security in a new homeland. Others saw the black towns as an opportunity to control their own destiny, politically and economically, without interference from whites. Many viewed the towns as a safe haven from groups such as the Ku Klux Klan. The organization of these black communities on the frontier landscape of Oklahoma followed the patterns of other pioneer western towns. They combined the elements often found in other emerging frontier places—utopian escapism when established by various religious and political sects seeking freedom from the social restrictions of the larger society; a "boom town" form of spontaneous development found in the rushes for gold, oil, and other natural resources; and promotional schemes that appealed to restless people wanting to migrate to a new area.[10]

The all-black towns began to decline following statehood. McCabe left Oklahoma in the summer of 1908 for Chicago where he lived in obscurity until his death in 1923.[11] The communities, left without their primary booster, never totally escaped their dependence on an economic system essentially controlled by whites. Furthermore, they experienced many of the same problems faced by all small town rural market centers, black or white. Improved highway networks bypassed them. The invention of the automobile allowed for more distant travel to larger urban centers offering a wider array of goods and services. Younger generations began to leave town for the big cities such as Tulsa and Oklahoma City where employment opportunities were greater. School and road funds were not forthcoming from a white-dominated state legislature. Low cotton prices and the agricultural recession of the 1920s, followed by the Great Depression of the 1930s, severely affected farming communities.

The all-black towns gradually lost population and many disappeared from the Oklahoma map. By the post-World War II period, only nineteen of the original twenty-eight remained. That number had decreased to thirteen in 1990. These thirteen towns have remained remarkably durable despite the many social, economic, and political problems they have suffered. They stand as historic reminders of a unique period in Oklahoma's history when blacks built homes, organized schools and churches, and constructed and operated businesses.

With the exception of Boley, a National Historic Landmark, little preservation work has been accomplished in the all-black towns of Oklahoma.[12] In 1983 the Oklahoma State University Department of Geography, under contract to the Oklahoma State Historic Preservation Office, conducted a survey of the surviving thirteen all-black towns in order to identify and evaluate historic properties. A total of twenty-seven properties were placed on the Oklahoma Landmarks Inventory and six of these were listed in the National Register of Historic Places.[13]

The most common house type surveyed in the all-black towns was the shotgun. Anthropologists have traced this unique form of folk architecture to seventeenth-century West Africa and contend that it has long been associated with black settlement in the United States.[14] It diffused from New Orleans, its American cultural hearth, to Oklahoma following a number of migration paths.[15] The floor plan of the shotgun was relatively simple—one room wide and two to three rooms deep. The name is derived from its elongated shape where one could fire a shotgun through the front door and the shot would pass through the house and out the rear without hitting anything in between. It was an inexpensive form of housing and could be easily and quickly constructed by local carpenters, both of which factors appealed to small town residents. Although none of the shotguns identified in the survey were recognized at the state or national level, they remain a viable part of the residential sections of the all-black towns.

The all-black towns provided a variety of goods and services for the surrounding agricultural areas. Boley, for example, boasted a population of approximately eight hundred at the time of statehood with an estimated two thousand more blacks living in the farming region around it.[16] Grocery stores,

Public Officials. African American residents of all-black communities held all local political power. The men in this photo comprised the Boley, Oklahoma, town council, *circa* 1907–1910. (Courtesy, Archives & Manuscripts Division of the Oklahoma Historical Society.)

blacksmith shops, barbershops, banks, and other businesses emerged as the "downtown" or central business district of these communities.

Several historic commercial buildings remain intact in the existing all-black towns. The only commercial property to receive National Register designation as a result of the 1983 survey was "The Rock Front," constructed in 1920. It has served the town of Vernon, established in 1895, in a variety of ways—grocery and dry goods store as well as a recreation center. The native sandstone building was occupied by the United States Post Office in 1990. Three other commercial structures were listed on the Oklahoma Landmarks Inventory, including Sharp's Grocery and the Red Bird Drug Store in Red Bird and the A.J. Mason Building in Tullahassee. All were constructed about 1910. Although most businesses in the all-black towns were small operations, their owners rendered a valuable service to those excluded from commercial establishments in white communities.

The all-black towns provided opportunities for local government organization, participation, and leadership. Residents quickly established a system of local government and offered services for their citizens. Water, streets, and other improvements were needed as well as police and fire protection. Taft City Hall, constructed in 1910, seven years after the town was founded, is the oldest remaining local government building in the existing all-black towns. The Red Bird City Hall, known locally as "The Court House," was built in the early 1930s. These two properties were placed in the National Register in 1985 as a thematic nomination. Two additional local government buildings, Langston City Hall and Red Bird City Jail, received Oklahoma Landmarks Inventory recognition.

By the early 1890s Oklahoma had created a system of public education for blacks. In 1892 Kingfisher established the first separate high school for blacks in the territory. From 1890 to 1897 territorial statutes provided for local option with the decision to segregate determined by popular ballot at the county level. In 1897 the territorial legislature adopted a statutory segregation law which was reaffirmed by the state constitution in 1907.[17]

Three public schools were placed in the National Register of Historic Places in 1985. The oldest of these buildings is Miller-Washington School in Red Bird. From the time of its construction in 1920 to the mid-1970s, it housed either the town's high school or elementary students. Julius Rosenwald Hall, built in 1921 in Lima, is the only educational institution in the all-black towns constructed with funds provided by the Rosenwald Foundation, a philanthropic organization that funded educational facilities for blacks in the American South. It is estimated that by 1930 approximately 10 percent of all black children in Oklahoma studied in school buildings erected with the aid of Rosenwald funds.[18] Rosenwald Hall served Lima's educational needs from 1921 to 1966 and in 1990 was still owned by the Lima School District. The W.E.B. DuBois Elementary School in Summit was one of the few educational facilities still in operation in 1990 in the all-black towns. Built in 1925, it has remained a vital community institution.

Six additional historic schools were erected in the mid-to-late 1930s under the auspices of the Works Progress Administration. These W.P.A. schools were recognized as Oklahoma Landmarks Inventory buildings in 1984. Located within or near the all-black towns are Carter G. Woodson School, Tullahassee; Langston City School, Langston; Tatums School, Tatums; Rock Hill School, vicinity of Vernon; Ross Hill School, vicinity of Grayson; and Mt. Zion School, vicinity of Rentiesville.

The centerpiece of black higher education in Oklahoma was situated near Langston. The Colored Agricultural and Normal University of Oklahoma (renamed "Langston University" in 1941) was established by the Oklahoma Territorial Legislature in 1897. In 1898 Inman E. Page, the school's first president, officially welcomed the first class and studies began in the Langston Presbyterian Church.[19] During Page's tenure to 1915, ten buildings were constructed on the campus, all of which have either been razed or significantly altered. Three buildings, however, constructed prior to 1930 were given Oklahoma Landmarks Inventory recognition based on survey documentation—the Power Plant, known by students and faculty as "the Boiler Room" (1915); the University Women's Dormitory (1928); and Moore Hall or the Administration Building (1929).

Each of these institutions reflected the significant role that education assumed in the all-black towns. The school was a primary agent in instilling a sense of community pride. Academically, it offered blacks an opportunity to acquire knowledge and gain skills to prepare them for future careers. Socially, it accorded young people the chance to participate in music programs, dramatic productions, and athletic events. The school was a stabilizing social force for black families during the era of racial separatism in Oklahoma.

Perhaps more important than the school as a source of community cohesion in the all-black towns was the church. Organized religion among blacks in Oklahoma dates to the 1830s when Baptists and Methodists began missionary activity in Indian Territory. By 1916 black church membership in Oklahoma reached approximately sixty thousand with the Baptists claiming more than two-thirds of that number. The African Methodist Episcopal and Colored Methodist Episcopal denominations divided the remainder.[20]

Six historic churches were identified in the survey and placed on the Oklahoma Landmarks Inventory. The oldest and best preserved church in the all-black towns is Mt. Zion, built about 1915, eight years after the town of Lima was founded. Originally a Presbyterian body, the congregation later changed its affiliation to the African Methodist Episcopal denomination. Constructed of native sandstone, the building reflects the permanent and stable nature of its religious and social role in the community. The oldest wood-frame church building in the all-black towns is Bethel Missionary Baptist of Tatums, erected in 1917 and listed on the National Register of Historic Places in 1995. Although a new church building was constructed nearby in 1969, the original structure, known to members as "Big Bethel," remained in use in 1990 as a fellowship hall and for Sunday school classes. Other historic church buildings include Secipio Baptist, Lima; St. Paul Baptist, Taft; St. Thomas Primitive Baptist, Summit; and Salter's Chapel African Methodist Episcopal, Langston.[21]

The church represented the one social institution over which blacks had total control. It was a powerful influence within each of the all-black towns. The church was the place to which blacks could turn for spiritual inspiration and escape from secular problems. It provided an opportunity for self-expression, recognition, and leadership, and it laid the foundation for social and economic reform in a segregated society.

What does the future hold for the thirteen all-black towns in Oklahoma? Will the historic buildings associated with the early development of the communities be preserved? The answer to these questions depends largely upon the broader questions concerning the fate of all small towns in Oklahoma. The keys to their continued existence focus on four issues: 1) school consolidation—the local school stands as a source of town pride and community cohesion and its loss has an adverse impact on this cohesion; 2) retention of post office facilities—a United States post office lends credibility to outsiders and government agencies and it usually keeps the town on the map; 3) economic revitalization—solidifying or broadening the economic base is imperative; and 4) the trend of rural/small town migrations to metropolitan areas—steps must be initiated to stem the tide of young residents and adults departing for larger cities to seek employment. Some of the existing all-black towns will undoubtedly decline, become "ghost towns," and disappear from the Oklahoma map. Many have already lost or are in the process of losing schools, post offices, businesses, and, more importantly, people.

However, several of the communities appear to retain characteristics that will keep them viable. Boley, Taft, and Langston, for example, have state-supported institutions. As long as Langston University is located on its present site, the town of Langston will survive. A number of goods and services, especially gas stations, convenience stores, cafes, and video shops will be needed to serve the student, faculty, and staff population who comprise a built-in set of consumers. Likewise, Boley and Taft have profited from the infusion of state funds. Taft in 1909 and Boley in 1923 became the centers for various state institutions, primarily orphanages, hospitals, and correctional facilities. Both towns retain that role with the John Lilly correctional unit located at Boley and the Jess Dunn facility at Taft. Each of these state agencies boosts the economy of the nearby towns.[22]

Although it is apparent that the all-black towns have not realized much in terms of population gains from the counterurbanization movement of the recent past, their function as "bedroom communities" should not be completely discounted.[23] Rentiesville, Summit, Red Bird, and Tullahassee are within commuting distance of either Muskogee or Tulsa via four-lane highways. These communities offer a number of advantages over the larger cities in an era when people are beginning to value their time with family and home more than dealing with traffic congestion, the high cost of living, pollution, and little sense of community pride. The peaceful small town lifestyle could be an attractive feature of the all-black villages in the future.

It also appears that the Oklahoma Main Street program, a division of the Department of Commerce, is starting to recognize the plight of small towns with populations of five thousand or less. Since its inception in Oklahoma in 1985, this program, initiated by the National Trust for Historic Preservation, has focused on communities with populations between five thousand and fifty thousand. Some five hundred Oklahoma communities, according to the 1990 census, contained populations below five thousand, including all of the all-black towns. The Main Street concept is concerned primarily with the economic restructuring of small towns by promoting special events related to retail trade, improving the appearance of the downtown through landscaping and building design, and attracting new businesses or revitalizing those already in existence. As always, state funding for such a new program is the question, but local residents are enthusiastic about the prospects of this plan.[24]

Finally, an appreciation for black history should be cultivated in the all-black towns as well as throughout the state. Black history should include more than teaching about famous persons and events at the national level. It also should emphasize local history and the preservation of buildings associated with local events and people. Historic buildings can reveal significant facts related to personalities, events and forces that molded and shaped the evolution of these unique communities.[25]

Perhaps Oklahoma needs a state-sponsored museum focusing on black heritage. An appropriate place for this site would be one of the all-black towns, particularly Boley, already designated as a National Historic Landmark with at least a dozen historic buildings constructed between 1910 and 1930. Located approximately ten miles north of U.S. Interstate 40, Boley is the logical choice because of its ability to attract visitors from Oklahoma and tourists from other states who travel along this major east-west route. The museum would not only bring the public's attention to the black history of Oklahoma, but also would aid in the economic revitalization of Boley.

After visiting Boley in 1908, Booker T. Washington wrote:

The Negro towns that have sprung up represent a dawning of race consciousness, a wholesome desire to do something to make the race respected: something which shall demonstrate the right of the Negro, not merely as an individual but as a race, to have a worth and permanent place in the civilization that the American people are creating.[26]

For those, past and present, who have participated in what Washington called a "bold experiment," there has been a sense of accomplishment—pride in place—as contributors to communities of, by, and for black people.

Notes

1. Jimmie Lewis Franklin, *Journey Toward Hope: A History of Blacks in Oklahoma* (Norman: University of Oklahoma Press, 1982) 9.
2. Arthur L. Tolson, *The Black Oklahomans, A History: 1541–1972* (New Orleans: Edwards Printing Company, 1972), 47–48.
3. United States Department of Interior, Bureau of Census, *Compendium of the Eleventh Census: 1890* (Washington, D.C.: United States Government Printing Office, 1893), 503.
4. United States Department of Interior, Bureau of Census, *Twelfth Census of the United States, 1900: Population* (Washington, D.C.: United States Government Printing Office, 1903), 553.
5. Kaye M. Teall, ed., *Black History in Oklahoma: A Resource Book* (Oklahoma City: Oklahoma City Public Schools, 1971), 169.
6. Daniel F. Littlefield, Jr. and Lonnie E. Underhill, "Black Dreams and 'Free' Homes: The Oklahoma Territory, 1891–1894," *Phylon*, 34 (December, 1973): 347.
7. Franklin, *Journey Toward Hope*, 13–15.
8. George A. Davis and O. Fred Donaldson, *Blacks in the United States: A Geographic Perspective* (Boston: Houghton Mifflin Company, 1975), 240.
9. For more detailed accounts of the establishment of the all-black towns, see Arthur Lincoln Tolson, "A History of Langston, Oklahoma: 1890–1950," (M.A. thesis, Oklahoma State University, 1952) and "The Negro in Oklahoma Territory, 1889–1907: A Study in Racial Discrimination," (Ph.D. diss., University of Oklahoma, 1966).
10. Mozell C. Hill, "The All-Negro Communities of Oklahoma: The Natural History of a Social Movement," *Journal of Negro History*, 31 (July, 1946): 254–257.
11. Tolson, *The Black Oklahomans*, 105.
12. The Boley Historic District was designated as a National Historic Landmark in 1975. The district consists of fourteen historic resources: ten commercial buildings, two churches, one structure, and one site. See Marcia M. Greenlee, "National Register of Historic Places Inventory-Nomination Form: Boley, Oklahoma Historic District," Oklahoma State Historic Preservation Office, Oklahoma City, Oklahoma.
13. George O. Carney, "Historic Resources of Oklahoma's Black Communities," Annual Report to the State Historic Preservation Office, 1983.
14. For various theories concerning the origin of the shotgun house, see John M. Vlach, "Sources of the Shotgun House: African and Caribbean Antecedents for Afro-American Architecture," (Ph.D. diss., Indiana University, 1975) and John M. Vlach, "Shotgun Houses," *Natural History*, 86 (1977): 50–57.
15. For a thorough discussion of shotgun diffusion into Oklahoma, see George O. Carney, "The Shotgun House in Oklahoma," *Journal of Cultural Geography*, 4 (1983): 57–71.
16. Tolson, *The Black Oklahomans*, 101.
17. Franklin, *Journey Toward Hope*, 27–28, 45–46.
18. *Ibid.*, 66.
19. For a book-length treatment of the history of Langston University, consult Zella J. Black Patterson, *Langston University: A History* (Norman: University of Oklahoma Press, 1979).
20. Franklin, *Journey Toward Hope*, 153–156.
21. An excellent account of churches in Langston and the importance of this social institution to the all-black community is Zella J. Black Patterson, *Churches of Langston* (Oklahoma City: Western Heritage Books, 1982).
22. Telephone interview with Oklahoma Department of Corrections officials (Research and Planning Division), April 24, 1991.
23. "Persons By Race and Hispanic Origin and Total Housing Units in Oklahoma," *1990 Census of Population and Housing*, Oklahoma State Data Center, Oklahoma Department of Commerce. This document gives 1990 census data for all incorporated places in Oklahoma.

Eleven of the thirteen all-black towns are included, Vernon and Lewisville being the exceptions.

24. "Will the Buffaloes Wallow on Your Main Street?" *Oklahoma Main Street: The Newsletter of the Oklahoma Main Street Program,* 5 (December, 1990): 1–2. The Oklahoma Main Street Program has proposed a Small Town program designed specifically for communities under five thousand population. Five regional meetings were held in March, 1991, to discuss the feasibility of this project.

25. "Afro-American History: Six Professionals Examine Major Issues in Black History at the Local Level," *History News,* 38 (February, 1983): 8–17.

26. Booker T. Washington, "Boley, A Negro Town in the West," *Outlook,* 88 (January, 1908): 28–31.

AMERICAN DAUGHTERS: BLACK WOMEN IN THE WEST

Glenda Riley

[This article originally appeared in *Montana: The Magazine of Western History*, Vol. 38, no. 2 (1988), pp. 14–27. Reprinted with permission.]

If historians of the American West and of the African American experience have ignored the contributions of western blacks, they have been especially negligent in chronicling the presence of black women on the western frontier. To be sure, African American women were much less numerous in the West than black men were. In states with a relatively large number of black residents who established towns and agricultural colonies—like Kansas and Oklahoma—black women comprised just under half of the African American settlers. In many other western states and territories, however, black men outnumbered black women by ratios of two (or more) to one. Only a very few African American women lived on the mining, cattle, and military frontiers—places where black men were present in significant numbers.

Some of the jobs available to black men on the frontier—such as in the military or the cattle industry—paid relatively well. But, as was true in the rest of the country, many African American men in the West made less money than white men did. As a result of this, a greater percentage of western black women than white had to seek employment outside the home to supplement their families' incomes. Economic necessity, therefore, forced many African American women on the frontier to work as domestics—the most typical means of employment for black women in all parts of the U.S. at that time. They became cooks, housekeepers, nannies, and laundresses for white families which, of course, afforded them less time to spend with their own husbands and children. Consequently, whether the West offered black women improved economic opportunity is uncertain.

Still, a few intrepid African American women prospered in the frontier West. Bridget "Biddy" Mason and Mary Ellen Pleasant were entrepreneurs (and civil rights activists) in late nineteenth-century California. Clara Brown made a fortune by investing her income from a small laundry into several mining properties in Colorado. A very few black women were able to enter the professions or obtain other white-collar jobs. Moreover, some—like stagecoach driver Mary Fields and boardinghouse operator Tish Nevins of Montana—gained a measure of notoriety even though their positions were not especially rewarding from an economic standpoint. Yet most African American women in the West (like their counterparts of other races) labored in relative obscurity—doing housework, raising children, participating in church and club work, and performing all kinds of other tasks necessary for surviving and, hopefully, enjoying life in an often harsh environment. And just as they have been consistently overlooked by historians because of their race and their gender, they often faced discrimination from fellow westerners for the same two reasons.

In the following essay, Glenda Riley highlights some of the experiences and accomplishments of African American women who lived in the West during the frontier era. She also notes, however, that historians need to do much more research to mine all the available sources—census records, diaries, newspaper articles, memoirs, and others—to tell the complete story of a double-minority group that made an impact on the West but has been all but invisible in standard historical accounts of the region's growth and development.

In 1946, a lively, highly informative autobiography of a black frontierswoman effectively challenged the prevalent stereotype that all female settlers were white. Few, if any, observers of the American West had thought that the strong, conquering Saint in the Sunbonnet or the delicate, dewy-eyed Madonna of the Prairie might occasionally be dark-complexioned rather than fair. Era Bell Thompson's *American Daughter* turned the usual conception of the lily-white western woman on its head.[1]

Yet, decades later, our knowledge of black frontierswomen has increased relatively little. Western black women still suffer from an unfortunate case of near-invisibility in the historical record. The chronicle of the American West continues to be commonly presented as one almost totally dominated by white Americans.[2] It is time to look at some of the inclusions and omissions of black frontierswomen by historians of the nineteenth- and twentieth-century trans-Mississippi West. And it is time to suggest some of the reasons why black women have been overlooked and what might be learned about them, their lives, and their contributions.

An immediate, but inaccurate, reaction to this objective might be that the necessary source materials do not exist. In fact, census materials contain much information about black women; and black women's diaries, letters, and memoirs are numerous. Many literate black women left written materials behind them. Others, both literate and not, have participated in oral interviews. With a little effort, the interviews can be found in archival collections, oral history projects, and published form. The Montana American Mothers Bicentennial Project of 1975–1976, for example, housed in the Montana Historical Society Archives in Helena, includes a short biography of "Aunt" Tish, a black frontier settler who ran a popular dining room and boardinghouse in Hamilton, Montana, during the early years of the twentieth century.[3] In the University of Wyoming's American Heritage Center in Laramie, there is a transcript of an interview with Sudie Rhone, who talks about a black woman's club movement on the Great Plains.[4] And in the pages of an article describing black people in South Dakota history there is mention of black brothels that catered to black troops stationed in the area during the 1880s, of black land promoter Mary Elizabeth Blair who was active professionally during the early 1900s, and of a number of other black working and entrepreneurial women during both these periods.[5]

If black women's sources exist, then why have they been largely overlooked? Clearly, they are not easy to find. A researcher must hunt them out and then supplement them with newspapers, statistical data, legal documents, police registers, wills, marriage certificates, bills of sale, property inventories, contracts of emancipation, and a wide variety of other records. But these problems are not unknown to the historian. It is more likely that antiblack sentiment is also responsible for the virtual absence of black women in western history. Because blacks in general, and black women in particular, have not been highly regarded by most Americans, their documents have not been widely or systematically collected and few investigators have protested the situation or tried to remedy it. Once recognized, however, such attitudes and the resulting dearth of scholarship can be changed.

Concerned historians who have attempted to begin exploring the lives of black women in the West have demonstrated that writing their history is both possible and desirable. In 1977, for example, Sue Armitage, Theresa Banfield, and Sarah Jacobus published a study of black women's communities in Colorado. Arguing that Colorado was the "most promising destination for blacks" during the late nineteenth century, the authors pointed out that

Colorado's black population began to increase after 1880, largely as a result of an influx of disillusioned Exodusters from Kansas. By 1910 blacks in Colorado numbered 11,453, most located in ghettos within white towns and cities. Black women not only lived and worked there, but they also pursued reform within communities through a sizable and active black women's club movement. The six oral history interviews with Colorado black women that comprise the bulk of the study whet the reader's desire for more information.[6]

A few years later, historian Lawrence B. de Graaf made an admirable attempt to unscramble census data regarding black women in the Rocky Mountain and Pacific Coast states between 1850 and 1920. He found that black women in these western areas bore fewer children and were of a higher median age than their counterparts in the South and tended to live in urban rather than rural areas. Like black women in Colorado, these women also noted the difficulties created for them by pervasive racial prejudice manifested in segregation policies, denial of their civil rights, exclusion from land purchases, and attempts to harass black settlers or drive them away entirely. As a consequence, black women workers often had to work at low-paid and extremely exhausting domestic and agricultural tasks. While de Graaf offered some answers, he also raised many questions that have received little follow-up by other investigators. De Graaf's conclusion that "black women would long remain an invisible segment of western society whose lives and accomplishments would remain known only within the confines of their race" is unfortunately still largely accurate.[7]

In a 1981 study of frontierswomen in Iowa, I also concluded that the re-creation of the history of black westering women would be a difficult and long process. Although frontier Iowa was generally antislavery in philosophy, its white citizens harbored noticeable prejudice against blacks. During the early settlement years, for example, Iowa did not countenance slavery and claimed to enforce fugitive slave laws, yet newspaper advertisements for runaway black indentured servants suggest that slavery existed under other guises. Prejudice also flared when blacks received jobs. Even in Grinnell, a liberal abolitionist town, a violent mob protested the arrival of four black male workers in 1860.[8]

More recently, historian Sandra L. Myres attempted to include black women in her study of westering women. She mentioned a few notable black women and the community efforts of black clubwomen and also explored the prejudicial attitudes of the time that helped make black women "an almost invisible part of the mythology of westering women." She explained that although blacks were "part of the westward migration rather than a native people encountered on the frontier, they were most often regarded, like Indians and

Mexicans, as an alien influence." She noted that following the Texas Revolution the government of the new republic passed legislation to enslave or expel free blacks in Texas. Myres added that in 1851 Indiana prohibited blacks from entering the state as did Illinois in 1853 and that colonization societies dedicated to sending blacks to Africa dotted the Midwest. She concluded that all over the West black westering women endured discriminatory treatment and isolation.[9]

All of these studies suggest that prejudice and discriminatory treatment of black frontierswomen are of long duration. They support a harsh assertion posited some years ago by historian William L. Katz. In assessing antiblack attitudes in such western regions as Iowa, he observed that "the black laws moved westward with the pioneers' wagons." He declared that statements made during the 1844 Iowa constitutional convention were clear examples of blatant racism. According to Katz, Iowans who argued that "we should never consent to open the doors of our beautiful state" to black settlers, that blacks "not being a party to the government, have no right to partake of its privileges," and that "there are strong reasons to induce the belief that the two races could not exist in the same government upon an equality without discord and violence" could lay no claim to the enlightenment and liberation that was widely assumed to characterize the West. Katz concluded: "The intrepid pioneers who crossed the western plains carried the virus of racism with them."[10]

Not all western settlers deserve Katz's harsh indictment. Thousands of whites aided blacks fleeing to freedom via the Underground Railroad, brought free blacks home with them after the Civil War, welcomed blacks as settlers, and worked for black civil rights.[11] Such evidence as a county manumission record showing that her master freed Mommia Travers at Fort Vancouver in 1851 or the Iowa court case involving a freed black woman married to a white man indicate that black frontierswomen occasionally drew positive sentiments and actions.[12]

An additional factor that is often cited for historians' neglect of black frontierswomen is the relative scarcity of blacks in the western population. But this raises questions. Is the smallness of a group sufficient reason to dismiss it from the annals of history? Is a group's size always proportional to its importance and contributions? And is it true that black frontierswomen were indeed scarce? Although the answer to all three queries would appear to be "no," only the last can be clearly proven. Census figures indicate that the number of black women in western states, particularly after the Civil War, was not minuscule. Thousands of them not only lived in most western states, but their ranks also increased over the years. Census data for seven selected Plains states during the fifty years following the Civil War document the absolute numbers, relative proportions, and increase of black women.

Federal census figures concerning black women can be supplemented by county records that often include both population figures and personal information. A county registry of free blacks in frontier Missouri between 1836 and 1861 listed approximately ten women and twenty men, but the records unfortunately gave little additional information about them. Another Missouri county, however, not only counted free blacks but noted age, gender, occupations, and places of origin. In 1850 sixteen free blacks lived in this county of over one thousand families. Five of the blacks were female, two of them cooks and three without paid occupations. In that same year in McLean County, Illinois, the population totaled 1,594, of whom 777 were white females, 777 were white males, 17 were black females, and 23 were black males. Among the black females were cooks, servants, and a twenty-year-old schoolteacher born in Kentucky.[13]

Compiling census figures, particularly on the county level, is a time-consuming and exhausting means of gathering information about black women in the West, but such data are a rich source of information. Given the dearth of material regarding black women and the frequent omission of them in western history, which is partially a result of this lack, census records are a resource well worth mining.[14]

Another factor that has contributed to widespread nearsightedness regarding black frontierswomen is the tendency to overlook female participation in historical movements. Black women and black men came to western regions very early in the settlement period. As early as June 24, 1794, a marriage between blacks, Jean and Jeanne Bonga, was recorded in Mickilmacknac Parish, later part of Minnesota. Many blacks entered the area with fur-trading expeditions, exploring forays, and the military. Beginning in 1820, officers and their families stationed at Fort Snelling in what is now Minnesota brought their slaves, both male and female, with them. By that time, there were already an estimated two thousand to three thousand blacks, both slave and free, in the upper Louisiana country.[15]

During the early nineteenth century, settlers from southern states also brought slaves into western regions. In 1822 a party of settlers traveling from Virginia to Missouri included four white men and their four black valets as well as "Mammy," a black woman servant ensconced in the cook and supply wagon. This family spent its first years in a log cabin with "Mammy" helping out inside while the white and black men broke the prairie sod outside.[16] Many other frontier families similarly relied on slave or free black women for help in raising children, doing domestic chores, and running inns and other family businesses.[17]

Even western states that loudly proclaimed themselves to be antislavery had their share of trappers, traders, soldiers, miners, and settlers who brought black slaves with them. The Iowa census of 1840 listed ten female and six male slaves even though the state had outlawed slavery. Although no slaves appeared in the Iowa census after that year, slaveholders circumvented the law. Some held blacks as indentured servants. As late as 1850, an advertisement in Iowa's *Burlington Tri-Weekly Telegraph* asked for the return of such a servant. Described as black, thirteen or fourteen years old, and with five years left to serve of her indenture, the girl was said to have been "decoyed" away by some "meddling person." Her owner claimed that "it would be an act of charity to her could she be restored" to him.[18]

Throughout the pre-Civil War years vestiges of slavery continued in Iowa. Female indentures served as cooks, nursemaids, and domestic servants.[19] Despite the antislavery movement and the activities of the Underground Railroad, proslavery sentiment ran strong, especially among the many migrants from southern states who had moved into southern Iowa seeking land.[20] The proslavery sentiment in these districts made them less amenable to the entry of free blacks than some expected or hoped, contrary to the egalitarian reputation of the frontier regions. But even antislavery Iowans were afraid of cheap black labor and the difficulties they believed would result from living and working with blacks. These whites supported the passage of black exclusion laws, denied blacks civil liberties in the state, regulated their behavior with "black laws," required a certificate of freedom from any free black entering Iowa, and often forced free blacks to post monetary bonds of $500 to ensure their "good behavior."[21]

In neighboring free Minnesota, both slaves and free blacks, including women, entered the region during the decades preceding the Civil War. Abolitionist sentiment, however, seemed to be more rife there than in Iowa, perhaps partly because of a smaller proportion of blacks in Minnesota's population. The residence at various army posts of a slave woman named Rachael during 1831–1834 led to her successful suit for freedom in 1835. The two-year stint of Dred and Harriet Scott at Fort Snelling in 1836–1838 eventually resulted in the Dred Scott Case of 1857. In 1849 the first territorial census recorded forty free blacks, thirty of whom lived in St. Paul. But during the 1840s and 1850s, both free blacks and fugitive slaves continued to enter Minnesota. This migration alarmed those who feared cheap black labor and "inundation" by blacks. Yet in 1860, when Eliza Winston accompanied her master on a vacation to Minnesota, she was able to enlist the aid of local abolitionists in seeking her freedom.[22]

Although black women evidently lived and left their marks in Iowa and Minnesota, little is said of them in the complex and sometimes voluminous historical accounts of these regions and of the black people living in them. Beyond the occasional mention of a female fugitive slave, a woman involved in a marriage or court case, or a free black woman employed as a domestic helper, washwoman, or day laborer, there is no systematic discussion of their roles or of the contributions of black women to the early development of these western regions.

The history of the Exodusters, a massive black migration to Kansas, Oklahoma, and other areas after the Civil War, is another example of historians slighting female participation in a major movement. Even though the census figures clearly demonstrate the presence of relatively large numbers of black women and a constant increase in the size of the black female population in Kansas and Oklahoma, black women generally appear only incidentally in historical accounts of the Exoduster movement.

The flight of the Exodusters from southern states to Midwest and Plains states during the later decades of the nineteenth century is well-documented. During these years, thousands of southern blacks traveled up the Missouri River and along other routes in an attempt to escape the evils of sharecropping, tenant farming, and antiblack sentiment. Seeking a better life in the "promised land," they sought employment in the cities or on farms, worked as cowhands, homesteaded, or created both rural and urban all-black communities. In the Midwest, Pulaski County, Illinois, contained a sizable black population by 1900. Plains colonies included Nicodemus, Kansas, established in 1877, Langston, Oklahoma, in 1891, and Dearfield, Colorado, in 1910.[23]

The story of the part played by black women in this migration to the Plains has not been researched and recorded even though diary entries, letters, and memoirs of both white and black women indicate that many Exodusters were female. Anne E. Bingham, for instance, recalled that she and her husband hired a family of six black Exodusters, two adults and four children, to help on their Kansas farm in 1880. Bingham remarked that the two adult Exodusters were reliable and diligent workers. She was particularly pleased to have the woman's services as washwoman. "She would carry a pail of water on her head with one hand to steady it," Bingham remembered, "and something in the other hand, and carry the clothes basket that way, too." Bingham was very sorry when the Exoduster family "got lonesome and finally went to town."[24]

The memories of several female Exodusters also offer enough information about black women to make the reader eager to learn more about them and their lives in the "promised land." According to Exoduster Williana Hickman, at the end of an exhausting railway journey from Kentucky to Kansas in 1878, her husband had pointed to "various smokes [*sic*] coming out of the ground and said, 'That is Nicodemus.'" Black families were living in dugouts almost at ground level, Hickman remembered. She reacted to the scene much as many of her white counterparts did: "The scenery to me was not at all inviting, and I began to cry." According to another newspaper story about early settlers in Nicodemus, a black woman who also arrived in 1878 began teaching a class of forty-five children in her new dugout home.[25]

Black women among homesteaders who settled throughout Nebraska, Dakota Territory, and other Plains states have yet to be studied. In North Dakota, for example, a group of black male and female homesteaders attempted to establish a farm community near Alexander in the southwestern part of the state in about 1910. Numbering only ten families at its peak, Alexander was not a success. Within a decade of the town's founding, all of its residents had dispersed to nearby towns and cities. More successful were the homesteading families of Ava Day in Nebraska and Era Bell Thompson in North Dakota. Day and Thompson both grew up on the Plains, far from the South their parents had known. But the difference that relocation made to women's lives in these and other cases like them remains unexamined. Further, we do not know whether black women homesteaded on their own as did so many white women during the 1890s and early 1900s. Nor have black women's contributions to the overall homesteading experience been noted.[26]

Although historians have not intentionally omitted black women in western history in order to imply that these women led puerile lives, that is often the result. The material reviewed here offers tantalizing glimpses of a fascinating but largely unexplored group of western settlers. It suggests that there is a great deal of available information and there are tremendous insights to be gained about black frontierswomen. But how should we proceed? A place to begin might well be black frontierswomen's domestic lives, a highly revealing area in the study of any group of women. Black women's writings point to great similarity between black and white women's daily lives in the West. Home and family were the focus of black women's lives, just as they were for white women, and they went about the care of both in similar ways.[27]

From the pioneer years in Minnesota comes the example of black settler Emily O.G. Grey who joined a growing black community in St. Anthony in 1857. Like many white women, Grey set up housekeeping in a converted barn and created cupboards and bureaus from packing boxes covered with calico.[28] Three decades later in neighboring St. Paul, Amanda Jennie Lee Bell married a barber and established a home. Her experiences in housekeeping, raising her family, and assisting with her husband's business also closely paralleled those of white women living in other pioneer western towns. And in North Dakota during the early 1900s, women in the family of Helen Johnson Downing followed traditional work patterns for girls and women and relied on books to ease their isolation just as white women settlers did.[29]

Black frontierswomen's employment is another rich area for investigation. Their work experiences, however, diverged widely from white women's, especially in rates and terms of employment. A higher percentage of black women than white worked outside of their homes. While white female workers ranged between 12 to 25 per cent of all teenage and adult white women, black female workers comprised as high as 40 to 50 per cent of all teenage and adult black women. Black women's relatively high employment level was largely due to economic necessity. Although both whites and blacks believed that women should work within the home, black women actually remained in the home far less than white women did. The realities of scarce and low-paid jobs for black men typically made employment a requirement for black women who had to contribute to family income. Black women not only had higher rates of employment than white women did, but racial prejudice also kept them from holding all but the more menial jobs. Despite their own reservations or ambitions to the contrary, poor wages, exhausting conditions, demeaning status, and heavy labor that these jobs usually entailed, black women took the positions most readily available to them.[30]

Most commonly, black women worked as domestics in western areas, although after the Civil War white western women, especially native-born women, began leaving domestic service for retail, sales, and clerical work as well as the professions. Employment as cooks, washwomen, dressmakers, nursemaids, and maids seemed to many white employers logical and appropriate derivations of the roles black women had fulfilled as slaves. Often called by such names as "Nigger Ellen," black servants received minimal wages sometimes supplemented by leftover scraps of food or cast-off clothing.[31] Black female servants were frequently described by their white employers as loyal, willing, and competent, while white—especially non-American-born—women often evoked their employers' enmity. Anna Ramsey of St. Paul wrote to her daughter that Martha, her black maid, performed many duties well, from housecleaning to packing the family's clothes for trips. Referring to her servant as "beloved" Martha, Ramsey regretted that old age necessitated Martha's retirement. On the other hand, a Bloomington, Illinois, woman did not think much of her black maid's abilities as a housekeeper but was delighted that her mother had sent the servant along with her as a companion on her journey to the West as a young bride.[32]

In other cases, black women earned local reputations as skilled workers when they carried their domestic talents out of the home and into the public arena. In Sioux City, Iowa, two black cooks during the 1860s vied with each other for the acclaim of their patrons. A woman cook referred to as "Black Ann" not only received the kudos of passengers on Mississippi steamboats, but she also earned enough money to buy her own freedom and that of her children. And in St. Paul, Minnesota, during the years following the Civil War customers praised the skills of a family of black women seamstresses.[33]

Despite the huge odds against black women progressing very far beyond employment as domestics, a considerable number parlayed their energy and abilities into such relatively high status positions as hotel or boardinghouse keepers and restaurant managers or owners. The most famous black boarding-house keeper was Mary Ellen "Mammy" Pleasant, a California pioneer who was also known for her charitable acts of assistance to needy blacks.[34] Other black women became entrepreneurs in a variety of businesses, including millinery shops, hairdressing establishments, and food stores. The most eminent of them was Sarah Breedlove Walker, better known as "Madame" Walker. She develop-ed "The Walker Method" of straightening black women's hair in St. Louis in 1905 and moved to Colorado in 1906.[35] Many women were real estate brokers, including Biddy Mason of Los Angeles, Clara Brown of Denver, and Mary Elizabeth Blair of Sully County, South Dakota. Most prominent of the group, Biddy Mason not only amassed considerable wealth, but she also spent huge amounts of time and money helping the less fortunate. Because of her charitable work she was called "Grandmother" Mason.[36]

A surprising number of black women became successful in a variety of professions. Young black women showed an interest in and talent for education, in spite of state and local attempts to prohibit them from attending school and laws that limited them to often poorly funded segregated schools. Ironically, because black women often lived in towns and cities, they gradually gained access to better educational facilities than those available to white rural women, which fostered a high rate of school attendance and graduation among black girls in the West. In addition, black families sometimes chose to educate daughters instead of sons to protect the girls from employment exploitation.[37] A number of these educated black women entered teaching, probably the profession most accessible to them because of the establishment of an increasing number of black schools around the turn of the century. As teachers in segre-gated schools or as founders of their own black schools, black female educators usually outnumbered black male educators in most western regions.[38]

Other achievement-oriented black women struggled to become nurses, doctors, journalists, and editors, but they succeeded in far fewer numbers than

Clara Brown. A former slave, Brown worked her way to Colorado as a cook for a wagon train. Arriving in 1859, she became a laundress and invested her money in real estate and gold mines. In 1881 white men in Denver elected her the first woman and first African American member of the Society of Colorado Pioneers. (Courtesy, Denver Public Library, Western History Department.)

black women who became teachers. Charlotta Spears Bass of Los Angeles particularly distinguished herself as a black woman editor. In 1912 she became editor of *The California Eagle* (published from 1879 to 1966), the oldest black newspaper on the West Coast. Through its pages she waged a fierce crusade for over forty years against racial segregation and discrimination against blacks. In 1952 she became the first black woman to run for the vice-presidency of the United States.[39]

Prostitution was the one "profession" left wide open to and, in fact, often urged on black women. Both economic necessity and negative images of black women pushed them toward criminal occupations, a pressure that they frequently resisted.[40] Thompson recalled being told by a white man in Mandan, North Dakota, that all black women were prostitutes.[41] Yet neither observers nor census takers noted large numbers of black prostitutes in the West. Occasionally, black brothels did coexist with sizable populations of black cowhands or black soldiers, but other black women in the area commonly scorned and reviled black prostitutes and madams.[42]

Another crucial topic to be examined in the history of black frontiers-women is the effect of racism. It is a subject and circumstance that most clearly differentiated them from their white counterparts. During her high school and college days in North Dakota, Era Bell Thompson frequently became the victim of prejudicial treatment that threatened to impair seriously or end her education. Eventually, she fled to Chicago in hopes of "blending in" with the black population there. Similarly, Dr. Ruth Flowers, the first black woman to graduate from the University of Colorado in 1924, spent her teenage years working as a dishwasher in a restaurant, resisting persistent racism that barred her from even enjoying an ice cream cone or a movie, and studying until early morning hours to get an education she hoped would free her from such trials.[43]

The prejudice and discrimination encountered by black females in the West point to the largest single variable affecting the lives of black western women: race and racism shaped their experiences in an incredible number of ways. Yet we know little about the development of racism in the West. Ava Day, whose family settled in the Overton area of Cherry County, Nebraska, in 1885, claimed that she met with very little prejudice during her childhood in the Nebraska Sandhills where her family raised cattle, brood mares, and mules. She recalled that her grandfather was white and her grandmother black. As Day explained, "Color never made a difference to Grandpa. You were a person and a man and a lady." She added that the family's neighbors felt much the same about the race issue, for they were friendly and helpful: "…everybody asked did you need anything from town—and brought it back by your house or left it at your gate."[44]

Era Bell Thompson also had some pleasant memories of white neighbors during her very early years in North Dakota. She claimed that when her family moved to the plains shortly before World War I they met with little discrimination. As she commented years later: "I was very lucky to have grown up in North Dakota where families were busy fighting climate and soil for a livelihood and there was little awareness of race." She recalled that neighbors befriended her family, especially a Norwegian family who brought supplies to the Thompsons at critical times. Thompson believed that North Dakota's high percentage of ethnic residents encouraged settlers to look on each other as equals, a situation that apparently changed as settlement increased, judging from the educational and career limitations placed on Thompson by racist attitudes and policies later in her life.[45]

Other black frontierswomen had different memories of prevailing attitudes toward blacks. For example, Sudie Rhone of Cheyenne, Wyoming, contradicted Thompson's view of race relations during the pre-World War I era. She noted that the black women's Searchlight Club, founded in 1904, was the only service group for black women at that time, adding that while black women could have joined white women's clubs, they seldom chose to do so. She believed that widespread prejudice and nonacceptance of blacks by whites kept the two groups of women segregated in this and many other activities.[46]

Rhone's observations about western women's service clubs pinpoint not only the racial prejudice that divided white women from black, but also lead to another subject for investigation: the activities and attitudes of black women reformers and civic activists. How widespread was the phenomenon of black women reformers and clubwomen? Did they typically attack the same social ills as did white women reformers, or did they attempt to solve race-related problems of black people? And did they ever join with white women, or did they work only within groups of black women? So little material exists on black women reformers in the West that it is impossible to give definite answers to any of these questions except the first one. Numerous black women throughout the West did become reformers and community activists. One Colorado woman stated that in black western communities where men worked long hours or were away seeking work, black women served as the "backbone of the church, the backbone of the family, they were the backbone of the social life, everything."[47] Other black women also wrote or spoke of the huge amounts of time and energy that they and their friends devoted to community improvement projects.[48] And records of black organizations, such as the Pilgrim Baptist

Church of St. Paul, founded in 1866, and the Kansas Federation of Women's Clubs, organized in 1900, reveal the number and diversity of black women's charitable organizations that existed from an early stage in the settlement of the West.[49]

Whether black women reformers attacked "black" problems and worked only with black women is not quite clear. Charlotta Pyles, a free black living with her family in Keokuk, Iowa, was a reformer. She and other family members joined together in a fundraising effort to buy their relatives out of slavery. During the 1850s, Pyles launched a speaking tour in the East to raise funds and converted her Keokuk home into a station on the Underground Railroad. To advance her cause, she joined with white abolitionists and helped many fugitive slaves escape to Canada.[50]

Unlike Pyles, numerous reform-minded black women chose or were forced by racial prejudice to cooperate only with other black women in reform activities.[51] Many of these joined the rapidly proliferating ladies' aid groups, charity associations, and missionary societies often associated with black churches. Black women reformers Emily Grey of St. Anthony and Amanda Bell of St. Paul, for example, attacked problems that particularly plagued black people, including inadequate health care, poverty, and substandard education.[52]

The General Federation of Women's Clubs' long-standing policy of accepting black women's organizations only as segregated locals pressured black women all over the United States to maintain their own service groups. Black clubwomen formed a parallel organization, the National Association of Colored Women, in 1896, and by 1915 it had fifty thousand members in twenty-eight state federations and over a thousand individual clubs. Should an investigator take the time to explore them, the records of these clubs might yield an abundance of information about black clubwomen in the West, such as Josephine Leavall Allensworth of California who helped organize the Women's Improvement Club that provided a public reading room and built playgrounds for children.[53]

There are many other topics in the history of black women in the West that are rife with unanswered questions. Little is known, for example, about western black women's participation in the woman suffrage movement. Because many black women in the South and the East organized their own suffrage groups, it is reasonable to believe that western black women did so as well. Because woman suffrage first became a reality in western territories and states, it might be significant to know if race was a positive or negative influence or any influence at all in this development. Black women's roles in temperance reform, the Grange, Populism, and in army forts are other subjects that need investigation. The black woman's relationship to American Indians and the physical environment of the West is virtually unexplored.

Historian Sue Armitage cautions that it is also necessary to consider regional differences in the lives and experiences of black women. In an unpublished paper and a bibliography of sources on black women in the Pacific Northwest written with Deborah G. Wilbert, she too raises the issues of domesticity, employment, racism, reform, and other germane topics but notes that the experience of a black frontierswoman in Kansas might vary greatly from that of a woman in Oregon. The point regarding regionalism is a highly significant one; era, class, and urban or rural residence are other important variables to be included in any study of black women in the West.[54]

Perhaps the ultimate question to be raised here is why the history of black women on the American frontier should be recovered. One obvious answer is that only by analyzing the history of all types of western women can their history and the history of the West itself ever be understood. Comparisons between black and white women will yield valuable insights about each group and about the larger group of women of which they were a major part. Moreover, despite racial prejudice, there are many ties between black and white women on the frontier. Anna Ramsey not only employed a black servant but also found herself strongly drawn to the enthusiasm and verve of the Tennessee Jubilee Singers who performed in the St. Paul Opera House to raise funds for black education. In the South, some women owned slaves while others, like Susan Vanarsdale, felt great sympathy for a female fugitive slave.[55] Black women, on the other hand, had to confront and interact with white women in almost every area of their lives, including employment, education, and social life. How, then, can the history of one group be written without the other?

Probably more crucial, however, is the issue of justice in restoring a historical heritage to black women in America. As Era Bell Thompson argued so well in *American Daughter,* black women were an integral part of the western and American traditions. It both impairs their sense of identity *and* unbalances the historical record to continue to overlook the role of black women in the development of the American West.

Notes

1. Era Bell Thompson, *American Daughter* (1946; reprint, St. Paul: Minnesota Historical Society, 1986).
2. Examples of historians who have attempted to reconstruct western black history but have included little or no material on black women are Jean I. Castles, "The West: Crucible of the Negro," *Montana the Magazine of Western History* 19 (Winter 1969): 83–85; William L. Katz, *The Black West* (Garden City, New York: Doubleday, 1971); Kenneth W. Porter, *The*

Negro on the American Frontier (New York: Arno Press and the New York Times, 1971);
Lawrence D. Rice, *The Negro in Texas, 1874–1900* (Baton Rouge: Louisiana State University
Press, 1971); W. Sherman Savage, *Blacks in the West* (Westport, Connecticut: Greenwood
Press, 1976). Richard White, "Race Relations in the American West," *American Quarterly* 38
(Bibliography edition, 1986): 397–416, has very little on blacks and nothing on black women.
A recent and refreshing collection of original essays and photographs of western blacks that
reflects the existence of women throughout is Marguerite Mitchell Marshall et al., *An
Account of Afro-Americans in Southeast Kansas, 1884–1984* (Manhattan, Kansas: Sunflower
University Press, 1986). For a discussion of the historiography of black women, see Gerda
Lerner, *The Majority Finds Its Past: Placing Women in History* (New York: Oxford University
Press, 1979), 63–82. Regarding racism, sexism, and black women, see Diann Holland
Painter, "The Black Woman in American Society," *Current History* 70 (May 1976): 224–227,
234.

3. Tish Nevins, American Mothers Bicentennial Project, 1975–1976, Montana Historical
Society Archives, Helena [MHSA].

4. Sudie Rhone, interview, November 8, 1979, University of Wyoming Heritage Center,
Laramie [WAHC]. Another useful collection is the Black Oral History Interviews, Holland
Library, Washington State University, Pullman.

5. Sara J. Bernson and Robert J. Eggers, "Black People in South Dakota History," *South
Dakota History* 7 (Summer 1977): 247, 251–252. See also Quintard Taylor, "Blacks in the
West: An Overview," *Western Journal of Black Studies* 1 (March 1977): 4–10. Suggestions for
locating black women's sources can be found in Deborah Gray White, "Mining the
Forgotten: Manuscript Sources for Black Women's History," *Journal of American History* 74
(June 1987): 237–242.

6. Sue Armitage, Theresa Banfield, and Sarah Jacobus, "Black Women and Their
Communities in Colorado," *Frontiers* 2 (1977): 45–51.

7. Lawrence B. de Graaf, "Race, Sex, and Region: Black Women in the American West, 1850–
1920," *Pacific Historical Review* 49 (May 1980): 289, 291, 296–297, 313. For an analysis of
black women in the Far West before the Civil War, see Michael S. Coray, "Blacks in the
Pacific West, 1850–1860: A View from the Census," *Nevada Historical Society Quarterly* 28
(Summer 1985): 90–121.

8. Glenda Riley, *Frontierswomen: The Iowa Experience* (Ames: Iowa State University Press,
1981), 88–91. The mob violence in Grinnell was described by Sarah Parker, letter to "Dear
Mother," March 10, 1860, State Historical Society of Iowa, Iowa City. For a discussion of
contradictory attitudes toward blacks, see Eugene H. Berwanger, *The Frontier Against
Slavery: Western Anti-Negro Prejudice and the Slavery Extension Controversy* (Urbana:
University of Illinois Press, 1967).

9. Sandra L. Myres, *Westering Women: The Frontier Experience, 1880–1915* (Albuquerque:
University of New Mexico Press, 1982), 85–86.

10. Katz, *The Black West*, 54, 50, 284. For a contrasting view of attitudes toward blacks in west
Texas, see George R. Woolfolk, "Turner's Safety-Valve and Free Negro Westward
Migration," *Journal of Negro History* 50 (July 1965): 185–197. For discussions of blacks in
Iowa, see Leola M. Bergmann, *The Negro in Iowa* (Iowa City: State Historical Society of
Iowa, 1969); Paul W. Black, "Lynchings in Iowa," *Iowa Journal of History and Politics* 10
(April 1912): 151–254; Louis Pelzer, "The Negro and Slavery in Early Iowa," *Iowa Journal of
History and Politics* 2 (October 1904): 471–484; Morton M. Rosenberg, *Iowa on the Eve of
the Civil War: A Decade of Frontier Politics* (Norman: University of Oklahoma Press, 1972);
Joel H. Silbey, "Proslavery Sentiment in Iowa," *Iowa Journal of History and Politics* 55
(October 1957): 289–318; Jacob Van Eck, "Underground Railroad in Iowa," *Palimpsest* 2
(May 1921): 129–193.

11. Riley, *Frontierswomen*, 94–99.

12. Fred Lockley, "Some Documentary Records of Slavery in Oregon," *Oregon Historical Quarterly* 17 (June 1916): 108; John E. Briggs, *History of Social Legislation in Iowa* (Iowa City: State Historical Society, 1915), 34–35.

13. Howard County, Missouri, Registry for Free Negroes, 1836–1861, and Cooper County, Missouri, United States Census, 1850, Volume I, manuscript census unpaginated, both in the Joint Collection of the University of Missouri Western History Society of Missouri Manuscripts, Columbia [Miss. Coll.]; McLean County, United States Census, 1850, McLean County Historical Society, Bloomington, Illinois, manuscript census unpaginated.

14. For studies regarding blacks that draw on census data, see Daniel M. Johnson and Rex R. Campbell, *Black Migration in America: A Social Demographic History* (Durham: Duke University Press, 1981); Elmer R. Rusco, *"Good Time Coming?" Black Nevadans in the Nineteenth Century* (Westport, Connecticut: Greenwood Press, 1975); Douglas Henry Daniels, *Pioneer Urbanites: A Social and Cultural History of Black San Francisco* (Philadelphia: Temple University Press, 1980).

15. Castles, "The West," 83; David Vassar Taylor, "The Blacks," in *They Chose Minnesota: A Survey of the State's Ethnic Groups,* ed. June Drenning Holmquist (St. Paul: Minnesota Historical Society Press, 1981), 73; Richard B. Morris, ed., *Encyclopedia of American History* (New York: Harper & Row, 1961), 159.

16. Eliza Byer Price, "Recollections of My Father, Samuel Dyer, 1905," Miss. Coll. For a discussion of the westward migration of southern slaveholders, see James Oakes, *The Ruling Race: A History of American Slave Holders* (New York: Alfred A. Knopf, 1982), 73–95.

17. Myres, *Westering Women,* 119; Adrienne Christopher, "The Story of Daniel Yoacham, Westport Pioneer Innkeeper," n.d., Delia Richerson McDaniel, diary, 1841, and James A. Ward, "Autobiography," n.d., Miss. Coll.

18. *Burlington Tri-Weekly Telegraph* (Iowa), August 27, 1850.

19. Ruth A. Gallaher, "Slavery in Iowa," *Palimpsest* 28 (May 1947): 158–160.

20. Silbey, "Proslavery Sentiment in Iowa," 189–191; Rosenberg, *Iowa on the Eve of the Civil War,* 14.

21. Pelzer, "The Negro and Slavery in Early Iowa," 471; Briggs, *History of Social Legislation in Iowa,* 34–35; William M. Donnel, *Pioneers of Marion County* (Des Moines: Republican Steam Printing House, 1872), 70–75.

22. Taylor, "The Blacks," in Holmquist, *They Chose Minnesota,* 73–74.

23. See Shirley J. Carlson, "Black Migration to Pulaski County, Illinois, 1860–1900," *Journal of the Illinois Historical Society* 80 (Spring 1987): 37–46; Roy Garvin, "Benjamin, or 'Pap,' Singleton and His Followers," *Journal of Negro History* 33 (January 1948): 7–23; Glen Schwendemann, "Wyandotte and the First 'Exodusters' on the Missouri," *Kansas Historical Quarterly* 26 (Autumn 1960): 233–249; "The 'Exodusters' on the Missouri," *Kansas Historical Quarterly* 29 (Spring 1963): 25–40; Nell Irvin Painter, *Exodusters: Black Migration to Kansas After Reconstruction* (New York: Alfred A. Knopf, 1977), 108–117; Robert G. Athearn, *In Search of Canaan: Black Migration to Kansas, 1879–1880* (Lawrence: The Regents Press of Kansas, 1978); George H. Wayne, "Negro Migration and Colonization in Colorado, 1870–1930," *Journal of the West* 15 (January 1976): 102–120; Mozell C. Hill, "The All-Negro Communities of Oklahoma: The Natural History of a Social Movement," *Journal of Negro History* 31 (July 1946): 254–268; Arvarh E. Strickland, "Toward the Promised Land: The Exodus to Kansas and Afterward," *Missouri Historical Review* 69 (July 1975): 376–412; Harold M. Rose, "The All-Negro Town: Its Evolution and Function," *Geographic Review* 55 (July 1965): 362–381; Nudie E. Williams, "Black Newspapers and the Exodusters of 1879," *Kansas History* 8 (Winter 1985–1986): 217–225.

24. Anne E. Bingham, "Sixteen Years on a Kansas Farm, 1870–1886," Kansas State Historical Society *Collections* 15 (1919–1920): 520–521.

25. Quoted in Glen Schwendemann, "Nicodemus: Negro Haven on the Solomon," *Kansas Historical Quarterly* 34 (Spring 1968): 14, 26. For a discussion of contemporary media images that usually represented Exodusters as male, see George R. Lamplugh, "The Image of the Negro in Popular Magazine Fiction, 1875–1900," *Journal of Negro History* 57 (April 1972): 177–189.

26. William C. Sherman, *Prairie Mosaic: An Ethnic Atlas of Rural North Dakota* (Fargo: North Dakota Institute for Regional Studies, 1983), 14; Ava Day, two letters to "Nebraska Historical Society," March 28, May 23, 1964, Nebraska State Historical Society, Lincoln [NHS]; "A Colored Man's Experience on a Nebraska Homestead," *Omaha World Herald,* February 11, 1899; Kathie Ryckman Anderson, "Era Bell Thompson," *North Dakota History* 49 (Fall 1982): 11–18; Era Bell Thompson, interview, September 16, 1975, State Historical Society of North Dakota, Oral History Project, Bismarck [NDOH]. See also Minnie Miller Brown, "Black Women in American Agriculture," *Agricultural History* 50 (January 1976): 202–212; Bernson and Eggers, "Black People in South Dakota History," 245–253.

27. See John A. Andrew, "Betsey Stockton: Stranger in a Strange Land," *Journal of Presbyterian History* 52 (Summer 1974): 157–166; Dorothy Bass Spann, *Black Pioneers: A History of a Pioneer Family in Colorado Springs* (Colorado Springs: Little London Press, 1978); Myres, *Westering Women,* 86.

28. Patricia C. Harpole, ed., "The Black Community in Territorial St. Anthony: A Memoir," *Minnesota History* 49 (Summer 1984): 42–55.

29. Eva Neal, Family Papers, 1881–1963, Minnesota Historical Society, St. Paul [Minn. H.S.]; Helen Johnson Downing, interview, September 16, 1975, NDOH. See also Taylor, "The Blacks," in Holmquist, *They Chose Minnesota,* 73–91.

30. De Graaf, "Race, Sex, and Region," 296; Katharine T. Corbett and Mary E. Seematter, "Black St. Louis at the Turn of the Century," *Gateway Heritage* 71 (Summer 1986): 44. For a discussion of blacks' expectations of women, see James Oliver Horton, "Freedom's Yoke: Gender Conventions Among Antebellum Blacks," *Feminist Studies* 12 (Spring 1986): 51–76.

31. Painter, *Exodusters,* 153; W. Sherman Savage, "The Negro in the Westward Movement," *Journal of Negro History* 25 (October 1940): 532–533; David M. Katzman, *Seven Days a Week: Women and Domestic Service in Industrializing America* (Urbana: University of Illinois Press, 1978), 82–85, 289–290.

32. Anna Ramsey, letter to "My Darling Children," March 31, 1876, "My Dear Daughter," February 2, December 8, 1876, Alexander Ramsey Family Papers, Minn. H.S.; *Bloomington Bulletin* (Illinois), January 26, 1899.

33. Phillip T. Drotning, *A Guide to Negro History in America* (New York: Doubleday, 1968), 67; Georgiana Packard, "Leaves from the Life of a Kansas Pioneer, 1914," Kansas State Historical Society, Topeka; Mattie V. Rhodes, Family Papers, 1968, Minn. H.S.

34. "Mary Ellen Pleasant," in *Notable American Women, 1607–1950,* 3 vols., ed. Edward T. James and Janet W. James (Cambridge, Massachusetts: Belknap Press, 1971), 3: 75–76; Bernson and Eggers, "Black People in South Dakota History," 250; D. Cheryl Collins, "Women at Work in Manhattan, Kansas, 1890–1910," *Journal of the West* 21 (April 1982): 33–40; Nevins, American Mothers Bicentennial Project, MHSA; "Washwomen, Maumas, Exodusters, Jubileers," in *We Are Your Sisters: Black Women in the Nineteenth Century,* ed. Dorothy Sterling (New York: W. W. Norton & Company, 1984), 355–394; Sylvia Lea Sallquist, "The Image of the Hired Girl in Literature: The Great Plains, 1860 to World War I," *Great Plains Quarterly* 4 (Summer 1984): 168.

35. "Sarah Breedlove Walker," in James, *Notable American Women,* 3: 533–534. For some other cases of black women entrepreneurs, see William L. Lang, "The Nearly Forgotten Blacks on Last Chance Gulch, 1900–1912," *Pacific Northwest Quarterly* 70 (April 1979): 54–55.

36. Donna Mungen, *Life and Times of Biddy Mason: From Slavery to Wealthy California Laundress* (n.p., 1976); Kathleen Bruyn, *"Aunt" Clara Brown: Story of a Black Pioneer*

(Boulder, Colorado: Pruett Publishing Company, 1970); Bernson and Eggers, "Black People in South Dakota History," 251.

37. Savage, *Blacks in the West*, 168–181; E. Wilburn Bock, "Farmer's Daughter Effect: The Case of the Negro Female Professions," *Phylon* 30 (Spring 1969): 17–26. For the "sex loophole" that helped black daughters get education, see Lerner, *The Majority Finds Its Past*, 69–70.

38. See Delilah L. Beasley, *The Negro Trail Blazers of California* (Los Angeles: Times Mirror Printing and Binding House, 1919), 123, 173–178; "California Colored Women Trail Blazers," in *Homespun Heroines and Other Women of Distinction*, ed. Hallie Qu. Brown (Xenia, Ohio: Aldine Publishing Company, 1926), 241–242; Rudolph M. Lapp, *Blacks in Gold Rush California* (New Haven, Connecticut: Yale University Press, 1977), 184; Corbett and Seematter, "Black St. Louis," 48. For black women practicing nursing see Day, letters, NHS; Elizabeth Cochran, "Hatchets and Hoopskirts: Women in Kansas History," *Midwest Quarterly* 2 (April 1961): 235; "Black Women in Colorado: Two Early Portraits," *Frontiers* 7 (1984): 21. For a black woman physician, see Armitage, Banfield, and Jacobus, "Black Women and Their Communities," 46; Susan H. Armitage, "Reluctant Pioneers," in *Women and Western American Literature*, ed. Helen Winter Stauffer and Susan J. Rosowski (Troy, New York: Whitston Publishing Company, 1982), 47.

39. See Thompson, interview, September 16, 1975, NDOH; James de T. Abajian, comp., *Blacks in Selected Newspapers, Censuses and Other Sources: An Index to Names and Subjects*, 3 vols. (Boston: G. K. Hall, 1977), 1: 221–222, 649, 716; "Charlotta Spears Bass," *Notable American Women: The Modern Period*, ed. Barbara Sicherman (Cambridge, Massachusetts: Belknap Press, 1980), 61–63; Gerald R. Gill, " 'Win or Lose—We Win': The 1952 Vice-Presidential Campaign of Charlotta Bass," in *The Afro-American Woman: Struggles and Images*, ed. Sharon Harley and Rosalyn Terborg-Penn (Port Washington, New York: Kennikat Press, 1978), 109–118.

40. For a fascinating study of black women convicts, see Anne M. Butler, "Still in Chains: Black Women in Western Prisons, 1865–1910" (paper presented before the Western History Association, Los Angeles, October 1987). The author thanks Anne Butler for sharing this research.

41. Thompson, interview, September 16, 1975, NDOH. For an analysis of the development of black women's sexual image, see Winthrop D. Jordan, *White Over Black: American Attitudes Toward the Negro, 1550–1812* (Chapel Hill: University of North Carolina Press, 1968), 150–151.

42. Bernson and Eggers, "Black People in South Dakota History," 247; Kenneth W. Porter, "Negro Labor in the Western Cattle Industry," *Labor History* 10 (1969): 327; Erwin N. Thompson, "The Negro Soldier and His Officers," in *The Black Military Experience in the American West*, ed. John M. Carroll (New York: Liveright, 1971), 182; Lang, "The Nearly Forgotten Blacks on Last Chance Gulch," 55. Nevins, American Mothers Bicentennial Project, MHSA, is an example of a black woman who detested a madam, Mammy Smith, reportedly the only other black in Hamilton, Montana. For black women's views of the myth of the "bad" black woman, see Gerda Lerner, ed., *Black Women in White America: A Documentary History* (New York: Vintage Books, 1973), 164–172.

43. Thompson, interview, September 16, 1975, NDOH; Armitage, "Reluctant Pioneers," 47–48; Armitage, Banfield, and Jacobus, "Black Women and Their Communities," 46.

44. Day, letters, NHS. See also Downing, interview, September 16, 1975, NDOH.

45. Anderson, "Era Bell Thompson," 11–12.

46. Sudie Rhone, interview, November 8, 1979, WAHC.

47. Armitage, Banfield, and Jacobus, "Black Women and Their Communities," 46.

48. Willard Gatewood, "Kate D. Chapman Reports on 'The Yankton Colored People,' 1889," *South Dakota History* 7 (Winter 1976): 28–35; Spann, *Black Pioneers;* Nellie Bush, interview, Indian-Pioneer Papers, Vol. 14, 53, Oklahoma State Historical Society, Oklahoma City.

49. "A Brief Resume of History," Pilgrim Baptist Church, ca. 1977, Minn. H.S. See also Elizabeth Lindsay Davis, *Lifting As They Climb* (Chicago: National Association of Colored Women, 1933); Marilyn Dell Brady, "Kansas Federation of Colored Women's Clubs, 1900–1930," *Kansas History* 9 (Spring 1986): 19–30; Gerda Lerner, "Early Community Work of Black Club Women," *Journal of Negro History* 59 (April 1974): 158–167.

50. Mrs. Laurence C. Jones, "The Desire for Freedom," *Palimpsest* 7 (May 1927): 153–163.

51. Rhone, interview, November 8, 1979, WAHC.

52. Harpole, "The Black Community," 44; Neal, Family Papers, Minn. H.S.; Rhone, interview, November 8, 1979, WAHC.

53. Savage, *Blacks in the West,* 187–188. See also Lerner, *The Majority Finds Its Past,* 83–93; Lerner, *Black Women in White America,* 437–478.

54. Susan H. Armitage and Deborah G. Wilbert, "Black Women in the Pacific Northwest: A Survey and Research Prospectus"; Armitage, "Black Women in the Pacific Northwest." The author thanks Sue Armitage for sharing this research. Particularly useful sources on black women in the Pacific Northwest are Quintard Taylor, "The Emergence of Black Communities in the Pacific Northwest, 1865–1910," *Journal of Negro History* 64 (Fall 1979): 346–351; Elizabeth McLagan, *A Peculiar Paradise: A History of Blacks in Oregon, 1788–1940* (Portland, Oregon: Georgian Press, 1980); Esther Mumford, *Seattle's Black Victorians, 1852–1901* (Seattle: Ananse Press, 1980). In addition, Melissa Hield and Martha Boethel's *The Women's West Teaching Guide: The Multicultural History of Women in the Nineteenth Century American West* is available from the Women's Studies Program at Washington State University, Pullman.

55. Anna Ramsey to "My Dear Daughter," June 27, 1875, Alexander Ramsey Family Papers, Minn. H.S.; Susan D. Vanarsdale, diary, 1847, Miss. Coll. It would also be useful to include Asian and Hispanic women.

STILL IN CHAINS: BLACK WOMEN IN WESTERN PRISONS, 1865–1910

Anne M. Butler

[This article originally appeared in the *Western Historical Quarterly*, Vol. 20 (1989), pp. 18–35. Copyright by the Western History Association. Reprinted with permission.]

Whether deserved or not, the American West of the frontier era has the reputation of having been a lawless place. The popular image of the region—perpetuated in books, movies, and television shows—is that it was replete with cattle rustlers, gunslingers, bank robbers, and other assorted desperadoes. Certainly, the frontier West had a significant number of outlaws, including several who were black. Moreover, most of the West's criminals—regardless of race—were men. Consequently, the African American women whose lives and crimes Anne M. Butler examines in the following essay hardly fit the profile of the stereotypical reckless western lawbreaker.

Butler begins by discussing the relatively large numbers of black women incarcerated in the frontier era in Louisiana and Texas prisons. Those two states were part of the slaveholding Confederacy and, thus, arguably more southern than western in character. Butler, however, considers conditions for African American women in their penitentiaries to be typical of the frontier because she finds parallels between prisoners' experiences there and in Kansas, Nebraska, and Montana— states whose white citizens were influenced only slightly by southern customs and racial attitudes.

The criminal justice systems of western frontier states discriminated against black women in a variety of ways, Butler alleges. They were more apt to be arrested and imprisoned for minor offenses than white women were. Their sentences were longer, prison guards mistreated them more often, and they were less likely to be pardoned, paroled, or put on probation than were Caucasian females. Like other historians, Butler believes that African American women were victimized for both sexual and racial reasons. But her view of the opportunities available to blacks in general—and women in particular—in the West is more pessimistic than that of the majority of scholars. To her, whether the West offered the average African American woman the hope of a better life than that available to her in other parts of the United States is questionable at best. Certainly, for black women who found themselves in western penitentiaries, the frontier had failed to place them beyond the reach of white male law enforcement officials who disdained members of their race and gender.

> ...the said Sarah King was one of a number of contraband Negroes brought to St. Louis from Alabama, who were huddled together in some miserable hut...and the child of this woman was found with a ten dollar gold piece in its possession...and upon the testimony of the child...being found with such a piece of money, she [Sarah King] was convicted and sentenced to two years.[1]

So wrote a petitioner seeking a pardon for Sarah King, an Alabama mulatto woman, whose legal difficulties in Missouri began sometime in the spring of 1864. The petitioner, Mrs. Lavina P. Jorden, who wanted King released to her for domestic service, assured governor Thomas Fletcher that the former slave had a husband away with the federal army, had a child who needed motherly attention, was a "good...trusty...patient and faithful" black woman, and that "the whole affair" was just a "kind of Negro fuss."[2]

Actually, "the whole affair" is suggestive of much more than a simple fuss. Nowhere in the country did opportunity seem more alluring after the Civil War than in the most promising of natural regions—the American West. It has been well documented that displaced persons—black and white, male and female— turned to the expanses of the frontier with hope for a more promising future.[3] The Far West beckoned as the "new" region, where Americans could put aside the antiblack, antislave preoccupations that had obsessed the cultures of North and South. In this emerging society, migrating blacks must have anticipated that the lingering vestiges of a slave society would dissipate in the face of a frontier tradition that allegedly judged people less by their color and more by their pluck and hard work.[4]

However, the Sarah King episode casts a shadow across such easy notions, so cherished in the nation's stereotypical vision of the West. The blatantly circumstantial evidence under which the Missouri court sent King to the state penitentiary raises the possibility that black women, especially within the context of their incarceration in western prisons, faced a frontier more hostile than expansive, more oppressive than egalitarian. These frontier penitentiaries have drawn their share of scholarly attention, but most accounts contain only a passing general reference to female prisoners and rarely give details about black women convicts as a group.[5] Yet records drawn from several state penal systems indicate that the freedom, the justice, the opportunity so often associated, however mythically, with the American frontier continued to elude black women long after the official demise of slavery. This paper does not suggest that black male prisoners enjoyed elements of freedom and justice while women did not. Prison registers and investigative reports give ample contrary documentation. Sample evidence can be found in any register or report cited in this paper that black men endured inhumane assaults on their dignity and the obliteration of their legal rights. However, an underlying thrust of this article rests on the notion that the significant dynamics of black womanhood have been ignored or de-emphasized in the process of suggesting that the most important result of slavery concerns its demoralizing impact on black men.[6] Whether part of a large Texas population or a small Montana group, black women found that racism, which had earlier been an energizing force of institutional slavery, retained its most powerful forms inside the penal system.

This article focuses, with only limited comparative pretenses, on the experiences of black women in western prisons. It does so in an effort to recapture one aspect of the black frontier, which deserves its own consideration as a western process. Racial comparisons in the saga of western development cannot be entirely appreciated until the black frontier assumes its own identity. Black westerners should not be expected to stand forever in the shadow of the white experience. Although the women here were few in number and scattered about the West, the fundamental commonality of their incarceration suggests that the full scope of frontier life for blacks has yet to be unraveled.

Although the punishment of slaves rested with owners before the end of the Civil War, occasionally blacks were turned over to the local courts. For example, in 1846 a fifteen-year-old mentally retarded slave, Nelly, was indicted for the murder of her infant. White citizens of the community, Warrenton, Missouri, petitioned on her behalf and asked for her release. They cited Nelly's youth, her mental limitations, the possibility that the child was stillborn, and emphasized that a public trial would be a social embarrassment to the widow and ten children of Nelly's recently deceased owner, the apparent father of her infant. Supported by a white community distressed for its own reputation, Nelly was pardoned October 14, 1846.[7]

By 1866 prison registers, in border and former slave states, began to show a dramatic rise in the number of blacks incarcerated, and, among them, more and more women. This was particularly true in Louisiana where, after 1869, the decentralized state penal system fell under the private control of a former Confederate officer, Major Samuel Jones. Dissatisfied with the loose structure of the penitentiary, Jones began to phase out convict leasing from Baton Rouge to levees, farms, and railroad labor camps around the state. He preferred to concentrate the prisoners at his isolated eighteen thousand-acre plantation, Angola, located on the eastern bank of the Mississippi River; Jones initiated his plan, transferring the Louisiana women convicts to that location in 1881.[8]

Louisiana's intimate economic and cultural bonding of blacks and whites, coupled with the state's extensive lands in the trans-Mississippi, make this particular "Gateway to the West" a sound base from which to cast a profile of the nineteenth-century black female prisoner. Between 1866 and 1872, sixty-seven women entered the Louisiana state prison system. Black and mulatto women accounted for sixty-four of those women. They ranged in age from thirteen to seventy-seven, and, but for one, all had been born in slave states. The convictions listed three murderers, one kidnapper, one leader of a riot, and three women committed without any criminal charges against them, apparently on the whim of officers in their home counties. The remaining fifty-six black women—including the girl of thirteen and the elderly woman of seventy-seven—faced sentences of three to twenty-four months for charges in some way connected to robbery or larceny.[9] Only one entry in the register identifies the stolen property, and its scant value indicates that in Louisiana a misdemeanor could mean a lengthy term at hard labor; a forty-eight-year-old mulatto woman found herself sentenced to three months in the state penitentiary, rather than the county jail, for stealing a shirt.[10]

Other aspects of these former slaves' lives can be extrapolated from the register data. Of the sixty-four black women remanded to state officials for this period, only five could read; of those five, one could write. In addition to their cultural deprivation, these women came to prison literally bearing the physical scars of their earlier lives. Generations of dietary deficiency told in their heights: only eight stood taller than five feet four inches, more than thirty measured five feet two inches or below. On these diminutive frames, the women carried weights that averaged between 120 and 140 pounds. Young women, many not yet twenty-five years old, had already sustained massive injuries. Blindness in one eye, the absence of all teeth, disfigurement from burns, disease, and wounds were the prisoners' usual distinguishing characteristics.[11]

The register listed the occupation of most women to be "common laborer," and the work they did, whether inside the prison or outside for a local citizen, was a continuation of the domestic labor and field drudgery of their slave days.[12] Those who thought to escape this dreary existence, might have been deterred by the story of Alice Dunbar. In 1868 Dunbar bolted from the superintendent's office after serving almost a full year of an eighteen month sentence. The authorities did not apprehend her until 1871, when she was returned to the state prison system.[13] Upon completion of her outstanding six months, Dunbar received her discharge; officials added no extension to her sentence, for, just as during slavery days, this fifty-one-year-old black woman had paid for her escape attempt—stripped to the waist and flogged with a cat-o-nine tails.[14]

This picture of black women of all ages—poor, abused, illiterate, and unjustly imprisoned—blended easily with other historical data about the most extreme treatment inflicted on former slaves in cultures of the Deep South, regardless of Louisiana's hefty territorial tilt into the Far West.[15] Yet Louisiana provided a foundation from which to assess the power of southern racial attitudes in the development of western communities, the tolerance of northerners for antiblack sentiment, and the transference of societal standards and values into frontier communities. Accordingly, more may be explained about the impact of the South on the ultimate regional identity of the trans-Mississippi West. Certainly, in relation to the subject of penal institutions, it seems clear that the experiences of Louisiana black convict women set a tone for the patterns found on the far frontier.

In Texas, for example, penal authorities consulted more than once with their Louisiana neighbors about prison management, and in the Lone Star State freed black women faced a judicial system not one bit friendlier.[16] In 1867 William Sinclair, an inspector for the Bureau of Refugees, Freedmen, and Abandoned Lands, sought executive clemency for former slaves detained at the Huntsville penitentiary.[17] Among the 220 blacks that Sinclair hoped to assist, he listed fourteen women, all of whom had been slaves. In a passionate letter to his superiors, Sinclair called the convicts "the innocent and unfortunate victims of their [former owners'] wrath and disappointment."[18] Convinced that the prisoners were guilty of little or no crime and outraged that most of them had been held in a county jail for at least six months prior to trial, Sinclair determined to document the injustices through interviews with each black convict.[19] Other than Elvira Mays, who had given her jailed husband a home-baked pie, the filling of which included an inedible axe, all these Texas black women were in prison for some type of thievery charge. Their thefts included stealing a hog, a nightgown, a pair of drapes, a petticoat, a pair of stockings, and $1.00. Sinclair found these women incarcerated in the state penitentiary for terms that ranged from two to five years at hard labor.[20]

By 1874 interested parties like Sinclair had retreated from Texas, and the control of the Huntsville penitentiary had passed into the hands of a private contractor. Any semblance of human decency inside the prison collapsed. Local Texans complained about the screams and groans that came from the prison or its surrounding rural labor camps; outside the state, prison reformers held the facility in low regard.[21] The charges of corruption had become so widespread that businessmen who retained a fifteen-year contract on Texas convict labor felt compelled to address the 1874 National Prison Congress at St. Louis, Missouri.

The speaker, Colonel A. J. Ward, who served as prison manager, assured the St. Louis delegates that by his presence he wanted the Texas penitentiary to be brought "into more...understood relations with the...workers in the cause of the prisons...."[22] He then outlined the Texas system. He declared it differed from any in the East because his prisoners were drawn from the "ignorant masses" and lacked "cleverness and intelligence." Ward attempted to soften his thinly disguised racial slurs by insisting that the prison operated on a plan for the reformation of the convicts. This included an appeal to self-respect, coupled with religious and educational opportunities, all supplemented by peaceful and cheery visits from family and friends. In an astonishing gesture, Ward invited members of the Prison Congress to visit Huntsville and make a firsthand inspection of its effective management.[23]

Ward's boldness and stupidity are indeed surprising in the wake of subsequent testimony leveled against him later in the same year. Granted, he had not inherited a penitentiary system in mint condition, but under his management the abuses toward prisoners reached new extremes.[24] The contours of Ward's administration became public knowledge when the U.S. Army decided to transfer into the Kansas State Penitentiary two groups of military prisoners found near death at Huntsville. Late in 1874 these prisoners, the barely living repudiation of Ward's earlier assertions about reformation and self-respect, provided some eye-witness accounts of how women fared with Colonel Ward as the overseer at Huntsville.[25]

For years officials had known that Huntsville conditions violated state laws that required segregation of the sexes in both living and work arrangements. Routinely, women and men shared a common bunkhouse or had adjacent cells and worked together in the cotton factory. These infractions seemed almost mild amidst the grisly reports of filth and brutality volunteered by the rescued military prisoners. They recounted a bleak tale of the fourteen women prisoners, at least twelve of whom were black; none had been extricated from Huntsville by the government inspector.[26]

According to the reports given in Kansas, Texas inmates of both sexes mingled without constraints during both work and leisure hours. Women convicts roamed the yard, carrying the infants conceived and born inside the penitentiary. Apparently, guards or male prisoners fathered these children, although inmates could be severely punished if sexual liaisons were discovered by the administration.[27]

The prison doctor, a white convict, repeatedly bragged of his coercive sexual relations with a black female prisoner, "Old Jane." During her imprisonment, Jane gave birth to a child of black and white parentage. The prisoners thought the convict doctor to be the father, although he received no punishment for the infraction. Perhaps his prison status as the doctor excused him. Jane had no privileges to save her from punishment for this pregnancy.

Immediately after the birth, the authorities separated the mother and newborn infant and closed Jane in the dungeon. Before she entered the isolation cell, Jane endured that special humiliation so often inflicted on women "offenders" through time; officials shaved her head.[28] The postponement of these penalties until after the child's arrival is without explanation, for certainly either could have been carried out during the pregnancy. There is the twisted possibility that, even in an environment as devoid of human dignity as a nineteenth-century rural prison, the aura generated by pregnancy might grant to women a temporary modicum of "protection" and "respect." That prison officials should find violence toward women so tolerable, but decree it to be suspended because of a pregnancy, highlights the distorted race and gender dynamics, not only on the frontier, but throughout American society.

If pregnancy abated the worst abuses, it was the only time that women prisoners could expect the slightest relief. Generally, the system spared women convicts no form of punishment. Guards hung women in the stocks so that the tips of their toes barely touched the ground. Women were beaten, raped, and forced to "ride" the wooden horse. Prisoners regarded this device, a pick-handle that had been embedded into an upright post, as the most brutal torture at Huntsville. A convict forced to straddle this apparatus had to dangle in space without moving. The inmates reported they felt a creeping paralysis spread through the genitalia, legs, and arms before they passed out.[29]

Through a parade of prison managers at Huntsville, women convicts found that very little changed over the next several years. In 1909 a committee investigating abuses in the penitentiary system visited a female camp a few miles from the Huntsville prison. In that camp, the committee found seventy-one women prisoners.[30] Of these, sixty-seven were black women. The four non-black convicts—three white women and one Hispanic—lived in quarters apart from the black women and performed the lighter domestic chores about the facility. Black women inmates toiled at all types of heavy field cultivation. The evidence of sexual misconduct by state employees working at the women's camp was so severe that the committee considered it too shocking for publication and refused to include the information in the final report.[31]

The Texas prison system, a rural agricultural operation, fashioned somewhat intentionally along the lines of the Louisiana penitentiary, had not much improved since the horrified government inspector, William Sinclair, made his report in 1867. Black women continued to outnumber whites, they still did the heavy labor of field hands, and they had little or no protection against physical and sexual assaults by male inmates and overseers.

Although in 1874 the Kansas authorities had publicized the Texas abuses with some degree of smugness, even a cursory look at the penal system in the former state suggests that it paralleled Huntsville more than officials wanted to acknowledge.[32] The 1874 happy boast of "point[ing] in triumph to the condition of our Kansas penitentiary" might not have been echoed by black women who served time in that prison.[33]

Between 1865 and 1906 the Kansas penitentiary received approximately two hundred women; of these at least 150 were black or mulatto females.[34] From the prisoner data, regularly recorded only after 1883, two items suggest some cultural changes for black women. First, these Kansas black women were generally taller than their Louisiana counterparts of two decades earlier, with the new average heights falling between five feet four inches and five feet six inches. Body scars from cuts and burns remained about the same. Perhaps more important, the literacy statistics of an earlier era had been almost reversed. From among approximately 125 women prisoners, 109 could read and write, an apparent affirmation of the oft made claim that blacks eagerly sought educational opportunities after the Civil War.[35] Other aspects of their experiences, however, had not changed very much.

Of the fifty women who entered the Kansas system between December 31, 1901, and January 7, 1906, thirty-two were black. Three of these women were older than thirty, twenty-four of them were between the ages of seventeen and twenty-five; only one had served a previous prison term in Kansas or elsewhere. Nine women were imprisoned for violent crimes such as arson or manslaughter; one woman was sentenced for bigamy. However, the majority of black women entered the Kansas penitentiary for a conviction related to robbery or larceny. Most received sentences of from one to five years, although one woman faced a term of eleven years. With the exception of two laborers and one seamstress, all these black women gave some form of housework—cooking, washing, cleaning—as their occupation.[36]

Cora Thomas. As a 20-year-old domestic worker, Thomas was sentenced to serve time in the Kansas State Penitentiary for the crime of grand larceny. (Courtesy, Kansas State Historical Society.)

The black women imprisoned in Kansas more than thirty-five years after the close of the Civil War continued to reflect the patterns prevalent among the Louisiana and Texas convicts. Most were young, poor women charged with crimes connected to the domestic services they performed. Although the Kansas recorder identified none of the missing property, it seems likely that white employers charged black domestics with thievery of items comparable to the stolen goods listed in the Texas register some years before.

The physical conditions in the prison also paralleled standards common in Louisiana and Texas. During an investigation into punishments at the Kansas State Penitentiary, matrons of the female ward testified that as late as 1910 strait jackets, handcuffs, and gags were routinely used to restrain female prisoners.[37] One warden had "rings…placed in the wall…of the female ward, for the purpose of extending the arms of prisoners for punishment, the…arms being fastened to a ring and extended above the prisoner's head."[38]

In 1905 Florence Akers, a twenty-year-old mulatto cook from Texas, received a sentence of from five to twenty-one years in the Kansas penitentiary on a charge of manslaughter.[39] The county attorney declared Akers to have "associates...of the worst class...their principle business [is] holding up and robbing people," and insisted she had operated with this gang in several Kansas and Missouri towns.[40] Akers conceded that everything in her past was not perfect, but denied her connection to the gang and hoped that, as this charge represented her first trouble with the law, she might be released to assist in the care of her insane sister, Lulu.[41] Other officials involved in the case tended to agree that Akers's main crime had been to be caught in a house of "tough women," who proceeded to testify against her. Over a period of five and one-half years, the arresting sheriff, the local jailer, a prison guard, and her lawyer all petitioned for her pardon. In 1910 the sheriff declared to Governor Walter Stubbs that Florence Akers had "served long enough for another's crime."[42] J. G. Bowers, a black guard at the penitentiary, wrote that he and his wife believed the young woman innocent and offered help after her release. That did not come until Akers had served more than five years for a murder she apparently did not commit.[43] The local jailer summed it up bluntly when he wrote to the governor, "Florence Akers was Railroaded."[44]

If so, she was not alone in Kansas, or in other states, some of which may appear remote from the most odious aspects of southern race relations. Linked to the national slavery debates by the Kansas-Nebraska Act, the latter state, overshadowed in history by the dramatic events that occurred in the former, always seemed peripheral to frontier race issues. Additionally, the preponderance of Scandinavian immigrants who plunged into farming on the Nebraska plains cast a European tone to area demographics that further distanced the state from border regions where black-white interaction might be expected.

Yet within the Nebraska penitentiary the patterns of incarceration for black women mirrored those of the deep southern frontier states in startling ways. Between 1869 and 1910, Nebraska imprisoned ninety women.[45] Of these, there were fifty-one black women, nine white women, a single native American, and one Hispanic. The records leave the racial identity of the remaining twenty-eight women unclear, although it seems certain that given the disproportionate number of blacks, some of these prisoners should be counted in that group.[46]

Among the black women, eleven had been convicted of a violent crime and had received sentences ranging from one to seven years. None of these women secured a gubernatorial pardon, and all, with one exception, served from one-half to three-fourths of her time before parole.[47] One prisoner, convicted of procuring, served two months in the state penitentiary for a crime usually penalized at the county level. The remaining thirty-nine black women went to the penitentiary for a charge of robbery or larceny. All of these convicts served the full amount of time before parole eligibility or a "good time" release.

The governor interceded for only one black woman, serving four years for robbery. He commuted her sentence so that she could be transferred to the insane asylum.[48]

Statistics for white women prisoners are difficult to compare since only nine can be identified with certainty in a forty-one year period. That small group included two convicted as bigamists, two sentenced for grand larceny, and five imprisoned for murder, manslaughter, or assault. These last five included two women with no occupations, one housekeeper, one dressmaker, and one prostitute. The two bigamists—one a nineteen-year-old chambermaid, the other a twenty-eight-year-old seamstress—entered guilty pleas and served until eligible for discharge. Of the two women convicted for grand larceny, one served her time and one received a pardon from the governor. Of the white women imprisoned for crimes of violence, one served until released for "good time," one died in prison, one shunted back and forth to the insane asylum, and two received gubernatorial pardons.[49]

Although the pool for comparison is small, the experiences of black and white women prisoners seem to have varied in Nebraska. In the first instance, white women simply did not enter the state penal system in numbers comparable to black women. This suggests that white women who broke the law, with the exception of some extremely poor ones who offended sexual social conventions, served their sentences at the local level. Generally, white women did not face the grand larceny and robbery convictions that included imprisonment in the state penitentiary, as did black women. Furthermore, although gubernatorial intervention remained limited, white women convicted of violent crimes appear to have had a better chance for executive pardon than black women.

Indeed, great distance from the pervasiveness of southern culture did not seem to enhance the situation for black women. Even in the face of the most flimsy evidence, juries did not hesitate to send black women to the state penitentiary. Such was the rueful discovery of Bessie Fisher, a black prostitute who moved to Butte, Montana, in 1901. Fisher shot and killed "Big Eva" Smith when the larger women lunged forward with threats of a beating. Despite the testimony of an eyewitness that Fisher fired in self-defense, the corroboration from the coroner's inquest, and the expectation of the prosecutor that the defendant would be acquitted, the jury returned a verdict of second degree murder.[50] Nineteen-year-old Bessie Fisher entered the Montana State Penitentiary where she became one of the twenty-three black women from among sixty female prisoners (ten white, twenty-seven not identified) incarcerated from 1888 to 1910.[51] There, despite her attorney's promise to secure a

Lida Gould. A deaf domestic worker, Gould was sentenced to serve two years in the Montana State Prison for theft of money. (Courtesy, Montana Historical Society.)

new trial, she languished for more than one-half of her twenty year sentence without the benefit of parole or pardon.[52]

From Louisiana to Montana, black women, burdened both by race and gender, juggled an uneasy relationship with western society. Most commonly, those who were arrested and convicted were young, uneducated women with negligible resources. When apprehended by the law, black women found a series of injustices set into motion: their crimes were often minor or nonexistent, serious charges materialized around the most questionable or circumstantial evidence, the issue of guilt or innocence became unimportant, prison sentences tended to exceed the seriousness of the crimes, parole and pardon procedures favored white female prisoners, and treatment inside the prisons emphasized brutality. If imprisoned wrongfully, a black woman's main hope for assistance lay with the concern of a good-spirited attorney, the efforts of a devoted family, or the desire of a local resident for cheap, docile labor. Without one of these sources, black women who entered state penitentiaries became forgotten citizens on the American frontier.

The experiences of black women in western prisons demand that historians ask more finely turned questions about the concepts of justice and equality in frontier communities, as well as the way in which social values were transmitted from region to region. Although black female prison populations never assumed large numbers, the constraints these women faced hardly varied from state to state. While all prisoners faced extreme treatment in nineteenth-century institutions, black women in the states surveyed were more likely to be sent to the state penitentiary, serve their full sentences, and be excluded from pardon procedures than white women who committed comparable crimes. The apparent indifference with which officials and private citizens tolerated questionable court procedures and prison atrocities points to the power of racial discrimination in the burgeoning West, regardless of a state's geographic location.

The evidence here suggests that southern antiblack attitudes permeated western communities close to and beyond the confines of Dixie. Within these five states there are indications that southern racial values remained a powerful force, regardless of the size of the black population. Whether there were many or few blacks in a state, authorities applied the penal code with haste and vigor against offenders. Racism, invincible as ever after the death of slavery, shaped the quality of life for blacks more than community regard for frontier pluck and individual hard work.

This serves to remind Americans that, once again, the meaning of opportunity in the West demands a reassessment to determine where, for whom, and under what conditions such a happy status existed. As for the black women listed in the prison registers of Louisiana, Texas, Kansas, Nebraska, and Montana, the West appears to have offered an uncertain freedom and little justice. Rather, these black women found that, in the West, a forge of racism reshaped the chains of slavery into the bars of a penitentiary.

Notes

1. Mrs. Lavina P. Jorden to Governor Thomas Fletcher, February 1865, Sarah King File, State of Missouri: Pardon Papers, Record Group [Hereafter RG] 5, Box 19, Missouri State Archives, Jefferson City, Missouri [Hereafter MSA].
2. Ibid.

3. For general treatment, see Richard A. Bartlett, *The New Country: A Social History of the American Frontier, 1776–1890* (New York, 1974); Norman Crockett, *The Black Towns* (Lawrence, 1979); Gerald McFarland, *A Scattered People: An American Family Moves West* (New York, 1987), esp. 175–245; Sandra L. Myres, *Westering Women and the Frontier Experience: 1800–1915* (Albuquerque, 1982), esp. 238–70; Randall Bennett Woods, *A Black Odyssey: John Lewis Waller and the Promise of American Life, 1878–1900* (Lawrence, 1981). Black migration to the frontier was, at least partially, impelled by a general feeling of optimism that, according to Benjamin Quarles, characterized the feelings of former slaves in the immediate post-war era. *The Negro in the Making of America* (New York, 1964), 126. Harold Hyman's assertion that in the first flush of Reconstruction, Republican politicians believed that, "States would no longer impose on individuals the desperate disabilities that slavery represented…" may further explain why black men and women turned to the West for social and political freedoms they suspected would be grudgingly offered in the Old South. See *A More Perfect Union: The Impact of the Civil War and Reconstruction on the Constitution* (Boston, 1975), 283.

4. With the emergence of black history in the 1960s, it became clear that the frontier experience of Afro-Americans had been largely ignored. Some of the first attempts to redress that neglect tended to affirm simply the presence of blacks on the frontier. For example, Philip Durham and Everett L. Jones, *The Negro Cowboys* (New York, 1965), and William Loren Katz, *The Black West* (Garden City, 1971). These authors did not entirely ignore western discrimination, but their goals seem to have been to document the black experience as a reality. Their works were followed by scholars who questioned more closely the quality of frontier justice for blacks. For example, Robert G. Athearn, *In Search of Canaan: Black Migration to Kansas, 1879–1880* (Lawrence, 1978); Thomas C. Cox, *Blacks in Topeka, Kansas, 1865–1915: A Social History* (Baton Rouge, 1982); Randall Bennett Woods, "Integration, Exclusion, or Segregation? The 'Color Line' in Kansas: 1878–1900," *Western Historical Quarterly,* 14 (April 1983), 181–98.

5. For examples see Garland E. Bayliss, "The Arkansas State Penitentiary Under Democratic Control, 1874–1896," *Arkansas Historical Quarterly,* 34 (Autumn 1975), 195–213; Gary R. Kremer and Thomas E. Gage, "The Prison Against the Town: Jefferson City and the Penitentiary in the 19th Century," *Missouri Historical Review,* 74 (July 1980), 414–32; Harvey R. Hougen, "The Impact of Politics and Prison Industry on the General Management of the Kansas State Penitentiary, 1883–1909," *Kansas Historical Quarterly,* 43 (Autumn 1977), 297–318; Paul G. Hubbard, "Life in the Arizona Territorial Prison, 1876–1910," *Arizona and the West,* 1 (Winter 1959), 317–30; William C. Nesheim, "A History of the Missouri State Penitentiary: 1833–1875," (master's thesis, University of Missouri-Kansas City, 1970); Gordon L. Olson, " 'I Felt Like I Must Be Entering…Another World': The Anonymous Memoirs of an Early Inmate of the Wyoming Penitentiary," *Annals of Wyoming,* 47 (Fall 1975), 152–90; James A. Wilson, "Frontier in the Shadows: Prisons in the Far Southwest, 1850–1917," *Arizona and the West,* 22 (Winter 1980), 323–42. Material about gender, race, and American prisons is found in Nicole Hahn Rafter, "Gender, Prisons, and Prison History," *Social Science History,* 9 (Summer 1985), 233–47, and by the same author, *Partial Justice: Women in State Prisons, 1800–1935* (Boston, 1985).

6. See also John Vodicka's "Prison Plantation: The Story of Angola," *Southern Exposure,* 6 (Number 4, 1978), 32–38. Vodicka claims that between 1870 and 1901 more than three thousand Louisiana convicts, almost all black men, died under the lease system. For black womanhood, see Bell Hooks, *Ain't I A Woman: Black Women and Feminism* (Boston, 1981), and Pauli Murray, "The Liberation of Black Women," in *Our American Sisters: Women in American Life and Thought,* 4th ed., ed. Jean E. Friedman et al. (Lexington, MA, 1987), 557–59.

7. Citizens' Petitions, Nelly ———— File, State of Missouri: Pardon and Parole Papers, RG 5, Box 3, MSA. For a general discussion see Herman Lee Crow, "A Political History of the Texas Penal System: 1829–1951," (doctoral dissertation, University of Texas, 1964), 85–86.

8. The process by which the Louisiana penitentiary came to be located at the Angola plantation stretched across a broad expanse of time. In 1835 the state moved its convicts from New Orleans to Baton Rouge. Under Jones's administration the relocation of prisoners to Angola was accomplished before his death in 1894. Assistant Warden Roger S. Thomas, Interview with author, Louisiana State Penitentiary, Angola, Louisiana [Hereafter LSP], 22 June 1987. See also, Assistant Warden Roger S. Thomas to Warden Frank C. Blackburn, Unpublished Reports, "The History of Angola Series," 24 September, 23 October, 27 December 1985, and 7 January 1986, Office of the Warden, LSP. See also, Vodicka, "Prison Plantation."

9. All data drawn from Louisiana State Penitentiary Register of Convicts Received: 13 February 1866–29 December 1889, Prisoners #1–9073, Office of the Warden, LSP. These years were summarized since it was an era when the Unionist government wanted to exert a strong hand in Louisiana, and it might be expected that blacks enjoyed some measure of legal protection from arbitrary arrest and imprisonment. Actually, by 1873 there was ample evidence that any such protection was rapidly collapsing. See William S. McFeely, *Grant: A Biography* (New York, 1982), 417–18.

10. Eugenie Comes, Prisoner #183, Louisiana State Penitentiary, Register of Convicts Received: 13 February 1866–29 December 1889, Prisoners #1–9073, Office of the Warden, LSP.

11. Ibid., passim. See especially entries for Prisoners #61, 94, 150, 217, 300, 301, 460, 726, 954, 1074, 1549, 1716, 2261, 2265, 2288, and 2289.

12. Assistant Warden Roger S. Thomas, Interview with author, 22 June 1987. Also see Assistant Warden Roger S. Thomas to Warden Frank C. Blackburn, Unpublished Reports, "The History of Angola Series," 12 December 1985, Office of the Warden, LSP. Domestic use of black female convicts was common in other states, as well. By 1865 ten black women inmates staffed the penitentiary kitchen at the Texas prison. See Crow, "A Political History," 85. Also, parole requests for black women most commonly stemmed from the desire of a local white woman to secure domestic help. See samples from records of the following states: Prisoner Files #1391, 3337, 948, and 21695, Arkansas Department of Corrections, Pine Bluff, Arkansas; Pardon and Parole Papers, State of Missouri, RG 5; Box 22, Folder 2; Box 23, Folders 7 and 17; Box 25, Folders 10 and 26; Box 31, Folder 10; MSA; and Pardon and Parole Files, Governor's Office, Kansas State Penitentiary, Box 1, Florence Akers; Box 2, Ella Anderson; Box 13, Ella Bradfield; Box 20, Annie Carmack; Box 36, Bertha Draper; Kansas State Historical Society, Topeka, Kansas [Hereafter KSHS].

13. Alice Dunbar, Prisoner #529, Louisiana State Penitentiary, Register of Convicts Received: 13 February 1866–29 December 1889, Prisoners #1–9073, Office of the Warden, LSP.

14. Assistant Warden Roger S. Thomas, Interview with author, 22 June 1987. Assistant Warden Roger S. Thomas to Warden Frank C. Blackburn, Unpublished Reports, "The History of Angola Series," 13 June 1986, Office of the Warden, LSP. By *de facto* policy this became a punishment reserved for black women, since officials almost never held white women inside the prison walls. Brutal physical punishments were not unknown in most nineteenth-century prisons. Nonetheless, black women often caught the greater brunt of such treatment. See Rafter, *Partial Justice*, 150–51.

15. For general treatment see, John Hope Franklin, *Reconstruction: After the Civil War* (Chicago, 1961); Rayford W. Logan, *The Betrayal of the Negro: From Rutherford B. Hayes to Woodrow Wilson* (New York, 1965); August Meier and Elliott Rudwick, *From Plantation to Ghetto* (New York, 1970); and McFeely, *Grant*.

16. Crow, "A Political History," 47, 69.

17. William H. Sinclair to Lt. J. F. Kirkman, 26 February 1867, Records of the Bureau of Refugees, Freedmen, and Abandoned Lands, RG 105, Texas, Assistant Commissioner,

Letters Received Register, vol. 1, 1866–67, Box 4, N-S, National Archives, Washington, D.C. The author thanks Barry A. Crouch of Gallaudet University for this research material.

18. Ibid., 3.

19. Ibid., 23.

20. Ibid., 8. Sinclair apparently failed in his efforts to correct this situation. A Reconstruction committee that convened in June 1868 recommended that most of the 160 convicts at the Texas penitentiary be granted executive clemency. See Crow, "A Political History," 47, 69.

21. Ibid., 101–103; *Public Institutions, Second Annual Report of the Board of Commissioners: Kansas State Penitentiary* (Topeka, 1875), 294; Michael A. Kroll, "The Prison Experiment: A Circular History," *Southern Exposure*, 6 (Number 4, 1978), 9; Blake McKelvey, "A Half Century of Southern Penal Exploitation," *Social Forces*, 13 (Number 1, 1934–35), 113–16.

22. Ward, Dewey, and Company Lessees, "The Texas State Penitentiary," from the *Transactions of the Prison Congress, 1874*, repr. *Public Institutions*, 339.

23. Ibid., 340–42.

24. Crow, "A Political History," 77, 96.

25. *Public Institutions*, 343–51.

26. One prisoner's testimony seems to suggest that two of the women prisoners were white. Ibid., 346.

27. Ibid., 346–49.

28. Ibid., 349, 351.

29. Ibid., 346–47.

30. The efforts of Texas officials to correct abuses by placing women in a separate female facility failed to produce the desired reform. None of several plans, for example, in 1895, 1907, or 1909 brought any real change. See Crow, "A Political History," 178, 197–98. See also Rafter, *Partial Justice*, 88–89.

31. Crow, "A Political History," 178.

32. Selection of Lansing, Kansas, as the site for the state penitentiary dated to 1867. Penal institutions dominated the history of Lansing and its neighbor, Leavenworth. The presence of federal, state, and military authorities shaped the economic and social direction of the people of both communities. It was not uncommon for local citizens to escort visitors on a guided tour through the Leavenworth prison, as late as 1908. See Sister Mary Celestia Letters, Prison Ministry File, 1908–1915, Archives, Sisters of Charity, Leavenworth, Kansas. Also, Sister M. Seraphine, D.C., Interview with author, 3 July 1987, Leavenworth, Kansas.

33. *Public Institutions*, 352. Harvey R. Hougen argues that Warden Henry Hopkins' administration from 1867 to 1883 was marked by a generally progressive spirit that faltered under later managements. In "The Impact of Politics," Hougen does not discuss women in the Kansas prison.

34. Prison records in Kansas were not always consistently maintained. Racial designations did not become a regular entry until after 1883. Therefore, the actual number of black female prisoners received may have been somewhat higher than noted here. See those prison registers after 1880, especially Statement of Convicts, Prison Ledger A, 1864–1919, KSHS. In the same agency, Pardon and Parole Files, 1863–1919 and photographs from the state penitentiary are useful in compiling prisoner information.

35. Failure to record all data for all prisoners makes an accurate reading of this material difficult. Sufficient information does appear to suggest patterns of change. See State Penitentiary, Statement of Convicts, Prison Ledgers, 1864–1906, passim, KSHS.

36. Kansas State Penitentiary Records, Prisoner Ledger I, Number 1–1953 (Series II), 1901–1906, passim, KSHS.

37. Affidavits of Mary Fitzpatrick and Elizabeth Simpson, 22 May 1914, Governor George Hodges Papers, Correspondence, 1913–1915, Board of Corrections: Investigations of Punishments, Box 33, KSHS.

38. Affidavit of Mary Fitzpatrick, 22 May 1914, Governor George Hodges Papers, KSHS.
39. Kansas State Penitentiary Records, Prisoner Ledger I, Number 1–1953 (Series II), 1901–1906, Prisoner #1629, KSHS.
40. Undated brief with remarks of Deputy County Attorney Dawson and Judge Stilwell, Florence Akers Parole File, Governor's Office; State Penitentiary, Pardon and Parole Files, Box 1, KSHS.
41. Ibid., Undated statement of Florence Akers.
42. Ibid., M. L. Ogg to Governor Walter Stubbs, 24 February 1910.
43. Ibid., J. B. Bowers to Governor Walter Stubbs, 18 March 1910.
44. Ibid., O. M. Johnson to Governor Walter Stubbs, 22 February 1910.
45. Nebraska began construction of a state penitentiary at Lincoln in 1870. Prior to that time only inferior local jails were available. Aaron M. Boom, "History of Nebraska Penal Institutions: 1856–1940" (master's thesis, University of Nebraska, 1951), 84. A separate prison for women was opened at York in 1920, although inmates could be returned to the male facility at Lincoln for disciplinary purposes. Mary R. Norquest, "Nebraska Center for Women: History," Unpublished report, n.d., Office of Records Management, Nebraska Center for Women, York, Nebraska.
46. All information about Nebraska prisoners drawn from Inmate Record Jackets; Inactive File, Project #3087, Microfilm Box 77, 18–22, Nebraska State Penitentiary, Nebraska State Penal Complex, Lincoln, Nebraska, and Nebraska State Penitentiary Descriptive Record, vol. 1–3, RG 86, Rolls 1 and 2, Nebraska State Archives, Lincoln, Nebraska [Hereafter NSA].
47. Prisoner Case #1075, 2082, 2359, 2433, 2806, 3116, 3475, 4026, 4165, 4583, 5308, Nebraska State Penitentiary Descriptive Records, vol. 1–3, RG 86, Rolls 1 and 2, NSA.
48. Prisoner #4630, Nebraska State Penitentiary Descriptive Record, vol. 3, RG 86, Roll 2, NSA.
49. Data drawn from Prisoner #164, 187, 327, 1797, 2029, 3769, 3938, 4376, 5175, Nebraska State Penitentiary, Descriptive Records, vol. 1–3, RG 86, Rolls 1 and 2, NSA.
50. *Butte Miner,* 13, 16, 17 May 1901.
51. State of Montana, State Prison Convict Register, 1879–1920; State of Montana, Description of Prisoners, vol. 6–8, 1885–1911, Old Montana Prison, Deer Lodge, Montana [Hereafter OMP].
52. State of Montana, State Prisoner Convict Register, 60; State of Montana, Description of Prisoners, vol. 7, 1901–1908, Case #1185, 537, OMP.

HELENA, MONTANA'S BLACK COMMUNITY, 1900–1912

William L. Lang

[This article originally appeared as "The Nearly Forgotten Blacks on Last Chance Gulch, 1900–1912" in the *Pacific Northwest Quarterly*, Vol. 70 (1979), pp. 50–57. Retitled and reprinted with permission.]

While some African American pioneers chose to found all-black agricultural colonies and towns, most migrated to existing communities where white residents constituted the majority of inhabitants. In many of these Caucasian-dominated cities, blacks created institutions and participated in activities that led to the development of a sense of community among each town's African American citizens. The larger the black population, of course, the easier it was to establish black civic and social organizations. Moreover, whites often contributed indirectly to the creation of segregated black western communities by denying their African American neighbors the opportunity to join and participate in white institutions.

During the late nineteenth and early twentieth centuries, Helena, Montana, was one such western town with a white majority and a significant black minority among its several thousand inhabitants. From the time of its founding as a gold mining camp called "Last Chance Gulch" in the early 1860s, blacks lived in Helena. They came as miners, servants of white families, and cowboys and soldiers who wanted to settle down. Other African Americans came later, apparently drawn to the area by friends and relatives who had come before. By 1910 the town's black community counted over four hundred members.

Not surprisingly, given the significant role religion has played throughout the course of African American history, the first organization founded by Helena blacks was a church. Other groups soon followed, some affiliated with black churches and some independent of them. These included literary societies, social and service clubs, and fraternal orders. African American businesses catered to the needs and wants of black Helenans. The city's white leaders forced black children to attend a segregated public school for awhile until they decided that the cost of operating such a separate facility was too great. In addition to learning together, blacks and whites often lived next door to each other in Montana's capital city. Yet this limited social interaction did not mean that Helena's whites considered or treated blacks as equals. The white press, for example, usually ignored African American activities unless they were of a negative nature such as fights and arrests.

Consequently, one of the most important of Helena's black institutions was a newspaper, the Montana Plaindealer. *Founded in 1906 by Joseph B. Bass, who migrated to Helena from Kansas, the* Plaindealer *existed for five years. It reported on events in and of interest to the black segment of Helena society. Also, Bass editorialized against perceived racially prejudicial actions of state and local white officials. As time passed, Bass became more vocal about discrimination and less content merely to report happenings within the African American community. This caused his white customers to cease advertising in his journal, and it folded for financial reasons in 1911. In the following essay, William L. Lang summarizes the development of Helena's black community and then discusses in detail the impact Bass and the* Plaindealer *had on that portion of the town's population in the early twentieth century.*

Contemporary residents of the state capital of Montana are usually surprised to learn that at one time over four hundred Afro-Americans made their homes in the city. A boomer mining camp in the 1860s, a financial and transportation center by the 1870s, the seat of territorial and state government, and reputedly the richest city per capita in the nation in 1911, Helena has a colorful past that is familiar to many: but few people know about the blacks on Last Chance Gulch. This essay examines the development of Helena's Afro-American community during the prosperous years after the turn of the century.[1]

It is not surprising that the history of a minority group on the frontier has been overlooked. In fairness, however, the lack of written records has made the historians' task particularly difficult. Contemporaries often ignored minorities and maintained a journalistic silence in order to deny their existence. In Helena, the press usually found newsworthy only the notorious incidents in the black community; a violent crime committed by a black or a humorous anecdote demonstrating the purportedly low intelligence of Afro-Americans merited news space. The ordinary activities and even the notable accomplishments of local blacks went unnoticed and unrecorded by most whites.[2]

In 1908, for example, when the *Montana Daily Record* published *The New Helena*, a descriptive pamphlet boosting a prosperous and ambitious city, the sizable black population received no mention. Though the publication lauded Helena's churches, fraternal orders and benevolent societies, civic improvement groups, and social clubs, it failed to report that similar black institutions were active. Nonetheless, blacks were at the time a progressive element in town and, despite their being omitted from the booster literature, had been a part of the population practically since Helena's first days.[3]

Mention of Afro-Americans appears in fragmentary accounts of the first pioneer activity in the Prickly Pear Valley. Reportedly an unidentified black was one of three men who first discovered gold deposits in the Helena area in August 1862. The U.S. census of 1870 reveals that seventy-one Afro-Americans resided in the city, constituting 2.3 percent of Helena's 3,106 inhabitants. Two decades later, the black community numbered 279 in a total population of 13,834. By 1910, when Helena's black population was at its height, there were 420 persons representing 3.4 percent of the city's 12,515 citizens.[4]

There is no single explanation for why blacks located in Helena. Employment opportunities for day laborers and domestic servants may have attracted some, judging from the occupations listed by blacks in the manuscript census of 1870. It is certain that a number of black servants, cooks and even families came to Helena with white families during and after the Civil War. Further, in the 1870s and 1880s, many black cowboys and soldiers chose to settle in Helena, if only briefly, because already a vibrant black community had developed. Around the turn of the century, a sizable portion of Helena's black population was peripatetic: blacks left for jobs in other towns and other states only to return and perhaps leave again. The attraction in Helena, apparently, was the solidity of the Afro-American community; it was a prosperous and comfortable home base.

Most blacks who settled in Helena prior to 1870 were natives of eastern and upper southern states. By 1880, however, natives of the lower South, Kansas, Colorado, and Missouri dominated the population. Migrants from these states continued to predominate: moreover, in the last two decades of the century, they seem to have come to Helena because relatives or friends had already settled there. In fact, former Kansas and Missouri residents practically formed small colonies within the black community.[5]

Families as well as single persons migrated to Helena, and the family groups, not surprisingly, provided the stable foundation for the whole community. At the core of the developing community was the church. As early as 1867, a clergyman named McLaughlin and several black families organized a church society that prospered throughout the 1870s. But it was not until 1888, when the Reverend James Hubbard of the Kansas Conference of the African Methodist Episcopal (AME) church established the St. James congregation, that Helena's blacks had a strong and well-organized national church. An active congregation, it provided religious instruction, established a literary society, organized a library, and directed a ladies' benevolent aid society. By 1894 the St. James Church had sufficient prestige to host the annual AME convention of the Kansas Conference.[6]

The existence of St. James Church and the Afro-American lodge of the Good Templars, which twenty blacks founded in 1879, points up the segregation in nineteenth-century Helena. Blacks found no opportunity to participate equally with whites in religious, social, or cultural organizations. Whites wanted blacks to remain separate, and, to emphasize that desire, the territorial legislature in 1872 passed a statute requiring school districts to segregate schools on the basis of race. Three years later, Helena established a separate black school when several black families attempted to enroll their children in the Hill Street School. Helena authorities founded the segregated school despite the fact that there were fewer than twenty potential enrollees. This decision sparked complaints from the black community, but whites generally approved and supported the segregationist principle. In subsequent years, however, Republican defenders of Afro-Americans, the state super-intendent of public instruction, and even Governor Benjamin F. Potts openly criticized segregated schools. Finally, due to financial considerations, the city's electorate voted to close Helena's segregated school in 1882.[7]

Segregation of black schoolchildren was not unusual in the late nineteenth century, since the frontier was anything but immune to the racial prejudice that swept the nation during the Jim Crow era. But distinctions should be made between the racial prejudice there and that which raged elsewhere in 1900. Race wars, lynchings, violent abuse, and other atrocities were unknown in Helena, where racial friction rarely generated more than occasional disagreements, personal animosities, and social slights. Helena's racism, though destructive and deplorable, consisted of what W.E.B. Du Bois called "those petty little meannesses."[8]

One explanation for the relative lack of racial conflict in Helena was the moderate size of the black population, which never constituted a social or economic threat to whites. Another factor was the absence of residential segregation. In many American cities at that time, there was a physical separation of black and white residential districts; often the demarcation was the railroad tracks or a county road. In Helena, however, it was almost impossible to define a black district, for Afro-Americans lived in nearly every residential section but the wealthiest of the city.

In the case of public amusement and entertainment, however, the situation was decidedly different. Black society and white society in Helena did not mix. One element of the black community frequented Clore Street, an area reputedly vice-ridden and dangerous after dark. Predictably, there were racial incidents on Clore Street, and whites viewed the area with suspicion. The majority of blacks, however, found their entertainment in organized social clubs and festivities. They accepted social segregation; perhaps freedom in housing made social restrictions in Helena less oppressive than they were elsewhere.

Despite the evidences of prejudice, there was in Helena a kind of positive atmosphere, best indicated by the personal success of some of the black citizens. Walter Dorsey, for example, arrived in Helena in 1891 from his native state of Missouri. For three years he worked as a steward at the prestigious Montana Club, but by 1894 he had opened a grocery business on Eighth Avenue. The enterprise prospered, and Dorsey purchased the building. He was a respected member of the community, active in the St. James Church, Odd Fellows Lodge, Masons, a local all-black band, and a debating society. William C. Irvin, an earlier arrival, worked as a porter until he received an appointment to the Helena police force in 1888. For nearly twenty years he acquitted himself well as a police officer and gained the respect of both black and white citizens. Active in the church, Odd Fellows, and a civic improvement association, Irvin was also a family man who owned a modest home in a newer section of Helena. By 1906 he had ventured capital with a partner in a local business. Perhaps the most aggressive of Helena's Afro-American businessmen was Lloyd V. Graye, who at one point held a majority interest in a cleaning establishment, a shoe shop, and two saloons. As a fellow Helenan suggested, a black businessman, "must be a hustler, and most any fair man must admire his pluck and perseverance."[9]

Many Helena blacks had pluck and perseverance, but even more impressive than the attributes of individuals was the dynamism of the black population as a whole. The St. James AME Church followed a pattern of growth and responsiveness to group needs that was typical of this community. Within a year after the formation of the church in 1888, the congregation constructed a handsome frame building with a limestone foundation and a steeple. Church members lost little time organizing a literary society, a Sabbath school, a women's benevolent association, a theatrical troupe, a nine-piece band, and even a baseball team. The congregation's leadership consisted of individuals representing nearly every occupation in the black community. Businessmen like Dorsey, Andrew J. Walton, and M.O.J. Arnett joined with

William C. Irvin. African Americans in Helena, Montana, had enough political clout with the town's white leaders to secure the appointment of Irvin to the city police force in 1888; he served as a policeman for nearly twenty years. This photo was taken by James Presley Ball, an African American who operated a studio in Helena from 1887 to 1900. (Courtesy, Montana Historical Society.)

waiter J. B. Reid, plasterer Ward Cole, janitor James Crump, porter Miles York, and printer Joseph Tucker to provide the church with a broad social foundation. St. James Church was truly a community institution.[10]

By 1900 service, fraternal, and social organizations competed with church-related groups for space on blacks' social calendars. The fraternal orders, which included two Masonic lodges, an Odd Fellows lodge, and the Household of Ruth and the Eastern Star, were somewhat cliquish and competitive, but they helped to stabilize Helena's black community. Women's benevolent societies, such as the "Busy Bees" and "Willen Workers," ministered to the needs of the unfortunate and raised money for the church.

The black population was large enough by the turn of the century to attract several traveling minstrel shows, but Helena's blacks also had local organizations that regularly sponsored gala activities. The Autumn Leaf Social Club, for example, organized events as diverse as "Buck and Wing" dancing contests and mandolin concerts. The Manhattan Social Club, which boasted a reading room, billiard parlor, and private dining room at its quarters on Main Street, was easily the most sophisticated club in town, and, though it was strictly "for men only," its members hosted more than a few grand socials.[11]

At church gatherings and Manhattan Club meetings alike, one subject certain to provoke discussion was politics. Although their numbers never made them a truly powerful electoral force in Helena, blacks interested themselves in local and national politics. In the 1860s and early 1870s, when Civil War political issues still evoked controversy, Afro-Americans often came under political attack. The Helena *Gazette*, for example, editorialized vitriolically against black suffrage in 1867. Democrats charged that blacks were little more than tools of the Republicans, and that some "unscrupulous white demagogues" even sent blacks "to the polls well liquored up to bully and insult white men." These charges were unfounded, but there is no denying that Republicans assiduously courted the black vote in Helena.[12]

Despite threats and accusations, Helena's blacks were not discouraged from political action. When the Fifteenth Amendment became a reality in 1870, Ben Stone and J. R. Johnson led their neighbors in a jubilant mass demonstration on Main Street, complete with "the firing of thirty-two guns from the hill...south of the city." The following year, an Afro-American political club, which was organized in part by Helena's Republicans, declared its intention to trumpet Republican William H. Claggett's candidacy for territorial delegate.[13]

In 1894 Helena blacks involved themselves once again in a controversial political issue. The story of the war between Helena and Anaconda for the designation as state capital is well known, but the part played in the third and last battle by the *Colored Citizen*, an Afro-American newspaper published briefly in Helena, is less familiar. J. P. Ball, Jr., the editor, campaigned vigorously on Helena's behalf during the newspaper's two-month existence in the fall of 1894. The *Colored Citizen* aimed at Montana's black voters, who Ball believed would be "the balance of power" in blocking the Anaconda Company's "iron claw of corporate infernalism which has always crushed out the black man from every factory and workshop." When the electorate selected Helena as the capital, Ball claimed no small part in the result.[14]

The *Colored Citizen*, however, was more than a mere mouthpiece for Helena's boosters. Its editor also chastised local racists and even suggested that they "be declared un-American." Ball apparently served two masters. In support of the city, he argued that Helena, unlike Anaconda, recognized "No Color Line"; in support of blacks, he exposed and denounced genuine prejudice— even in Helena. Despite ample evidence that white politicians financed Ball's paper for the sole purpose of promoting the city, the *Colored Citizen* benefited local Afro-Americans: it was their public defender, if only for two months.[15]

By the first decade of the new century, Helena's black community had a new spokesman to replace J. P. Ball. Joseph B. Bass came to Helena from Topeka, Kansas, in early 1906. He arrived full of energy, ambition for his race, and commitment to community involvement. In his thirty-three years of residence in Topeka, Bass had participated in AME church activities, reform politics, and some newspaper work. Whether or not he moved to Helena with journalism in mind, he was in town hardly long enough to acquaint himself with the area before he began publishing the *Montana Plaindealer*. And from the outset, Bass and his paper had a decided and positive effect upon Helena's black community.

"With this issue we make our initial bow to the public," Bass told awaiting readers of the *Plaindealer* on March 16, 1906. In an opening expression of modesty, he disclaimed any intention of assuming instant leadership of the black community and stated that "our only aim shall be for the progress and uplifting of a race with which our destiny is forever linked." Indeed, the eight-page paper was not overpowering in appearance, and Bass's modesty was appropriate; still, a discerning reader could surmise that the *Plaindealer* would not be an idle paper. "Our mission," Bass explained, "shall be at no time to stir up strife, but rather to pour oil on troubled waters," but he also warned that he would "stand up for the right and denounce the wrong." As the *Plaindealer* quickly demonstrated, J. B. Bass was a progressive in politics, and his paper's motto, "Peace, Prosperity, and Union," indicated a strong Republican affiliation.[16]

Operating out of a small office at 17 South Main Street, Bass and his assistant, Joseph H. Tucker, published the *Plaindealer* on a weekly basis from 1906 to 1911. Bass's printing business, supplemented by advertisements and subscriptions, kept the paper solvent, and there is no evidence of silent business partners or other financial resources. Editorials appeared on page one, along with national news items of interest to the black community; the remaining pages included regional, state, and local news.

A black Helenan reading the *Plaindealer* in 1906 might have read the week's editorial and glanced at the major news items, but he was certain to study the local news section. Herein Bass provided a genuine service to Helena blacks, for these columns engendered community identity and involvement. Church activities, vital statistics, unusual experiences, awards and honors, and gossip all found a place in the *Plaindealer*, and readers faithfully checked to see if they or their friends appeared in print. One device Bass used, a column he called "The Plaindealer Would Like To Know Why," must have created minor sensations when he poked fun by asking why "A certain gentleman who attended the Ball last week did not have his full dress complete?" and "The Owl saw two of the Smart Set on Joliet and Cutler Sts. at a late hour Wednesday night?" Though such entertainment items undoubtedly attracted readers, Bass's real purpose was to stimulate genuine progressive action among Afro-Americans in Helena.[17]

Black progressivism, it should be noted, was distinct from white progressivism. White progressives sought to reform beleaguered institutions. But Afro-Americans in 1900 had yet to be accepted into American life or allowed access to American institutions; they met discrimination at every turn. Since emancipation, blacks throughout the nation faced a continuing challenge to improve their condition and thereby establish a recognized and equitable position in society. Progressivism for blacks, then, was the effort to acquire the rights, opportunities, and rewards that America seemed to offer. Among blacks themselves a national debate raged over the means by which progressive aims could be best accomplished. Some leaders urged self-help and economic development as the most efficient way to racial advancement; others argued that the acquisition of political and social rights should be the first priority. By the first decade of the twentieth century, Booker T. Washington of Tuskegee Institute and W.E.B. Du Bois of Atlanta University stood as the acknowledged national proponents of the two strategies of black progressivism.[18]

J. B. Bass consistently prodded Helena's blacks to undertake self-help projects and business enterprises. Like Washington, he believed that economic development rather than strident demands for rights brought the desired results. "We advise our young men to go to work or engage in some legitimate business," Bass wrote in 1906, because "by doing something they will not only command greater respect for themselves but it will redound to the credit of the race and community as well." The shiftless and the idle, he reminded his readers, "are the weights upon our progress." His was a gospel of industry, thrift, and work.[19]

The ideas, speeches, and activities of Booker T. Washington figured prominently in the *Plaindealer*'s pages. Bass regularly excerpted articles and editorials from Washingtonian newspapers such as the New York *Age* and the Washington (D.C.) *Bee*. He also put the suggestions of the Sage of Tuskegee into action: due primarily to Bass's efforts, Helena's black community had by 1908 created two progressive organizations founded on the self-help principle. First, in 1907, a small group that included Bass, tailors Arnett and Harry Saulsburg, Manhattan Club president Harry C. Simmons, and printer J. L. Ellis formed a Helena chapter of the National Negro Business League. The league, which Washington himself founded in 1900 with the aid of Carnegie money, promoted the establishment of black-owned businesses. In Helena the league met regularly to discuss business problems; it provided some financial support for new businesses; and it sent delegates to national conventions. Then in January 1908, a second self-help group, the Afro-American Building Association, incorporated under the laws of Montana.[20]

The Afro-American Building Association focused on an ambitious program of economic development, that is, it formed "for the purpose of buying real estate and erecting buildings." The *Plaindealer* endorsed its program as "a splendid investment for the colored citizens of Helena." The eight-member board of directors included three women, two of whom operated businesses of their own—a beauty salon and a "physical culture club" for women. Bass declared that the association was a "giant stride in the betterment of the condition of the race in this section," and he believed that it would attract more blacks to Helena. Although there is no evidence that the association actually constructed any buildings, Frank Mitchell's Atlantic Restaurant and Jessie Waggener's Crown Cleaners received support from the organization.[21]

Business and economic development was not the only focus of Helena's progressive-minded blacks. Community improvement, a major concern of both black and white progressives, took on special significance for blacks. Local struggles to improve conditions were part of the greater effort to better the black man's position, uplift the entire race, and hasten the day of genuine acceptance by white Americans. Fired with this vision and hope, Bass used the *Plaindealer* to challenge his neighbors and pressure them into working for civic progress.[22]

As Bass told his readers, civic progress demanded that the blacks organize their community, unify it, cleanse it of immoral elements, encourage its dynamic members, and defend it from racist attacks. The first priorities were unity and local initiative. "The greatest hope for the ultimate solution of the problems…of our race," he said, "is our ability to get together." In 1907, for example, when representatives of a national Colored Co-Operative League tried to organize in Helena, Bass editorialized in support of the cooperative principle but against the league. "Let's get together on a movement of our own," he suggested, "and not one that requires us to pay high tribute to some insatiable nabob of which we know nothing about." Black Helenans benefited from information and expertise provided by the National Negro Business League, but Bass held firmly to the belief that only local cooperative activities would increase self-esteem and also win approval from whites: "With our people working together, we shall be in a position to command the respect and commendation of our more favored friends of the opposite dominant race."[23]

Bass and fellow progressives challenged defeatist attitudes among Helena blacks and succeeded in stimulating that sense of group pride that every ethnic population desires. It was a pride born of achievement and nurtured by the optimistic faith that acceptance was forthcoming. Fred Spearman, a waiter and later civil service employee, told *Plaindealer* readers: "The Negro is the mighty force he is in the world today only because he has demonstrated in competitive struggle that he possesses power." The black man, Bass proudly claimed, could compete with anyone. When Charles Mason and his professional crew of black waiters from Hot Springs, Arkansas, came to Helena's famed Broadwater Hotel and Natatorium, for example, Bass could not resist comparing their expertise to the "bum service" previously provided by "the young white men who were imported here as waiters."[24]

Bass, Spearman, and other progressives commended the active, moral, and achievement-oriented life. Of all their community organizations, the St. James Literary Society best emulated such values. Under the initial guidance of the Reverend W. T. Osborne, Walter Dorsey, Mrs. Eugene Baker, and Joseph Clark, the society grew quickly after its founding in November 1906, boasting over one hundred participants at its weekly meetings. The society provided black Helenans with a forum for discussion of community issues, an audience for performing artists, and an opportunity for local poets, playwrights, and essayists to present their work. Bass called the society "an intellectual treat"; he believed the group would keep Helena's blacks "in the front ranks of progress," doing their part "in the solution of the great problems that confront us."[25]

While recitals, plays, and socials drew considerable interest, the St. James Literary Society debates created real excitement. Furious discussions often followed the formal debates on controversial topics such as "Resolved, that the Negroes of the South enjoy more prosperity than in any other section of the U.S."; "Resolved, that slavery was a benefit to the Negro race"; and "Resolved, that woman suffrage is detrimental to the welfare of the nation." These debates forced blacks to evaluate the progress of the race and, more importantly, the actual condition of Helena's black population. Moral standards in the community, concerned Afro-Americans agreed, needed to be raised so that the misbehavior of a few would not condemn the majority. It was particularly painful to black progressives that whites took special notice of the criminal and deviant elements among Helena blacks and ignored the achievements of average citizens. The mere existence of black prostitutes, pimps, hustlers, and gamblers in Clore Street dives confirmed for whites the worst black stereotypes. Situations demanding a defense of this immoral element in the black community against an outraged and prejudiced white citizenry posed a genuine dilemma to Bass and other progressives.[26]

A case in point is the Nora Mentzel trial in 1906. Mentzel, a rather well-known Clore Street prostitute, killed a black soldier in the course of an argument. Though the *Independent* and the *Montana Daily Record* reported the whole affair accurately, the reports dwelt on lurid details and the antics and opinions of Leon Lacroix, the prosecutor and county attorney. Lacroix's charge to the jury, which the *Record* called "a masterful effort, at times reaching the stage of eloquence," succinctly expressed a widely held view. "It is time that the respectable white people of this community rise in their might and assert their rights." Bass angered quickly when he heard such sentiments, because he knew that all too often white saloonkeepers and gamblers enticed blacks and relied on their patronage.[27]

Although progressive blacks did not defend Nora Mentzel's morality, they protested against her being used to make race once again the target of generalized attacks. Bass, in a pained and angry reaction to Lacroix, asked Helena to "give us credit for what we do.... we are law-abiding." He reminded whites that "the moral degenerates are the weight upon us, as they are upon your race, and this is no fault of the whole race." The jury found Mentzel not guilty of murder by reason of self-defense, but for Helena's blacks the issue was not her guilt or innocence. Criminal behavior strengthened white prejudice, and it was clear that the black community needed to speak out plainly against immorality, defend its reputation, and contest prejudice aggressively.[28]

Consequently, the *Plaindealer* began to advocate civil rights. Bass demanded that Helena treat its citizens on an equal basis. Refusing to maintain the low civil rights profile typical of the followers of Booker T. Washington, Bass and other activists rejected retreat-and-accommodation tactics. "Negro rights in the north, prejudice against the Negro in the north," Annie Walton wrote in the *Plaindealer*, "is just as intense as that in the south, only the North plays the hypocrite to the contrary." According to Walton, Helena blacks should recognize the truth about whites: "the northern white man never did want the Negro on equal rights with him and he knows he is playing the hypocrite all the time." Afro-Americans might be encouraged to improve their condition through business, Walton reminded her readers, but soon "you will hear the northern white brother say, 'Oh it is too bad he or she is colored, they ought to have been a Jew.'"[29]

Walton and other Helena blacks mixed the self-help doctrine with a strong defense of political and civil rights. Not exclusively committed to Washington's views, they embraced many of the ideas and tactics of Du Bois, whose Niagara movement stressed the acquisition of equal rights over self-help and economic development. The truly challenging aspect of Du Bois-style militancy was its rejection of hypocrisy and self-deception. Although many blacks continued to accommodate whites whenever politically or economically expedient, others—even business people like Annie Walton—accepted the Du Bois example, gave vent to their anger, and stripped the hypocrisy off themselves and their neighbors.

By 1908 the *Plaindealer* had become an ideologically interesting mixture: it exhorted blacks to protest yet it urged them to quiet industry. Bass and other progressives found it increasingly difficult to remain silent when discrimination and prejudice threatened their integrity and racial pride. What good was it to bolster community pride if prejudice robbed blacks of their rights and freedom? The more Bass questioned, the less Washingtonian the *Plaindealer's* tone became. By 1911, when Walton wrote her strident piece, the paper verged on militancy. Perhaps Bass swung toward Du Bois too quickly for most Helena blacks, and this may partially explain the demise of the *Plaindealer* that year. One thing is certain: local conditions caused Bass's move to militancy.

In 1906, for example, when the *Independent* maliciously belittled Afro-American improvement, stating that "the average Negro likes pork chops better than work" and that blacks "have a genius for self-maintenance without working," Bass was anything but quiet. In response to the insult that "repose is the natural attitude of the Negro," Bass assailed the *Independent's* views as "dull, stupid, and disingenuous." Go south of the Mason-Dixon Line, he instructed, "and any 12 years old school child can tell you who furnishes the labor that puts on the market the great productions of the South." According to Bass, the *Independent's* editor had outdone the notorious southern racist "Pitchfork" Ben Tillman, and Helena's blacks would not stand for it. The *Plaindealer*, at times as strident as Du Bois himself, defended the black community time and again, and particularly in two separate instances in 1908 and 1909.[30]

On May 5, 1908, William R. Holland, who was described by the *Record* as "a colored man wearing large and flashy diamonds, with clothes to correspond," found that he had transgressed a recently enacted law prohibiting the unauthorized wearing of an insignia of a fraternal order. Holland, who played ragtime piano in a Clore Street brothel, was a member of the International Benevolent and Protective Order of Elks of the World, the Afro-American Elks organization. For several days he had displayed a diamond-studded Elks pin inscribed with the legend "B.P.O.E."; local white Elks members moved to have him arrested, maintaining that Holland was masquerading as a "real" Elk when in fact he was not. This unusual law resulted from fears generated when the Butte Elks, the only black lodge in Montana, proposed expansion in 1906. That year Helena Elks warned other white fraternal orders that a black invasion was in the offing, and when the legislature met in 1907 there was considerable support for a bill introduced by W. H. Haviland, a Butte Democrat, which was designed to protect white fraternal orders from similar Afro-American orders by making unauthorized insignia-wearing unlawful. After little debate the bill passed unanimously on February 13, 1907, providing penalties of a $200 fine and ninety days in jail.[31]

Thus, when William Holland walked about Helena wearing his Elks pin in the spring of 1908, the white Elks recognized that he was recruiting for the expanding Butte lodge. Armed with the new law, they acted swiftly. In response to Holland's arrest, the *Plaindealer* carried an editorial entitled "Jim Crowing"; in it, Bass defended the black Elks organization and declared the law "distinctive class legislation," "an outrage" that had no place in a civilized community. "Any old bum be he with a white face could use the button and no notice would be taken of the same," Bass contended, but an upstanding black had no rights. A jury of white Helenans found Holland guilty, and Judge Samuel W. Langhorne, noting what he called Holland's impudence, fined him $100. Holland, standing on principle and with the support of the *Plaindealer*, refused to pay and went to jail. Bass charged that Langhorne, Deputy County Attorney Edward Phelan, and others involved in the case were themselves members of the Elks and were hardly objective in prosecuting the case.

Holland's lawyer, Charles Spaulding, agreed and appealed the decision to the state supreme court on June 29, 1908.[32]

Spaulding, who had previously defended Nora Mentzel, argued that the legislation violated the equal protection clause of the Fourteenth Amendment and constituted a poorly disguised effort to discriminate against blacks. On July 18, 1908, Chief Justice Theodore Brantly, expressing the opinion of a unanimous court, agreed that the law was discriminatory and in violation of the Fourteenth Amendment. "Speaking generally," Brantly wrote, "all persons in the community are free to use or wear any article they please." Yet the court dodged the racial issue altogether. It invalidated the law on the basis of a section that exempted wives and daughters of members from prosecution, ruling against sexual—not racial—discrimination. What may have constituted an early victory for women's rights in Montana left the Jim Crow issue in a somewhat ambivalent state. Nonetheless, Bass rightfully boasted that Jim Crow laws in Montana could be challenged and that they had suffered a defeat. As black progressives claimed victory, another test loomed on the horizon.[33]

Democratic State Senator Charles S. Muffly of Winston, representing Broadwater County, had introduced a bill in 1907 prohibiting mixed racial marriages. The legislation failed in 1907, but Muffly reintroduced it in 1909. "The Tom-Toms have been beaten, the tocsin sounded," Bass wrote in February of that year, "and one, the honorable Mr. Muffly of Broadwater, has achieved fame, if not fortune, by the passage in the Senate of the Montana Legislature, of a real Jim Crow law." Bass geared up the *Plaindealer* for a contest with "the Ben Tillman of the Northwest," and at once set about portraying Muffly as a veritable Jeff Davis, an "unregenerate Democratic fire eater" who snorted racist sentiments, played the demagogue's role, and encouraged racial prejudice. How could Montanans be taken in, Bass asked, when Muffly rose in the senate shouting, "Oh Lord, save us from being devoured by inter-marriages between blacks and whites!"[34]

"An Act Prohibiting Marriages between White Persons, Negroes, Persons of Negro Blood, and between White Persons, Chinese and Japanese, and making such Marriage Void; and prescribing punishment for Solemnizing such Marriages," became law on March 3, 1909. Though the antimiscegenation bill passed narrowly—and only after considerable amendment and at least one major floor fight in the house—it nevertheless was a great blow to blacks in the Treasure State. "Montana has joined the Jim Crow Colony alongside of Mississippi, South Carolina, Texas, and Arkansas," Bass blasted in boldface across the front page; "God help us!" The white press, notably Helena's *Treasure State*, supported the law: "the black man is not the equal of his white contemporary...and Jim Crow laws won't hold him down if he deserves to rise." To this Bass replied, "Just as well to tell us even if you are in prison, if you deserve to be free you shall be."[35]

Bass was particularly critical of the Republicans who voted for Muffly's bill. They were traitors to their principles and the nation. It was tragic, Bass cried, that "the blacks were slain in the house of their friends." To emphasize his point, he published the names of "four degenerate Republicans" advertisement-style on the front page. Despite his fulminations the law stood. Nevertheless, Bass and the *Plaindealer* made it clear that Helena's black community was not without a voice in protest. In April 1909, Henry J. Baker, J.E.W. Clark, Arnett, Bass, and others created the Afro-American Protective League to bring political pressure in defense of blacks' rights.[36]

The league, at least through 1910, seems to have been effective in identifying and protesting discrimination, most commonly the discriminatory administration of justice. Blacks frequently faced charges for gambling, disorderly conduct, and other disturbances, but whites usually escaped punishment for the same activities. By September 1911, yet another organization had been founded to protect Helena blacks. The Colored Progressive League, composed of over sixty active members, pledged itself to expel black pimps, prostitutes, and hustlers from the city and to defend Afro-Americans unjustly harassed by racist authorities.[37]

Publication of the *Montana Plaindealer* ended in 1911. For several months before the paper's demise, Bass pleaded with subscribers to renew, and he publicly asked those who owed money to pay their debts promptly. His job printing business, which had carried a major portion of the newspaper's financial burden, had dropped off since 1909. Perhaps Bass's increasing militancy, particularly the organization of the Afro-American Protective League, turned customers away; perhaps the quality of printing had declined and business suffered as a result. Whatever the reason, with the end of the *Plaindealer*, black Helena lost its most effective progressive voice.

In subsequent years, Helena's black population declined sharply from its height in 1910. By 1920 there were only 220 blacks in a total population numbering 12,037, and in 1930 only 131 in 12,094 persons. There is no single cause for the decline. Helena's population decreased slightly between 1910 and 1920, probably as a result of the heavy draft calls Montana experienced during World War I. Many of Helena's blacks were called to fight; it is also likely that blacks in Helena responded to the lures of war-related jobs in the Midwest and on the Pacific Coast. By mid-century, only eighty-eight blacks remained in a total population of 17,581, and by 1970 the census revealed only forty-five blacks residing in a city of 22,730.[38]

During the progressive era, Helena's blacks formed a strong and viable community characterized by racial pride, pragmatism, and group-oriented action. Their experience demonstrates that the behavior of minorities on the frontier resembled that of their counterparts in more developed regions; further, it suggests that Afro-American political strategies were influenced more by local conditions than by ideological convictions. The story of Helena's blacks constitutes an important chapter in the urban history of the frontier West.

Notes

1. Last Chance Gulch, named by the four prospectors who found gold there in 1864, became Helena in 1865. By 1875 it was the territorial capital, and it incorporated in 1881. In 1894, after statehood, Helena was selected as Montana's permanent capital.

2. Although articles on blacks in the West have appeared sporadically over the last forty years, it was not until the 1960s that the subject drew much attention. Since then, scholars have studied Afro-Americans in California, Colorado, Kansas, Oregon, and the Southwest, but they have largely ignored the history of urban blacks. Lawrence B. De Graaf, in "Recognition, Racism, and Reflections on the Writing of Western Black History," *Pacific Historical Review*, Vol. 44 (1975), 22–51, surveys the literature and suggests where research is needed. Some of the best recent literature on the black West includes: Arlen L. Fowler, *The Black Infantry in the West, 1869–1891* (Westport, Conn., 1971); William L. Katz, *The Black West* (Garden City, 1971); William H. Leckie, *Buffalo Soldiers: A Narrative of the Negro Cavalry in the West* (Norman, Okla., 1967); Kenneth W. Porter, *The Negro on the American Frontier* (New York, 1971); W. Sherman Savage, *Blacks in the West* (Westport, Conn., 1976).

3. Charles D. Greenfield, ed., *The New Helena: A Series of Articles Descriptive of the Capital City of Montana* (Helena, 1908).

4. *Montana Territorial Directory for 1868* (Helena, 1868), 47; *The Statistics of the Population of the United States, Ninth Census,* Vol. I: 1870 (Washington, D.C., 1872), 196; *Report on Population of the United States at the Eleventh Census: 1890,* Part 1 (Washington, D. C. 1895), 467; *Thirteenth Census of the United States Taken in the Year 1910,* Vol. II: Population (Washington, D.C., 1913), 1159.

5. See manuscript census schedules for Montana Territory, 1870 and 1880 (microfilm), Montana Historical Society (MHS), Helena. Information about the transience of Helena's black population is gleaned from the files of the Helena *Colored Citizen,* 1894, and Polk's Helena city directories, 1895–1915, MHS.

6. Helena *Weekly Herald,* July 31, 1867; Sept. 27, 1888. *Colored Citizen,* Oct. 8, 1894.

7. *Laws, Memorials and Resolutions of the Territory of Montana* (Deer Lodge, 1872), 627 (hereafter cited *Laws* with appropriate year). The law remained in force in several Montana cities until its repeal in 1895. Helena *Daily Independent,* Jan. 26, 1875; Dec. 2, 1876. *House Journal of the Ninth Session of the Legislative Assembly of the Territory of Montana, 1876* (Helena, 1876), 340 (hereafter cited *House Journal* with appropriate year); Helena *Daily Herald,* Dec. 20, 1876. For a brief discussion of the school issue, see: J. W. Smurr, "Jim Crow Out West," in *Historical Essays on Montana and the Northwest,* ed. J.W. Smurr and K. Ross Toole (Helena, 1957), 180–82.

8. Eugene H. Berwanger, *The Frontier Against Slavery: Western Anti-Negro Prejudice and the Slavery Extension Controversy* (Urbana, Ill., 1967); V. Jacque Voegeli, *Free But Not Equal: The Midwest and the Negro during the Civil War* (Chicago, 1967).

9. *Montana Plaindealer* (Helena), June 27, Sept. 14, 1906; Jan. 10, 1908 (hereafter cited *Plaindealer* with appropriate date).

10. *Colored Citizen*, Sept. 3, 1894.

11. *Plaindealer*, June 8, Nov. 18, 1906; April 3, 1908. Helena city directories, 1895–1900; treasurer's account book, Helena Second Baptist Church (Negro), MHS.

12. Helena *Gazette*, June 15, July 13, 1867; *Rocky Mountain Gazette* (Helena), Aug. 6, 1873 (quotation).

13. *Herald*, April 15, 1870 (quotation); July 11, 1871. Republicans Wilbur Fisk Sanders and Col. Wiley S. Scribner were instrumental in urging blacks to organize politically.

14. *Colored Citizen*, Sept. 17, Oct. 29 (quotation), 1894.

15. *Ibid.*, Sept. 3, 24, 1894. On the political role of the *Colored Citizen*, see: Rex C. Myers, "Montana's Negro Newspapers, 1894–1911," *Montana Journalism Review*, No. 16 (1973), 17–22.

16. *Plaindealer*, March 16, 1906.

17. *Ibid.*, Oct. 12, 1906 (first quotation); June 14, 1907 (second quotation).

18. August Meier, *Negro Thought in America, 1880–1915: Racial Ideologies in the Age of Booker T. Washington* (Ann Arbor, 1963), 100–120, 190–206; Louis R. Harlan, *Booker T. Washington: The Making of a Black Leader, 1856–1901* (New York, 1972); Elliott M. Rudwick, *W.E.B. Du Bois, Propagandist of the Negro Protest* (New York, 1968).

19. *Plaindealer*, April 27, 1906.

20. *Ibid.*, April 26, June 14, July 19, Aug. 9, 1907; Meier, 124–27.

21. *Plaindealer*, Jan. 10 (first quotation), 24 (second quotation), 1908. The board of directors included Nathaniel Ford, M.O.J. Arnett, James Crump, George W. Alexander, William C. Irvin, Mary Matthews, Mattie Simmons, and Lenora Johnson.

22. On black progressivism, see: Lester C. Lamon, "Progressivism Was Not 'For Whites Only': The Black Progressive Reformers of Nashville, Tennessee, 1906–1918," *Indiana Academy of the Social Sciences Proceedings,* 3rd Series, Vol. 9 (1974), 103–12; Linda O. Hines and Allen W. Jones, "A Voice of Black Protest: The Savannah Men's Sunday Club, 1905–1911," *Phylon,* Vol. 35 (1974), 193–202.

23. *Plaindealer*, May 11, 1906 (third quotation); May 24 (first quotation), Nov. 1 (second quotation), 1907.

24. *Ibid.*, April 12, 1907; June 26, 1908 (Fred Spearman, "The Negro a World Force").

25. *Plaindealer*, Feb. 1, 1907.

26. *Ibid.*, March 13 (first quotation), May 1 (second quotation), Dec. 7 (third quotation), 1908.

27. *Montana Daily Record* (Helena), March 23 (quotation), 24, 1906 (hereafter cited *Record* with appropriate date); *Independent*, March 20, 23, 26, 1906.

28. *Plaindealer*, March 30, 1906 (quotation); *Record*, March 26, 1906. Mentzel was not entirely free, however, for she was charged with conspiracy to commit perjury along with Joseph H. Tucker, Clover "Bad Boy" Smith, and L. L. Grisson. She was, in fact, apprehended as she boarded an outward-bound train.

29. Annie Walton to editor, in *Plaindealer*, March 24, 1911.

30. *Independent*, June 1, 1906 (first quotation); *Plaindealer*, June 8, 1906 (second quotation).

31. *Record*, May 5, 1908 (quotation); *Plaindealer*, June 24, 1906; *Laws*, 1907, pp. 24–25; *House Journal*, 1907, pp. 259, 271, 283.

32. *Plaindealer*, May 15, 1908.

33. *Reports of Cases Argued and Determined in the Supreme Court of Montana, 1908* (San Francisco, 1909), 393–407; *Plaindealer*, July 31, 1908.

34. *Plaindealer*, Feb. 12, 1909.

35. *Laws*, 1909, pp. 57–58 (first quotation). For the legislative history of Muffly's senate bill 34, see: *Senate Journal of the Eleventh Session of the Legislative Assembly of the State of Montana, 1909* (Helena, 1909), 46, 171, 282, 291; *House Journal*, 1909, pp. 55, 238, 287, 300, 368. The senate vote was 15 to 11; after one defeat on the floor, the bill passed the house by a final vote

of 42 to 18. *Plaindealer*, March 5, 1909 (second quotation); *Treasure State* (Helena), Feb. 20, 1909 (third quotation).

36. *Plaindealer*, Feb. 12 (first quotation), April 24 (second quotation), July 30, 1909.

37. See editorials in *Plaindealer*, April 2, Oct. 30, 1909; May 26, Sept. 8, 1911.

38. *Fourteenth Census of the United States,* Vol. III: *Population: 1920* (Washington, D.C., 1922), 584; *Fifteenth Census of the United States: 1930, Population,* Vol. III, Part 2 (Washington, D.C., 1932), 48; *A Report of the Seventeenth Decennial Census of the United States: Census of Population: 1950,* Vol. II, Part 26 (Washington, D.C., 1952), 39; *1970 Census of Population,* Vol. I, Part 28 (Washington, D.C., 1973), 62.

THE DEVELOPMENT OF AFRICAN AMERICAN NEWSPAPERS IN THE AMERICAN WEST, 1880–1914

Gayle K. Berardi and Thomas W. Segady

[This article originally appeared as "The Development of African-American Newspapers in the American West: A Sociohistorical Perspective" in the *Journal of Negro History*, Vol. 75 (1990), pp. 96–111. Retitled, adapted, and reprinted with permission.]

As the preceding essay shows, whenever possible African American pioneers usually sought to create a sense of community on the western frontier of the late nineteenth and early twentieth centuries. Consequently, they often established all-black settlements or black neighborhoods in already existing "white" towns. Living in close proximity to fellow African Americans, therefore, was a key aspect of the process of creating the sense of community that characterized much of western African American settlement.

Another element of the phenomenon, however, was that white westerners frequently refused to allow African Americans to become part of integrated communities. Although most historians believe that whites in the West subjected black pioneers to less prejudice than was the case in other parts of the country, race consciousness was still prevalent on the frontier. Consequently, western Caucasians customarily preferred not to socialize with their black neighbors, and they typically excluded blacks from their clubs and other organizations. This rejection by white society, therefore, served to nurture the urge African American pioneers had to form their own close knit communities. Often, one indication of the cohesiveness of a black community was that one or more of its members began publishing a newspaper.

In the following essay, Gayle K. Berardi and Thomas W. Segady examine western African American newspapers of the frontier era. They find that these journals not only fostered a sense of community among black pioneers, but also that they followed traditions established by the black press that existed in the eastern United States in the early nineteenth century. When white newspapers refused to publicize activities in the black community, African Americans would begin their own news organs to advertise and promote noteworthy happenings in their churches, fraternal lodges, and social clubs. Black newspaper owners—like white ones—sold advertising space to bring in necessary revenue, and this aspect of the news business also provided an informative service to readers. Finally, black editors filled their journals' pages with state, national, and international news that they hoped would be of interest to their subscribers. In all of these ways, therefore, black newspapers served to strengthen the bonds of community that united the majority of western black pioneers. In so doing, they helped to make the African American contribution to the settlement and development of the western frontier more significant and more enduring.

Historical accounts of the development of African American newspapers in the United States are replete with stories of success and failure. However, what is missing from the collection of histories is an analysis of the newspapers that were written by and—in most cases—owned by African Americans in the U.S. West. The numerous African American papers that were printed in the West seemed to serve many of the same purposes as other African American papers that existed throughout the country. One of their chief functions was to provide the reader with information regarding the African American communities. As a result, the papers served to establish an African American identity in the communities that countered the stereotypes perpetuated by the communities as a whole, which were often fostered by the white-owned press.

The African American press has a long history in the United States. Its beginning in 1827 can be linked to the growing discontent among African Americans and a small group of whites over the issue of slavery. From 1827 to the Civil War period, the press was committed to addressing African Americans' grievances concerning their lack of economic, political and social freedoms.[1]

In addition to being a crusader for African American freedoms, the press became a means of responding to the reporting found in white newspapers. For example, *Freedom's Journal,* the first African American publication (1827), was distributed in New York City as a response to the negative reporting about African Americans found in the white newspaper, the New York *Enquirer.* The second major African American publication, the *Weekly Advocate,* was published from 1837 to 1842 in New York City and was supported by those involved in the abolitionist movement.

These early newspapers were not entirely devoted to articles that contained purely news items. Articles about local community and church activities were plentiful, as well as articles describing the best method for cleaning soiled shirts or remedies that would cure the common cold. This content should not be dismissed as trivial, however; it provided valuable information regarding everyday concerns of a growing, increasingly literate African American population.

Although the beginnings of African American newspapers were in the eastern part of the United States, it was not long before similar papers appeared in the West. The papers in the West, however, were not as well organized or funded as those in the East and, thus, were not in existence for long periods of time. In addition, the papers in the West tended to be shorter in length than those published in the East and also more often were printed in pamphlet form. The early western papers also tended to print more opinion and local news than news about national and international events. However, the emphasis seemed to satisfy readers eager to learn about local happenings in their new environment.

As the number of papers increased during the late nineteenth century, their content began to change. Papers began running stories that dealt with science, art, literature, and drama. Thus, many of the papers began to lose their provincial appearance and to become more cosmopolitan sources for news about a variety of events from a wider geographic range.

The reasons for the upsurge in the publication of African American newspapers at this time are manifold. Among these, the most significant are: (1) that the African American population was becoming better educated and literate; (2) African Americans began earning more money and thus were able to purchase newspapers; (3) religious organizations were able freely to publish their own newspapers which encouraged the distribution of all types of papers and the growth of literacy among African Americans; (4) African Americans were given the right to vote and thus were linked with the political system, specifically political parties; (5) the wide-spread availability of newspapers increased their circulation and the interest in organizing and printing new ones; and (6) editors of newspapers were accorded a high status and given an important place in the community which influenced the viability of locally published newspapers.

As African Americans moved to the West and to the North, owners and editors of papers developed an interest in the plight of their developing communities. Editors encouraged writers to explore the conditions within these communities and, if possible, make suggestions for change. The African Americans who relocated to new areas were anxious to find out about changing economic and political conditions as they directly affected them and their family members. In addition, these papers provided individuals with a means to find a niche in the new communities they were settling in, and perhaps, to reestablish contact with lost friends and relatives. This certainly was the case for many African Americans settling in the West.

During the period 1880–1914, the movement West brought a continuously rising wave of inhabitants. The population of the eleven Rocky Mountain and Pacific Slope states in 1880, as reported by the Bureau of the Census, stood at slightly over two million. By 1910 this figure had virtually doubled, to just under four million (3,853,934).[2] The motivation for white settlers during this time could be described as the "pull" toward riches, land, and greater economic opportunity. On the part of African Americans, however, the movement could be described more adequately as being "pushed" out of their former environment by conditions that had led to escalating oppression. Both tacitly and overtly, the way was being paved for diminishing African American opportunities for achieving equality in the South after the promise brought by the Emancipation.

This steady diminishment of rights often took the form of political themes that became translated into policy. In 1877, President Rutherford B. Hayes, a Republican, traveled to the South on a goodwill tour. During this trip, Hayes announced his "Let Alone" policy, in which he announced to African Americans that their "...rights and interests would be safer...if Southern whites were 'let alone' by the federal government."[3] The wholesale abandonment of the embryonic freedoms of African Americans was underway, and the "Let Alone" policy became the *modus operandi* of subsequent legislation and legal decisions.

In 1883 the Supreme Court declared unconstitutional the Civil Rights Act of 1875, which had attempted to provide equal access for all citizens to hotels, theaters, and other public places. The Court ruled that the Fourteenth Amendment prohibited discrimination by the states; it did not, however, address the practice of discrimination by private individuals.

The South took full advantage of this ruling to reestablish new lines of segregation and discrimination, which had broken down, and racism in its worse forms became epidemic. The "convict-lease" system, in which large numbers of African Americans were tried for relatively minor crimes, became prevalent. Once sentenced, they were forced to work off their obligations by performing free labor for individual planters, or for the state. One consequence of this was the shrinking of the legitimate labor pool for African Americans; the work was done by prisoners. With respect to skilled labor, African Americans constituted the majority of the South's artisans before the Civil War.[4] Within thirty years, however, they were a small fraction of this labor force, largely as a result of being barred by unions that prohibited African American members. When African Americans were able to reclaim their former occupations, it was usually by defying the unions and crossing picket lines. Thus, the work was temporary, low-paying, and further exacerbated prejudice and discrimination.

An even more brutal fact of life for African Americans living in the South during this time was the prevalence of public executions that occurred outside the law. Between 1882 and 1900, vigilantes lynched 3,011 African American citizens, with the vast majority of these in the South. Grounds for lynching included charges of "insulting whites" and "having bad manners."[5] The South was not alone in its renewed practice of racism, however. The North also quickly adopted the "Let Alone" policy, although it was perhaps more insidious by virtue of its being intellectualized. Books carrying the theme of the inherent racial inferiority of African Americans began to appear, some with such unambiguous titles as *The Negro: A Beast* (1900), and *The Negro: A Menace to American Civilization* (1907).[6]

Between the years 1880 and 1900, racial injustice had escalated to the point that one author has labeled it "cradle to grave" segregation.[7] In many parts of both the North and the South, playgrounds and even cemeteries were segregated; in one town in the South, an African American found himself in trouble because his horse drank from the same trough as horses owned by whites. Increasingly, African Americans faced a structurally induced inability to alter this situation. Six southern states adopted the "Grandfather Clause," which distinguished between poor, uneducated African Americans and poor, uneducated whites. The clause stated that only those individuals whose ancestors (their "grandfathers") had voted in elections before 1867 remained eligible to vote. Since no African Americans in the South possessed that right in 1867, they were disfranchised *en masse*. In Louisiana, for example, the number of African American voters dropped from 130,000 to 1,342 six years after the grandfather clause was adopted.[8]

The opportunity for African Americans to participate, even in a limited way, in their own communities was systematically denied.[9] *Plessy v. Ferguson* in 1896 marked the capstone of the "Let Alone" policy.[10] It is in light of these factors that the beginnings of the exodus to the West can best be understood. It should be noted that there is little evidence, on the part of African Americans, that a change in geographic location brought the promise of increased political freedom and economic opportunity. There is also little evidence that they perceived Horace Greeley's famous shibboleth, "Go West Young Man," to be intended for them. For the most part, the response of white settlers took one of two forms: either to deny African Americans their rights on the grounds that granting them would leave whites open to demands from other racial and ethnic groups for rights that had already been denied; or to deny African Americans entrance into the newly developing communities in the West entirely. An example of the first attitude is found in an editorial from an Oregon newspaper in 1865, which anticipated the political dilemmas approaching with the movement west of African Americans: "If we make the African a citizen, we cannot deny the same right to the Indian or the Mongolian."[11]

The wish to avoid confronting this dilemma led to direct action. A series of "Exclusionary Laws," which were passed in Oregon between 1844 and 1857, went so far as legally requiring African Americans to leave the territory within three years' time. "Anyone in violation of the law would suffer a whip lashing, to be repeated after six months if they still refused to leave."[12] African Americans residing in Liberty, Oregon, in 1893 were "requested" to leave town; in 1904, police in Reno, Nevada, rounded up the African Americans who were unemployed and expelled them from the city.[13]

Despite this enforced marginality, African Americans continued to arrive in the West in greater numbers. Highly literate, they brought with them the requisite ability to form viable communities in the West, and to express their growing presence through newspapers that they owned and operated. In 1905 an African American citizen of Telluride, Colorado, irate over the treatment of his race by local unions, submitted a passionate appeal that was printed in a leading newspaper of the day, the *Colorado Statesman*. The editorial stated: "We, the Negro citizens of the United States are enfranchised voters; are as much so as any other race or nationality in this country, and when we are accepted as such and are accepted in any organized union without discrimination then I will give unions my support, and not until then, for we are collectively citizens in this country and not individual citizens. Consequently, we should unite as a whole and as individuals."

Similar sentiments among African Americans during the early twentieth century were widespread. This editorial remark, however, is of special interest for two important reasons. First, the *Statesman* was both owned and operated by African Americans, and its masthead alleged that it was the "organ of the colored people in Colorado, Wyoming, Montana, Utah, and New Mexico." Its range of coverage was perhaps greater and its circulation larger than others, but in reality the *Statesman* was only one of several African Americans newspapers flourishing in this region during the years 1880–1914.

Second, an important clue to the role of these newspapers is provided by the placement of this letter to the editor on page one of the *Statesman*. There was no gratuitous inclusion on an obscure inside page of these opinions from African American citizens. This paper, and the many that existed alongside it, was intended to represent the interests of the local African American community in a manner that found no expression in any other medium. Gunnar Myrdal, in his classic work, *An American Dilemma*, wrote in 1944 that: "The importance of the Negro press for the formation of Negro opinion, for the functioning of all other Negro institutions, for Negro leadership and concerted action generally, is enormous."[14] This observation captures the unique historical importance of the African American press, and this significance was keenly felt in the developing American West, where African Americans were routinely excluded from the pages of white-owned publications. This exclusion occurred, during this period, in all regions of the country. One of the earliest African American papers—the *Ram's Horn*—was begun when Willis A. Hodges was refused space for African American news in a white-owned newspaper, the *New York Sun*. Hodges was curtly informed: "The *Sun* shines for all white men, and not for colored men."[15] The history of the African American press in the West thus documents the history of African Americans' struggles to survive as individuals—and beyond that, to establish a collective identity.

The observation that much of the African American experience has been lost is not new. However, this appears to be even more pronounced in the West than in other regions. The failure to consider the important evidence of the African American contribution to the cultural identity and progress of the West stems, in part, from the widely held belief that the history of the West is unique. The late nineteenth-century American West has been considered, in many historical accounts, to be an unsettled area, with entire communities that were temporary or even transient—more like settlements or camps than cities.[16] What has become central, in most historical accounts and certainly in the popular imagination, is the depiction of the individual spirit in conquering the "frontier." As a result, the formation and importance of communities and the groups in them in the frontier West have been largely excluded, if not lost completely.

Settlements in the late nineteenth-century West are commonly believed to have been distinctive "kinds" of communities, in the respect that they were "boom towns." They were expected, in most cases, to have a temporary existence. Consequently, they also exhibit a relatively low "degree" of community, in the sense of establishing any lasting relationships among their members. As a result, many historical accounts have proceeded to document the "colorful past" of these towns, whose inhabitants' sense of community was perceived as marginal or absent entirely.

Thus, the historical emphasis on the emerging cities as a special transitory type of community has tended to obscure any consideration of their sustained development. Ample evidence exists suggesting that members of these communities formed close, interpersonal ties, much as in older, established areas. What is missing in many historical accounts of these towns is the realization that, for their inhabitants, these communities became lifelong residences.[17] This implies, then, that the towns consisted of a substantial number of individuals who perceived their existence in the towns to be more or less permanent. The result of this was that a cultural life emerged that was characteristic of stable, "permanent" communities, and the life-world of these individuals imparted a highly developed cultural existence to the towns that otherwise would appear to be highly implausible.

This permanence is best seen in the newspapers and journals of the day. They strove to provide not only a sense of community for the towns' residents, but also promoted an emerging cultural life within the towns. As David Halaas has stated:

> Unlike their eastern counterparts who worked in a stable environment where law and familiar institutions were of long standing and taken as a matter of course, early Western journalists directed their editorial energies toward introducing the trappings of culture and civilization.[18]

Thus, communities in the West in which African American newspapers existed during 1880–1914 were unique in several respects. First, the rapid growth of the African American population in this region either paralleled or outpaced the growth of the West generally. Second, the majority of the communities that emerged during this period shared a common characteristic: they experienced a period of rapid growth, becoming for a period "boom towns," with all the attendant intensification of activity and social problems that remain characteristic of communities of this nature. Third, these communities were largely cut off, at least for a period, from much of the information regarding the outside world. Thus, the new members turned to the media generally within the communities for information. Lastly, as various minority groups entered these communities, they were forced to form separate cultural identities, as they were excluded from the informational sources of the dominant groups. The response appeared to be, in the West as in all other regions of the country, the rapid development of an African American owned and operated press. This press depicted African Americans involved in the creation of thriving, culturally distinct communities with social and political concerns that have long been ignored.

For African Americans living in the West during this period, newspapers were the only mass medium of information exchange. Thus, in a region where the literary and other cultural achievements of African Americans have received scant attention, forty-three African American newspapers were in existence between 1880 and 1914.[19] While this number may appear at first to be excessively large, it only underscores the existence of a growing literate African American community; between 1870 and 1910, the overall literacy rate for African Americans rose from 20 percent to 70 percent. This sharp rise in literacy in turn resulted in the proliferation of African American newspapers.[20]

With this surge in development, a bifurcation of function with respect to the emerging newspapers appeared during this period. Several of these newspapers performed the role of providing national coverage taken from eastern papers such as the *New York Herald* and the *Boston Globe*. However, the national coverage in these papers was augmented by other newspapers that provided full coverage of virtually nothing but local and regional news. This intense concentration on local affairs was a natural outgrowth of the role of the newspapers in boom towns. In this capacity, they provided a basis for a sense of community in a population that consisted largely of individuals who had recently migrated to the area, and who were often cut off from traditional relationships. In light of this, one eastern observer wrote that westerners appeared to be "starved" for local news.[21]

However, the "communities" that were identified by the papers often tended to be highly selective, reflecting racial and ethnic biases within the rapidly growing towns. Thus, the clientele to which the newspapers catered tended to be members of the established majority group, and stories and editorials often reflected their prejudices toward outgroups. For early western newspapers this presented a profound dilemma, as African Americans were the one racial outgroup that resided firmly within the bounds of these early communities themselves. The African American population comprised an integral component in the founding of many of these early cities. For the newspapers, the concern quickly became one of representing their own interests rather than the interests of everyone in the community. The fate of the papers was often more closely tied to the concerns and biases of select community leaders than newspapers in "established" communities, and this was reflected in the content of the papers.[22]

These leaders all too often harbored a common sentiment of prejudice toward the black communities within their towns. It was perhaps inevitable that many white-owned newspapers began to run stories that often exhibited an extremely negative slant—termed "race angling" by some authors—in reporting the activities of the black population residing in their communities.[23] For example, the June 10, 1899, *Cripple Creek Weekly Tribune* reported that: "Last night there was a free-for-all colored fight on Myers [Avenue], between Fourth and Fifth, in which even women were mixed up in [sic], but there were no skulls broken."[24] This quote appears to reflect the negative coverage accorded the African American communities. More overtly prejudicial coverage was also in evidence, however, as illustrated by this news item (not an editorial) from the same paper on January 13, 1890: "Pueblo [Colorado] has a colored mail carrier, and now some of the colored folks of this burg thing [sic] they ought to either have one or a member of the police force."

Thus, when any group of blacks was mentioned, it tended to be in stories reflecting negative characteristics. Significantly, it appears that attempts by African Americans to sponsor positive cultural activities within their own communities were ignored not only by the newspapers, but were also excluded entirely from the towns' directories of the period. An examination of selected directories during this time indicates that the only African American organizations recognized and listed in them were churches.

Three obvious effects are discernible regarding the treatment by whites of African Americans in the West during this period. First, there appeared to be a concerted effort to deny the African American population within these cities any affiliation with the white communities. Second, there was a disavowal of the existence of any African American *community* in the subjective sense. Third, there was often an attempt to identify and label negatively individual African American members of the communities. This distinction served as an attempt to portray African Americans as deviants or isolates within the total community, and to de-emphasize their community basis. It appears that these newspapers took elaborate steps to identify individual African Americans who had violated community norms, while denying their status as a cultural community with a closely knit system of organizational linkages. Certainly, any attempts to portray or recognize the presence of cohesive African American communities were fairly nonexistent in the newspapers that purported to represent the entire populace.

During the time that African Americans were being condemned, ridiculed, or ignored by these newspapers, however, the African American communities themselves exhibited signs of increasing organization. This can be seen, for example, through the number of African American service organizations that developed and the cultural activities reported in newspapers owned and operated by members of the African American communities. The sustained growth of these newspapers, in turn, indicated the presence of a highly literate population. The literacy rate for African Americans approached 90 percent in the West by 1910, twice the literacy rate for African Americans living in the South at that time.[25] These newspapers not only reflected, but served to galvanize, the growing sense of the African American community within them. For example, the Colorado Springs *Sun* was founded in 1897 with the purpose of "fulfilling the need of an independent, reliable organ, wherein the Afro-Americans of this city…could find expression of their best thought and material progress." This publication listed seven lodges in Colorado Springs for the town's African Americans, who numbered one thousand at the time. The same publication also reported the existence of three "secret societies" for African Americans, which provides evidence of a stable, thriving community reflective of the general trend in the West during this period.

In format, these newspapers were oriented toward reporting local events, as were the other community newspapers. A substantial amount of each paper was dedicated to news within the local African American communities—ranging from reports about political activities (including calls for involvement) to rummage sales at local churches. In the 1890s discussions of civil rights were also commonly found in the African American newspapers of the West. Additionally, many articles forcefully called for the representation of African Americans in state and local governments.

With this, it can be seen that these newspapers provided African American residents of frontier towns with a sense of community. In addition, they served to indicate some of the avenues available for establishing relations with the wider community. These relations often tended to be of a political rather than a social nature, however. Enoch Waters has asserted that the struggle that African Americans waged to resist deprivation of their rights became expressed primarily in the content of their newspapers.[26] For example, the *Denver Statesman* (often referred to by other African American newspapers as "the leading race journal of the West") circulated petitions each week, calling for its patrons to endorse and return this statement:

> Believing that for the Negro especially the call for united action is imperative, to ameliorate our hard condition industrially and politically I endorse the move to incorporate the Negroes of this state into local leagues with representatives in a state body. I will give my presence and aid toward formulating plans for union and making it effective.

At the same time that the call for political unification was prominent in these papers, the cultural activities of the African American communities

S. Douglas Russell. African Americans published several newspapers on the western frontier of the late nineteenth and early twentieth centuries. Russell published a few newspapers in Oklahoma, including the *Western Age* in the all-black town of Langston. (Courtesy, Archives & Manuscripts Division of the Oklahoma Historical Society.)

were also highly evident. For example, the *Statesman* during the same period announced cultural events for the African American communities, including "grand balls" with accompanying orchestras.

The cultural community of African Americans in frontier western towns thus included a wide range of social and political activities. The picture that gradually emerges is one of a unified response by African Americans to the prejudice and discrimination that they encountered in the wider community. Contrary to accounts in the newspapers owned by whites, which tended to portray African Americans as isolated individuals possessing a status apart from any group, an inspection of African American newspapers in these same communities indicates the degree to which African Americans were able to encounter the unique problems confronting them by forming identifiable reference groups with strong personal bonds.[27]

Therefore, the conclusion may be reached that the growing African American population during this period of western history very often created viable communities. It is also clear that social scientists have failed to study this significant development. This failure is, in part, a result of an unfortunate tendency to focus on the *dissolution* of community (particularly in the subjective sense) of various minority groups.[28] Consequently, the few historical accounts that do exist reflect both ignorance of and distortion of the existence of African American communities in the West. Thus, by taking either the individual or the entire community as the fundamental unit of historical analysis, the important dimension of the unification of minority populations has been obscured and, in some instances, totally neglected. Historically, this sense of community may be difficult to recover, as even tangible evidence of its existence (newspapers, periodicals, directories, sources for obtaining oral histories) begin to disappear. However, only with the recovery and critical analysis of these documents will the significant role of African Americans on the western frontier be fully comprehended.

Notes

1. Roland Wolseley, *The Black Press, U.S.A.* (Ames, Iowa, 1971).
2. Source: U.S. Census Reports, 1880 and 1910.
3. Ethel R. Dennis, *The Black People of America* (New York, 1970), p. 169.
4. Ibid.
5. Ibid.
6. Charles Carroll, *The Negro: A Beast* (St. Louis, 1900). Robert Shufeldt, *The Negro: A Menace to American Civilization* (Boston, 1907).
7. Dennis, *The Black People of America*, p. 185.
8. Ibid., p. 179.

9. Although southern white Populists had worked for African Americans' rights, their outlook slowly changed. By the time that the denial of voting rights became widespread in the South, Populists lent their support to those who added to the African Americans' political oppression.

10. In this landmark case the Supreme Court established the separate but equal doctrine. In effect, the Court ruled that segregation alone did not violate the Constitution: "Laws permitting and even requiring their separation in places where they are liable to be brought into contact do not necessarily imply the inferiority of either race to the other" (*Plessy v. Ferguson,* 163 U.S. 537, 1896). The result of this ruling was the development of a system of racial segregation throughout the U.S., but particularly in the South, that required separate facilities for African Americans and whites. This form of segregation was institutionalized by the Jim Crow laws.

11. Patricia Nelson Limerick, *The Legacy of Conquest: The Unbroken Past of the American West* (New York, 1987).

12. Although obviously not enforced, an exclusionary clause remained on the books in Oregon until 1926. Elizabeth McLagan, *A Peculiar Paradise: A History of Blacks in Oregon, 1788–1940* (Portland, Oregon, 1980).

13. Ibid.

14. Gunnar Myrdal, *An American Dilemma* (New York, 1944), p.75.

15. Armistead Price, "The Negro Newspaper in the United States," *Gazette: International Journal For Mass Communication Studies,* 2, 3 (1956), 141–149.

16. Limerick, *The Legacy of Conquest.*

17. See, for example, Marshall Sprague, *Money Mountain* (Lincoln, Nebraska, 1979).

18. David Halaas, *Boom Town Newspapers: Journalism on the Rocky Mountain Mining Frontier, 1859–1881* (Albuquerque, New Mexico, 1981).

19. These newspapers existed in only six states: Colorado had sixteen, California fifteen, Montana four, Utah three, Washington three, and Oregon two.

20. Georgetta Campbell, *Extant Collections of Early Black Newspapers: A Research Guide to the Black Press, 1880–1915* (Troy, New York, 1981).

21. Halaas, *Boom Town Newspapers.*

22. The extremes to which some of the papers actually went in order not to offend their readers is indicative of their precarious position in the community. For example, the *Rocky Mountain News* located its printing facilities in the middle of a live creek to avoid offending citizens living in different towns on either side of the creek.

23. Wolseley, *The Black Press, U.S.A.*

24. In identifying the street on which the fight took place (not a common practice in stories of this kind), the negative slant of the press become apparent: the street was notorious for its harboring of prostitutes.

25. Source: U.S. Census Reports, 1910.

26. Enoch Waters, *American Diary: A Personal History of the Black Press* (Chicago, 1987).

27. William Freudenberg, for example, has found an increase in reference group bonds as community-wide associations decrease in contemporary boom towns. See William Freudenberg, "Community Structure," unpublished manuscript, University of Denver, 1987.

28. Daniel Rodgers, *The Work Ethic in Industrial America: 1850–1920* (Chicago, 1978).

THE AFRICAN AMERICAN FRONTIER: A BIBLIOGRAPHIC ESSAY

Roger D. Hardaway

[This is an original article written specifically for inclusion in this volume.]

Books and articles on western African Americans, once quite rare, have proliferated in recent years. Moreover, the trend appears to be one that will continue for some time. Multiculturalism, which was popular in the United States during the civil rights era of the 1960s and 1970s before waning temporarily, is back in vogue as the twentieth century gives way to the twenty-first. Consequently, any bibliographic essay on any aspect of a minority group's historical experiences in the United States is sure to be incomplete (and somewhat outdated) by the time it is published. The following comments are intended, therefore, to be instructive and enlightening—if not exhaustive.

Only a few general works on the African American frontier experience exist. In a discerning essay surveying the literature then extant, Lawrence B. de Graaf argued in the mid-1970s in "Recognition, Racism, and Reflections on the Writing of Western Black History," *Pacific Historical Review* 44 (1975): 22–51, that most of the works available on blacks in the American West were designed simply to point out their presence on the frontier to readers who had incorrectly assumed that almost no African Americans had ever lived in the West. A year later, pioneering black historian W. Sherman Savage published *Blacks in the West* (Westport, Connecticut: Greenwood Press, 1976). This survey, whose author was eighty-six years old, marked the culmination of over a half century of collecting tidbits of information from sparse and disparate sources. Critics alleged that it was a narrative without analysis, but it remains today the best general history available. Also useful is *The Black West* by William Loren Katz (4th ed., New York: Touchstone Books, 1996), a popular history for general readers. The author describes it as a "pictorial history," and its extensive array of photographs is its chief attraction. Another photographic history is John W. Ravage, *Black Pioneers: Images of the Black Experience on the North American Frontier* (Salt Lake City: University of Utah Press, 1997). Kenneth Wiggins Porter, *The Negro on the American Frontier* (New York: Arno Press and The New York Times, 1971), is a useful collection of fourteen journal articles published by the author between 1932 and 1969; several, however, are concerned with the frontier east of the Mississippi River. A survey article is Quintard Taylor, "From Esteban to Rodney King: Five Centuries of African American History in the West," *Montana: The Magazine of Western History* 46, no. 4 (1996): 2–17. A few documents relevant to western African Americans are included in Herbert Aptheker, ed., *A Documentary History of the Negro in the United States* (New York: The Citadel Press, 1951).

A few studies of African Americans in individual western states are required reading for those interested in the western black experience. The best state history is Elmer R. Rusco, *"Good Time Coming?": Black Nevadans in the Nineteenth Century* (Westport, Connecticut: Greenwood Press, 1975). Equally important is Rudolph M. Lapp, *Blacks in Gold Rush California* (New Haven, Connecticut: Yale University Press, 1977), which—despite its title—is a general history of African Americans in the Golden State in the late nineteenth century. Jimmie Lewis Franklin has written two volumes about Oklahoma's African American population; *Journey Toward Hope: A History of Blacks in Oklahoma* (Norman: University of Oklahoma Press, 1982) is a more detailed and ambitious work than is *The Blacks in Oklahoma* (Norman: University of Oklahoma Press, 1980). Also useful for the Sooner State is Arthur L. Tolson, *The Black Oklahomans, A History: 1541–1972* (New Orleans: Edwards Printing Co., 1972). Texas African American history is surveyed in Alwyn Barr, *Black Texans: A History of African Americans in Texas, 1528–1995* (2d ed., Norman: University of Oklahoma Press, 1996); and in Lawrence D. Rice, *The Negro in Texas, 1874–1900* (Baton Rouge: Louisiana State University Press, 1971).

Several volumes by amateur historians have limited scholarly value but may be of some help to those researching African Americans in particular western states. These include Delilah L. Beasley, *The Negro Trail Blazers of California* (Los Angeles: By the author, 1919; reprinted, San Francisco: R and E Research Associates, 1969); Sue Bailey Thurman, *Pioneers of Negro Origin in California* (San Francisco: Acme Publishing Co., 1952; reprinted, San Francisco: R and E Research Associates, 1971); Barbara J. Richardson, compiler, *Black*

Directory of New Mexico: Black Pioneers of New Mexico, A Documentary and Pictorial History (Rio Rancho, New Mexico: Panorama Press, 1976); Gene Aldrich, *Black Heritage of Oklahoma* (Edmond, Oklahoma: Thompson Book and Supply Co., 1973); Marguerite Mitchell Marshall, *An Account of Afro-Americans in Southeast Kansas, 1884–1984* (Manhattan, Kansas: Sunflower University Press, 1986); Thomas P. Newgard and William C. Sherman, *African-Americans in North Dakota: Sources and Assessments* (Bismarck, North Dakota: University of Mary Press, 1994); and Elizabeth McLagan, *A Peculiar Paradise: A History of Blacks in Oregon, 1788–1940* (Portland, Oregon: Georgian Press, 1980). Three such works exist for Arizona: Gloria L. Smith, *Black Americana in Arizona* (revised ed., Tucson: Trailstones Industries, Inc., 1992); Richard E. Harris, *Black Heritage in Arizona* (Phoenix [?]: By the author, 1977); and Harris, *The First Hundred Years: A History of Arizona Blacks* (Apache Junction, Arizona: Relmo Publishers, 1983). A regional amateur history is Martha Anderson, *Black Pioneers of the Northwest, 1800–1918* (Portland, Oregon: Pioneer Publishing Co., 1980).

The black presence in many western states has not yet been examined in book-length detail. Useful scholarly articles include Ronald G. Coleman, "Blacks in Utah History: An Unknown Legacy," in Helen Z. Popanikolas, editor, *The Peoples of Utah* (Salt Lake City: Utah State Historical Society, 1976); Sara L. Bernson and Robert J. Eggers, "Black People in South Dakota History," *South Dakota History* 7 (1977): 241–270; and Jesse T. Moore, Jr., "Seeking a New Life: Blacks in Post-Civil War Colorado," *Journal of Negro History* 78 (1993): 166–187.

A few articles have analyzed census records to gain some insight into western blacks; among these are Michael S. Coray, "Blacks in the Pacific West, 1850–1860: A View from the Census," *Nevada Historical Society Quarterly* 28 (1985): 90–121; Coray, "Negro and Mulatto in the Pacific West, 1850–1860: Changing Patterns of Black Population Growth," *Pacific Historian* 29, no. 4 (1985): 18–27; Coray, "Influences on Black Family Household Organization in the West, 1850–1860," *Nevada Historical Society Quarterly* 31 (1988): 1–31; K. Keith Richard, "Unwelcome Settlers: Black and Mulatto Oregon Pioneers," *Oregon Historical Quarterly* 84 (1983): 29–55 and 172–205; Eugene S. Richards, "Trends of Negro Life in Oklahoma as Reflected by Census Reports," *Journal of Negro History* 33 (1948): 38–52; and Monroe Billington, "A Profile of Blacks in New Mexico on the Eve of Statehood," *Password* 32 (1987): 55–60, 90.

A few bibliographies are helpful in locating materials on western African Americans. General collections—some of which are outdated but still useful—include James deT. Abajian, compiler, *Blacks and Their Contributions to the American West: A Bibliography and Union List of Library Holdings Through 1970*

(Boston: G. K. Hall and Co., 1974), which is especially valuable for California items; Lenwood G. Davis, *Blacks in the American West: A Working Bibliography* (2d ed., Monticello, Illinois: Council of Planning Librarians, 1976); Davis, *Blacks in the Pacific Northwest, 1788–1972* (Monticello, Illinois: Council of Planning Librarians, 1972); Quintard Taylor, "Bibliographic Essay on the African American West," *Montana: The Magazine of Western History* 46, no.4 (1996): 18–23; and Roger D. Hardaway, *A Narrative Bibliography of the African-American Frontier: Blacks in the Rocky Mountain West, 1535–1912* (Lewiston, New York: The Edwin Mellen Press, 1995). Two bibliographies with substantial sections on western blacks during the frontier era are Rodman W. Paul and Richard W. Etulain, compilers, *The Frontier and the American West* (Arlington Heights, Illinois: AHM Publishing Corp., 1977); and Richard W. Etulain, editor, *The American West in the Twentieth Century: A Bibliography* (Norman: University of Oklahoma Press, 1994). State bibliographies include Lucille Smith Thompson and Alma Smith Jacobs, *The Negro in Montana, 1800–1945: A Selective Bibliography* (Helena: Montana State Library, 1970); Hazel E. Mills and Nancy B. Pryor, *The Negro in the State of Washington: 1788–1969* (Olympia: Washington State Library, 1970); Lenwood G. Davis, *Blacks in the State of Utah: A Working Bibliography* (Monticello, Illinois: Council of Planning Librarians, 1974); and Davis, *Blacks in the State of Oregon, 1788–1971* (Monticello, Illinois: Council of Planning Librarians, 1971).

The first African Americans to sojourn to the American West were members of European exploring parties. The Spanish conquistadors who came to the Southwest brought several African slaves with them. The best known of these enslaved conquerors was Estevanico (also known as "Stephen," "Estevan," "Esteban," and "Estebanico"), a survivor of an ill-fated expedition who—along with three white conquistadors—meandered across Texas from 1528 to 1536 and later traveled to Arizona and New Mexico. His story, including his death at the hands of Zunis in New Mexico in 1539, has been the subject of several biographies. While none is satisfying, the best is John Upton Terrell, *Estevanico the Black* (Los Angeles: Westernlore Press Publishers, 1968). Two adequate essays on Estevanico are William J. Buchanan, "Legend of the Black Conquistador," *Mankind* 1 (February 1968): 21–24, 93, reprinted in John M. Carroll, editor, *The Black Military Experience in the American West* (New York, Liveright Publishing Corp., 1971); and Jeannette Mirsky, "Zeroing in on a Fugitive Figure: The First Negro in America," *Midway* 8 (June 1967): 1–17. Estevanico and other African conquistadors are discussed in Richard R. Wright, "Negro Companions of the Spanish Explorers," *American Anthropologist* 4 (1902): 217–228, which has been reprinted at least twice—in *Phylon* 2 (1941):

325–333; and in August Meier and Elliott Rudwick, editors, *The Making of Black America: Essays in Negro Life & History* (New York: Atheneum, 1969).

Other works that examine briefly early black explorers and their descendants in the Southwest include, for California, Jack D. Forbes, "Black Pioneers: The Spanish-Speaking Afroamericans of the Southwest," *Phylon* 27 (1966): 233–246; and, for New Mexico, Carroll L. Riley, "Blacks in the Early Southwest," *Ethnohistory* 19 (1972): 247–260. Articles arguing that many more descendants of blacks lived in New Mexico during the Spanish colonial era than official records indicate include Adrian Bustamente, " 'The Matter Was Never Resolved': The *Casta* System in Colonial New Mexico, 1693–1823," *New Mexico Historical Review* 66 (1991): 143–163; and Jim F. Heath and Frederick M. Nunn, "Negroes and Discrimination in Colonial New Mexico: Don Pedro Bautista Pino's Startling Statements of 1812 in Perspective," *Phylon* 31 (1970): 372–378.

Two articles debating the possibility that the Indian leader of the seventeenth-century Pueblo Revolt against the Spanish invaders was descended from a black explorer are Fray Angelico Chavez, "Pohe-yemo's Representative and the Pueblo Revolt of 1680," *New Mexico Historical Review* 42 (1967): 85–126; and Stefanie Beninato, "Pope, Pose-yemu, and Naranjo: A New Look at Leadership in the Pueblo Revolt of 1680," *New Mexico Historical Review* 65 (1990): 417–435.

The first major exploring body sent to the American West by the United States government included one African American venturer. Known simply as "York," this man was an important member of the Lewis and Clark Expedition that traveled from St. Louis to the Oregon coastline and back from 1804 to 1806. The slave of expedition co-leader William Clark, York is mentioned several times in the various journals published by Clark and other expedition members. Robert B. Betts has written from the available sketchy historical record as good a biography of York as is likely ever to be published in *In Search of York: The Slave Who Went to the Pacific with Lewis and Clark* (Boulder: Colorado Associated University Press, 1985).

The purchase and exploration of Louisiana in the first decade of the nineteenth century led to the establishment of the fur trade in the American West, especially in the Rocky Mountains and the Pacific Northwest. The owners of fur companies hired men to go to the West and either trap beaver and other fur-bearing animals or trade with Indian trappers. These rugged individuals explored the West, became knowledgeable of Indian culture, and—often through self-promotion—became larger-than-life legendary adventurers. Among these so-called "mountain men" were a few African Americans. Best known of the black mountain men was Jim Beckwourth who lived among the

Jim Beckwourth. A fur trapper and "mountain man," Beckwourth first went to the West in the 1820s. Adopted by the Crows, he became a war chief of their tribe for several years in Montana and Wyoming. Later in life, he served as an army scout and discovered a pass used by travelers going to California through the Sierra Nevadas. (Courtesy, Wyoming Division of Cultural Resources.)

Crows of Wyoming and Montana for many years, spent several years in California guiding settlers through the Sierra Nevadas, and resided as an old man in Colorado where he farmed, worked as a store clerk, and scouted occasionally for the U.S. army.

In 1854 Beckwourth began dictating his life story—including liberal embellishment of the circumstances of his deeds and misdeeds—to newspaperman Thomas D. Bonner. Two years later, Bonner published *The Life and Adventures of James P. Beckwourth, Mountaineer, Scout, Pioneer, and Chief of the Crow Nation of Indians* (New York: Harper and Brothers, 1856). The volume made Beckwourth famous but historians generally dismissed it as consisting of more fantasy than reality. Nevertheless, several editions of the memoir have been published, the best of which is that edited by Delmont R. Oswald (Lincoln: University of Nebraska Press, 1972). By systematically separating the facts from the fiction, Oswald has added historical value to an entertaining narrative. Oswald has also produced an excellent, brief profile of this most famous African American mountain man in "James P. Beckwourth," in Leroy R. Hafen, editor, *The Mountain Men and the Fur Trade of the Far West,* vol. VI (Glendale, California: Arthur H. Clark Co., 1968). Several authors have written book-length treatments of Beckwourth's life based upon the Bonner volume, but the only one that is a solid effort for adult audiences is Elinor Wilson, *Jim Beckwourth: Black Mountain Man and War Chief of the Crows* (Norman: University of Oklahoma Press, 1972).

Another black mountain man about whom a substantial amount of information exists is Edward Rose who also lived with the Crows and some of whose exploits Beckwourth allegedly appropriated for his autobiography. Most of what is known about Rose derives from a newspaper article written in 1828 by an admiring white army officer, Reuben Holmes. This article, edited by Stella M. Drumm, was reprinted under the title, "The Five Scalps," in the journal *Glimpses of the Past* 5 (January-March 1938): 3–54. The Rose biography in the Hafen set cited above, Willis Blenkinsop, "Edward Rose," in vol. IX (1972), is not particularly inspiring. Neither is Harold W. Felton, *Edward Rose: Negro Trail Blazer* (New York: Dodd, Mead and Co., 1967), a volume written primarily for adolescent readers.

Information on other black fur traders appears in Kenneth Wiggins Porter, "Negroes and the Fur Trade," *Minnesota History* 15 (1934): 421–433, reprinted in his compilation, *The Negro on the American Frontier,* cited above. Biographical sketches of two other blacks in the fur industry are in the Hafen collection: A. P. Nasatir, "Jacques Clamorgan," in vol. II (1965); and Kenneth L. Holmes, "James Douglas," in vol. IX (1972).

In the 1840s and 1850s slaveholders took several of their black chattels with them as they joined the burgeoning westward movement. And while much has been written about the political struggle that occurred in the 1850s over slavery in the western territories, surprisingly little scholarship deals with the institution of western slavery itself. Two of the better essays on the subject are those by W. Sherman Savage and Newell G. Bringhurst reproduced in this volume. The most significant book on the topic is Eugene H. Berwanger, *The Frontier Against Slavery: Western Anti-Negro Prejudice and the Slavery Extension Controversy* (Urbana: University of Illinois Press, 1967). Berwanger argues persuasively that northerners who moved to the frontier were opposed to the existence of slavery not because they thought it was immoral but because they did not want blacks—free or slave—living near them. Klaus J. Hansen presents a similar thesis in "The Millennium, the West, and Race in the Antebellum American Mind," *Western Historical Quarterly* 3 (1972): 373–390. Northerners going to the West, he argues, saw the region as a land of opportunity where they could create a perfect society so long as African Americans were not allowed to enter and, thus, ruin this "virgin land." A good, brief summary of the peculiar institution in the western territories is Bringhurst, "Slavery in the West," in Randall M. Miller and John David Smith, editors, *Dictionary of Afro-American Slavery* (Westport, Connecticut: Greenwood Press, 1988).

Legalized slavery existed in four western jurisdictions. Texas entered the Union in 1845 as a slave state; both Utah and New Mexico, created as territories by the Compromise of 1850, enacted slave codes in the ante-bellum era; and the United States government allowed Native Americans to enslave African Americans in Indian Territory. Texas slavery is discussed in Elizabeth Silverthorne, *Plantation Life in Texas* (College Station: Texas A & M University Press, 1986); and in Randolph B. Campbell, *An Empire for Slavery: The Peculiar Institution in Texas, 1821–1865* (Baton Rouge: Louisiana State University Press, 1989).

Slavery in the Mormon theocracy of Utah is addressed by Jack Beller, "Negro Slaves in Utah," *Utah Historical Quarterly* 2 (1929): 122–126; James B. Christensen, "Negro Slavery in Utah Territory," *Phylon* 18 (1957): 298–305; and Dennis L. Lythgoe, "Negro Slavery in Utah," *Utah Historical Quarterly* 39 (1971): 40–54. Mormon antiblack attitudes—including but not limited to slavery—are explored by Newell G. Bringhurst, *Saints, Slaves, and Blacks: The Changing Place of Black People Within Mormonism* (Westport, Connecticut: Greenwood Press, 1981); and by Lythgoe, "Negro Slavery and Mormon Doctrine," *Western Humanities Review* 21 (1967): 327–338.

New Mexico's slave code is discussed in the context of that territory's antiblack policies in Loomis Morton Ganaway, *New Mexico and the Sectional Controversy, 1846–1861* (Albuquerque: University of New Mexico Press, 1944); and in Alvin R. Sunseri, "A Note on Slavery and the Black Man in New Mexico, 1846–1861," *Negro History Bulletin* 38 (1975): 452–459.

Black slavery as practiced among the so-called Five Civilized Tribes in Indian Territory is the subject of several important works including Theda Perdue, *Slavery and the Evolution of Cherokee Society, 1540–1866* (Knoxville: University of Tennessee Press, 1979); R. Haliburton, Jr., *Red Over Black: Black Slavery among the Cherokee Indians* (Westport, Connecticut: Greenwood Press, 1977); Daniel F. Littlefield, Jr., *Africans and Seminoles: From Removal to Emancipation* (Westport, Connecticut: Greenwood Press, 1977); Littlefield, *Africans and Creeks: From the Colonial Period to the Civil War* (Westport, Connecticut: Greenwood Press, 1979); and Wyatt F. Jeltz, "The Relations of Negroes and Choctaw and Chickasaw Indians," *Journal of Negro History* 33 (1948): 24–37.

Although slavery never officially existed in either California or Oregon, several southern slaveholders moved to those areas and took their slaves with them. Delilah L. Beasley, "Slavery in California," *Journal of Negro History* 3 (1918): 33–44, surveys the institution as practiced in the first Pacific Slope state including the time before the United States acquired the area. For the debate over slavery in Oregon, see D. G. Hill, "The Negro as a Political and Social Issue in the Oregon Country," *Journal of Negro History* 33 (1948): 130–145; T. W. Davenport, "Slavery Question in Oregon," *Quarterly of the Oregon Historical Society* 9 (1908): 189–253 and 309–373; and Fred Lockley, "Some Documentary Records of Slavery in Oregon," *Quarterly of the Oregon Historical Society* 17 (1916): 107–115.

Slaveholders in both Oregon and California ignored those areas' "free" status until the courts began to issue antislavery decisions. A precedent-setting case in Oregon, holding that "slaves" were free because slavery did not legally exist in the territory, is explored in Fred Lockley, "The Case of Robin Holmes v. Nathaniel Ford," *Quarterly of the Oregon Historical Society* 23 (1922): 111–137. In two celebrated cases, the California supreme court held that slavery did not exist in the Golden State but nevertheless sought to return control of the defendants to their masters for transport back to the South and bondage. See Ray R. Albin, "The Perkins Case: The Ordeal of Three Slaves in Gold Rush California," *California History* 67 (1988): 214–227, 287–289; Rudolph M. Lapp, *Archy Lee: A California Fugitive Slave Case* (San Francisco: Book Club of California, 1969);

and William E. Franklin, "The Archy Case: The California Supreme Court Refuses to Free a Slave," *Pacific Historical Review* 32 (1963): 137–154.

A few works have examined the lives of free blacks who lived in the West during the slavery era. Not surprisingly, much of this scholarship deals with Texas, a slave state whose African American population surpassed that of the remainder of the West combined in the mid-nineteenth century. For the pre-statehood era, see Harold Schoen, "The Free Negro in the Republic of Texas," *Southwestern Historical Quarterly* 39 (1936): 292–308; 40 (1936): 26–34 and 85–113; 40 (1937): 169–199 and 267–289; and 41 (1937): 83–108. Based upon his research of Texas free blacks, George R. Woolfolk concluded that African Americans who were not slaves had more social and economic opportunity in the West than in other areas of the United States; see "Turner's Safety Valve and Free Negro Westward Migration," *Pacific Northwest Quarterly* 56 (1965): 125–130; reprinted, *Journal of Negro History* 50 (1965): 185–197. Andrew Forest Muir has examined free blacks in selected Texas jurisdictions in "The Free Negro in Harris County, Texas," *Southwestern Historical Quarterly* 46 (1943): 214–238; "The Free Negro in Fort Bend County, Texas," *Journal of Negro History* 33 (1948): 79–85; and "The Free Negro in Jefferson and Orange Counties, Texas," *Journal of Negro History* 35 (1950): 183–206.

Several works have been published about free blacks in other western areas. These include Quintard Taylor, "Slaves and Free Men: Blacks in the Oregon Country, 1840–1860," *Oregon Historical Quarterly* 83 (1982): 150–173; Philip M. Montesano, *Some Aspects of the Free Negro Question in San Francisco, 1849–1870* (San Francisco: R and E Research Associates, 1973); Richard B. Sheridan, "From Slavery in Missouri to Freedom in Kansas: The Influx of Black Fugitives and Contrabands Into Kansas, 1854–1865," *Kansas History* 12 (1989): 28–47; and Daniel F. Littlefield, Jr., and Mary Ann Littlefield, "The Beams Family: Free Blacks in Indian Territory," *Journal of Negro History* 61 (1976): 16–35.

Texas was the only state considered in this study that underwent post-Civil War Reconstruction. A general history of that era in the Lone Star State is James M. Smallwood, *Time of Hope, Time of Despair: Black Texans During Reconstruction* (Port Washington, New York: Kennikat Press, 1981). Some of the discrimination that whites in Texas exhibited toward freed African Americans during the Reconstruction era is discussed in Barry A. Crouch, "A Spirit of Lawlessness: White Violence; Texas Blacks, 1865–1868," *Journal of Social History* 18 (1984): 217–232. See, also, Greg Cantrell, "Racial Violence and Recon-struction Politics in Texas, 1867–1868," *Southwestern Historical Quarterly* 93 (1990): 333–355.

Because slavery also existed in Indian Territory, however, the U.S. government's Reconstruction policies affected society there, too. The *Chronicles of Oklahoma* has published three essays on this subject; see Parthena Louise James, "Reconstruction in the Chickasaw Nation: The Freedmen Problem," 45 (1967): 44–57; Hanna R. Warren, "Reconstruction in the Cherokee Nation," 45 (1967): 180–189; and Walt Willson, "Freedmen in Indian Territory During Reconstruction," 49 (1971): 230–244. Some of the legal problems faced by ex-slaves in the Choctaw and Chickasaw nations during and after the Reconstruction era are discussed in Thomas F. Andrews, "Freedmen in Indian Territory: A Post-Civil War Dilemma," *Journal of the West* 4 (1965): 367–376.

The work of the most important federal agency created during Reconstruction is the focus of Barry A. Crouch, *The Freedmen's Bureau and Black Texans* (Austin: University of Texas Press, 1992). An earlier, shorter work on the same topic is Claude Elliott, "The Freedmen's Bureau in Texas," *Southwestern Historical Quarterly* 56 (1952): 1–24. Perhaps the most enduring legacy of the Freedmen's Bureau was the rudimentary educational system it created for ex-slaves. The agency's pedagogic efforts are examined in Alton Hornsby, Jr., "The Freedmen's Bureau Schools in Texas, 1865–1870," *Southwestern Historical Quarterly* 76 (1973): 397–417. That African Americans desired education so much that freed slaves founded schools without waiting for the Freedmen's Bureau to do so is the theme of James M. Smallwood, "Early 'Freedom Schools': Black Self-Help and Education in Reconstruction-Texas, A Case Study," *Negro History Bulletin* 41 (1978): 790–793. In an additional article on the subject of public education for blacks in the late nineteenth-century West, James C. Carper argues in "The Popular Ideology of Segregated Schooling: Attitudes Toward the Education of Blacks in Kansas, 1854–1900," *Kansas History* 1 (1978): 254–265, that African Americans there desired integrated education but were denied the opportunity by prejudiced whites.

A few scholarly works have looked at the establishment of colleges for ex-slaves and other blacks in Texas and Oklahoma. The Freedmen's Bureau and other organizations founded higher educational institutions in Texas immediately after the Civil War as Michael R. Heintze shows in *Private Black Colleges in Texas, 1865–1954* (College Station: Texas A & M University Press, 1985). State-supported institutions founded in the late nineteenth century are examined, for Texas, by George Ruble Woolfolk, *Prairie View: A Study in Public Conscience, 1878–1946* (New York: Pageant Press, 1962); and, for Oklahoma, by Zella J. Black Patterson, *Langston University: A History* (Norman: University of Oklahoma Press, 1979).

Along with freedom came political power for western African Americans. Because Texas underwent Reconstruction, the black community in that state exercised a significant measure of political influence for some time; this power diminished, however, in the last few years of the nineteenth century (as was the case in all of the "reconstructed" states) as is shown by Merline Pitre in *Through Many Dangers, Toils and Snares: The Black Leadership of Texas, 1868–1900* (Austin, Texas: Eakin Press, 1985). Philip M. Montesano explores the tie between politics and religion in "San Francisco Black Churches in the Early 1860's: Political Pressure Group," *California Historical Quarterly* 52 (1973): 145–152; church leaders in that city were able to organize their congregations to protest discriminatory state laws. Secular black leaders managed to influence city political practices in another western town almost a half century later as William Lang shows in "Tempest on Clore Street: Race and Politics in Helena, Montana, 1906," *Scratchgravel Hills* 3 (Summer 1980): 9–14. See, also, Eugene H. Berwanger's article in this volume on black activists in post-Civil War Colorado and works about individual political leaders, cited below.

While most western African Americans gladly supported the Republican Party during the frontier era, some argued that the GOP took their support for granted and, thus, did little to better the social and economic conditions of black voters. This belief caused some western blacks to become Democrats while others looked to third parties for political salvation. Activities of African Americans in Texas and Kansas on behalf of the People's Party are examined by Jack Abramowitz in "The Negro in the Populist Movement," *Journal of Negro History* 38 (1953): 257–289, a study that concentrates on the South. William H. Chafe, "The Negroes and Populism: A Kansas Case Study," *Journal of Southern History* 34 (1968): 402–419, presents a more detailed explanation of why frustrated Republicans in one western state opted for a third party; essentially, Chafe argues, the Populists offered Kansas African Americans more patronage positions than the GOP was willing to give. That economic hard times as well as dissatisfaction with the Republican Party caused some western blacks to support the Socialist Party in the early twentieth century is the theme of H. L. Meredith, "Agrarian Socialism and the Negro in Oklahoma, 1900–1918," *Labor History* 11 (1970): 277–284.

Publications on the buffalo soldiers abound, but four books stand out above all others. The definitive work on the black cavalry is William H. Leckie, *The Buffalo Soldiers: A Narrative of the Negro Cavalry in the West* (Norman: University of Oklahoma Press, 1967), which stresses the soldiers' role in fighting Indians. Arlen L. Fowler's *The Black Infantry in the West, 1869–1891* (Westport, Connecticut: Greenwood Publishing Corp., 1971; reprinted, Norman:

University of Oklahoma Press, 1996) is designed to give the infantry the recognition Leckie gives the cavalry; Fowler, however, concentrates on the non-combat duties of the infantry (which did much less Indian fighting than did the cavalry). Monroe Lee Billington examines both the cavalry and the infantry in all aspects of their military experiences—fighting and otherwise—using one western territory as a case study in *New Mexico's Buffalo Soldiers, 1866–1900* (Niwot: University Press of Colorado, 1991). Another volume that focuses on both types of buffalo soldiers in one western state and emphasizes the prejudice they encountered from the dominant white society in the post-Indian wars era is Garna L. Christian, *Black Soldiers in Jim Crow Texas, 1899–1917* (College Station: Texas A & M University Press, 1995).

Several other general works on African American soldiers have some value. John M. Carroll, editor, *The Black Military Experience in the American West* (New York: Liveright Publishing Corp., 1971), is a compilation of fifty-eight articles of varying length and historical merit. Jack D. Foner, "The Socializing Role of the Military," in James P. Tate, editor, *The American Military on the Frontier* (Washington, D.C.: Office of Air Force History, 1978), postulates that serving as a soldier in the West offered better opportunity for black men than was available to them in the East. Foner also has significant chapters on buffalo soldiers in two books he authored: *The United States Soldier Between Two Wars: Army Life and Reform, 1865–1898* (New York: Humanities Press, 1970); and *Blacks and the Military in American History: A New Perspective* (New York: Praeger Publishers, 1974). Thomas D. Phillips, "The Black Regulars," in Allen G. Bogue, Thomas D. Phillips, and James E. Wright, editors, *The West of the American People* (Itasca, Illinois: Peacock, 1970), is a good, brief overview of the role of the buffalo soldiers in the frontier West.

African American soldiers on the western frontier are also examined in other worthwhile studies. Biographical information on individual soldiers is included in Frank N. Schubert, *On the Trail of the Buffalo Soldier: Biographies of African Americans in the U.S. Army, 1866–1917* (Wilmington, Delaware: Scholarly Resources Inc., 1995), and in Schubert, *Black Valor: Buffalo Soldiers and the Medal of Honor, 1870–1898* (Wilmington, Delaware: Scholarly Resources Inc., 1997). Henry O. Flipper, one of three black officers (other than chaplains) in the U.S. army in the late nineteenth century, left a slim unpublished autobiography that Theodore D. Harris edited and published under the title *Negro Frontiersman: The Western Memoirs of Henry O. Flipper, First Negro Graduate of West Point* (El Paso: Texas Western College Press, 1963). That Flipper's dismissal from the army for financial misconduct was unfair is the theme of Bruce J. Dinges, "The Court-Martial of Lieutenant Henry O. Flipper:

An Example of Black-White Relationships in the Army, 1881," *American West* 9, no. 1 (1972): 12–17, 59–61. Another article highlighting the prejudice African American soldiers encountered in the West is Frank N. Schubert, "Black Soldiers on the White Frontier: Some Factors Influencing Race Relations," *Phylon* 32 (1971): 410–415. Monroe Billington, "Civilians and Black Soldiers in New Mexico Territory, 1866–1900: A Cross-Cultural Experience," *Military History of the Southwest* 19, no. 1 (1989): 71–82, discusses both the positive and negative exchanges that occurred when African American soldiers and white civilians came into contact with each other on the frontier.

Articles detailing the general experiences of black troopers at lonely, isolated frontier posts include Ronald G. Coleman, "The Buffalo Soldiers: Guardians of the Uintah Frontier, 1886–1901," *Utah Historical Quarterly* 47 (1979): 421–439; Lee Myers, "Mutiny at Fort Cummings," *New Mexico Historical Review* 46 (1971): 337–350; Erwin N. Thompson, "The Negro Soldiers on the Frontier: A Fort Davis Case Study," *Journal of the West* 7 (1968): 217–235; Monroe Billington, "Black Soldiers at Fort Selden, New Mexico, 1866–1891," *New Mexico Historical Review* 62 (1987): 65–80; and Thomas G. Alexander and Leonard J. Arrington, "The Utah Military Frontier, 1872–1912: Forts Cameron, Thornburgh, and Duchesne," *Utah Historical Quarterly* 32 (1964): 330–354. A more detailed history of a fort at which black cavalrymen served contains much information on the soldiers' military and off-duty activities; see, Frank N. Schubert, *Buffalo Soldiers, Braves, and the Brass: The Story of Fort Robinson, Nebraska* (Shippensburg, Pennsylvania: White Mane Publishing Co., 1993), reprinted as *Outpost of the Sioux Wars: A History of Fort Robinson* (Lincoln: University of Nebraska Press, 1995). These works should be compared with that of Michael J. Clark, reprinted in this volume, detailing the experiences of black infantry troops at a fort adjacent to an urban area.

Specific experiences of various African American military units are the subject of several works. Two articles discuss the role of the Ninth Cavalry in the 1892 Wyoming cattleman dispute known as the Johnson County War: Robert A. Murray, "The United States in the Aftermath of the Johnson County Invasion," *Annals of Wyoming* 38 (April 1966): 59–75; and Frank N. Schubert, "The Suggs Affray: The Black Cavalry in the Johnson County War," *Western Historical Quarterly* 4 (1973): 57–68. Robert M. Utley, "The Buffalo Soldiers and Victorio," *New Mexico Magazine* 62, no. 3 (1984): 47–50, 53–54, examines the black cavalry's role in harassing a major Apache leader in Arizona in 1879 and 1880. Elvis Eugene Fleming, "Captain Nicholas Nolan: Lost on the Staked Plains," *Texana* 4 (1966): 1–13, relates the oft-told story of the ordeal of several Tenth Cavalry troopers who were lost without water for several days in western

Texas and eastern New Mexico in 1877. A delightful article, Marvin E. Fletcher, "The Black Bicycle Corps," *Arizona and the West* 16 (1974): 219–232, recounts the army's use of Montana infantry troops to experiment with the popular two-wheeler as a potential military transport vehicle in the late 1890s.

The U.S. army commissioned five African American ministers as chaplains in the late nineteenth century and assigned them to all-black units. A short survey of these two Baptists and three Methodists is included in Earl F. Stover, *Up From Handymen: The United States Army Chaplaincy, 1865–1920* (Washington, D.C.: Department of the Army, 1977). Biographies of two of these men are William Seraile, *Voice of Dissent: Theophilus Gould Steward (1843–1924) and Black America* (Brooklyn, New York: Carlson Publishing Co., 1991); and John Phillip Langellier and Alan M. Osur, "Chaplain Allen Allensworth and the 24th Infantry, 1886–1906," *Smoke Signal*, no. 40 (1980), reprinted in *Brand Book 4* (Tucson: Tucson Corral of the Westerners, 1984), which relies heavily upon Charles Alexander, *Battles and Victories of Allen Allensworth* (Boston: Sherman, French and Co., 1914). See, also, Stover, "Chaplain Henry Plummer: His Ministry and His Court-Martial," *Nebraska History* 56 (1975): 20–50. On the role of the black chaplains in teaching buffalo soldiers to read and write, see Miller J. Stewart, "A Touch of Civilization: Culture and Education in the Frontier Army," *Nebraska History* 65 (1984): 257–282.

A few black men who were not buffalo soldiers accompanied U.S. military expeditions to the western frontier. G. M. Bergman, "The Negro Who Rode With Fremont in 1847," *Negro History Bulletin* 28 (October 1964): 31–32, profiles briefly Jacob Dodson, a personal servant of military mapmaker John Charles Fremont. Martin Hardwick Hall, "Negroes With Confederate Troops in West Texas and New Mexico," *Password* 13, no. 1 (1968): 11–12, mentions a few slaves of southern troops involved in the trans-Mississippi theater of the Civil War. A major biography of an African American army scout is Joe DeBarthe, *Life and Adventures of Frank Grouard*, Edgar I. Stewart, editor (Norman: University of Oklahoma Press, 1958). Two articles on a black scout and interpreter who rode and died with General George A. Custer in Montana in 1876 are Roland C. McConnell, "Isaiah Dorman and the Custer Expedition," *Journal of Negro History* 33 (1948): 344–352; and Robert J. Ege, "Braves of All Colors: The Story of Isaiah Dorman, Killed at the Little Big Horn," *Montana: The Magazine of Western History* 16, no. 1 (1966): 35–40.

Scholarship on blacks in the mining industry is sparse. W. Sherman Savage authored a pioneering article, "The Negro on the Mining Frontier," *Journal of Negro History* 30 (1945): 30–46. Rudolph M. Lapp, *Blacks in Gold Rush California*, and Elmer R. Rusco, *"Good Time Coming?": Black Nevadans in the Nineteenth Century,* both cited above, have much information on African American miners in those states' mineral rushes. Two poorly written essays chronicling individual black miners who supposedly struck it rich but kept the location of their mines secret are Carol Ann Muller, "Nigger Ben McLendon and His Lost Gold Mine," *Journal of Arizona History* 14 (1973): 379–384; and J. Frank Dobie, "The Lost Nigger Mine," in *Coronado's Children: Tales of Lost Mines and Buried Treasures of the Southwest* (New York: The Literary Guild of America, 1931). An article on African American coal miners, in addition to that of Robert A. Campbell in this volume, is Mark Stern, "Black Strikebreakers in the Coal Fields: King County, Washington—1891," *Journal of Ethnic Studies* 5, no. 3 (1977): 60–70. Information on blacks on the mining frontier can be found, for Idaho, in George M. Blackburn and Sherman L. Ricards, "Unequal Opportunity on a Mining Frontier: The Role of Gender, Race, and Birthplace," *Pacific Historical Review* 62 (1993): 19–38; and, for Montana, in Paul A. Frisch, " 'Gibraltar of Unionism': Women, Blacks, and the Anti-Chinese Movement in Butte, Montana, 1880–1900," *Southwest Economy and Society* 6 (1984): 3–13. Malcolm Edwards, " 'The War of Complexional Distinction': Blacks in Gold Rush California and British Columbia," *California Historical Quarterly* 56 (1977): 34–45, argues that black miners left the Golden State and went to the British Columbia gold fields because of discriminatory treatment in California.

African American cowboys have been the subjects of only a limited number of works. Beginning in the 1950s two English professors and amateur historians published a few articles on black cowhands. The focus of the work of these academics, Philip Durham and Everett L. Jones, was that fiction writers and moviemakers had purposely neglected to chronicle the contributions made by blacks to the western cattle industry. Their research led them to issue a general history entitled *The Negro Cowboys* (New York: Dodd, Mead, and Co., 1965; reprinted, Lincoln: University of Nebraska Press, 1983). Their efforts stimulated several historians to investigate the role African Americans played in the cattle kingdom, the chief product of which was the article by Kenneth Wiggins Porter included in this volume. Two book-length biographies of black cowboys written in the 1970s are Bailey C. Hanes, *Bill Pickett, Bulldogger: The Biography of a Black Cowboy* (Norman: University of Oklahoma Press, 1977); and Franklin Folsom, *Black Cowboy: The Life and Legend of George McJunkin* (2d ed., Niwot, Colorado: Roberts Rinehart Publishers, 1992). A short biography of an early twentieth-century western black cowboy is Walker D. Wyman and John D. Hart, "The Legend of Charlie Glass," *Colorado Magazine* 46 (1969): 40–54. A significant autobiography that is entertaining but of questionable veracity is Nat Love, *The Life and Adventures of Nat Love, Better*

Bill Pickett. A cowboy on a large Oklahoma ranch for many years, Pickett invented the rodeo event of bulldogging and performed it all over the United States and in several foreign countries. (Courtesy, Nebraska State Historical Society.)

Known in the Cattle Country as "Deadwood Dick" (Los Angeles: By the author, 1907; reprinted, Lincoln: University of Nebraska Press, 1995). An oversized, coffee table picture book with limited historical value is Paul Stewart and Wallace Yvonne Ponce, *Black Cowboys* (Denver: Black American West Museum and Heritage Center, 1986).

Two major books have examined the exodusters who went to Kansas after Reconstruction ended in the South: Robert G. Athearn, *In Search of Canaan: Black Migration to Kansas, 1879–1880* (Lawrence: The Regents Press of Kansas, 1978); and Nell Irvin Painter, *Exodusters: Black Migration to Kansas After Reconstruction* (New York: Alfred A. Knopf, 1977). One of the leaders of the migrants is profiled in Roy Garvin, "Benjamin, or 'Pap,' Singleton and His Followers," *Journal of Negro History* 33 (1948): 7–23. Some of their experiences are the subject of several articles including Glen Schwendemann, "Wyandotte and the First 'Exodusters' on the Missouri," *Kansas Historical Quarterly* 26 (1960): 233–249; Schwendemann, "The 'Exodusters' on the Missouri," *Kansas Historical Quarterly* 29 (1963): 25–40; and Arvarh E. Strickland, "Toward the Promised Land: The Exodus to Kansas and Afterward," *Missouri Historical Review* 69 (1975): 376–412. Nudie E. Williams, "Black Newspapers and the Exodusters of 1879," *Kansas History* 8 (1985–1986): 217–225, surveys the attitudes of several eastern and a few Kansas African American editors toward the exodus. The stories of four communities founded by blacks in Kansas are Schwendemann, "Nicodemus: Negro Haven on the Solomon," *Kansas Historical Quarterly* 34 (1968): 10–31; C. Robert Haywood, "The Hodgeman County Colony," *Kansas History* 12 (1989–1990): 210–221; Gary R. Entz, "Image and Reality on the Kansas Prairie: 'Pap' Singleton's Cherokee County Colony," *Kansas History* 19 (1996): 125–139; and Joseph V. Hickey, " 'Pap' Singleton's Dunlap Colony: Relief Agencies and the Failure of a Black Settlement in Eastern Kansas," *Great Plains Quarterly* 11 (1991): 23–36.

That many Kansas exodusters later homesteaded in Colorado is shown in George H. Wayne, "Negro Migration and Colonization in Colorado—1870–1930," *Journal of the West* 15 (January 1976): 102–120. The most well-known all-black agricultural colony in Colorado was Dearfield on the state's northeastern plains. Frederick P. Johnson, "Agricultural Negro Colony in Eastern Colorado," *Western Farm Life* 17 (May 1, 1915): 5, 12, is merely a long interview with Oliver T. Jackson, Dearfield's founder. Karen Waddell, "Dearfield.... A Dream Deferred," *Colorado Heritage* (1988, no. 2): 2–12, is a general history of Jackson's creation of that colony and its eventual failure. Daniel Gibson, "Blackdom," *New Mexico Magazine* 64, no. 2 (1986): 46–47, 50–51, profiles an all-black agricultural colony in eastern New Mexico, while Lonnie G. Bunch III, "Allensworth: The Life, Death and Rebirth of an All-Black Community," *Californians* 5 (November/December 1987): 26–33, is about a California settlement. Dearfield, Blackdom, and Allensworth all suffered financial and organizational problems, and none could survive the economic hard times of the 1920s.

Colorado homesteaders. The western frontier offered many African Americans opportunities that might not exist for them elsewhere in the United States — including the chance to own their own land and homes. This family posed in front of their Colorado homestead in the 1880s. (Courtesy, Denver Public Library, Western History Department.)

All-black towns were more numerous in Oklahoma than all other western states combined. The pioneering article on Oklahoma's black settlements is Mozell C. Hill, "The All-Negro Communities of Oklahoma: The Natural History of a Social Movement," *Journal of Negro History* 31 (1946): 254–268. The most thorough general survey of the topic is the article by George O. Carney in this volume. Several journal articles present the history of individual all-black towns in the Sooner State; among them are Linda C. Gray, "Taft: Town on the Black Frontier," *Chronicles of Oklahoma* 66 (1988–89): 430–447; Jere W. Robinson, "Edward P. McCabe and the Langston Experiment," *Chronicles of Oklahoma* 51 (1973): 343–355; Kenneth Marvin Hamilton, "Townsite Speculation and the Origin of Boley, Oklahoma," *Chronicles of Oklahoma* 55 (1977): 180–189; and Hamilton, "The Origin and Early Developments of Langston, Oklahoma," *Journal of Negro History* 62 (1977): 270–282. That African Americans hoped for a better life in Oklahoma's all-black towns is the theme of William E. Bittle and Gilbert L. Geis, "Racial Self-Fulfillment and the Rise of an All-Negro Community in Oklahoma," *Phylon* 18 (1957): 247–260, reprinted in August Meier and Elliott Rudwick, editors, *The Making of Black America: Essays in Negro Life & History*, cited above; Martin Dann, "From

Sodom to the Promised Land: E. P. McCabe and the Movement for Oklahoma Colonization," *Kansas Historical Quarterly* 40 (1974): 370–378; and Daniel F. Littlefield and Lonnie E. Underhill, "Black Dreams and 'Free' Homes: The Oklahoma Territory, 1891–1894," *Phylon* 34 (1973): 342–357. Hamilton has combined his research on African American communities into the book, *Black Towns and Profit: Promotion and Development in the Trans-Appalachian West, 1877–1915* (Urbana: University of Illinois Press, 1991); it includes chapters on Nicodemus (in Kansas), Boley and Langston (in Oklahoma), and Allensworth (in California). Also useful is Norman Crockett, *The Black Towns* (Lawrence: The Regents Press of Kansas, 1979), which profiles Nicodemus, Boley, and Langston as well as the Oklahoma town of Clearview. On black settlements in general, see Harold M. Rose, "The All-Negro Town: Its Evolution and Function," *Geographical Review* 55 (1965): 362–381.

Several significant studies have examined African American communities within larger white societies. Blacks in three of California's most populous cities are discussed in Lawrence B. de Graaf, "The City of Black Angels: Emergence of the Los Angeles Ghetto, 1890–1930," *Pacific Historical Review* 39 (1970): 323–352; Gail Madyun and Larry Malone, "Black Pioneers in San Diego, 1880–1920," *Journal of San Diego History* 27 (Spring 1981): 91–114; Douglas Henry Daniels, *Pioneer Urbanites: A Social and Cultural History of Black San Francisco* (Berkeley: University of California Press, 1990); and Albert S. Broussard, *Black San Francisco: The Struggle for Racial Equality in the West, 1900–1954* (Lawrence: University Press of Kansas, 1993).

Studies of African American communities in western cities outside California include Thomas C. Cox, *Blacks in Topeka, Kansas, 1865–1915: A Social History* (Baton Rouge: Louisiana State University Press, 1982); relevant parts of Bradford Luckingham, *Minorities in Phoenix: A Profile of Mexican American, Chinese American, and African American Communities, 1860–1992* (Tucson: University of Arizona Press, 1994); and Quintard Taylor, *The Forging of a Black Community: Seattle's Central District from 1870 Through the Civil Rights Era* (Seattle: University of Washington Press, 1994). Amateur efforts include Joseph Franklin, *All Through the Night: The History of Spokane Black Americans, 1860–1940* (Fairfield, Washington: Ye Galleon Press, 1989); Esther Hall Mumford, *Seattle's Black Victorians, 1852–1901* (Seattle: Ananse Press, 1980); and Eddie Faye Gates, *They Came Searching: How Blacks Sought the Promised Land in Tulsa* (Austin, Texas: Eakin Press, 1997). See also, Quintard Taylor's general study, "The Emergence of Black Communities in the Pacific Northwest: 1865–1910," *Journal of Negro History* 64 (1979): 342–354; Nupur Chaudhuri, " 'We All Seem Like Brothers and Sisters': The African-American Community in

Manhattan, Kansas, 1865–1940," *Kansas History* 14 (1991–1992): 270–288; C. Robert Haywood, " 'No Less a Man': Blacks in Cow Town Dodge City, 1876–1886," *Western Historical Quarterly* 19 (1988): 161–182; and William L. Lang's article on Helena, Montana, reproduced in this volume.

Surprisingly little scholarship exists on the role of religion as a unifying force in western black communities; the history of one congregation in a white-dominated town is Mamie O. Oliver, "Boise's Black Baptists: Heritage, Hope, and Struggle," *Idaho Yesterdays* 40, no. 3 (1996): 23–30. On the importance of black-owned newspapers to the establishment of a sense of community in towns with white majorities see Rex C. Myers, "Montana's Negro Newspapers, 1894–1911," *Montana Journalism Review* 16 (1973): 17–22; and the article by Gayle K. Berardi and Thomas W. Segady that is included in this volume. The development of African American newspapers in one western territory is examined in Nudie Williams, "The Black Press in Oklahoma: The Formative Years, 1889–1907," *Chronicles of Oklahoma* 61 (1983): 308–319. A single African American newspaper is the subject of Arnold Cooper, " 'Protection to All, Discrimination to None': The *Parson's Weekly Blade*, 1892–1900," *Kansas History* 9 (1986): 58–71.

Only a scant number of scholars have studied the experiences of African American women in the West. Other than the essays by Glenda Riley and Anne M. Butler that are included in this volume, the best work on the subject is Lawrence B. de Graaf, "Race, Sex, and Region: Black Women in the American West, 1850–1920," *Pacific Historical Review* 49 (1980): 285–313. See, also, Roger D. Hardaway, "African-American Women on the Western Frontier," *Negro History Bulletin* 60, no. 1 (1997): 8–13. A book-length treatment of the history of African American women in one western state is Ruthe Winegarten, *Black Texas Women: 150 Years of Trial and Triumph* (Austin: University of Texas Press, 1995), which contains many photographs of the subjects profiled within its pages. William Loren Katz, *Black Women of the Old West* (New York: Atheneum, 1995), is a slim volume for adolescents.

The endeavors of black women to establish social organizations in the West have been the focus of a few scholarly works. Lynda F. Dickson has published two studies of the efforts of African American women in Denver to create clubs that gave them an enhanced sense of self-worth while presenting a good image to women of the dominant white community: "Toward a Broader Angle of Vision in Uncovering Women's History: Black Women's Clubs Revisited," *Frontiers: A Journal of Women's Studies* 9, no. 2 (1987): 62–68; and "African American Women's Clubs in Denver, 1890s–1920s" in Sucheng Chan, Douglas Henry Daniels, Mario T. Garcia, and Terry P. Wilson, editors, *Peoples of Color in the American West* (Lexington, Massachusetts: D.C. Heath and Co., 1994). Another article on such organizations in a western plains state is Marilyn Dell Brady, "Kansas Federation of Colored Women's Clubs, 1900–1930," *Kansas History* 9 (1986): 19–30. Attempts of black women to create a sense of community in three early twentieth-century western towns are explored by Sue Armitage, Theresa Banfield, and Sarah Jacobus in "Black Women and Their Communities in Colorado," *Frontiers: A Journal of Women's Studies* 2, no. 2 (1977): 45–51. The struggles of African American women (mostly ex-slaves) to balance home, family, and work obligations in one Texas city are examined by Barry A. Crouch, "Seeking Equality: Houston Black Women During Reconstruction," in Howard Beeth and Cary D. Wintz, editors, *Black Dixie: Afro-Texan History and Culture in Houston* (College Station: Texas A & M University Press, 1992).

The lives of at least four western African American women who lived during the frontier era have received scholarly treatment. Dolores Hayden, "Biddy Mason's Los Angeles, 1856–1891," *California History* 68 (Fall 1984): 86–99, 147–149, discusses the intriguing life of a woman born a slave in Mississippi who went to Utah and California with her Mormon master, sued for her freedom, and bought several real estate parcels that made her twentieth-century descendants quite wealthy. Another Mormon black woman's life is profiled by Henry J. Wolfinger in "A Test of Faith: Jane Elizabeth James and the Origins of the Utah Black Community," in Clark Knowlton, editor, *Social Accommodation in Utah* (Salt Lake City: University of Utah American West Center, 1975). Kathie Ryckman Anderson, "Era Bell Thompson: A North Dakota Daughter," *North Dakota History* 49 (1982): 11–18, is about a woman who was born in Iowa, grew up in early twentieth-century North Dakota, and went on to become an editor of *Ebony* magazine; Thompson's autobiography is *American Daughter* (Chicago: University of Chicago Press, 1946). Elizabeth Amelia Hadley Freydberg has produced a biography of a pioneering black female aviator from Texas with *Bessie Coleman: The Brownskin Lady Bird* (Hamden, Connecticut: Garland Publishing Co., 1994); see, also, Doris L. Rich, *Queen Bess: Daredevil Aviator* (Washington, D.C.: Smithsonian Institution Press, 1993).

Two book-length biographies of western black women are of questionable historical value. Helen Holdredge, *Mammy Pleasant* (New York: Putnam, 1953), relates the story of a shadowy woman in late nineteenth-century California who operated a boardinghouse that may have been a brothel. Kathleen Bruyn, *"Aunt" Clara Brown: Story of a Black Pioneer* (Boulder,

Colorado: Pruett Publishing Co., 1970), tells of a former slave who became wealthy and respected in the Colorado mining country.

Three informal reminiscences of individual black women give some insights into the loneliness members of their race and gender often endured on the western frontier: Glenn Chaffin, "Aunt Tish: Beloved Gourmet of the Bitter Root," *Montana: The Magazine of Western History* 21, no. 4 (1971): 67–69, is about a woman who ran a boardinghouse in Hamilton, Montana; Gary Cooper, "Stage Coach Mary," *Ebony* 14 (October 1959): 97–100, recalls Mary Fields, who drove a stagecoach and owned a laundry in Cascade, Montana; and M. Lilliana Owens, "Julia Greeley, 'Colored Angel of Charity'," *Colorado Magazine* 20 (1943): 176–178, is about a domestic servant who lived in Denver. Two privately printed pamphlet-length memoirs tell the stories of two Colorado families in the frontier era and contain much information on the women in those families; they are Wilbur P. Ball, *Black Pioneers of the Prairie* (Fort Collins, Colorado: Commercial-PWS Printers, 1988); and Dorothy Bass Spann, *Black Pioneers: A History of a Pioneer Family in Colorado Springs* (Colorado Springs, Colorado: Little London Press, 1978).

More African American men than women have been profiled in scholarly publications. Several articles discuss the careers of black politicians in post-Civil War Texas. These include Ann Patton Malone, "Matt Gaines: Reconstruction Politician," in Alwyn Barr and Robert A. Calvert, editors, *Black Leaders: Texans for Their Times* (Austin: Texas State Historical Association, 1991); Merline Pitre, "Richard Allen: The Chequered Career of Houston's First Black State Legislator," in Howard Beeth and Cary D. Wintz, editors, *Black Dixie: Afro-Texan History and Culture in Houston,* cited above; Alwyn Barr, "Black Legislators of Reconstruction Texas," *Civil War History* 32 (1986): 340–352; Carl H. Moneyhon, "George T. Ruby and the Politics of Expediency in Texas," in Howard N. Rabinowitz, editor, *Southern Black Leaders of the Reconstruction Era* (Urbana: University of Illinois Press, 1982); Randall B. Woods, "George T. Ruby: A Black Militant in the White Business Community," *Red River Valley Historical Review* 1 (1974): 269–280; Jack Abramowitz, "John B. Rayner—A Grass-roots Leader," *Journal of Negro History* 36 (1951): 160–193; and Paul Douglas Casdorph, "Norris Wright Cuney and Texas Republican Politics, 1883–1896," *Southwestern Historical Quarterly* 68 (1965): 455–464. Randall Bennett Woods has produced a masterful biography of a Kansas political leader in *A Black Odyssey: John Lewis Waller and the Promise of American Life, 1878–1900* (Lawrence: The Regents Press of Kansas, 1981), while W. Sherman Savage, "The Influence of William Alexander Leidesdorff on the History of California," *Journal of Negro History* 38 (1953): 322–332, is about a San Francisco politician.

Two articles have examined the dual careers that William Jefferson Hardin fashioned as a civil rights activist in Colorado and a territorial legislator in Wyoming: Eugene H. Berwanger, "William J. Hardin: Colorado Spokesman for Racial Justice, 1863–1873," *Colorado Magazine* 52 (1975): 52–65; and Roger D. Hardaway, "William Jefferson Hardin: Wyoming's Nineteenth Century Black Legislator," *Annals of Wyoming* 63, no. 1 (1991): 2–13. An essay comparing Hardin's efforts to secure voting and other rights for Colorado's black men to those of Charles H. Langston, who sought to accomplish the same things in Kansas, is Berwanger, "Hardin and Langston: Western Black Spokesmen of the Reconstruction Era," *Journal of Negro History* 64 (1979): 101–115. Two California equal rights activists are the subjects of Rudolph M. Lapp, "Jeremiah B. Sanderson: Early California Negro Leader," *Journal of Negro History* 53 (1968): 321–333; and Philip S. Foner, "Reverend George Washington Woodbey: Early Twentieth Century California Black Socialist," *Journal of Negro History* 61 (1976): 136–157. Lapp is the author of an additional work on the struggle for equal rights in the early years of California statehood: "Negro Rights Activities in Gold Rush California," *California Historical Society Quarterly* 45 (1966): 3–20. See, also, a final essay by Lapp: "The Negro in Gold Rush California," *Journal of Negro History* 49 (1964): 81–98.

A few articles have focused upon African American attorneys in the frontier West; these include Gary R. Kremer, "For Justice and a Fee: James Milton Turner and the Cherokee Freedmen," *Chronicles of Oklahoma* 58 (1980–81): 376–391; Lawrence O. Christensen, "J. Milton Turner: An Appraisal," *Missouri Historical Review* 70 (October 1975): 1–19; Albert S. Broussard, "McCants Stewart: The Struggles of a Black Attorney in the Urban West," *Oregon Historical Quarterly* (1988): 157–179; and Nudie E. Williams, "The African Lion: George Napier Perkins, Lawyer, Politician, Editor," *Chronicles of Oklahoma* 70 (1992–93): 450–465. Mifflin Wistar Gibbs, *Shadow and Light: An Autobiography with Reminiscences of the Last and Present Century* (Washington, D.C.: By the author, 1902; reprinted, Lincoln: University of Nebraska Press, 1995), is the first-person account of a man who lived in California and British Columbia for several years before settling down to a law practice in Arkansas.

Several articles also examine African American U.S. marshals in Oklahoma; most of the essays are by Nudie E. Williams, and most of the scholarship is on the lives of two lawmen, Bass Reeves and Grant Johnson. Daniel F. Littlefield, Jr., and Lonnie E. Underhill write about both of these peacekeepers in "Negro Marshals in the Indian Territory," *Journal of Negro History* 56 (1971): 77–87. Williams has authored a quartet of articles: "Black Men Who Wore the 'Star'," *Chronicles of Oklahoma* 59 (1981): 83–90; "Black

Men Who Wore White Hats: Grant Johnson, United States Deputy Marshal," *Red River Valley Historical Review* 5, no. 3 (1980): 4–13; "Bass Reeves: Lawman in the Western Ozarks," *Negro History Bulletin* 42 (1979): 37–39; and "United States vs. Bass Reeves: Black Lawman on Trial," *Chronicles of Oklahoma* 68 (1990): 154–167.

Several books and articles profile successful black businessmen. Forbes Parkhill, *Mister Barney Ford: A Portrait in Bistre* (Denver: Sage Books, 1963), is the biography of a man who became wealthy in the restaurant and hotel business in Colorado and Wyoming; the work, however, is of questionable historical value. John H. Monnett and Michael McCarthy, "Lewis Price," in their volume, *Colorado Profiles: Men and Women Who Shaped the Centennial State* (Evergreen, Colorado: Cordillera Press, 1987), tells of a man who founded a newspaper before making and then losing a fortune in the real estate business. John H. Paynter, "Joseph D.D. Rivers," *Journal of Negro History* 22 (1937): 289–291, is a long obituary notice summarizing the more important events in the life of a Denver newspaper publisher. Bruce A. Glasrud, "William M. McDonald: Business and Fraternal Leader," in Alwyn Barr and Robert A. Calvert, editors, *Black Leaders: Texans for Their Times*, cited above, is about a man who was a banker, teacher, civic leader, and Republican Party activist. Two men involved in the ranching business are discussed in Hettye Wallace Branch, *The Story of "80 John": A Biography of One of the Most Respected Negro Ranchmen in the Old West* (New York: Greenwich Book Publishers, Inc., 1960), an admiring memoir written by the daughter of D.W. Wallace, the Texas cattleman who is the subject of the slim, poorly crafted volume; and in Todd R. Guenther, " 'Y'all Call Me Nigger Jim Now, But Someday You'll Call Me Mr. James Edwards': Black Success on the Plains of the Equality State," *Annals of Wyoming* 61, no. 2 (1989): 20–40.

Other articles on western black men who lived during the frontier era offer a potpourri of interesting people who led varied lives. Robert W. O'Brien, "George Washington, Founder of Centralia," *Negro History Bulletin* 5 (1942): 194, 197, 215; and W. Sherman Savage, "George Washington of Centralia[,] Washington," *Negro History Bulletin* 27 (1963): 44–47, are about a Washington homesteader and town builder. Another early Washington settler is the subject of John Edwin Ayer, "George Bush, the Voyageur," *Washington Historical Quarterly* 7 (1916): 40–45; and of Ruby El Hult, "The Saga of George W. Bush: Unheralded Pioneer of the Northwest Territory," *Negro Digest* 11 (September 1962): 88–96. D. B. McGue, "John Taylor—Slave-Born Colorado Pioneer," *Colorado Magazine* 18 (1941): 161–168, is a poorly written essay about a man who was a buffalo soldier, settler, and interpreter for local courts. A successful and respected farmer is profiled in Darold D. Wax, "Robert Ball Anderson: Ex-Slave, A Pioneer in Western Nebraska, 1884–1930," *Nebraska History* 64 (1983): 162–192. Janis Hebert, "Oscar Micheaux: A Black Pioneer," *South Dakota Review* 11 (Winter 1973–74): 62–69, is about a South Dakota homesteader who left the plains and became an important movie producer in the early twentieth century. Another man who made a contribution to the arts is the subject of Joan R. Sherman, "James Monroe Whitfield, Poet and Emigrationist: A Voice of Protest and Despair," *Journal of Negro History* 57 (1972): 169–176. Deborah Willis, editor, *J. P. Ball: Daguerrean and Studio Photographer* (New York: Garland Publishing, Inc., 1993), includes a short biography of a photographer who lived and worked in Helena, Montana, and Seattle, Washington, during the late nineteenth and early twentieth centuries; all 218 known photographs that Ball took are reproduced in this volume. The life of a minister who became a newspaper publisher is examined in D. G. Paz, "John Albert Williams and Black Journalism in Omaha, 1895–1929," *Midwest Review* 10 (1988): 14–32. A ship's captain stationed in California is the subject of E. Berkeley Thompson, "Black Ahab: William T. Shorey, Whaling Master," *California Historical Quarterly* 51 (1972): 75–84. Augusta Hauck Block, "Old Lige," *Colorado Magazine* 19 (1942): 154–156, tells of Elijah Wentworth, self-proclaimed Denver town crier in the late nineteenth century.

Finally, the question of the amount of prejudice African Americans experienced in the frontier West is a topic that several authors have addressed in the course of examining larger themes. One article that focuses almost exclusively on the issue of racism is the one by Randall B. Woods that is included in this volume. Eugene H. Berwanger has written a major work on the struggle of western blacks to secure political equality, including the right to vote; *The West and Reconstruction* (Urbana: University of Illinois Press, 1981) holds that white westerners generally resisted granting the franchise to blacks until officials in Washington, D.C., forced them to do so. William M. King argues in *Going to Meet a Man: Denver's Last Legal Public Execution, 27 July 1886* (Niwot: University Press of Colorado, 1990) that Colorado's criminal justice system treated blacks more harshly than it did whites in the late nineteenth century.

White prejudice against African Americans could be subtle or overt. Caucasian officials often held antiblack attitudes that affected the way they formulated public policy and conducted governmental affairs. Albert Castel argues in "Civil War Kansas and the Negro," *Journal of Negro History* 51 (1966): 125–138, that white Kansans supported the Civil War and the Radical Reconstruction program because they wanted to preserve the Union and punish the South—not to help blacks (against whom they often discriminated). Stanley

R. Davison and Dale Tash, "Confederate Backwash in Montana Territory," *Montana: The Magazine of Western History* 17, no. 4 (1967): 50–58, contend that Montana's white leaders were also antiblack in philosophy; they enacted prejudicial laws and administered justice in a racially discriminatory manner. Prejudice against African Americans sometimes resulted in violence in the West as it did in other parts of the country. Genevieve Yost, "History of Lynchings in Kansas," *Kansas Historical Quarterly* 2 (1933): 182–219, examines extralegal violence and shows that a disproportionate number of people lynched in Kansas during the frontier era were black. John H. Monnett and Michael McCarthy investigate an especially brutal example of western-style lynching in "Preston Porter," in *Colorado Profiles: Men and Women Who Shaped the Centennial State*, cited above; the victim, a sixteen-year-old African American male, who may have been retarded, was burned at the stake by three hundred white ranchers for allegedly raping and murdering a thirteen-year-old Caucasian girl.

Several articles have explored the discriminatory statutes enacted by white westerners to prevent African Americans from experiencing the constitutional guarantee of equality under the law. These include William Hanchett, "Yankee Law and the Negro in Nevada, 1861–1869," *Western Humanities Review* 10 (1956): 241–249; J. W. Smurr, "Jim Crow Out West," in J. W. Smurr and K. Ross Toole, editors, *Historical Essays on Montana and the Northwest In Honor of Paul C. Phillips* (Helena: Western Press, Historical Society of Montana, 1957); and Harmon Mothershead, "Negro Rights in Colorado Territory (1859–1867)," *Colorado Magazine* 40 (1963): 212–223. William M. King focuses on school segregation laws in "Black Children, White Law: Black Efforts to Secure Public Education in Central City, Colorado, 1864–1869," *Essays and Monographs in Colorado History* 3 (1984): 55–79. Roger D. Hardaway has examined the statutes of two western states that prohibited African Americans from marrying outside their race; see "Prohibiting Interracial Marriage: Miscegenation Laws in Wyoming," *Annals of Wyoming* 52, no. 1 (1980): 55–60; and "Unlawful Love: A History of Arizona's Miscegenation Law," *Journal of Arizona History* 27 (1986): 377–390.

Obviously, the African American western experience has spawned many historical publications in recent decades. Nevertheless, the works cited above (and those that have gone unmentioned) leave much room for further inquiry. The record is incomplete; the whole story of black pioneers in the American West of the frontier era is yet to be told. Surely, therefore, much additional scholarship will be forthcoming as more and more historians search for clues to complete the saga of African Americans on the western frontier.

APPENDIX

The African American Population on the Western Frontier, 1850–1910

	1850	1860	1870	1880	1890	1900	1910
Arizona			26	155	1,357	1,848	2,009
California	962	4,068	4,272	6,018	11,322	11,045	21,645
Colorado		46	456	2,435	6,215	8,570	11,453
Dakota			94	401			
Idaho			60	53	201	293	651
Kansas		627	17,108	43,107	40,710	52,003	54,030
Montana			183	346	1,490	1,523	1,834
Nebraska		82	789	2,385	8,913	6,269	7,689
Nevada		45	357	488	242	134	513
New Mexico	22	85	172	1,015	1,956	1,610	1,628
North Dakota					373	286	617
Oklahoma					21,609	55,684	137,612
Oregon	207	128	346	487	1,186	1,105	1,192
South Dakota					541	465	817
Texas	58,558	182,921	253,475	393,384	488,171	620,722	690,049
Utah	50	59	118	232	588	672	1,144
Washington		30	207	325	1,602	2,514	6,058
Wyoming			183	298	922	940	2,235
Totals	59,799	188,091	227,846	451,129	587,398	765,883	941,176

Source: United States Bureau of the Census

CONTRIBUTORS

GAYLE K. BERARDI (Ph.D., University of Colorado) is Associate Professor of Political Science at the University of Southern Colorado and the author of several articles in scholarly journals.

EUGENE H. BERWANGER (Ph.D., University of Illinois) is Professor of History at Colorado State University and the author of several books, including *The Frontier Against Slavery: Western Anti-Negro Prejudice and the Slavery Extension Controversy* and *The West and Reconstruction.*

MONROE LEE BILLINGTON (Ph.D., University of Kentucky) is Professor of History Emeritus at New Mexico State University and the author of several books, including *New Mexico's Buffalo Soldiers, 1866–1900.*

NEWELL G. BRINGHURST (Ph.D., University of California, Davis) is Instructor of History and Political Science at the College of the Sequoias in Visalia, California, and the author of *Saints, Slaves, and Blacks: The Changing Place of Black People Within Mormonism.*

ANNE M. BUTLER (Ph.D., University of Maryland) is Editor of the *Western Historical Quarterly,* Professor of History at Utah State University, and the author of *Gendered Justice in the American West: Women Prisoners in Men's Penitentiaries.*

ROBERT A. CAMPBELL (Ph.D. candidate, Simon Fraser University) is Instructor of History at Capilano College in North Vancouver, British Columbia, and the author of *Demon Rum or Easy Money: Government Control of Liquor in British Columbia from Prohibition to Privatization.*

GEORGE O. CARNEY (Ph.D., Oklahoma State University) is Professor of Geography at Oklahoma State University and the editor of *Fast Food, Stock Cars, and Rock-n-Roll: Place and Space in American Pop Culture.*

MICHAEL J. CLARK (Ph.D., University of Utah) is Professor of Ethnic Studies at California State University, Hayward and the author of several scholarly articles.

ROGER D. HARDAWAY (D.A., University of North Dakota; J.D., University of Memphis) is Associate Professor of History at Northwestern Oklahoma State University and the author of *A Narrative Bibliography of the African-American Frontier: Blacks in the Rocky Mountain West, 1535–1912.*

WILLIAM L. LANG (Ph.D., University of Delaware) is Director of the Center for Columbia River History in Vancouver, Washington; Professor of History at Portland State University; the co-author of *Montana: A History of Two Centuries*; and the author of *Confederacy of Ambition: William Winlock Miller and the Making of Washington Territory.*

KENNETH W. PORTER (Ph.D., Harvard University) was Professor of History Emeritus at the University of Oregon at the time of his death in 1981 and the author of several books, including *The Negro on the American Frontier.*

GLENDA RILEY (Ph.D., Ohio State University) is Alexander M. Bracken Professor of History at Ball State University and the author of several books, including *The Female Frontier: A Comparative View of Women on the Prairie and the Plains* and *A Place to Grow: Women in the American West.*

W. SHERMAN SAVAGE (Ph.D., Ohio State University) was Professor of History Emeritus at Lincoln University in Jefferson City, Missouri, at the time of his death in 1980 and the author of *Blacks in the West.*

THOMAS W. SEGADY (Ph.D., University of Denver) is Associate Professor of Sociology at Stephen F. Austin State University and the author of *Values, neo-Kantianism, and the Structure of Weberian Methodology.*

RANDALL B. WOODS (Ph.D., University of Texas) is Distinguished Professor of History at the University of Arkansas and the author of several books, including *A Black Odyssey: John Lewis Waller and the Promise of American Life, 1878–1900.*

INDEX